LIFT
EVERY
VOICE

Constructing Christian Theologies
from the Underside

Susan Brooks Thistlethwaite
& Mary Potter Engel, Editors

HarperSanFrancisco

A Division of HarperCollins*Publishers*

For our children

James
Bill
Douglas
Sam
Miriam

Credits are found on page 330.

Library of Congress Cataloging-in-Publication Data

Lift every voice: constructing Christian theologies from the underside / Susan
    Brooks Thistlethwaite & Mary Potter Engel, editors.
        p.   cm.
      ISBN 0-06-067992-1 :
        1. Liberation theology. I. Thistlethwaite, Susan Brooks, 1948-
          II. Engel, Mary Potter.
BT83.57.L53   1990   89-45558
230'.046—dc20   CIP

93   94   MAL   9   8   7   6   5

Contents

Acknowledgments

One of the great joys of completing any manuscript is publicly acknowledging all the people and institutions who made the project possible. We wish to express our deep gratitude to: Yvonne Delk and the United Church of Christ Office for Church in Society for bringing the two of us together at a meeting in Washington, D.C. in November, 1986, where the idea for this book was conceived.

Mary would like to thank particularly United Theological Seminary for a sabbatical in the spring of 1987 that afforded much-needed time for the initial stages of this venture; the Association of Theological Schools for its generous grant in 1987; the staff and faculty at United, especially Mary Bednarowski and Clyde Steckel, who provided valuable support throughout the work on the manuscript; and Win, husband and friend, for his ordinary and extraordinary support during the entire project.

Susan would like to thank especially the Chicago Theological Seminary for a sabbatical in 1988 that was indispensible for bringing this manuscript to completion; the staff and colleagues at CTS, especially Kenneth Smith, Graydon Snyder, Linda Parrish, Roz Russell, Deb Baxter, Lorolee Brown, and Max Havelick; the students of the constructive theology classes who were willing to put up with many drafts of their class text; and Dick, James, Bill, and Douglas for their love and support.

Mary and Susan thank each other for all the pleasures of women joining efforts. The order of names on the cover is entirely arbitrary, arrived at by the flip of a coin. This project was equally conceived, labored over, and brought to fruition by both Mary and Susan and the alternation of editors' names in the text reflects this. Mary and Susan wish to extend their expression of the delights of women working together to include Jan Johnson, editor, colleague, friend.

Mary Potter Engel, &
Susan Brooks Thistlethwaite, 1989

Introduction: Making the Connections Among Liberation Theologies Around the World

MARY POTTER ENGEL
and SUSAN BROOKS THISTLETHWAITE

This textbook is an introduction to the theological task from the perspective of the theologies of liberation. It is, in fact, not wholly correct to say that the theologies of liberation share a perspective, for each liberation theology, whether Black, Hispanic, feminist, or Latin American, is characterized by its distinctive viewpoint. What these different theologies do share is their commitment to social justice.

In the past twenty years an explosion has taken place in Christianity. All around the world popular movements are rising up out of the culture of silence and finding their voices.[1] In Latin America, Asia, Africa, and North America the spirit is moving and communities of the oppressed are forming, crying out against their suffering and the social, political, economic, and religious structures that give rise to that suffering. But that is only half the story. These cries of protest are the signs not of a mass outpouring of hatred and revenge, but of a movement committed to working for liberation toward abundant life. Realizing that "only justice can stop a curse,"[2] these communities have begun a new practice of Christianity, experimenting with new ways of being the church, engaging in the practice of justice, and reflecting critically on the meaning of this practice. Theology done in these communities grows out of solidarity with those suffering and in need and is rooted in particular social justice contexts.

In the course of their work toward liberation, these communities have given birth to theologians and spiritual leaders who accept the responsibilities of being "organic intellectuals." Grounded in the life and practice of these specific communities and accountable to them, these theologians have accepted as their tasks the representation of the community, the articulation of a foundation for the intra- and extra-communal demands, and the specification of the fundamental elements appropriate to the community's possibilities for knowledge and analysis of reality.[3] In other words, the "organic intellectuals" of the liberation movements around the world, or liberation theologians, are not part of an intellectual elite that fabricates ideas for the theologically illiterate and helpless masses. Rather, they are formally trained individuals who, because they are engaged in the struggle for liberation of a particular community and committed to it, contribute their skills of analysis to their community's discernment of the way of life. As Anita Hill and Leo Treadway put it, these theologians are advocates who do not speak "to or for" certain communities, but "with and on behalf of" them.

This crucial shift in the role of the theologian from individual scholarly authority to reflective community advocate is perhaps most evident in the growing number of theological working groups and collectively-authored publications in liberation theology. A theological working group formed the discussion upon which Juan Luis Segundo based his five-volume series, *Theology for Artisans of a New Humanity*. Three recent volumes, *Your Daughters Shall Prophesy, God's Fierce Whimsy*, and *Revolutionary Forgiveness*, were all written by theological collectives.[4] Whether actually written down by individuals or collectives, liberation theology is clearly a communally-based and authorized theology, with liberation theologians lending their voices to the movements of which they are a part.

Many responsible teachers of systematic theology today have sought to include in their courses representatives from the theologies of liberation. Those who have participated in the making of this volume, however, contend that it is not possible to force theologies which represent radical methodological shifts into other normative theological schemas. New wine bursts old wineskins. The location of theological doctrines in an overall constructive schema determines their meaning. This volume proposes a new constructive outline, beginning with contextual method. In order to enter the theological task from liberation perspectives, it is necessary to begin by learning its method, an approach characterized by a commitment to doing theology contextually, communally, and concretely.

CONTEXTUALITY

Our intent in bringing together these diverse voices is not to suggest that in the end there is a kind of liberation theological Esperanto, a single language shared by all. That would be to make the same mistake liberation theologians have accused North American white male theologians of making: namely, to assume that there is one universal theology. On the contrary, liberation theologies have argued from the beginning that social location is important, that the context in which one does theology significantly shapes the method, content, and structure of theology.[5] By bringing together this variety of liberation theologians, therefore, we intend to underline the differences among them that occur because each comes out of a different social, economic, political, and cultural context.

There are two reasons for emphasizing the differences among liberation theologies. It concretely demonstrates the general point that all liberation theologies have made from the beginning: that all theology, including so-called universal theology, is inevitably and inescapably contextual and must acknowledge its limits. And it corrects the common misunderstanding that many white North American theologians and Christians have of liberation theologies. In their attempts to understand this novel movement many have inadvertently lumped all liberation theologies together, ignoring the differences among them. The First World's invention of the term *Third World* is one example of this. As Shiva Naipaul comments, the term itself exhibits imperialism, for it is a term of bloodless universality that robs individuals and societies of their particularity. In the spirit of clarity we go forth and denude them. Adapting the opening sentence of *Anna Karenina,* we might say that each society, like each family, is unhappy in its own way.

Even the one banner of "third worldhood" is as absurd and denigrating as the old assertion that all Chinese look alike. People look alike only when you cannot be bothered to look at them closely.[6] "Third World" then is "a flabby concept," and "an ideological instrument of the West."[7] As Naipaul suggests, to throw Asian, African, and Latin American all together in one heap is to miss the very real differences among them. The same may be said of all liberation theologies: North American feminist liberation theologies, gay and lesbian liberation theologies, Black liberation theologies, Native American theologies, Latin American liberation theologies, and *minjung* theologies. They are not clones. They are not interchangeable. Each has its own peculiar interests, emphases, viewpoints, analyses, and aims, dependent upon the requirements of its own particular social context.

For example, while Latin American theologians have focused their attention on developing the notions of human agency, freedom, and history (see chapter 9), Native American and feminist theologians have concentrated more on constructing a new view of nature. Or, while North American Black theologians and Latin American theologians have contributed new understandings of evil as structural and systemic, feminists have offered creative ways of understanding sin as self-denial (see chapter 11). For this reason it is as important to speak of liberation theologies as liberation theology.

In order to emphasize the contextuality of all theology and the specific contexts of different liberation theologies, we have included a wide variety of theologians in this text. Though our selection is not exhaustive, and is, indeed, flawed by the absence of certain voices, we hope to provide enough diversity to allow the reader listening to these new voices to discern the differences among them and to learn that "one of the greatest honors we can confer on other people is to see them as they are, to recognize not only that they exist but that they exist in a specific way, and have specific realities."[8]

This recognition of diversity is equally important on the individual level. No one of our contributors presents her- or himself as (or should be taken as) *the* spokesperson for her or his particular community. They are certainly voices responding to and accountable to their communities, advocates within and on behalf of particular communities, but by no means are they irreplaceable or exclusive representatives.

The distinctiveness of social location in liberation theologies has not always led to celebration of diversity and a search for connections with one another. It has also led to unnecessary divergences. Many liberation theologians, while advocating liberation from the oppression they are familiar with, have remained blind to other forms of oppression. Thus, while working to liberate individuals and societies from one particular form of oppression they have perpetuated others. For example, in the earliest years of Black theology, male Black liberation theologians ignored sexism altogether, concentrating on racism from a Black male perspective and assuming this included every Black. When Black feminist liberation theologians challenged them, they began to change.[9] For many years Latin American liberation theologians, focusing on economic exploitation, also ignored sexism, though they, too, have responded to recent criticisms from women within their movements.[10] White North American feminist theologians have long ignored classism and racism, focusing on sexism *from a white middle-class perspective* and assuming their description of the problems and possibilities included all women. Challenged by Black, Native American, Hispanic women and women of the Two-Thirds World, some have begun to change.[11] And, until recently, almost all liberation theologians have ignored heterosexism and homophobia and sexual and domestic abuse as significant modes of oppression. Liberation theologians have begun to recognize that these "isms" form an interlocking chain of oppression, which collectively may be called patriarchy. This recognition is now replacing old arguments over which oppression is the root of all others or, alternatively, the neglect of any oppressions beyond one's own immediate experience. Much more still needs to be done in this direction. The connections among the liberating responses to those interlocking oppressions require much deeper investigation than they have yet received. We are talking about the need to recognize both the particularity of context and the links between the structures of oppression. Gail Peterson's distinction between solidarity and alliances illustrates this idea. In a study of women's groups composed of Black, Hispanic, white, Jewish, and Christian lesbian and heterosexual women, Peterson and her colleagues discovered that both solidarity and alliances are important to liberation movements. Solidarity she defines as "the knowledge of, respect for, and unity with persons whose identities are in certain ways common with one's own" (e.g., with those who share a similar racial, economic, sexual orientation, or religious context or concrete experience of oppression). She defines alliances as "the knowledge of, respect for, and commitment between persons who are in essential ways different but whose interests are in essential ways akin" (e.g., among those who have chosen to work together for social reconstruction).[12] In other words, the single task of liberation entails both recognition of the particularities of personal and social contexts *and* recognition of the interconnections among struggles against oppression in those different contexts. This is as true for those trying to understand various liberation movements as it is for those immediately engaged in them. Otherwise, we are in danger of substituting a narrow, constricting, and closed particularism for the false objectivity and universalism of dominant theologies.

Though liberation theologies are embedded in different contexts and give rise to distinct voices that are not interchangeable, monotonal, they are also linked. As we listen to them, then, we need to listen for harmonies and points of convergence. One of the clearest ways to do this is by focusing on their shared method.

CONTEXT AND METHOD

If each of these liberation theologies is unique because of its context, what justifies including them in a single volume on liberation theology? The answer lies in the general approach to theology that these different theologies share and that distinguishes them from other types of theology. This shared method, characterized by a commitment to doing theology contextually, emerged early as the distinguishing feature of liberation theologies and has remained its single most significant indicator.

Contextuality is an often misunderstood premise of the theologies of liberation. It does not mean what North American Protestant liberals have often meant by this word. Liberalism, the opening of theological reflection to the modern world, views theology as rational discourse necessary in a world that challenges Christianity's basic claims. Protestant liberalism in North America understands itself as contextual theology because it takes individual human experience, an obvious point of commonality between religion and the secular world, as the starting point for theological reflection. In this contemporary North American liberal sense, then, context often means "me and my personal experience."[13]

By contrast, when a liberation theologian speaks of context, s/he means that one's *social location* is central to the theological task. Social location is not particular to the individual. It is a perspective shared by others of the group or class. For example, when Goba says "Our blackness is a given thing," he is not referring to his personal reaction to having been born Black. Rather, he is speaking of the socio-economic-political construction of what it means to be a Black person in capitalist-apartheid South Africa. That is what context means in his theology.

One meaning of contextuality in liberation method, therefore, is one's shared social location. It is this understanding of context that must be kept in mind as one hears liberation theologians speaking of contextual theology. As Goba states, "Every context of a political struggle has tremendous influence on the political perceptions of those who engage in it." In his landmark work, A Theology of Liberation, Gustavo Gutiérrez begins his theological reflection only after a lengthy critique of the economic policy of developmentalism in Latin America. He argues that the Latin American context is one of structured economic and political dependence, and that it is this socio-economic-political situation that conditions his Christian theological reflections.[14]

These perceptions structured by political struggle are called an ideology. An ideology is a deeply held, comprehensive, and interlocking set of beliefs about the nature of the world and how the world works. Ideology has often been used as a pejorative term to indicate perceptions distorted or warped by unreflective prejudice. Yet recently scholars in the field of the sociology of knowledge have shown that all knowledge is structured by social, political, and economic factors.[15] There is no such thing as objective knowledge free of ideological taint. "Each society has a regime of truth, its 'general politics' of truth," wrote Michel Foucault.[16] That is, what counts for the known, that which is true, is a function of what a given society accepts as true. Thus there are no truly objective knowers, only knowers who are or who are not critically aware of the context of their deeply held beliefs and the advantages and limitations of their belief system. Awareness of one's own and others' ideological bent is called critical consciousness. Lack of such awareness is often called false consciousness or ideological blindness. To call to our attention this reality, liberation theologians often engage in ideology critique, using the tools of economics, sociology, or political science.

Not all liberation theologians find ideology critique the most adequate or appropriate way to analyze their contexts. Native Americans, for example, along with minjung and other Asian theologians, do not share the intellectual heritage of Euro-Americans and do not find even its most radical tools of critique congenial. Many theologians in these cultural situations share a commitment to contextualize via narrative. They employ folktales, stories, poems, and chants to set and reflect on context. Doing theology contextually in their case is better understood as extending the imaginative horizon. As Young-chan Ro points out, they prefer mythos to logos as a way of transforming theology so that it can become a theology of transformation.

Feminist contributors to this volume often find themselves sharing several contexts, and feminist method reflects this. In patriarchal culture women are objects and not agents. That is, women are socialized by their culture to perform the roles (mostly private, not public) assigned to them, and these roles are not flexible. So a woman/academic finds herself able to move in more than one context, e.g., in 1) the traditional women's world of home maintenance and child nurture and 2) the male academic world of ideas and publications, but she cannot combine them into a third context of 3) women's academics, because this context does not exist. Black women sometimes have several additional spheres since Black culture in a racist society is itself constricted. Black women do not share the same "women's experience" as white women, even when both groups are constricted by sex. Lesbians will add another sphere of constriction, and so forth. Each patriarchal context (Asian, Latin American, South African, North Atlantic, etc.) will divide these spheres differently.

Feminist method should therefore be contextually adaptable. While Mary Daly has argued "patriarchy appears to be 'everywhere'. . . even outer space and the future have been colonized,"[17] her analysis seems to assume that patriarchy looks the same everywhere. She does not acknowledge the particular permutations of patriarchy in different social, political, economic, and cultural contexts. Feminist liberation theologians tend to break down their analyses of patriarchy and interface them with other modes of critique such as class and race. Adrienne Rich offers a comprehensive definition of patriarchy: "Patriarchy is the power of the fathers; a familial-social, ideological, political system in which men—by force, direct pressure, or through ritual, tradition, law and language, customs, etiquette, education and the division of labor—determine what part women shall or shall not play, and in which the female is everywhere subsumed under the male."[18]

All of these ways of analyzing context, the sociopolitical, the imagistic horizon, and the feminist are represented in the chapters that follow. While these modes of analysis may differ from one another, they are similar in that context is not interpreted individualistically or intra-psychically. These latter characterize modern liberalism. Further, the emphasis on the central role that context plays in the theological task distinguishes theologies of liberation from much of the neo-orthodox tradition, which so radically separated God's revelation from the vagaries of the human situation.

COMMUNAL AND CONCRETE

Theologies of liberation are profoundly *communal* theologies serving to express and explain the faith, hope, and charity of the community of Christians.[19] They are also *concrete*, practical, and historical theologies, grounded in and continually referring to the actual practice of Christian communities in particular times and places.[20] For this reason the traditional shorthand definition of theology as "GodTalk" does not adequately describe liberation theologies. They are better understood as *GodWalk,* to use Frederick Herzog's term.[21]

Liberation theology as GodWalk is built upon the dialectical relationship between theory and practice, between theological reflection and the life of the Christian community lived toward liberation. This differentiates it from deductive (classic orthodox) and inductive (classic liberal) theologies. Active commitment to a specific struggle for liberation, far from being a distorting and unfortunate occurrence, is the first necessary element in this theology. Critical reflection upon the communal practice that one is engaged in is the second. Both are continually related to one another. One implication of this, in traditional terms, is that a new relationship between faith and life is being envisioned that calls into question the dominant understanding that relieved theology and religious life of all political decisions and responsibilities. No longer are faith and life, theology and politics split apart, nor are abstract principles imposed upon the life of faith. Instead, liberation theologies stress the obligation of the Christian community and Christian theology to reflect and act upon their responsibilities in *history*.

PROPHETIC AND CONSTRUCTIVE

Liberation theology is also prophetic and constructive. It is both a theology of protest against unjust social orders and a theology aimed at social transformation toward greater justice for all. This twofold task is reflected in the definition of liberation offered by Ismael García. Liberation, he says, "expresses the longing to be free from all that represents a significant limit to the realization of one's potential, as well as the desire to be free to realize one's potential to the fullest."[22] This understanding of liberation and theology assumes that human beings are agents in history rather than merely passive victims of oppression or pitiful sufferers; that individuals are the subjects of history who are collaborating in the making of history, rather than the objects of the conquerors' history. Thus, another of the goals of liberation theology, in addition to prophetic criticism of unjust structures and social transformation, is the empowerment of individuals.

The inspiration and guidelines for this prophetic criticism and social transformation come from many sources, as the reader will note in the various chapters: the experience of faith; the experience of oppression; the scriptures; the Christian tradition; non-Christian instruments of social analysis (class, race, or gender analyses); and a wide variety of art forms, including poetry, folktales, novels, and popular songs. Though the way these materials or sources are integrated varies from one theologian or community to another (e.g., feminist theologians generally tend to use more contemporary poetry and popular songs than other forms of liberation theology), all liberation theologians agree on one basic principle for the use of any source: suspicion. All sources, whether Marxist analyses, ancient Christian texts, the scriptures, or "classic" literature, must be used critically and approached with the suspicion that they further the dominant mode of oppression. (See chapters 19 and 20.)

CONCEPT AND STRUCTURE OF THE VOLUME

As the above comments imply, this text has three aims. The first aim is to dispel the romantic notion that liberation theology is an exotic phenomenon existing "over there" or "out there" in "foreign" countries by including North American Black, Native American, feminist, and gay and lesbian liberation theologies. The second aim is to correct the idea that liberation theology is a uniform movement by introducing readers to the variety of liberation theologies that have arisen in different parts of the world. The third aim is to describe the relationship among the various struggles against oppression and to illustrate the basic method common to liberation theologies that identifies them and that challenges mainstream theology.

There is a fourth aim of this text, which may, indeed, be the most significant one: to stress the point that liberation theologies are developing as full-fledged *constructive* alternatives to dominant theologies. Their challenge is not only to the method but to the content and structure of Christian theologies as well. Liberation theologies, then, also call for the liberation of Christian theology from oppressive concepts and structures.

From its first appearance on the scene liberation theology has been met with harsh criticism. It has been called "a modern-day anti-Christian heresy," "trendy theology," "genitive theology," or, at best, "occasional theology." Too few have considered it as a serious constructive challenge to theological method and to the structure and content of theology.[23] Three significant works demonstrate that the goal of liberation theologies is the complete transformation of Christian theology. Each of these books is a constructive liberation theology covering all the major doctrinal *loci* of the tradition: James Cone's *A Black Theology of Liberation*, the five-volume series by Juan Luis Segundo, et al., entitled *Theology for Artisans of a New Humanity*, and Rosemary Radford Ruether's *Sexism and God-Talk*.[24] Anthologies of liberation theology and works on liberation theology to date have not paid sufficient attention to this challenge.[25]

We have organized this volume with this constructive task in mind, deliberately selecting a different order of topics than is usually found in volumes of Christian systematic theology. We have chosen to reorder the topics to reflect more accurately the concerns, emphases, and goals of liberation theologians.

This is significant for a number of reasons. First, liberation theology is not just a slightly different look at Christian theology from different perspectives. We cannot simply insert a liberation chapter into the old structure of a systematic course and think we have understood its full meaning. On the contrary, the full meaning of liberation theological reconstructions of specific doctrines comes out when they are seen in their own systematic context. This point was made by Schleiermacher in the nineteenth century, when he observed (by way of justifying his own reordering of the Christian system) that the meaning of a doctrine was in part determined by its place in the total system.[26] We may call this concern with the placement of doctrines in a system the theological location, which is analogous to liberation theologians' concern with social location. It is for this reason that we have chosen to order the volume in a way that may at first appear confusing to the reader familiar with traditional Christian systematic theologies.

The point of reordering the theological *loci* in this way is to stress that liberation theologies challenge the method *and* the content of dominant theologies. Liberation theologies are not about rearranging the furniture in the house of theology, or even about redecorating or remodeling the house. Rather, they are about rebuilding the foundation (method) and redesigning the floorplan (categories).

What is the rationale for the ordering of topics in this textbook? We begin with part 1 on method, context, and commitment because this alternative approach to theology is the key to understanding the entire movement and the work of the individual theologians. In this section the contributors focus on the importance of context and commitment and discuss the nature and method of theology in this new model.

We have included the topics of revelation and the relation of Christianity to other religions in this section because it is here that these questions have come up for liberation theologians. As one reconsiders the appropriate sources for theology and the development of a theology of critical reflection on faith and social justice, the question of if and when to use non-Christian sources is intensified. Examples include the debates within North American Black liberation theology about the use of African folk religions, the debate within feminist theology about Goddess religions, the debate within Native American liberation theology about the use of their own religious traditions, and the debate surrounding Latin American liberation theology about Marxism.[27]

Part 2 focuses on the doctrine of God. We have isolated this from the remainder of the *loci* in order to highlight the distinctive questions within the doctrine of God that arise within liberation theologies, such as "What does the power of God or the judgment of God mean?" (chapter 6), or "How is God related to the threat and possibility of nuclear war?" (chapter 7). Part 2 illustrates the manner in which liberation theologians approach this most traditional of theological doctrines. Two things the reader should not expect in part 2 are 1) a discussion of "classical" theological issues, such as formal versions of the trinity and 2) a metaphysical argument for the reality of God. Part 2 could have been located at the end of the volume, to point out that the pertinent issue in the doctrine of God for liberation theologians is not the reality of God in itself (aseity) but God in relation to the world.

The location of the discussion of eschatology in part 3, between the discussions of God and the multifarious workings of God's grace in the world, is meant to highlight the fact that eschatological vision has fueled many liberation movements and theologies. The vision of the reign of the gracious God in the world in love and justice (or the "kindom of God" as Isasi-Díaz puts it) has guided and sustained those struggling with oppression. The shared hope that the ongoing transformation of society in light of the kindom of God is possible has inspired oppressed peoples to begin to work for change and to persevere in that work in the face of otherwise overwhelming opposition.

Hence eschatology is no longer "the last things" but "those things in our midst." The stress is on a God acting in history and on the need to discover God's direction for abundant life in the midst of our ambiguous and conflict-ridden history. Prophecy, then, so intimately connected to eschatological vision and hope, does not involve predicting the future or mapping out the endtimes, but discerning God's activity in the world now, the meaning of that activity for the community of faith, and the appropriate response. The ultimate vision or hope that one holds, as chapter 8 suggests, affects this process of discernment.

Everything after "eschatology" comes under the heading of "grace," by which we mean the dynamic presence, power, and activity of God continually working to bring the world toward greater wholeness through justice and love. We believe this common term and the distinction between various ways or modes of God's relation to the world in parts 4 and 5 underscore the importance of the ongoing generative and regenerative connection between God and the world in liberation theologies. This connection in turn serves as the foundation for the strong connection between faith and life, theology and politics. Part 4 discusses creating and governing grace, part 5 reconciling, liberating, and sanctifying grace.

Creating and governing grace has been an important concern to all liberation theologians, though in different ways. Their radical revisioning of the relation between God and the world, between faith and life, focuses on the notion of human beings as agents collaborating with God to reshape the world in love and justice. Liberation theologies differ in their view of the relation of human beings to the rest of nature. Latin American and North American Black liberation theologians, because of their emphasis on history and politics, have tended to emphasize the distinctiveness of human beings in the world and their freedom in relation to nature, while Native American and feminist liberation theologians have tended to stress the interdependence of human beings and nature and the limits of human freedom within nature.

We have placed sin and evil in this part not in order to suggest, in neo-orthodox fashion, that the doctrine of humankind can be confused with or reduced to the doctrine of sin, but to make the point that human beings experience equally an original righteousness and an original sinfulness. For this reason part 4 includes discussion of the human ways of participating in the destruction as well as the creation of the world. Furthermore, traditional theologies, especially under Neoplatonic influences, have emphasized stasis as divine and have denigrated change and decay. Liberation theologians hold that change is a necessary and indeed graceful part of life. Change as transformation is critical in unjust human situations.

Part 5, on healing, liberating, and sanctifying grace, is the largest in the entire volume. It highlights another dominant concern of liberation theologies and challenges other theologies with the need to witness to the continuing empowerment of the spirit in our individual and social lives and in the larger economic and political world. We begin part 5 with a chapter on healing grace in order to stress that our recognition of possibilities for healing and liberation, and our relation to Jesus Christ, are dependent upon the empowering spirit of God constantly at work all around us, among us, and in us.

Part 5A, on christology, focuses on the specific ways in which Christian communities make their claims about and are witnesses to the presence and activity of that empowering spirit of God. Part 5B, on church, ministry, and spirituality, highlights the fact that in Christian liberation movements this empowering spirit is experienced most vitally *in community,* an experience that has not always been adequately recognized in Western theologies. Our search for a chapter on the sacraments was unsuccessful. The power of communal sign-acts to bind communities in solidarity, to call them to remembrance and resistance, and to nourish and renew them in their struggles for justice and love is experienced in base communities all over the world. Liberation theologians are just beginning to reflect upon this new experience and formulate new models of the sacraments.[28]

Our location of the scriptures in this part on sanctifying grace and at the end of the volume is especially significant. Under the influence of orthodoxy and neo-orthodoxy, many systematic theologians discussed the scriptures at the beginning of their theologies, under the epistemological doctrine of revelation. We have placed the discussion of the scriptures within the larger discussion of the empowering spirit of God in community in order to emphasize three key points of liberation theologies. First, the way we come to know God is not primarily through propositional statements deposited in a text, but in the midst of our struggles in faithfulness for justice and love. The scriptures are an indispensable guide in these struggles, but not necessarily the first or only source for reflection. Second, the scriptures, as one of the most powerful agents of liberation, belong to the whole people of God. They do not belong to formally trained exegetes alone; they are the *church's* book. And third, the scriptures must always be interpreted *in, by,* and *for* particular justice-seeking communities. This is an important alternative to the more rationalistic, elitist, and individualistic models still operating in many Western theologies and churches today.

Far from suggesting that the scriptures are inessential or a mere addendum to theology, placing discussion of the scriptures last accents their fundamental importance. Whatever situation liberation theologians face, the scriptures play a cardinal role in their reflections. Our placement of them at the end should be understood as a rounding out of the discussion of basic issues of method with which the volume begins.

Overall, the entire structure is trinitarian, proceeding from God as the End of Life (or, as Segundo says, "the One Ahead of Us"), through God as Source of Life ("the One Before Us"), to God as Gracious Sustainer, Liberator, and Enlivener of Life ("the One with Us").[29]

STRUCTURE AND BIOGRAPHY

Theology emerges out of particular contexts. Those who contribute to a book of constructive theology bring their own context to it. The lengthy treatment of grace in this book, a category usually only given a short section in traditional systematics, is due to the particular experience of grace amongst the participants.

The Latin American liberation theologian Leonardo Boff, in writing on *Liberating Grace,* makes the point that we must not ignore "biographical conditioning factors" in interpreting why grace is usually seen by Christian theologians as the much desired but wholly unmerited bridge over the experience of alienation and despair. Paul, Augustine, and Martin Luther, three men who have set the terms for the Western discussion of grace, were all people who "suffered the painful experience of alienation and a deep inability to carry out the human project of holiness."[30] Their views on grace are "rooted in a profound existential pessimism."[31] They all experienced their religion in opposition to their daily life and its character. This is true as well for the great modern Protestant Paul Tillich, who said that the fundamental human dilemma is estrangement.[32] "Their theology and piety never took conscious note of the historical mediations of grace, of the gratuitousness in their own day-to-day lives, of the presence of grace in countless profane dimensions."[33] In fact, they missed the ordinariness of the reality of grace.

The biographies of the participants in this volume are vastly different from those of classical theologians of the past. They are all members of nondominant groups. Paul, Augustine, Martin Luther, and Paul Tillich—as educated male ecclesiastics—were members of three dominant groups in their societies. Women, people of color, and non-Western peoples have had less experience of the artificial freedom from daily routine that membership in a dominant group brings. They have tended to take note of the presence of grace in nature, in politics, in human interests, and in human growth and development. Theirs is a view of grace less estranged from human life and work. God's movement in the world, these writers would say, is not so *extra*-ordinary after all.

FINAL COMMENTS

Three final qualifying comments are necessary at this point. First, though the sequence of our chapters may confuse some readers at first, the material is not inaccessible. The chapters can be read in sequence as a counterpoint to dominant theological systematic orders, or they can be read out of sequence to fit in with more traditionally organized systematic theology courses. In the latter case, classroom discussion of the way in which theological location affects the meaning of particular doctrines is important and should draw on the outline and the introductory chapter of the volume.

Second, though the sequence of our chapters is significantly different from those found in most dominant theologies, it is not wholly different. Perhaps we could have been even bolder. We assume that this will indeed happen in future systematic liberation theology texts. We do not claim that the order we have chosen is *the* systematic order for liberation theologies. Quite clearly it is not. In fact, many of our contributors would not order things in exactly the same way, given the choice. The sequence of topics in this volume represents only our joint attempt to reorder Christian theology to reflect the concerns, emphases, and goals of this new model of theology called the theology of liberation. The result is, therefore, not a collection of essays, nor an anthology. Rather, it is a volume in constructive liberation theology which we hope will be useful in a number of ways, specifically, either as a systematic text for a course on liberation theology or as a supplement and constructive challenge to traditional systematic theology courses in method, content, and structure.

Lastly, a word of caution. This book will not tell you much if you enter it as a tourist. Learning the method of the theologies of liberation, understanding the commitment to doing theology contextually, communally, and concretely, means asking yourself, "In my social location, where is justice struggling to be born and how can I help?" As Audre Lorde has written, "Survival is not an academic skill."[34]

"Lift every voice and sing / 'til earth and heaven ring / Ring with the harmony of liberty."[35] Thus begins the familiar empowering hymn of

Black Christian communities in North America. It is our hope that this volume of constructive Christian theology from the perspective of liberation communities will enable students to begin to hear the many different individual voices rising out of these communities today and their harmony in God's song of liberation for all peoples and the whole earth.

Part 1

THEOLOGICAL METHOD: COMMITMENT AND CONSTRUCTION

Introduction to Part 1

What is faith? What is theology? What are its tasks and sources? What method is most appropriate for accomplishing its tasks? What is revelation? What is the relationship between Christianity and other religions? These are the fundamental questions Christian theologians have raised for centuries and which liberation theologians are raising again today. The freshness of their answers stands out here more than in other areas, because changes in answers to basic questions are bound to have greater consequences. Perhaps the quickest introduction, then, to the distinctiveness and challenge of liberation theology is by way of its responses to these kinds of questions.

Goba's response to the question "What is faith?" sounds several liberation themes. Faith, the root of theology, emerges in the context of a specific struggle. It is defined not primarily as belief or assent to correct ideas as determined by others, but as the liberating action of "radical spontaneity." This definition follows the lines of the Protestant Reformation of the sixteenth century, but departs from it in two significant ways. Luther and others also defined faith in terms of trust rather than belief and demanded that each person be responsible for his or her own faith and not rely on another's. In developing this view, North American Protestantism has tended to associate faith with the individual, to distinguish it sharply from revolutionary activity, and to confine it to the life of the "soul." Liberation theologians challenge all three of these modifications. First, as Goba says, "faith must be deprivatized." It is a social reality that is defined by the people and for the people. Second, it is characterized less by quiet obedience than by a "spirit of resistance." Finally, it is related to every aspect of life, outer as well as inner aspects. While not all liberation theologians agree with Goba's Christocentric approach to faith, they share his characterization of it as social, active, political, and liberating.

For example, Isasi-Díaz stresses similar themes in her response to the question "What is theology?" From a liberation perspective, theology, as critical reflection upon the Christian way of life, is concerned with "the right praxis" and not the right belief (p. 31). Though this concern with orthopraxis has sometimes been interpreted as establishing a new fundamentalism, this is not the case. For theology's task is not to establish the right practice for all time but to reflect critically on the practice of the gospel in specific times and places. This is why liberation theologians speak of theology as "the second step."[1] Theology's task is not to determine the correct beliefs which are then applied to everyday life. It is not the first step, from which the Christian community's practice is then deduced. The practice of justice is the first step, to which theology, the second step, responds. It is this sense in which Isasi-Díaz's comments about the interconnection of theology, ethics, and spirituality must be understood. She is not suggesting that theology be reduced to either one of the other two, but that it be grounded in the moral and ritual practices of communities of resistance and solidarity.

That first step of praxis has sometimes been identified with Christian charity. Isasi-Díaz argues that since charity is so often misunderstood as one-directional (therefore paternalistic) and passive, "the appropriate present-day expression of the Gospel demand that we love our neighbor" is "solidarity." Solidarity is characterized by mutuality and praxis. Her description of solidarity with the oppressed by their friends and solidarity among the oppressed is an important elaboration on the liberation theme of "the preferential option for the poor." In her essay one sees evidence of a shift in the theological paradigm that reflects the turn not only to the subject but to the *political* subject.

The political subject, Ro argues, is also the *religious* subject. His chapter raises the question of the nature and task of theology in a different way. Questioning the appropriateness of the West's conceptual approach to liberation theology, he suggests a narrative approach instead. Like Isasi-Díaz, he sees theology as grounded in experience and activity, but he stresses the religious symbols, myths, and rituals of the Korean people as a way into that experience. This shift results in different sources for theology. For Ro social and political analyses are not the only essential sources for theology: the stories of the people are also essential. This viewpoint is evident in the chapters by Song and Charleston as well.[2]

The chapters by Ro, Song, and Charleston all speak to the fundamental concern with the appropriate sources of theology and a method for relating them. Charleston offers a provocative look at the question of how one identifies and uses sources in theology and raises the issue of the use of experience in liberation theologies. He says, "I am announcing the privilege of my own people to interpret the Christian canon in the light of Israel's experience but also in the light of their own experience" (p. 59). In this statement one sees the commitment to using a method of critical correlation, as well as the partiality and use of new sources that this entails.

Liberation theologians have committed themselves to a method that, broadly speaking, correlates the social and cultural experience of oppression and liberation with the Christian witness. This method associates many liberation theologies with a larger paradigm shift in theology that David Tracy calls a method of "mutually critical correlation."[3] Thus the relationship between Christianity and contemporary experience is a complex one in which the two terms are related in different ways at different times. Segundo has called this continuing change the "hermeneutic circle."[4] Without such a circle theology becomes conservative rather than liberating. The goal is not simply the translation of traditional Christian symbols into new language, however, but the resymbolization of Christianity and culture out of this creative encounter. As Ruether has said, "Human experience is the starting point of the circle of interpretation. . . . If the symbol does not speak authentically to experience, it becomes dead and is discarded or altered to provide new meaning."[5]

This method entails a different understanding of the Bible and revelation, as well as theology. As Segundo says, "the Bible is not the discourse of a universal God to a universal man [sic]. Partiality is justified because we must find, and designate as the word of God, that *part* of divine revelation which *today,* in the light of our concrete historical situation, is most useful for the liberation to which God summons us."[6] (For further discussion of this see the chapters on scripture in this volume.) Christian theology, then, is always characterized by partiality rather than by the neutrality of Greek thought. And it is opened up to new sources that reflect the present-day experiences of different peoples, as is evident in the chapters by Ro, Charleston, and Song.

Ro points to the use of stories of *han* and the ritual of the mask dance in *minjung* theology. Charleston urges that Native American experience that has been handed down through their traditions as an "Old Testament" be brought into relation with the Christian witness. Song uses many sources from the non-Christianized Asian world and speaks of bringing together the Asian context and the Christian revelation "with one stroke of an Asian brush" (p. 62). His argument for the necessity of doing so is important for understanding liberation theology. He points out that the Barthian position that theology always critiques culture is no longer an adequate method for theology, for it is grounded in a split between heaven and earth. This comment is reminiscent of Latin American theologians' rejection of the Augustinian and Lutheran legacies of two kingdoms, which taught Christians to neglect the social and political context in which they lived.[7] Song's description of the liberation alternative as a "gravity-bound" theology applies to liberation theologies in other contexts as well.

The implications of this method for revelation are important. From this viewpoint revelation is seen not as breaking into history from above or afar but as present in the ordinary events of our existence here on earth—as in a peach tree in bloom. This view is not far from that of some Latin American theologians, who state that "We don't bring Christ to culture. Christ is already there!" As Song says, "One of the most important things Jesus did, it seems to me, was to free his followers from fear of their context and to make them realize its revelatory significance" (p. 68). This radically incarnational theology accompanying a praxis-based method is common to Black and feminist liberation theologies as well.

One way in which liberation theologies are suspicious of the new paradigm of mutual critical correlation can be seen in their critiques of the recent trend among liberal Christian theologians to speak of conversation, or a community of discourse. While they admit that religious experience is ambiguous and pluralistic, liberation theologians do not agree that the way forward lies through "genuine conversation" or genuine community of inquiry,[8] especially if community is understood as an academic guild rather than as the smaller hermeneutical communities of shared commitment that are engaged in struggles for justice. As Westhelle says, "Community is not a forum for discussion of interests that brings together people of good will. Community is possible when it begins with the fundamental equity of those who are displaced" (p. 139). Without this understanding of community, conversation itself becomes but another form of imperialism, with Western, white, privileged persons setting the agenda. And when this is the case, liberation theologians are choosing not to enter the conversation, deliberately stepping back from it in order to respond to the prior and more urgent needs of justice.

CHAPTER 1

What Is Faith? A Black South African Perspective

BONGANJALO GOBA

CONTEXT AND COMMITMENT

Christian commitment and faith in the South African context are rooted in the current struggle for liberation. This is inevitable because in this context, faith has a challenge to respond to the ongoing crisis of brutal repression. Such a faith threatens those whose faith is rooted in cultural and economic privilege. But for me as a Black South African Christian, genuine faith is always vulnerable no matter where we are, because economic, political, and cultural forces throughout the world reflect the inherent evil of oppression.

The dynamics of oppression shape our faith not in a passive fashion but through the spirit of prophetic vigilance. It is a faith which seeks to affirm life amidst terror and chaos. It is this faith that shapes the life of the Christian community as it engages in the resistance against tyranny. Being part of this community has added a very important dimension in my life, which I shall try to describe in this brief statement. To have faith in Jesus is to oppose apartheid. One could go on to say that to have faith in Jesus is to participate in struggles for justice and peace wherever they are pursued. For me as a Black South African Christian, this is what makes my faith and that of many other Christians vital and exciting.

CONSTRUCTION

To raise questions about the nature of faith in the South African situation poses a serious theological challenge. This is particularly true in the Black church context, where to be faithful, to be committed to the liberating vision of Christ, is a matter of life and death. This brief statement seeks to articulate the kind of faith that is emerging within the current struggle for liberation in South Africa.

What is becoming clear is that faith embraces every aspect of life, particularly in situations of extreme repression. Faith becomes a response to some of the pressing problems that confront any Christian community that seeks to be obedient to the imperatives of the gospel. Faith becomes a challenge to state categorically that to accept Jesus Christ as savior is revolutionary and has subversive implications. This is why Allan Boesak maintains that "Black theology is the expression of the faith of Black Christians. It says that in spite of white manipulation (slavery, sons of Ham, theology of apartheid) the gospel is still God's liberating word. It says that the covenant God of the Torah and the prophets cannot be possessed, least of all by oppressors. God cannot be overcome, least of all by the Pharaohs, the Baals and the Dragons of this world."[1]

In the current struggle for liberation a new perception of faith is emerging. This new vision of faith is expressed in Black theology and in the *kairos* movement.* It is a contextual faith which comes out of the commitment to the struggle but which also responds to the imperatives of the gospel. This has tremendous significance, especially for the Black Christian community in South Africa. It challenges the prevailing distortions of white faith, a faith that continues to justify the ideology of apartheid. But more than that, it is a new faith which seeks to vindicate the liberating word of God not simply as a gift to the Black Christian community alone, but to the entire community of the people of God.

The other significance of the emerging faith within the Black struggle for liberation is that, for the first time, the oppressed are responsible for their faith. Their faith does not depend on the white ecclesiastical structures or on the traditions imposed by early white missionaries. Their faith is born in the womb of the struggle itself. Their faith affirms life and challenges the forces of darkness. *The Kairos Document* celebrates this new faith. This faith represents a new *kairos,* a moment of truth, a commitment to a liberated and liberating faith in Jesus Christ (Hebrews 11:1).

THE CHALLENGE OF THIS NEW FAITH WITHIN THE CURRENT STRUGGLE FOR LIBERATION

As they articulate this new faith in the struggle for liberation, Black Christians are discovering that they are doing theology. Theology is critical reflection on the praxis of faith. Faith is an expression of a commitment based on a profound relationship with Christ as we participate in the struggle for liberation. Our faith in Christ gives us this mandate to do theology. As Karl Barth puts it, "Faith is the condition *sine*

---

*The *kairos* movement refers to a group of South African church people, clergy, lay, theologians and ethicists, Black, white and mixed race, who signed *The Kairos Document*. This document was produced by discussion groups responding to the crisis of faith anti-apartheid work poses for theology and church. The document critiques "state theology" and "church theology" and proposes a "prophetic theology" and "call to action." At the time of publication (September 13, 1985), over 150 people from sixteen churches and groups had signed. Since then many others have added their names.

qua non of theological science. This is to say, faith is the event and history without which no one can become and be a Christian. . . . Faith is the special event that is constitutive for both Christian and theological existence. Faith is the event by which wonderment, concern, and commitment that make the theologian a theologian are distinguished from other occurrences which, in their own way, might be noteworthy and memorable or might be given the same designation."[2]

A theology based on this involved faith of the Black Christian community is a response to the prevailing context of violence and death. Faith is shaped by the spirit of resistance. Yet faith adds a critical dimension to the nature of that resistance. There is a dialectical process here which indicates how the dynamics of faith emerge in a particular struggle. This faith points to a new kind of spirituality that is radically on the side of those who are marginalized and oppressed. We are reminded of the linkage of spirituality and action in the prophetic vision of Jesus when he stood in the synagogue to declare his mission. "The Spirit of the Lord is upon me, because He has annointed me to preach good news to the poor. He has sent me to proclaim release to the captives and recovering of sight to the blind, to set at liberty those who are oppressed, to proclaim the acceptable year of the Lord" (Luke 4:18–19).[3]

This faith challenges the Black Christian community to develop a critical understanding of the context. We must begin to do a social analysis that unravels the contradictions of the apartheid society. This analysis exposes previous limitations within the Black Christian community, its failure to come to grips with the destructive consequences of this policy of economic and racial genocide.

But this new deprivatized faith has created a deep crisis within the Christian community. It is a crisis which forces Christians to take sides in the current struggle in South African society. As the authors of *The Kairos Document* put it, "The time has come. The moment of truth has arrived. South Africa has been plunged into a crisis that is shaking the foundations, and there is every indication that the crisis has only just begun and that it will deepen and become even more threatening in the months to come. It is the *kairos* or "moment of truth" not only for apartheid but also the church."[4] Elsewhere the document says, "A crisis is a judgment that brings out the best in some people and the worst in others. A crisis is a moment of truth that shows us up for what we really are. There will be no place to hide and no way of pretending to be what we are not in fact. At this moment in South Africa the church is about to be shown up for what it really is, and no cover-up will be possible."[5]

The Black Church has no other option but to be at the center of the struggle. But it must also provide a context in which a vision of a new society can be shaped. I believe the Black theological movement can offer radically new models of how the Black church can begin to be a catalyst for radical change in the South African society today.

BLACK THEOLOGY AND THE REDEFINITION OF FAITH
OF THE BLACK CHURCH

When Black theology emerged in the South African scene in the late sixties it brought a new and radical understanding of faith.[6] Its major contribution was the redefinition of faith within the context of the Black struggle, taking as its point of departure the Black religious experience. The dynamics of this new perception of faith are visible in its address to the current political situation.

One of the issues that has confronted the Black Christian community in South Africa is how does our faith in Christ relate to our experience of oppression as Black people? The question has been raised because the dominant white churches and their theologies have promoted a privatized notion of faith. They claim a kind of political neutrality and theological innocence about the situation. Theirs is a private faith which supports the prevailing racial and economic status quo. The separation of religion and politics continues to be promoted by white-dominated churches because of political expediency and not for theological reasons. It is this privatization of faith which supports the apartheid state and which is being challenged by Black theology.

Faith in Black theological reflection begins by affirming our blackness as the people of God. Yes, our "blackness is a given thing."[7] What authenticates our faith, however, is its anchor in Jesus Christ. The struggle to affirm our blackness in the South African situation is also a statement about our faith, because it points to the uniqueness of our relationship with Christ in our struggle to dismantle apartheid, both in the church and in society. This faith represents a counter-ethos because it seeks to expose and shake the foundations of the South African society.

This new, radical, and liberating faith provides us a new sense of identity, one which does not simply expose the contradictions of our society—but also highlights the uniqueness of our blackness, especially within a white, racist, and capitalist society. A new identity and a fresh interest emerge in the celebration of our cultural values and in those institutions within the Black community that have been negated by white Western Christianity. It is a faith that authenticates our experience, opening up new possibilities for theological creativity within our communities. It is a faith that embraces every aspect of life, providing a new spirituality for involvement in the current struggle for liberation, or as Simon Maimela puts it:

To accept Christ and the qualitatively different life that he offers is for blacks tantamount to revolting against and denouncing the present unjust and life-denying social structures. Indeed, those who have experienced the Spirit of Christ and his gospel have no alternative but to call for a new society, to call for a fundamental re-direction of human relations, and to call for the death of the Old

Adam and the end of the sinful human existence represented by our society so that the creation of the new humanity in Christ might come to be.[8]

What is very exciting about this new faith or this radical spirituality is that theological reflection becomes a communal effort, or, to use my favorite term, theology becomes a communal praxis.[9] This is a contextual faith, arising out of a particular struggle. A very good example of this is *The Kairos Document.* I believe this contextual faith is a product of a certain way of doing theology. The theological method which is responsible for this contextual faith has certain characteristics which I believe are critical for any theology seeking to address its particular context.

First, this method begins with life experience—not merely private life experience, but the collective life experience of pain, oppression, and dehumanization. The focus here is both on the personal and social dimensions of human experience as they are affected by structures of society. In the South African context, what becomes critical is the prevailing racial and economic order of apartheid, which is the source of Black oppression. For Black Christians living in this context, faith becomes a critical response to this policy of racial and economic genocide. All questions related to the meaning and relevance of faith become tested as they try to respond to the context. As Black Christians get involved in the struggle for liberation, they begin to raise critical questions about who God and Christ are for them in this situation.

The theological hermeneutic that shapes Black faith evolves as Black Christians raise these serious questions about God, Christ, and the church in their context. In raising these questions they are compelled to debunk the prevailing theological categories of the dominant white theological establishment. We see this hermeneutic of suspicion in many theological statements coming from the Black Christian community, bringing out new theological insights about the various aspects of the affirmations of the Christian faith. For example, God becomes the God of the oppressed. God in this new context of faith is no longer neutral in the face of blatant oppression, exploitation, and suffering. God takes sides. Again in this new context of faith, Christ becomes the liberator, the one who liberates both Blacks and whites from the bondage of apartheid.

Starting from a collective life experience of oppression involves a rereading of the scriptures. As Black Christians approach scriptures out of a particular experience, they bring new questions to the text, which we can see especially in *The Kairos Document.* This rereading of the scriptures plays a significant role in the redefinition of faith. It is also key in the new Black Christian identity that is evolving in the South African context today. Faith in this context is not an appendage to life, something outside or privatized, but the central axis which shapes and directs every aspect of life.

The second critical characteristic of this new faith is its communal aspect, which expresses the solidarity of faith. This I believe is unique because it points to the concept of corporate personality.[10] The embodiment of the community in the individual and the dialectical relationship between the individual and community is made clear. This solidarity in faith as part of the expression of the people of God means theology is no longer the monopoly of professional theologians. The community becomes the theologian. The community articulates a new faith which expresses solidarity in the struggle for liberation. It is a communal faith which inspires a spirituality of solidarity and involvement.

Here again we encounter an exciting development. There is a new understanding of the church, especially the mission of the church. The church is no longer simply a group of individuals who share a common faith and yet are divided in their commitment to the struggles of justice and peace. The church represents a communal praxis of faith, one that critiques and opens the possibilities of transforming life. The pervasive individualism which we see in bourgeois liberal Christianity has no place in this new expression of faith. Such a communal expression of faith in the South African context is the beginning of the confessing movement, whose goal is to dismantle the system of apartheid.[11]

The third characteristic of this new faith is its commitment to social analysis. What makes this new expression of faith exciting is the ability to identify the structures of oppression. Because this faith represents an attempt to respond critically to the current political context characterized by institutional sexism, racism, and flagrant economic exploitation, there is a commitment to social analysis. This involves a critical understanding of the social forces and institutions that embody the ideology of apartheid.

How does this new social analysis within Black theological reflection express itself? It begins by taking seriously the collective pain and the experience of oppression reflected in the lives of the people. It explores how people feel about their oppression, how they understand their situations. Social analysis begins by creative listening, especially to the anger and cries of the people. It begins by taking seriously the vision of the people with its limitations and possibilities. This social analysis represents what the authors of *The Kairos Document* call the moment of truth, a decisive moment which calls for radical alternatives in a particular sociopolitical context. It calls for a radical faith, one that is prophetic and relevant. This faith fosters a new kind of sociopolitical consciousness.

The second aspect of this social analysis involves critical understanding of all the instruments of repression, the ideological apparatus of the state which is reflected in the structures of society. In unraveling these structures, through use of the social sciences, the Christian community begins to identify the forces of evil. There is considerable debate about what kind of social analysis is appropriate in expressing the Christian vision, and there are serious ideological divisions among Christians about this. Within the South African context we have two opposing forms of social analysis. These are represented by what is referred to by Lebamang Sebidi as the "race-analyst position" and the "class-analyst" position. He makes the following observation about the first one: "What do the race-analysts say in general? For them the basic ingredient in the South African, three-hundred-year conflict is race. The primacy of racial ideology or political racial factors, they say, should be obvious to any unbiased analyst of the South African problematic. This is their point of departure."[12] Further, "The protagonists of the race-analysis approach do not see how the struggle of the people, at least at this stage, would be anything but a nationalistic struggle. They point to the obvious fact that in this country the so-called "non-whites" are oppressed, excluded, discriminated against as a black nation, and not as a class. And, therefore, the proper response to this blatant and obvious national oppression is some form of nationalism—not classism."[13]

This kind of race-analyst position has dominated the social analysis found in Black theology. The issue of institutional racism has been central in Black critical theology because it identified clearly the nature of the oppressive structures that are responsible for racial genocide. But because of the complexity of the problem, one senses a shift also in Black theological reflection. There is a shift toward the class-analyst position. As Lebamang Sebidi observes, "Class-analysts inveigh against what they see as the superficiality of the race analysis of the South African situation. They feel that race analysis arbitrarily isolates the South African struggle not only from struggles against world capitalist exploitation, but also from liberating currents that have been a long-standing feature along the borders of this country."[14]

He goes on to state:

South African blacks are oppressed not primarily because they show a different skin colour, but because, basically, their economic interests are antithetical to those who are the economically dominant class. So whilst the conflict manifests itself in forms that are racial, its origin is decidedly non-racial. Its origin is a collective attempt to protect group-interests; the land, water, pasture, and later the mines, manufacturing industry, and commerce. It is, therefore, not race relations that one should study and focus on, but class-relations.[15]

These two conflicting perspectives are mentioned here to indicate that the emergence of this new contextual faith within the Black church is very much affected by the ideological conflicts of our time, which reflect different political perceptions about the context. But these also demand different kinds of theological hermeneutics. The tension between these two approaches to social analysis cannot be resolved at a theoretical level, but will emerge as each approach takes much more seriously the interrelatedness of the variables of race, class, and gender in the forging of a new Christian communal praxis. I believe this new communal praxis is embodied in the theological insights of the authors of *The Kairos Document,* which to my mind avoids theoretical exclusiveness.

The possibilities of a much more comprehensive kind of social analysis are embodied in Cornel West's new approach to Black theology as a critique of capitalist civilization. According to Cornel West such an approach:

1. Presupposes a sophisticated understanding of the internal dynamics or power relations of a society or civilization. This understanding requires a social theory whose aim is to demystify present ideological distortions or misreadings of society, to bring to light who possesses power and wealth, why they do, how they acquired it, how they sustain and enlarge it, and why the poor have little or nothing.
2. Is integrally linked with a praxis of faith or political movement which is capable in the near future of fundamentally transforming the present order.
3. Is capable of ushering forth a new order, or organizing, administering, and governing a more human social order.[16]

But because social analysis alone is not enough to promote a Christian vision, the third aspect is theological reflection. This entails critical reflection about the praxis of faith in the ongoing struggle for liberation. In this aspect, faith grapples with issues of life and death. Based on a particular social analysis, Black theological reflection brings the word of God to address the structures of bondage and points to new alternatives. The Black Christian begins to reclaim some of the fundamental theological motifs of the Christian faith and their implications for the Black Christian community based on the scriptures and the prophetic traditions of the church. This is the hermeneutic of suspicion which brings out the radical implications of our faith as it relates to every aspect of Christianity, whether this involves discussion about sin, grace, spirit, or the church. The authors of *The Kairos Document,* for example, identify three kinds of theologies in the South African context: state theology, church theology, and prophetic theology. While social analysis identifies the social forces and institutions that promote oppression, theological reflection becomes a critical response of faith seeking to transform those structures of oppression.

The fourth aspect of social analysis is the development of a Christian communal praxis of faith committed to the transformation of the existing social order. One of the most important shifts in Black theological reflection in South Africa is that our faith makes a radical difference in our life and especially in the present oppressive context. Faith is validated by political praxis. This communal praxis in the South African context means faith compels us to be involved in the struggle for liberation. This faith commits us to a preferential option for the poor and the oppressed.

This communal praxis represents an attempt by the Black Christian community to redefine the mission of the church and to explore new strategies of engaging in the process of radical social change. The authors of *The Kairos Document* encourage us to support the political campaigns of the people, such as consumer boycotts and stayaways. They also call for the radical transformation of church activities: "The Church has its own specific activities, Sunday services, communion services, baptisms, Sunday school, funerals and so forth. It also has its specific way of expressing its faith and its commitment, that is in the form of confessions of faith. All these activities must be reshaped to be more fully consistent with the prophetic faith related to the *kairos* that God is offering us today."[17]

The authors maintain that this communal praxis also involves the call for civil disobedience. If the South African political system of apartheid represents tyranny, then the Black Christian community has no choice but to engage in acts of civil disobedience:

In the first place the church cannot collaborate with tyranny. It cannot or should not do anything that appears to give legitimacy to a morally illegitimate regime. Secondly, the church should not only pray for a change of government, it should also mobilise its members in every parish to begin to think and work and plan for a change of government in South Africa. We must begin to look ahead and begin working now with firm hope and faith for a better future. And finally the moral illegitimacy of the Apartheid regime means the church will have to be involved at times in civil disobedience. A church that takes its responsibilities seriously in these circumstances will sometimes have to confront and to disobey the state in order to obey God.[18]

CONCLUSION

As I have tried to show, faith in the South African context is at the very heart of the struggle for liberation. Our faith as members of the Black Christian community compels us to challenge apartheid and all forms of human oppression. To have faith in Christ is a risky business, one which makes us vulnerable and at worst exposes us to the possibilities of a painful death. But this faith also represents the radical hope that in the face of oppression we have a responsibility to affirm life as we participate in the struggle for justice and peace. Faith in Christ is revolutionary, for it calls for resistance in any situation of oppression and dehumanization. This faith is at the center of any creative theological task that tries to respond courageously to the imperatives of the gospel of our Lord Jesus Christ.

RECOMMENDED READING

From South Africa: A Challenge to the Church. Closter, NJ: Theology in a Global Context Program, 22 Tenakill St., 1988.

Maimela, Simon. *Proclaim Freedom to My People: Essays on Religion and Politics.* Braamfontein, South Africa: Skotaville, 1987.

Nolan, Albert. *God in South Africa: The Challenge of the Gospel.* Grand Rapids, MI: Eerdmans, 1988.

CHAPTER 2

Solidarity: Love of Neighbor in the 1980s

ADA MARÍA ISASI-DÍAZ

CONTEXT AND COMMITMENT

I am a Cuban activist theologian struggling to develop a *Mujerista* theology that is rooted in and has as its source the experience of Hispanic women. I have lived away from my country most of my adult life because of circumstances beyond my control and I think of myself as living in exile. This is the context within which I have struggled to find my voice and my mission. I now know that finding my voice has been part of my mission, a mission which now calls me to struggle to create a platform in the theological world for my voice and the voices of my Hispanic sisters.

As a *Mujerista* I do not see myself as part of a minority group, a marginalized group. It is a fact that at present *Mujeristas,* as well as all Hispanics, have no way of influencing the society in which we live; our values and ideals are not part of the norm of society. As a *Mujerista* I believe that we need to change radically the society in which we live. Simply influencing society will not result in the changes that are needed to bring about peace with justice in our world. That is why we *Mujeristas* understand ourselves along the lines of the biblical concept of the "remnant." Like the biblical remnant we are not an integral part of society. Our mission is to challenge oppressive structures which refuse to allow us to be full members of society while preserving our distinctiveness as Hispanic women.

We also apply this understanding of ourselves as a remnant to our theological task and to our role as theologians. We see *Mujerista* theology as a distinctive contribution to the theological enterprise at large which challenges particularly nonliberative theological understandings. For us theology is a praxis—a liberative praxis having as its goal the liberation of Hispanic women which cannot take place at the expense of any other oppressed group. As *Mujerista* theologians we straddle the academic theological world and the Hispanic women's community. Hispanic women are indeed my community of accountability. But I am an academically trained theologian and wish to maintain a dialogue with all liberation theologies. Therefore, *Mujerista* theology must be understandable both to Hispanic women and to liberation theologians. Our theological method must be a liberative praxis; at the same time we must be able to explain our methodology in such a way that it impacts in no matter how limited a degree the whole theological world.

For me the struggle is life, *la vida es la lucha*. To do *Mujerista* theology is an intrinsic part of my struggle for liberation. To do *Mujerista* theology is to attempt to live life to the fullest, to be about justice and the self-determination of all peoples. To do *Mujerista* theology is to believe that God stands in solidarity with us, Hispanic women.

CONSTRUCTION

Solidarity must replace charity as the appropriate Christian behavior—ethical behavior—in our world today. This constitutes a significant methodological shift, for there is an essential difference between solidarity and charity. Charity, the word we have used most often when talking about love of neighbor, has been implemented mainly by giving of what we have in abundance, a one-sided affair. Obviously that is not all that charity means, but I think that, in general, this is how it is understood and used. I am not saying that giving is never an appropriate and even necessary way of loving. I do believe, however, that giving is an ethical behavior today only if it is understood and carried out within the context of solidarity.

Solidarity is the appropriate present-day expression of the gospel demand that we love our neighbor. This demand, I contend, is what salvation is all about—the goal of Christianity.[1] Therefore, if salvation depends on love of neighbor, and if love of neighbor today is expressed through solidarity, then solidarity is a *sine qua non* of salvation. And who is our neighbor? Our neighbor, according to Matthew 25, is the least of our sisters and brothers. Our neighbor is the poor, the oppressed, with whom we must stand in solidarity.[2]

THE MEANING OF SOLIDARITY

The true meaning of solidarity is under serious attack and runs the risk of being drastically changed. The proof of this is how fashionable its usage has become, how easily it rolls off the tongues of all sorts of speakers, how unthreatening it is. If the true meaning of solidarity were understood and intended, visible radical change would be happening in the lives of those who endorse it with their applause. Solidarity is *not* a matter of agreeing with, of being supportive of, of liking, or of being inspired by, the cause of a group of people. Though all these might be part of solidarity, solidarity goes beyond all of them. Solidarity has to do with understanding the interconnections among issues and the cohesiveness that needs to exist among the communities of struggle.

Solidarity is "the union of fellowship [sic] arising from the common responsibilities and interests, as between classes, peoples, or groups; community of interests, feelings, purposes, or action; social cohesion."[3] Solidarity moves away from the false notion of disinterest, of doing for others in an altruistic fashion. Instead it is grounded in "common responsibilities and interests," which necessarily arouse shared feelings and lead to joint action.

The true meaning of solidarity can best be understood if it is broken down into its two main interdependent elements: mutuality and praxis. Both of these elements will be examined at length later in the chapter, but from the very beginning it must be clear that neither of them is to be considered more important, central, or necessary than the other. Mutuality and praxis are inexorably bound; they have a dialogic, circular relation in which one is always understood in view of the other. There is no dichotomy between them, nor are they to be understood in a dualistic fashion. Furthermore, mutuality and praxis as intrinsic elements of solidarity cannot be conceived or understood as abstractions. They are grounded in the historical situation; their specificity is defined by the socio-economic-political circumstances of the persons involved.

The goal of mutuality and praxis, of solidarity, is to create participation in the ongoing process of liberation through which Christians become a significantly positive force in the unfolding of the "kin-dom"[4] of God. At the center of the unfolding of the kin-dom is the salvific act of God. Salvation and liberation are interconnected. Salvation is gratuitously given by God: it flows from the very essence of God—love. Salvation is the love between God and individual human beings and among human beings. This love relationship is the goal of all life—it constitutes the fullness of humanity. Therefore, love sets in motion and sustains the ongoing act of creation in which the person necessarily participates, since love requires, per se, active involvement of those who are in relationship.

Our ongoing act of creation, our work to transform the world, is both cause and effect of the struggle to have a love relationship with others, including God. This work of transformation—to become a full person and to build the human community—is the work of salvation.[5] There can be no salvation without liberation, though no single act of liberation can be totally identified with salvation in its fullness. As Gustavo Gutiérrez has said, "Without liberating historical events, there would be no growth of the Kingdom [sic] . . . we can say that the historical, political, liberating event is the growth of the Kingdom [sic] and is a salvific event; but it is not the coming of the Kingdom [sic], not all of salvation."[6]

The main obstacle to the unfolding of the kin-dom is the alienation from God and from each other experienced by all persons and understood only through social categories.[7] This alienation is what in theology has been traditionally called sin. Sin always affects the totality of the person and the relationship with God and with others for which the person was created and, therefore, sin always affects society and is a concrete historical reality. "Sin appears, therefore, as the fundamental alienation, the root of a situation of injustice and exploitation."[8]

In order for the person to become fully human—to be in a love relationship with God and with others—justice has to prevail. "As virtue, justice is a trait of character empowering and disposing an agent to act in ways constitutive of human flourishing."[9] This is why the unfolding of the kin-dom of God is made possible when just structures and situations exist. "This is the reason why effort to build a just society is liberating."[10] This is why "action on behalf of justice and transformation of the world fully appear . . . as a constitutive element of the preaching of the Gospel."[11] And, finally, this is why Christianity can be reaffirmed as containing some truth, "not because of its origins, but because it liberates people now from specific forms of oppression."[12]

Solidarity with the oppressed and among the oppressed has to be at the heart of Christian behavior, because the oppression suffered by the majority affects everyone. This solidarity demands a preferential option for the poor. This preferential option is not based on the moral superiority of the poor; it does not mean that personally those who are oppressed are better, or more innocent, or purer in their motivations. The preferential option is based on the fact that the point of view of the oppressed, "pierced by suffering and attracted by hope, allows them, in their struggles, to conceive another reality. Because the poor suffer the weight of alienation, they can conceive a different project of hope and provide dynamism to a new way of organizing human life *for all*."[13]

The epistemological privilege of the poor makes it possible for them to conceive of a new nonalienating reality for all. Oppression and poverty limit love since love cannot exist in the midst of alienation. Oppression and poverty are "a slap in the face of God's sovereignty."[14] The alienation brought about and maintained by oppressive structures is a denial of God. Gutiérrez recalls, "as a Bolivian campesino, Paz Jimenez, put it . . . with an insight that is profoundly biblical: 'an atheist is someone who fails to practice justice toward the poor.'"[15]

Who are the poor and oppressed? First of all, the poor and the oppressed in this context "always implies collective and social conflict."[16] The poor and the oppressed are those who are marginalized, whose participation in the sociopolitical life is severely restricted or totally negated. The poor are living persons whose struggle for survival constitutes their way of life. "Concretely, to be poor means to die of hunger, to be illiterate, to be exploited by others, not to know that you are being exploited, not to know you are a person."[17] The poor and the oppressed suffer from very specific forms of oppression—sexism, racism, classism.

These specific oppressions, however, are not self-contained realities in the world today, but are interconnected parts of a worldwide system of domination in which the few oppress the many.[18] This system of domination permeates every aspect of society: ideology, religion, social mores, government, businesses, families, relationships.

In order to effectively change such a worldwide reality, solidarity is a must both as a theory and as a strategy.[19] As a theory solidarity stands against the theory of oppression[20] and reconceptualizes every aspect of society in every part of the world. As a strategy solidarity indicates the path to follow in order to change society radically. The magnitude of this task is such that only worldwide action can effectively undo and replace oppression.

The starting place of solidarity as a theory is the particularity of the oppressions suffered by those who are exploited and marginalized. As a theory solidarity insists on the interconnections of the oppression. This creates a commonality of interests among the oppressed and between the oppressed and those who stand in solidarity with them. Solidarity as a theory insists on the centrality of mutuality, on the importance of a new order of relationships opposed to any and all forms of domination. This constructive task has to go hand in hand with the deconstructive task of denouncing the understandings and theories which support the present structures of domination. Therefore, solidarity must continuously denounce hierarchy as a structure which sets a few, eventually only one, over the many.

As a strategy solidarity has to be politically effective. Though there is no place for purist understandings in strategical considerations, solidarity as a strategy must not sacrifice any one group of oppressed people for the sake of another group. As a strategy solidarity must be about radical structural change. The goal is not the participation of the oppressed in present societal structures but rather the replacement of those structures by ones in which full participation of the oppressed is possible. No strategy can wait for a perfect time to be carried out, or until all the internal problems and inconsistencies are solved. As with all strategies, there is risk involved; as with all human realities, the understanding and implementation of solidarity is and will always be imperfect. But this should never delay creating a community of solidarity committed to change oppressive structures.

The theoretical aspect of solidarity is intrinsically linked to its strategic component.[21] The theoretical and strategic considerations of solidarity correspond to its two main elements: mutuality and praxis. The strategy of solidarity carries out the theoretical understandings at the same time that it provides the ground for the reflection needed to elaborate the theory. The theory of solidarity provides the goal for the strategy of solidarity at the same time that it gives the strategy an inherent way of evaluating its progress and critiquing itself. It is solidarity as a strategy which demands of the theory an ever greater clarity and demands that it be historically rooted. The internal relation of theory to strategy within solidarity demands a dialogic, circular understanding of the elements of solidarity—mutuality and praxis.

THE PRAXIS OF MUTUALITY: FRIENDSHIP

Common interests—the heart of solidarity—are what move Christian behavior from the one-sidedness of charity to mutuality. These common interests are a reality in our world today. Two world wars, multinational corporations, the threat of global annihilation, the global spread of AIDS, the worldwide political influence and control of the superpowers, acid rain, the deterioration of the ozone layer—all of these are examples of the bases for common interests today.

What about mutuality among the oppressed? Mutuality among the oppressed is set in motion by becoming aware, by a moment of insight which creates a suspicion about oppression. Almost anything can create the spark which moves people "from a 'naive awareness,' which does not deal with problems, gives too much value to the past, tends to accept mythical explanations, and tends toward debate, to a 'critical awareness,' which delves into problems, is open to new ideas, replaces magical explanations with real causes, and tends to dialogue."[22]

Paulo Freire calls this process "conscientization" and insists that it involves praxis and is not just an intellectual understanding apart from action.[23] Critical awareness makes the oppressed understand the real causes of oppression and the need to engage with others in changing the situation which marginalizes them. This process of conscientization is not something that happens once and for all. Conscientization is a "permanent effort of man [sic] who seeks to situate himself [sic] in time and space, to exercise his [sic] creative potential, and to assume his [sic] responsibilities."[24]

Mutuality among the oppressed is not a given. Though it is true that many of the oppressed do depend on other oppressed people to survive, frequently the oppressed do not see their common interests because they have to fight each other for the few crumbs that fall from the table of the oppressors. In many ways the oppressed depend for their survival on those who control the society in which they live—their oppressors. To even begin to envision the possibilities that they can create when they stand in solidarity with each other, the oppressed have to be willing to stop looking for and accepting the "charity" of their oppressors. To turn from the "charity" of the oppressors to solidarity among themselves requires great willingness to take risks. This going beyond the isolated self is followed by creating strategies, solidarity among them, in order to carry out their struggle for liberation. The implementation of these strategies will keep their hopes alive and, together with the vision of their own liberation, it will give them the courage to risk and sustain the struggle.

Mutuality between the oppressed and the oppressor also starts with a process of becoming aware. To become aware does not stop with individual illumination but necessarily moves to establish dialogue and mutuality with the oppressed.[25] The first word in this dialogue is uttered by the oppressed. The oppressors who are willing to listen and to be questioned by the oppressed begin to cease being oppressors—they become "friends" of the oppressed.[26] This word spoken by the oppressed is "at times silent, at times muzzled; it is the face of the poor . . . of oppressed people who suffer violence."[27] This word is often spoken through demonstrations, boycotts, and even revolution. This word imposes itself "ethically, by a kind of categorical imperative, which is well determined and concrete, which the 'friend' as 'friend' listens to freely. This word . . . appeals to the 'friend's' domination and possession of the world and even of the other, and questions the desire for wealth and power."[28]

This word uttered by the oppressed divests those who allow themselves to be questioned by it of whatever they have totally appropriated. This word carries in its very weakness the power to judge the desire for wealth and power. It also is able to signify effectively the real possibility of liberation for those oppressors who allow themselves to be questioned. The leap the oppressors must take in order to be questioned is also made possible by the efficacious word uttered by the oppressed. The word uttered by the oppressed carries the real possibility of this qualitative jump and can be the liberating force which pushes the "friends" to take the leap that will put them in touch with the oppressed. This word also makes it possible for the "friends" to question and judge the oppressive structures which they support and from which they benefit, and to become cocreators with the oppressed of new liberating structures.

The "friends" answer the initial word uttered by the oppressed not only by questioning their own lives but also by responding to the oppressed. This response is born of the critical consciousness of those who allowed themselves to be critiqued and who take responsibility for their own consciousness. This response therefore becomes a word and an action which helps the oppressed in their process of conscientization. The response of the "friends" is one of the enabling forces which help the oppressed to become agents of their own history. This response of the "friends" enables the oppressed to rid themselves of the oppressor they carry within themselves. This moves the oppressed away from seeking vengeance, from wanting to exchange places with the oppressors. This response of the "friends" enables the oppressed to understand that they must not seek to participate in oppressive structures but rather to change radically those structures.

In many ways the "friends" are often harshly victimized by society at large because they have been part of the oppressors and know how to thwart the control and domination which keeps the oppressors in power.

Furthermore, "friends" can prick the conscience of the oppressors in ways the oppressed cannot, because the "friends" know the manipulations and the betrayals that the oppressors must make to stay in power. The "friends" are able to demystify the world of the oppressors from within, to expose its weakness and incoherence, to point out its lies. One must not lose sight, however, that it is not the word uttered by the "friends" which initiates the process of conscientization for the oppressor. It is the word uttered by the oppressed, the one which starts the dialogic process which results in mutuality based on common interests—especially liberation. The oppressors who have become "friends" and the oppressed derive their courage to persist in the long struggle which begins with conscientization from their vision of liberation.

Mutuality among the oppressed and between the oppressed and their "friends" is not simply a matter of mutual understanding and support, though that is or could be a very positive side effect. Mutuality as an element of solidarity must push the oppressed and their "friends" to revolutionary politics.[29] Mutuality must urge them to envision and work toward alternative systems, or they will not be able to sustain the revolutionary momentum that makes liberation possible.[30] Mutuality must enable the oppressed and their "friends" to stay away from easy, partial solutions which might alleviate the situation of oppression but do not lead to liberation.

In order to maintain the revolutionary momentum the oppressed and their "friends" must work constantly to maintain the commitment to mutuality alive and strong. Commitment to mutuality means *"willingness to do something* for or about whatever it is we are committed to (at least to protect it or affirm it when it is threatened),"[31] and this follows upon a "sense of *being bound* to whomever or whatever is the object of [this] commitment."[32] Commitment gives other persons or a cause claim over oneself, thus establishing or strengthening mutuality between the self and the other. It is, as Margaret Farley argues, "a relation of binding and being-bound, giving and being-claimed."[33]

Commitment to the mutuality established among the oppressed and between the oppressed and the "friends" is essential because it provides assurance to others and strength to the person who is committed. Commitment is required if mutuality as an element of solidarity is to be the basis for praxis, because "it undergirds the very possibility of human communication."[34] Mutuality as an element of solidarity based in commonality of interests demands commitment to action. Without action mutuality becomes a "soft word," a passing whimsical reaction which is often privatized and removed from the public sphere, from the political reality of the struggle for liberation.[35] The actions resulting from true commitment become the framework of mutuality; they are the signs and deeds of mutuality and the efforts that ensure the future of mutuality.[36] It is precisely these actions which express and constitute mutuality that in a limited but real way begin to make liberation present. Actions born out of commitment to mutuality are eschatological glimpses which clarify the vision of liberation and make faithfulness to the vision possible. Liberation is not a condition that already exists and is simply waiting for the oppressed to grasp it. Rather, liberation is a historical possibility that takes form and shape according to the actions of the oppressed and their "friends." Liberative actions born out of commitment to mutuality, therefore, are not only glimpses of the future but eschatological actions making parts of the future present.

Commitment to mutuality among the oppressed and between the oppressed and their "friends" cannot be taken lightly because of the eschatological actions which are part of its framework. This commitment involves all aspects of one's life and has a lifelong permanency. The way in which the commitment is lived out might change. At times the person might be much more intentional about carrying out the implications of the commitment than at others. How the commitment is carried out might also vary according to circumstances. But to betray the mutuality established by placing oneself in a position of control and domination over others is to betray the commitment made. This is a betrayal of the other and a betrayal of oneself, because of the commonality of interests that exists whether one recognizes it or not. The betrayal, which most of the time occurs by failing to engage in liberative praxis rather than by a formal denunciation of the commitment, results in the "friends" becoming oppressors once again and in the oppressed losing their vision of liberation. Such betrayal, then, effectively delays liberation and, therefore, at least makes more difficult the unfolding of the kin-dom of God.[37]

CONCLUSION

Solidarity as a praxis of mutuality is indeed an intrinsic element of the process of liberation and salvation. It is through solidarity with the "least" of our sisters and brothers (Matt. 25) that the gospel command to love our neighbor as ourselves finds expression in our world today. By examining the process through which solidarity is established and the politically effective praxis through which it is expressed, we come to understand what our ethical behavior is to be today, if we are to call ourselves Christian.

RECOMMENDED READING

Chopp, Rebecca S. *The Praxis of Suffering.* Maryknoll, NY: Orbis, 1986.
Farley, Margaret. *Personal Commitments.* San Francisco: Harper & Row, 1986.
Gutiérrez, Gustavo. "Liberation Praxis and Christian Faith." In *Frontiers of Theology in Latin America,* ed. R. Gibellini. Maryknoll, NY: Orbis, 1974.

———. *The Power of the Poor in History.* Maryknoll, NY: Orbis, 1984.
Sobrino, Jon, S.J., and Juan Hernandez Pico, S.J. *Theology of Christian Solidarity.* Maryknoll, NY: Orbis, 1985.
Welch, Sharon D. *Communities of Resistance and Solidarity.* Maryknoll, NY: Orbis, 1985.

CHAPTER 3

Symbol, Myth, and Ritual: The Method of the *Minjung*

YOUNG-CHAN RO

CONTEXT AND COMMITMENT

In my view, theology as a form of intellectual reflection on the Christian tradition is facing a unique challenge today. In terms of its methodology, theology can no longer enjoy the privilege of being based on "special revelation." Nor can it any longer assume that it is a privileged discipline separate from other forms of human inquiry for spirituality and religious life. Theology must be fully *incarnated* in society and culture. The nature and goal of theology must not be defined purely in the realm of the church, for the church, and by the church alone.

Traditional theologians often view the study of the broad context of human religiosity, history of religions, or religious studies with two kinds of false perception: a false sense of superiority and a false sense of insecurity. The former results from the *hubris* inherent in the belief that the methodology of Christian theology is unique and preordained and thus must be protected from all other forms of human investigation (such as the history of religions approach). This attitude assumes that theology is, methodologically speaking, *sui generis*. The latter is caused mainly by ignorance, as is evident in the belief that interpreting theology or constructing theology from other than theological points of view is inadequate and dangerous, because it may undermine the very assumptions on which Christian theology itself is based.

Having been trained in both theology and religious studies, I believe that theology can gain much from religious studies and history of religions. This is true especially when we study a new theological movement such as *minjung* theology. Traditional Western categories and theological formulae may not be sufficient for understanding and interpreting the deeper implications and diverse ramifications of nontraditional and non-Western forms of theology. For this reason, I am committed to bringing a new perspective to the interpretation of new theological movements emerging in the non-Western world. *Minjung* theology is to be examined and reflected in the whole context of Korean culture, spirtuality, and social values. The significance of *minjung* theology, despite its obvious contribution to the development of sociopolitical dynamics in Korea, goes beyond the limits of a political theology or a social ideology. *Minjung* theology, in my view, proposes a new way of *doing* theology.

I live at a crossroads in a double sense. Intellectually, I am committed to doing theology by crossing the boundaries between Christian texts and non-Christian contexts. Culturally and existentially, as a native Korean, I am committed to exploring the significance of the texts of Korean and other Asian traditions in light of modern Western contexts. Both fields contribute to my work of developing a fully incarnated theology.

CONSTRUCTION

This chapter is a preliminary exploration of the significance of *minjung* theology from the viewpoint of the phenomenology and history of religion. *Minjung* theology is a theological movement and a religious phenomenon. It is such a rich and complex phenomenon that it requires a much broader perspective than Christian theology usually provides. So far its social and political significance have been greatly emphasized. But it cannot and must not be reduced to a social philosophy or a political ideology. The source of *minjung* theology is found in a profound religious experience of the Korean people. To call attention to this I have adopted a history of religions approach to *minjung* theology, the rationale for which is given below.

First, Christianity itself is a religious tradition. Approaches such as history of religions, phenomenology of religion, comparative and cross-cultural analysis, and dialogue among religions will shed light on a deeper dimension of Christianity in general and *minjung* theology in particular.

Second, for a proper understanding, interpretation, and appreciation of *minjung* theology, we have to explore more than the Christian categories of human religious experience. Although the main figures of the *minjung* theology movement are Christian theologians or lay intellectuals and the main structure of *minjung* theology is dependent upon the Christian theological framework, the implications of *minjung* theology are far broader. Several Korean *minjung* theologians (e.g., Suh Nam-dong, Kim Yong-bock, and Hyun Young-hak) have already shown interest in extending the discussion of *minjung* theology to non-Christian realms of experience. That they have moved in this direction indicates the need for a history of religions approach to formulate *minjung* theology's basic assumptions and interpret its full significance.

Third, *minjung* theology as a system of thought requires a cultural form of expression. Understanding Korean forms of religiosity and spirituality, therefore, is necessary for a proper interpretation of the cultural history, socioeconomic tradition, and even "social biography" of Korea.

Fourth, theology (*theos* + *logos*) in Western intellectual and cultural traditions is essentially a *logos*-oriented system rather than a *mythos*-appreciating activity. A history of religions approach will be more helpful in illuminating this *mythos* dimension of *minjung* theology.

Fifth, *minjung* theology is a clear and conscious attempt to develop a Korean theology. Although traditional Western theologies, and even contemporary theologies such as liberation theology and Black theology, have influenced the formation of *minjung* theology, the method of *minjung* theology goes beyond traditional Western categories. In breaking these boundaries, *minjung* theology has already transformed conventional theological method and structure.

To limit my discussion, I will develop only the last two points: the dynamics of transformation in *minjung* theology. Theology, if taken seriously, is an intellectual formula and a form of confession or a statement of faith.[1] In other words, theology as a serious intellectual discipline includes an existential commitment. Theology, in this sense, takes the form of a political ideology. Theology is the *theoria* of believers' *praxis.* Theory and praxis are mutually interpenetrating. *Minjung* theology, like liberation theology, aims at the transformation of society and political conditions. *Minjung* theology was formed and developed in the social and political context of Korea. It has successfully functioned as the most powerful intellectual force in the transformation of the social and political structures of contemporary Korea.

This is not, however, what makes *minjung* theology unique. In the process of serving as the most effective religious movement, intellectual power, and political ideology of social transformation in Korea, *minjung* theology has developed a distinctive way of doing theology that challenges traditional Western theology's content and method. The task, then, of *minjung* theology is twofold: to transform the socioeconomic structure of Korean society and to transform theology itself. The former aims at external transformation and the latter at internal transformation. Neither can be achieved without the other.

Korean *minjung* theologians have been deeply aware of the dynamic interrelationship of external (socio-economic-political or ecclesiastical) and internal (theological) transformation. In my view, *minjung* theology itself results from the interrelationship between the two forms of transformation. Both types of transformation have existed throughout the history of religious traditions in the East and West. In order to transform church structures, the sixteenth century reformers transformed the interpretation of the scripture. In order to transform social conditions, the Chinese neo-Confucianist Chu Hsi reconstructed and rearranged the basic Confucian texts. Chinese Buddhism involved a Chinese adaptation of Indian Buddhism and a Chinese transformation of Indian Buddhism in order to transform Chinese culture and society. Won-hyo, Chinul, T'ogye, and Yulgok, some of the most distinguished Buddhist and Confucian scholars of Korea, have attempted to transform Buddhism and Confucianism in order to transform their societies. Mao Tse-tung transformed Marxism into Maoism in order to transform and unify China. Kim Il-sung transformed Communism into the ideology of *chuche* (a place we can learn) in order to transform North Korean society.

One of the most exciting aspects of the *minjung* theology movement is its dynamic twofold power of transformation. In the process of serving as an effective political ideology, intellectual movement, and religious passion for the transformation of Korean society, *minjung* theology found itself undergoing a profound self-transformation. Although *minjung* is still in the making and far from taking a definitive form, it has a discernible identity. How might that identity be described? It is too simple to classify it along with liberation theologies as a Third World theology; or with Black theologies as an ethnic, racial theology; or with feminist theologies as a marginal theology.[2] Korean *minjung* theologians often discuss the similarities between these theologies and *minjung* theology. We share, for example, a commitment to resist dominant political and social powers. But we also discuss the differences, for in spite of all the similarities, we believe *minjung* theology cannot and must not be simply a Korean version of liberation or Black theology. One of the clearest points of difference between many other liberation theologies and *minjung* theology may be seen in its theological method.

To avoid an extended comparison between liberation theologies and *minjung* theology, I will confine myself to one preliminary methodological observation. Most liberation theologies have not yet overcome the traditional Western way of doing theology. Their logic is still very dependent on Western ways of thinking. That is, they are characterized by patterns of reflection that are analytical, dialectical, and conceptual. A dialectical method assumes a dichotomy between the real and the ideal and believes that truth is to be found in the process of dialectical struggle between the two opposing sides of this dichotomy.

The logic of *minjung* theology stands in contrast to this. It is neither analytical nor dialectical but rather synthetic and dialogical. A dialogical method assumes reality is nondualistic; it is not separated into black and white, good and evil, God and human, male and female, etc. Further, a dialogical way of thinking seeks the truth about this reality in relationships rather than in dichotomy.

The dialogical method is not unique to *minjung* theology, for all Korean spiritual and religious traditions reflect this way of thinking. It does differentiate it from many other liberation theologies, however. Different ways of thinking arise out of different cultural contexts. Although other liberation theologies (especially Black theologies) and *minjung* theology share similar social and political contexts, they do not necessarily share the same religious and cultural context. For this reason the theological responses of *minjung* may not be the same as those in Black theologies. Korean cultural traditions, for example, have developed under the influence of several religious traditions, including native shamanism. The Korean people have inherited a single racial and linguistic tradition, but their cultural and religious experiences are grounded in rich and diverse traditions. *Minjung* theology, then, consciously or unconsciously, reflects all these cultural and spiritual traditions.

MINJUNG THEOLOGY: SYMBOL, MYTH, AND RITUAL

Minjung theology, a latecomer to the scene of Third World theology (not third-class theology), has learned a lot from other liberation theologies, particularly in the area of social awareness and analysis. In its beginning stage in the early 1970s it was heavily influenced by political theology (Jürgen Moltmann's *Theology of Hope*) and South American liberation theology (Gustavo Gutiérrez's *Theology of Liberation* and others). In its later stages, however, *minjung* theology has made a significant turn. It has moved from a focus on theology of transformation, blending social awareness and analysis of the Korean society with the Christian tradition, to a focus on the transformation of theology, analyzing and interpreting the basic assumptions of Christian faith from the Korean social and cultural point of view. This distinction between theology of transformation and the transformation of theology is a preliminary one and may oversimplify the complex development of *minjung* theology. For one thing, it should be noted that these two processes may occur simultaneously. Nonetheless, in the history of the emergence of *minjung* theology, a transition from the former to the latter is discernible. And, the most serious and original theological challenge of *minjung* theology to Christian theologies in general and liberation theologies in particular is to be found in this distinctive direction we have taken toward the transformation of theology. In order to demonstrate the validity of this thesis, I would like to call attention to this shift in the work of Suh Nam-dong, Hyun Young-hak, and Kim Yong-bock, especially as it relates to the following three dimensions of religious experience: symbolization, remythologization, and ritualization.

SYMBOLIZATION

One of the controversies regarding *minjung* theology concerns the exact definition of the term *minjung*. It is not translatable into English; it is undefinable, even for Koreans. Although many theologians and sociologists have attempted to define the *minjung*, they have not reached a clear consensus. At its broadest, it refers to all oppressed peoples. Sociologist Han Wan-sang's definition of the *minjung* is frequently mentioned as an acceptable definition, at least on a conceptual level: "The *minjung* are those who are oppressed politically, exploited economically, alienated sociologically, and kept uneducated in cultural and intellectual matters."[3] This definition, however, inaccurately implies that the *minjung* are limited to a certain social class. The idea of the *minjung* must not be interpreted in terms of the proletariat, because the *minjung* cannot be reduced to a social class or political entity. *Minjung* cannot be grasped in terms of sociological and political concepts alone, for the *minjung* is a living, dynamic, human, social reality that includes a religious dimension. Kim Yong-bock makes a clear distinction between the *minjung* and the proletariat for this reason.

This difference between the *minjung* and the proletariat entails different views of history. *Minjung* history has a strong transcendental or transcending dimension—a beyond-history—which is often expressed in religious form. There is a close relation between religion and the *minjung*'s perception of history. Even if *minjung* history does not involve a religious element in an explicit manner, its folklore or cultural elements play a transcending function similar to religion in the perception of history.[4]

The religious element of the *minjung* is so significant for Kim Young-bock that he denies it can be reduced to any kind of concept: "*Minjung* is not a concept or object which can be easily explained or defined. *Minjung* signifies a living reality which is dynamic. This living reality defines its own existence, and generates new acts and dramas in history; and it refuses in principle to be defined conceptually."[5]

Minjung as a living reality has become a symbol for the people who identify themselves as the *minjung*. As a symbol it is direct and immediate. It does not need a concept, for it comes to us without mediation. A symbol is a comprehensive way of experiencing reality that does not require an intellectual articulation or philosophical analysis. Concepts require explanation, description, and justification. A symbol is irreducible and transcends any form of conceptual framework. A defined symbol is no longer a symbol. A conceptualized symbol is a corrupted symbol. A symbol explained is a symbol that has vanished.

This does not mean that the idea of *minjung* is so vague and obscure that any people can identify themselves as the *minjung*. On the contrary, far from an abstract idea, the *minjung* is a clear and concrete reality. *Minjung* is a form of self-understanding and self-identifying experience. That is, *minjung* is an irreducible experience in which one finds his or her self-identification. As symbol, *minjung* has an inclusive power that enables people to participate in it.

Minjung theology has transformed the word *minjung* from a concept to a symbol. Although there is no concrete, physical symbol (such as the cross or the star of David) associated with *minjung*, it nevertheless operates as a symbolic structure of reality for people in Korea, because of its characteristics of unmediated knowledge and the transparency of experience. In other words, *minjung* is not a concept for theological definition, but a living religious symbol in which people can fully participate and with which they can completely identify. What then is the core of that experience which enables us to identify ourselves with the *minjung*? What is the content of the experience in which the *minjung* identify themselves with this symbol?

HAN: THE SPIRIT OF THE MINJUNG

So far I have argued against any attempt to conceptualize *minjung*. How then may we identify *minjung*? One fundamental element that runs through the whole experience of *minjung* is *han*. *Han*, another untranslatable word, is a definitive form of human experience for those who are the *minjung*. With the experience of *han*, common people become the *minjung*. *Han* is in part a negative or passive notion implying the cumulative unresolved feeling that arises out of people's experience of injustice. But *han* is also a positive psychosocial energy which can be expressed in sociopolitical power or spiritual-religious transcendence.

Korean *minjung* theologians (especially Suh Nam-dong and Kim Yong-bock) have developed the idea of the *minjung* and *han* as a symbolic reality. Yet Suh Nam-dong, for example, never bothers to define *han* in his essay, "Towards a Theology of *Han*."[6] In a footnote to this article the translator and the editor of the volume explain the idea of *han* and attribute this explanation to Suh Nam-dong. "*Han* is a deep feeling that rises out of the unjust experiences of the people. 'Just indignation' may be a close translation of *han*, but it evokes a refined emotion yearning for justice to be done [translator]. The author offers this explanation: *han* is the suppressed, amassed, and condensed experience of oppression caused by mischief or misfortune so that it forms a kind of 'lump' in one's spirit [editor]."[7] This explanation runs counter to Suh's own theological method. Suh deliberately did not attempt to define the concept of *han*. Instead, assuming a dialogical method and the symbolic power of *han*, he begins by *telling* two tragic stories about events in contemporary Korea. After telling these stories, Suh simply says "This is *han*." From my perspective it is important to point out that Suh takes a different approach to understanding *han*. It is the stories that tell what *han* is. *Han* cannot be understood without listening to the stories. We must listen to the *story* of *han*. *Han* may not unfold itself without the telling of stories. This approach represents a significant departure from the method of traditional Western theology. I call this part of *minjung* theological method "deconceptualization."

REMYTHOLOGIZATION

Han, the spirit of the *minjung*, cannot be conceptualized, yet it must be expressed, captured, and realized in life. The unfolding story of *han* is so real and so powerful that the story of *han* must be told and retold. *Minjung* theology is therefore a theology of stories and narration. Western theology *(theos + logos)* is a *logos*-oriented system that extracts *logos* from *mythos*. One of the most remarkable attempts of this kind is found in Rudolf Bultmann's theology, so appropriately termed "demythologization." In contrast, *minjung* theology has rediscovered the power of myth and the need for remythologization. The story must be told, not analyzed or conceptualized. Thus, *mindam* (folklore) is the mode of theology in the *minjung* theology movement. *Mindam* is the house of *han* in which the spirit of the *minjung* dwells. *Mindam* is also the mode of preaching in *minjung* theology. *Minjung* speaks through the mode of *mindam*. The *han* of the *minjung* is incarnated in *mindam*. Therefore, *minjung* theology is *mythos*- not *logos*-oriented theology. For myth-making is understood to be essential to *minjung* theology, because *han* must be told, heard, touched, felt, and resolved. *A tragedy is not a tragedy until it is told.* *Mindam* is the unique mode of speaking and telling in which the message of *han* may be heard. In this sense, the medium is the message. History becomes story. Story becomes a paradigm of history.

RITUALIZATION

Life is a process of ritual (Mingok). Life must be lived, not contemplated. Native Korean spirituality (for example, shamanism) has totally integrated the spiritual realm and the physical realm. *Minjung* theology rediscovered the gist of Korean spirituality in the traditional Korean mask dance. The mask dance is the ritual aspect of *minjung* theology. *Minjung* is a theology of the body. The body contains the mind. The *minjung* feel pain and suffering, joy and ecstasy in the ritual of the mask dance. The mask dance is an experience of transcendence, the moment of the spiritual transformation from *han* to *dan* (the sublimation of *han* through self-denial).

CONCLUSION

By grounding itself in the symbols of the *minjung* and *han,* the power of story-telling, and the ritual of the mask dance, *minjung* theology has made a significant turn. It has moved beyond being a theology of transformation of the social-economic-political reality to becoming a theology that is transformed from a *logos*- to a *mythos*-orientation.

RECOMMENDED READING

Commission on Theological Concerns of the Christian Conference of Asia. *Minjung Theology.* Maryknoll, NY: Orbis, 1981.

Lee, Jung Young, ed. *An Emerging Theology in World Perspective: Commentary on Korean Minjung Theology.* Mystic, CT: Twenty-Third Publications, 1988.

CHAPTER 4

The Old Testament of Native America

STEVE CHARLESTON

CONTEXT AND COMMITMENT

I come from Oklahoma. I was born in the southern part of the state in a small town called Duncan. My grandfather and great-grandfather were Presbyterian ministers. Like most people in our tribe, the Choctaw Nation, they were Presbyterians who preached and sang in Choctaw. My own family was tied up with the oil fields. We moved out of Duncan and went up to Oklahoma City as the jobs changed. That means that I experienced a number of different churches. I was baptized a Southern Baptist, but I've known everything from Roman Catholic to Unitarian to the Baha'i faith. I think that's partly because Oklahoma Indian life can be so eclectic. There are dozens of tribes to go along with dozens of churches. Things are very mixed in Oklahoma. It's a cultural patchwork quilt laid down over ranch land, red dirt, and eastern timberland. I've inherited some of that mixture and it's followed me around wherever I've gone.

I am an Indian. I am a Christian. Being both wasn't always easy. Like many other Native People, I've known my share of confusion, frustration, anger, and struggle. But I've also known a lot of hope, joy, and visions. So the two balance each other out. Today I feel comfortable talking about Christianity as a faith that emerges from Native America. I came to that feeling after many years of travel through different Native communities. I would credit a great many Native men, women, and children (Traditional, Christian, and a little of both) as being my real teachers. They helped me to grow up and find the sense of spiritual balance that I think is central to life. Of course, keeping the balance takes a lifetime, but at least I have a place to stand.

The place I stand is in the original covenant God gave to Native America. I believe with all my heart that God's revelation to Native People is second to none. God spoke to generations of Native People over centuries of our spiritual development. We need to pay attention to that voice, to be respectful of the covenant, and to be unafraid to lift up the new covenant as the fulfillment of the ancient promise made to the Native People of North America. That means seeing Jesus not as a white plastic messiah taken off the dashboard of a car and dipped in brown to make things look more Indian, but a living Christ that arises from the Native covenant and speaks with the authority and authenticity of Native America.

I have been talking about what I call a Native People's Christian theology for over fifteen years. I started out when I was one of only four Native People in seminary and I am still doing it today. So I feel a deep commitment to this new theology. I want to do all that I can to help bring Native People together. That means healing the false divisions brought into our tribes by Western colonialism. It means helping Native People who think of themselves as being either Traditional or Christian find common ground, a common center. In time, it will mean carrying the voice of Native America around the world to join with millions of other Christians in a second reformation. I may not be around for that time, but I want to help make it happen by proclaiming the indigenous theology of this continent.

And that brings me full circle, because I also believe that theology is autobiography. If we are really honest about all of this, about all of the millions of words we produce each year on theology, we have to admit that when we start out trying to talk about God, we usually wind up talking about ourselves. At least, between the lines. So, I think you can read Oklahoma in what I have to say: and Presbyterian preachers baptizing Native People in the river, and Choctaw camp meetings, and some struggle to be made whole. I also hope that you can hear commitment, energy, and strength, and that you recognize the power of God to help and to heal and a messiah who is changing the world.

CONSTRUCTION

Imagine a supermarket: not one of the small local convenience stores, but a really big supermarket, the kind of place with aisle after aisle of things from which to choose. The shelves are loaded. There are hundreds of different brands. There are different departments or sections. The merchandise is carefully organized to make shopping easier. This is a real American store, a place that testifies to our abundance and our right to choose for ourselves.

Now imagine that instead of groceries, this supermarket sells theologies. As you roll your cart along the aisles, what do you see? Dozens of different brands: a theology for every taste. There is a department for basic Western theologies, the old standbys. There are sections reserved for feminist theology, for Black theology, for liberation theology. There are shelves for African theology and Asian theology. There is even a gourmet section for New Age theologies. At first glance, it seems that this supermarket has a Christian theology from every culture and community. Almost. But not quite. Something is missing. As strange as it may seem, the Great American Religious Supermarket is incomplete. It has some shelves that are standing empty. Go down the aisles and try to find the section for a Native People's Christian theology. It isn't there. Look for a department called Native American or American Indian Christian theology. Still not there. The fact is: in all of the abundance of Christian theologies flooding the religious marketplace in contemporary America, one is conspicuous by its absence. There is no strong presence of Native American Christians in the theological marketplace.

Why? That's the simple but profound question that needs to be answered. Why have Native People not entered visibly into the Christian debate? Why is there no quickly recognizable Christian theology from Native America? Why not several brands for Native Americans to choose from? Why not a whole shelf of theologies from Native Christian theologians? Is it because they are content to let others do the talking for them? Or are there other reasons that need to be examined, understood, proclaimed?

"Conspicuous by their absence." That's the phrase I used and I wonder if you caught it? There is an irony in using those words, because I doubt if Native People have really been conspicuous by their absence. I doubt it, because I have rarely heard the question "Why?" asked before. Not too many Christians seem troubled by the absence of a Native People's Christian theology. I think if we are honest with one another, we will admit that most religious shoppers have gone down the aisles and never noticed that Native People were missing. They assumed that the supermarket was complete: new products arrive daily, old products are repackaged—new and improved theologies, special sales on hot items. In all of the abundance, in all of the excitement, I don't believe many people have noticed a few empty shelves. This fact alone raises another question. Why have so very few people questioned the absence of Native Americans? Given the proliferation of theologies from many racial, cultural, ethnic, and economic communities, given the rise of theologies from the feminist community, given the increased awareness on the part of consumers of theology—why has the absence of Native People's theology gone unnoticed?

If we tackle that question first, we may find that we are starting to surface some clues to the more fundamental reasons for Native America's silence in the Christian debate. Here is a place to begin: many people may have overlooked the absence of a Native People's Christian theology because they assumed it was covered by the supermarket sections reserved for spirituality. I think that's a fair guess. After all, there are many shelves these days loaded with works on Native American spirituality. Some are historical, others are anthropological or biographical; some are journalistic accounts by white authors who went to live with the Indians and returned to share the exotic secrets they discovered. In fact, there has been something of a minor gold rush in Native American "spirituality," with lots of people writing about it. What is described as Native American spirituality crops up in all kinds of places, especially in the gourmet section of the theological supermarket. In a style not too far removed from the 1960s and early 1970s, it's become chic to be Indian again, or, at least, to know an Indian, particularly if that Indian is a medicine person. It's romantic, earthy, "creation-centered."

The Native spirituality craze, therefore, may account for the neglect of a Native People's Christian theology. Well-intentioned shoppers may have simply thought that this talk about spirituality was the voice of Native America in the religious dialogue. And up to a point, they're right. Traditional Native spirituality does represent a major and crucial voice for Native People. It is a voice that has frequently been misquoted, distorted, or co-opted, but it's a voice nonetheless. I am certainly not prepared to argue against a legitimate role for that spirituality. In fact, I am going to argue that this spirituality is something extremely central to Native America, and to the Christ, and faith. Still, the spirituality section alone does not complete the supermarket. It is still not an expression of a Native Christian viewpoint. As good (or bad) as these works may be at articulating Native tradition, they do not offer a clear voice for Native American Christianity. They are not a Native People's Christian theology. Instead they are the source for materials for that theology—they are reference points, or commentaries.

THE OLD TESTAMENT OF NATIVE AMERICA

So far, we've said that the answer to why most people have ignored the absence of a Native People's Christian theology is because they thought they were getting it through Native "spirituality." But that still doesn't explain why the theology itself is missing. Now, we have a clue to follow. What would happen if instead of speaking about Native American spirituality we began speaking of an Old Testament of Native America? What would that do for us?

Well, first of all, it would give us a new vocabulary in dealing with what we've been describing as Native spirituality. For example, a great many of those books in the supermarket would become Old Testament commentaries. They would be books about the source material of Native America's Old Testament. Books about the traditions of Old Testament times, about the culture of Old Testament times, about the personalities of Old Testament times, and the theology of Old Testament times. We might start treating them more seriously and critically, since they would be describing the foundational theology for a contemporary Christian theology. They would have to be weighed and judged on a much finer scale than we have been accustomed to. The authors of these books would begin to seem like Old Testament scholars, not hack writers. Their standard of scholarship would be open to public inspection and criticism. Tossing off a book about "living with an Indian medicine woman" might not qualify as research so easily anymore. We would want to know how accurate the work was. How genuine. How consistent with any tradition. If Raph Nader were a theologian, he would be proud of us for our new sense of comparison shopping.

What about the Old Testament scholars themselves? Who would they be? My own guess is that the gold rush would be over. Instead of Western writers hacking away at Native spirituality, we would begin to see the emergence of more theologians from within the Native community itself. That might not be as romantic, exotic, or exciting as what we've been used to, but I expect it would be a great deal more valuable. Native American women and men could finally speak for themselves, not as gurus for Western theological science fiction, but as reputable scholars for an Old Testament tradition. Their voices would be clear and distinct. They would be listened to seriously. These speakers would not necessarily be Christian, but they would be treated with respect by the Christian community, just as Jewish scholars are respected. Their contribution to the larger interfaith dialogue would be profound. It would change us. It would open us up to a whole new dimension in theological exploration.

As a result, attitudes toward Native People and their Tradition would alter. Naming that Tradition an "Old Testament" is a powerful statement of recognition for Native America. It says that Native People are not just historical curiosities, footnotes for Western colonial expansion, but the living members of a world-class religious heritage. Since the first Western missionary or anthropologist walked into a native community, the Tradition of Native America has been called everything but an Old Testament. It has been named by others. It has been named by the West, not the People themselves. It has been called "superstition," "tribal religion," "nature worship," "animism," "shamanism," "primitive," "Stone Age," "savage," "spirituality," anything and everything, but never an Old Testament. The namers themselves have had mixed motives, some innocent, some racist, some just ignorant. But the results have been the same: the names attached to the Old Testament of Native America have consigned that Tradition to the backwaters of serious Christian scholarship. Native American spiritual tradition has been considered the proper study of historians, ethnologists, anthropologists, or even the gourmet writers of the New Age, but not for most Christian theologians. There is a big difference for Western theologians between a "spirituality" and a "theology," just as there is between a "tradition" and the "Old Testament." By claiming the right to name the Tradition an Old

Testament, Native America would be walking into the private club of Christian theology, even if that means coming in uninvited.

Finally, shifting our vocabulary to Old Testament language gives us an answer to that original question: Why hasn't there been a Native People's Christian theology? The whole purpose of such a theology would be to talk about the New Testament. It would be the Native perspective on Jesus and the gospels, on Paul, eschatology, redemption, salvation, sin, resurrection, community, grace, love, and God. To truly be a "Christian" theology, it would have to cover the whole range of ideas that form the Christian understanding of the New Testament. It would also have to be directly related to what we have always called the "Old Testament," i.e., the Old Testament of Israel. You can't have one without the other.

And there's the problem: you can't have a "new" testament if you don't have an "old" testament. Christians have invented those adjectives to distinguish between the original covenant relationship between God and the people and the "new" relationship established through the person of Jesus as the Christ. For Western People those distinctions work. For Native People they don't work.

Why? Because Native People also have an "old" testament. They have their own original covenant relationship with the Creator and their own original understanding of God prior to the birth of a Christ. It is a Tradition that has evolved over centuries. It tells of the active, living, revealing presence of God in relation to Native People through generations of Native life and experience. It asserts that God was not an absentee landlord for North America. God was here, on this continent among this people, in covenant, in relation, in life. Like Israel itself, Native America proclaims that God is a God of all times and of all places and of all peoples. Consequently, the "old" testament of Native America becomes tremendously important. It is the living memory, the living tradition of a people's special encounter with the Creator of Life.

So what are Native People supposed to do with that memory when they pick up the New Testament? Forget it? Pretend it doesn't matter? Assume that millions of their ancestors were just ignorant savages who didn't have any ideas about the reality of God in their lives? Was God just kidding around? Was the Creator passing off disinformation onto Native America? Was it just a joke?

It should be painfully obvious that Native People have only one choice to make. To erase the collective memory of Native America would not only be a crime against humanity, but a macabre theological position that would so limit the nature of God as to cease to be Christian. Or Jewish. God is the God of all time, of all space, of all people. Moreover, God relates to humanity through love, not through disinformation. When God spoke to Native America, it wasn't a joke. It wasn't primitive. It wasn't Stone Age. It wasn't nature worship. It wasn't superstition. It was the call of God to all people to draw near, to listen, to believe, and to love. Did

Native America hear this call? Yes. Did Native America encounter God? Yes. Did Native America remember that encounter and try to explain it to their children? Yes. Did they always get it right? No. Like any human community, Native America is finite and fallible. Its "old" testament is full of mistakes, false starts, guesses, hopes, dreams, wishes, just like any other Old Testament. And yet it is also full of truth, prophecy, and promise. It reveals something genuine and precious. It tells us a little more about the Creator we call God.

When Native People were denied access to that religious legacy, when they were told that their Old Testament was nothing more than a grab bag of primitive superstitions, when they were forbidden to share the memory with their own children, when they were commanded to undergo spiritual amnesia, to lose their memories, to go blank, to forget their own story and let others do the naming for them, it was exactly at this moment that any "New" Testament was jerked away from them. We need to press this point again: you cannot have a "new" testament if you do not have an "old" testament. You cannot fulfill what you do not have. The shelves are empty of a Native People's Christian theology because the theologians who would fill them have been brainwashed. They have been told to be content with another People's story, and to forget their own. They have been reduced to silence. It is the silence of any man or woman who cannot remember their own name. Who cannot remember where they came from. Who cannot remember having a family. Who cannot remember having a home. It is a silence of terror and of dread. An insane silence. A silence of isolation. The silence of a People who have been exiled from the love of their God.

THE TRIBE OF ISRAEL/THE TRIBE OF AMERICA

The reason for proclaiming an Old Testament of Native America is to break the silence. It is my intention to be a Christian theologian. To be a Native Christian theologian. But I cannot do that if I am not allowed to name myself. To name my tradition, and to use it. I cannot write about Jesus of the gospels or the letters of Paul if I don't interpret them through the truth as I try to understand it. That means the truth of the original covenant that God maintained with Israel, the truth of the witness to Jesus as the Christ as it is upheld in the "new" covenant, and the truth of the covenant between God and the Native People as it is revealed in the ancient testimony of Native America. Like any theologian from any community that retains its memory of God through tradition, I have to work with at least three primary sources: the Old Testament of Israel, the New Testament of the Christian scriptures, and the Old Testament of my own People. The three are integral. They cannot be separated.

In saying this I am very aware of the negative reaction it can produce among Christians, among Jews, and among Native People themselves. The words "old" and "new" testaments account for part of that reaction.

The words certainly are not accurate, nor do they promote interfaith understanding. The term *Old Testament* is too pejorative; it leaves the impression that it is something we can dismiss, something that has been replaced, something secondary. I know that within the Jewish community there is a strong reaction when Christians describe the Bible in this way. And yet, I feel bound by the words, as they have become a shorthand for signifying distinctions. At least for now. At least until people begin to accept the Native Old Testament for what it is. Then in a few years' time, we can bypass the words "Old Testament of Native America" and begin to speak of the Native Covenant.

Until that time, I want to push for recognition of a Native American Old Testament, even if it evokes a strong reaction from all directions. To be honest, *because* it evokes a strong reaction. The kind of silence I have described is not going to be broken by whispers, but by shouts. Therefore, I announce the Old Testament of Native America and invite others to do the same. Even if the language is imprecise, it is familiar language. It telegraphs a clear message across a wide spectrum. It makes Christians uncomfortable. It makes Jews uncomfortable. It makes Native People uncomfortable.

The discomfort arises because all of us have been conditioned to think of *the* Old Testament. Good, bad, or indifferent: we all know what we mean. We say *the* Old Testament and we know that we are referring to the first 39 books of the Bible. That's the Christian position, of course, but it is understood by both Native People and the Jewish community when Christians use the term in conversation or discourse. We all assume that there is only one Old Testament, just as Christians assert that there is only one New Testament. Challenging that assumption makes people nervous. To use the term *Old Testament* conventionally seems to question the validity of the traditional canon.

It also opens a closetful of theological and doctrinal issues. Can there be more than one "Old Testament"? If so, then what is the relationship between them? What is their relationship to the "New Testament"? Does one supplant the other? Where is the final claim on truth? Can the Christ be said to fulfill other Old Testaments? Wouldn't that be heresy at best and syncretism at worst? I doubt that I will be able to answer all of these questions here, anymore than I may be able to reassure all concerned that the Old Testament of Native America is a valid idea. Still, I think there are some basic points that may be covered and that may prove to be helpful.

First, my own awareness of a Native American Old Testament began to grow while I was sitting in an introductory Old Testament class during my first year of seminary. The professor described what was unique about the religious worldview of ancient Israel. He said that Israel, unlike its neighbors, had a special understanding of the relationship between God and humanity. This was the covenant between a single God and a particular People. It involved the promise of a homeland. It was sustained by the personal involvement of God in history. It was communicated through the prophets and the Law. It made Israel a nation. It brought them together as a People.

It was the most simple, important, understanding of the Old Testament that we share as Christians. And yet, during that lecture, I couldn't help but make a list of comparisons in my mind. Each time the professor mentioned some aspect of the Old Testament story that was "unique" to early Israel, I was reminded of my own Tradition and People. To help you understand what I mean, I will repeat that list in abbreviated form:

1. God is one.
2. God created all that exists.
3. God is a God of human history.
4. God is a God of all time and space.
5. God is a God of all People.
6. God establishes a covenant relationship with the People.
7. God gives the People a "promised land."
8. The People are stewards of this land for God.
9. God gives the People a Law or way of life.
10. The People worship God in sacred spaces.
11. God raises up prophets and charismatic leaders.
12. God speaks through dreams and visions.
13. The People maintain a seasonal cycle of worship.
14. The People believe God will deliver them from their suffering.
15. God can become incarnate on earth.

These fifteen items for comparison each merit more discussion, but the point I wish to make is simply that the religious worldviews of ancient Israel and ancient Native America have much in common. This is not to say that their understandings were identical. There are many variations on the theme not only between the two communities, but within them as well. What is striking, however, is that for many key concepts the two traditions run parallel. Like Israel, Native America believed in the oneness of God; it saw God as the Creator of all existence; it knew that God was active and alive in the history of humanity; it remembered that the land had been given to the people in trust from God. Native People accepted the revelation from God as it was given to them through prophets and charismatic leaders; they recognized sacred ground and holy places in their worship; they maintained a seasonal liturgical calendar; they had a highly developed belief in the incarnational presence of God and expected that presence to be revealed in times of strife or disaster. Is it strange, therefore, that Native Americans would consider themselves to be in a covenant relationship to their Creator or that they would think of themselves as a People "chosen" by God? Take the names which the People used for themselves in their own languages and you get a clear sense of this: in the tribal languages, the many nations of Native

America announced their identity as "The People" or "The Human Beings." Moreover, they tied this identity to the land given to them by God. It was this land-based covenant that gave them their identity as "The People," as the community special to a loving God.

Comparisons, of course, and especially sketchy ones, don't "prove" any claim to an Old Testament for Native America. I don't intend for them to. Their function is only to illustrate the depth of the Native Tradition itself. Talking about an Old Testament which emerges from the genius of Native America is not a wild leap into the unknown. There are sound theological reasons for taking the Native heritage seriously. It embodies the collective memory of an encounter with God that should cause any theologian to stop and think. As with Israel, this memory was transmitted through all of those channels that make up any Old Testament: through stories, histories, poetry, music, sacraments, liturgies, prophecies, proverbs, visions, and laws. The mighty acts of God in North America were witnessed and remembered. They were interpreted and passed on. Taken all together, they constitute an original, unique, and profound covenant between God and humanity.

If this is true then we are confronted with a problem. Suppose that we do allow Native People to claim an "Old Testament" status for their Tradition. Then what do we do with "the" Old Testament? What is the relationship between the two? What is the relationship to the "New" Testament?

An immediate answer is that we will have to be more concise when we speak of the original covenant with ancient Israel. We won't be able to use that word *the* in quite the same way. As Christians, we're going to have to make some elbow room at the table for other "old testaments." Not only from Native America, but from Africa, Asia, and Latin America as well. That's another door that is opening up in Christianity, and I doubt that anyone is going to be able to close it again. The fact is, Christians must permit the same right for other peoples that they have claimed for themselves. God was as present among the tribes of Africa as God was present among the tribes of America, as God was present among the tribes of Israel. Consequently, we must be cautious about saying that God was "unique" to any one people; God was in a special relationship to different tribes or in a particular relationship with them, but never in an exclusive relationship that shut out the rest of humanity.

This understanding broadens our dialogue about the connections between old testaments. It allows us to say that while there was nothing "unique" about God's relationship to either Native America or ancient Israel, there are elements to both that were special or particular. Obviously, for Christians, the concern focuses on christology. As a theologian of Native America, I can feel comfortable (not to mention orthodox) in saying that it was into the Old Testament People of Israel that God chose to become incarnate. Consequently, the story of this community becomes of primary importance to me. I need to honor, as well as understand, the Old Testament of Israel as the traditional culture into which God came as a person. In this way, the Old Testament of the Hebrew People remains central to my faith as a Christian and vital to my reading of the Christian scriptures.

At the same time, I can stand on my own Old Testament Tradition and let it speak to me just as clearly about the person, nature, and purpose of the Christ. I maintain that this Christ fulfills both Old Testaments. In the Pauline sense, I can assert that while as a man Jesus was a Jew, as the risen Christ, he is a Navajo. Or a Kiowa. Or a Choctaw. Or any other tribe. The Christ does not violate my own Old Testament. The coming of the Christ does not erase the memory banks of Native America or force me to throw away centuries of God's revealing acts among my People. But let me be careful about this: I am not glossing over the Old Testament of Native America with the Western whitewash of a theology that gives out a few quick platitudes about the "Christ of all cultures." When I speak of a fulfillment of Native America's Old Testament, I mean just that: a Christ that emerges from within the Native Tradition itself; that speaks of, by, and for that Tradition; that participates in that Tradition; that lives in that Tradition. Grounded in the Old Testament of Native America, it is the right of Native People to claim fulfillment of Christ in their own way and in their own language. I am not looking simply to paint the statues brown and keep the Western cultural prejudices intact. I am announcing the privilege of my own People to interpret the Christian canon in the light of Israel's experience, but also in the light of their own experience. Whether this interpretation is compatible with Western opinions is open for discussion.

The Old Testament of Native America, therefore, does not replace the Old Testament of Israel. It stands beside it. The Native People's claim to truth is not a competition with other traditions. The answer to the question about the relationship between the two Old Testaments is this: they do not cancel one another out (anymore than they are cancelled out by the New Testament); rather, they complement each other. I firmly believe that if the Christian faith is ever to take root in the soil of Native America, both testaments will be needed. Native People can read through the New Testament from both perspectives and see the gospel far more clearly for themselves. In turn, the gospel can speak to the Tradition with far more clarity. And here's a critical point: when we talk about the "fulfillment" of the Old Testament by Christ, we are describing the dual role of Christ in both confirming and correcting a People's memory. There was much in the memory of Israel that Jesus confirmed; there was also a great deal that he sought to correct. The same applies to the Old Testament memory of Native America. There is much that the Christ confirms and much that stands corrected. No Old Testament has a monopoly on perfection. The two traditions stand side-by-side under the fulfillment of Christ. As Native People begin to actively use their own Old Testament in reading the Christian scriptures they will find strengths that were missing from the experience of Israel, just as they will find weaknesses that need to be changed.

In the end, the naming of an Old Testament of Native America should not be a cause for alarm among any group or People. It is not a threat, but a hope. Our knowledge of God will not be diminished by this act of a People to regain their memory, but enhanced. The testimony of Israel will remain central to all Christians, Western and Native alike. The Tradition of Native People will be as changed by the gospel of Christ as it changes our understanding of that gospel. Native People will discover that they can read and understand both the Old and New Testaments of the Bible with a much clearer vision. Suddenly, they will start to make sense. Not the sense of the West perhaps, the imported versions of truth handed down from a community that fears it has lost its own Old Testament, but the common sense of any People that remembers, that recounts, that reasons, that reveals, and that responds. The "old" and the "new" will merge. They will enter deeply into the Kivas and Lodges of Native America and come back out stronger than we ever dreamed possible.

THE SECOND REFORMATION

In the next century, the Christian church is going to experience a second major reformation. It will be far more powerful than the one we knew in sixteenth century Europe. For one thing, it will be international, not just regional. It will cross over not only denominational lines, but also over lines of color, class, gender, and age. It will be more important than the last reformation because it will change the way people think and feel about themselves. While the West will participate in this reformation, it will not play a dominant role. The leaders of the coming reformation will be women. They will be from Africa, Asia, Latin America, and Native America. They are being born right now.

One of the guiding theologies of the second reformation will be the Christian theology of Native America. The emergence of that theology is already taking place. Not that too many people have noticed yet. In the centers of Western religious power, the revolution occurring in Native America is far too distant and obscure to be disturbing. It only shows up occasionally, for example, at meetings to discuss "Indian ministries," at conferences on racism or spirituality, and in books like this one.

The Native People's Christian theology is being overlooked, because it is being born in silence. That silence is so strong, so pervasive, so smothering that even the shout of a human voice cannot escape it. Not alone. But with each day that passes, more and more voices are beginning to take up the cry. In little backwater reservation chapels. In urban slums. In Arizona and Alaska and Minnesota and California and Manitoba. In sweat lodges and camp meetings. In Christian homes and Traditional homes. In Cheyenne homes and Mohawk homes. In Tribes all across Native America.

Native People are shouting into the silence of Western colonialism. They are shouting their names. They are saying that they are still the Tribe of the Human Beings. The Memory is coming back and with it the voice of a whole nation. Against that kind of power, no silence will long endure.

The midwife to the Native Reformation is the Old Testament of Native America. It is going to give birth to a cry of freedom. Old divisions between the People will be healed. The Traditional and the Christian People will once again become whole. The spiritual center of the Tribe will be regained and the People will unite as a family once more. With their combined strength they will begin to reclaim their rightful Tradition. It will not be "old." It will not be "new." It will be alive—right here and right now.

In the next century, the Old Testament of Native America is going to be fulfilled.

RECOMMENDED READING

Allen, Paula Gunn. *The Sacred Hoop: Recovering the Feminine in American Indian Tradition.* Boston: Beacon, 1986.

Beck, Peggy V., and Anna L. Walters. *The Sacred: Ways of Knowledge; Sources of Life.* Tsaile, AR: Navajo Community College Press, 1977.

Black Elk Speaks: Being the Life Story of a Holy Man of the Oglala Sioux, as told to John G. Neihardt. Lincoln: University of Nebraska Press, 1988.

Brown, Joseph Epes. *The Spiritual Legacy of the American Indian.* New York: Crossroad, 1984.

Capps, Walter Holden, ed. *Seeing with a Native Eye: Contributions to the Study of Native American Religion.* New York: Harper & Row, 1976.

Deloria, Vine, Jr. *God Is Red.* New York: Dell, 1973.

Gill, Sam. *Native American Religions: An Introduction.* Belmont, CA: Wadsworth, 1983.

——. *Native American Traditions: Sources and Interpretations.* Belmont, CA: Wadsworth, 1983.

Waters, Frank. *Book of the Hopi.* New York: Penguin, 1977.

——. *Masked Gods: Navajo and Pueblo Ceremonialism.* Athens: Ohio University Press, 1950.

CHAPTER 5

Context and Revelation with One Stroke of an Asian Brush

C. S. SONG

CONTEXT AND COMMITMENT

Is Christian theology possible from perspectives other than those of Western Christians? Is it viable when it uses idioms different from those in traditional Christian theology? Is it possible to develop Christian theology in the contexts not directly related to Judeo-Christian cultures?

These are some of the fundamental questions that started me thinking about fundamental issues related to the articulation of the Christian faith. I am still conscious of them as I continue my theological efforts. It is not that I try to answer these questions. Rather, they serve as the impetus to challenge Christian theology from the cultures within which Christianity developed into a major religious force.

In my view, Christian theology in Asia, for example, should face fundamental ideas and norms considered to be sacrosanct in traditional theology. It should not be just a variation of the contents and methods of traditional Christian theology in the West. Nor should it be a Christian theology just clothed in the language, ideas and names borrowed from the indigenous culture. Christian theology in Asia would, then, be like the Chinese herb medicine with the same ingredients cooked two or three times by refilling the pot with water, *huan t'ang pu huan yau,* as the Christian expression has it. Christian theology in Asia until recently has, in most cases, been this kind of theology. It still prevails today in some Asian countries.

I am not, however, saying that Christian theology in Asia should be different from Christian theologies elsewhere for the sake of being different. What I am urging is the authenticity of doing theology in the contexts that are different from the "Christian" West in some very fundamental ways. If this is the case vis-a-vis traditional Christian theology, it is also true vis-a-vis new theological developments in the West such as feminist theology, liberation theology, or process theology.

Revelation is, of course, one of the time-honored concepts in Christian theology. The way it is understood has shaped ways in which Christians believe and theologians do their theology. It is one of what I call fundamental theological concepts that have to come under fresh theological scrutiny. What a different and exciting theological world will be disclosed to us when we find a new key to unlock the mystery of God's revelation! It will be at once an awesome and fascinating experience. This is what I attempted to do in this chapter.

CONSTRUCTION

This is the story of how a Chinese Zen monk, Fo-têng Shou-hsün (1079–1134), reached his enlightenment:

Fo-têng Shou-hsün began to study Zen under Kuang-chien Ying. He came later to Tai-p'ing where Fo-chien [a Zen master] resided, but was at a loss how to take hold of Zen. He put a seal on his bedding and made his vow: "If I do not attain the experience of Zen in this life, this will never be spread to rest my body in." He sat in meditation during the day, but the night was passed standing up. . . .

Seven weeks thus elapsed, when Fo-chien gave a sermon saying, "A world of multiplicities is all stamped with the One." This opened the eye of Shou-hsün. Fo-chien said, "What a pity that the lustrous gem has been carried away by this lunatic!" He then said to Hsün, "According to Ling-yün, 'Since I once saw the peach bloom, I have never again cherished a doubt.' What is this when no doubts are ever cherished by anybody?"

Hsün answered, "Don't say that Ling-yün never cherishes a doubt; it is in fact impossible for any doubt to be cherished anywhere even now."

Chien said, "Hsün-sha criticized Ling-yün, saying, 'You are all right as far as you go, but you have not yet really penetrated.' Now tell me where is this unpenetrated spot."

Hsün replied, "Most deeply I appreciate your grandmotherly kindness."

Chien gave his approval to this remark. Thereupon, Hsün produced the following stanza:

All day he has been looking at the sky yet without lifting his head,
Seeing the peach in full bloom he has for the first time raised his eyebrows:
Mind you, however, there's still a world-enveloping net;
Only when the last barrier-gate is broken through,
There is complete rest.[1]

VOW-MAKERS, NAVEL-STARERS, AND SKY-GAZERS

"A world of multiplicities" was the context for Shou-hsün, the Zen monk. For the unenlightened, the world is hidden behind "an unpenetrated spot." They may make vows not to sleep, not to eat; they will remain immobile until they penetrate the unpenetrated spot. They may meditate day and night, staring at their own navel until it begins to emit words of truth. Or they may pray without ceasing, gazing at the sky waiting for it to break open and a ray of revelation to shine forth. But all this is to no avail.

Vow-makers, navel-starers, and sky-gazers remain unenlightened. But then their eyes catch sight of the peach in full bloom. This is a commonplace sight, a most ordinary phenomenon in nature, a seasonal routine. But the unpenetrated spot in the world of multiplicities is penetrated; its last barrier-gate is broken through. A mind is enlightened. A mystery disclosed. Something extraordinary is revealed. Context and revelation are linked up. "A world of multiplicities" is perceived as "stamped with the One."

Christian theologians in Asia are a little like vow-maker, navel-starer, and sky-gazer combined. We vow to penetrate the Asian soul formed and nourished by centuries of pain and suffering. We strive to break through the barrier-gate of the Asian spirit steeped in Asian philosophical systems and religious beliefs. We realized that here we have the virgin soil for Christian theology. Christian faith must get into this virgin soil of Asia. If Asian theologians will not do it, who will? If they *cannot* do it, who can? And how? These are the questions before us.

That is why many Asian theologians are preoccupied with methodology. There must be a method to go about this task. If only we knew and possessed it! If only we had the magic wand of the fairy godmother! A pumpkin would instantly turn into a beautiful carriage and mice would change into lovely stallions, carrying the future princess to the royal ball. Instant method, instant theology, instant marriage of the gospel and the Asian heart. . . . But alas, the beautiful carriage and the lovely stallions are not real. When the magic spell is broken, everything returns to what it has always been. Theology and the Asian soil still seem millions of light-years apart. The *Asian* context and the *Christian* revelation remain strangers passing by each other without a nod of acknowledgement.

There is something of the navel-starer in us. It is right to be a little self-critical: "Know yourself!" This is not only the injunction of Socrates, the Greek sage, but also the insight of Oriental sages such as Confucius and Gautama the Buddha. Truth is within you. You possess the Buddha nature in you. But as we turn inward to ourselves in search of the truth, we discover that we are odd theological creatures! We become a little confused. Have not some traditional schools of theology taught us that truth comes to us from outside? Is it not an alien body taking hold of our *tabula rasa*? Is this not what revelation essentially means? Is not denial of what we are the beginning of theological wisdom? So, we find ourselves faced with a kind of theological dilemma: to be a Christian theologian or an Asian humanist. We face the danger of falling between the two stools of context and revelation.

But some questions remain. Does God require us to be a *tabula rasa* before God is willing to disclose the secret to us? Does God ask us to jump out of our skin before God will have anything to do with us? I do not believe God attaches such a condition to revelation. Besides, could even the most staunch theologians of the "otherness" of God and the "purity" of revelation honestly claim that their God-experience has nothing to do with their own cultural traditions and historical environments? I think theologians have to be a little more sensible. God seems to be a sensible God who knows that we cannot help being human with all our personal, cultural, historical, and religious accretions. That is why the Word had to become flesh, to become one of us in a full sense—with flesh and blood. Asian theologians do not have to spend a lot of time and energy trying to invent a theological method. They just have to be brave and sensible. Asian theology has to be a "sensible" theology. How else can we follow and experience the "sensible" God amid Asian flesh and blood?

If being a navel-starer gives us discomfort, we are tempted to become sky-gazers. The vast span of space above us awes and inspires us. It lifts our hearts from the pettiness of this earth that pursues us with its mundane problems and troubles. It frees our soul from the din of this world that gives us no rest. It is where God and the hosts of heaven reside.

This is not an outdated primitive cosmology that we who live in an age of science and technology have outgrown. It is still very much embedded in our subconscious mind and from time to time it makes its appearance in our theological speculation. God's help comes from the august sky. When heaven opens, God speaks. This is essentially revelation. Heaven is the context of God's revelation. God creates separate contexts irrespective of what and where we are. That is why we tend to go for a "gravity-free" theology—a theology that speculates about what God is like as an ontological being. Gravity-free theology spends most of its time trying to figure out how many angels can dance on a needlepoint. It makes every effort to draw a line between the saved and the unsaved.

But God's theology is a "gravity-bound" theology. "God loved the world so much that he gave his only Son" (John 3:16). Love is essentially gravity-bound. When it becomes gravity-free, it is no longer love. It turns into a force that repels. It is hate, rejection, alienation, condemnation, and death. But God is drawn to the world through gravity-bound love. God's love in Jesus Christ is grace, acceptance, communion, salvation, and life. The mark of this gravity-bound love is suffering: the cross. No magic can bring context and revelation together in theology. No theological method needs to be invented to test how revelation is at work in a particular contest. Such a test is blasphemous and sacrilegious, for God has already united our context with revelation through gravity-bound love: God's suffering love. Human longings and struggles for grace, acceptance, communion, salvation, and life in Asian settings are the contexts of revelation for Christian theology in Asia. This is where gravity-bound theology should begin and end.

THE PEACH TREE IN FULL BLOOM

Seeing the peach tree in full bloom, Shou-hsün, the Zen monk, raised his eyebrows. Something struck him. The fullness of the tree poses a striking contrast to a body thin and tired due to fasting and lack of sleep. In seeing the tree, he realized truth does not come by making vows not to eat and sleep, by staring—all tangled up in his own inadequacy and worthlessness—at his own navel, or by gazing at the sky, leaping into the world of illusion. Truth is right there in front of you. That innocent-looking peach tree beckons you. That full-blossomed tree extends its hand to you. It speaks to you in the language you can understand: the language of beauty and grace. It discloses to you the mystery of nature: the mystery that sustains life. It reveals to you the power of the divine: the power of love that overcomes frost, snow, and wind to bring a peach tree to full bloom.

It is all there before your eyes. But you have been making vows, sealing your bedding, and putting away your bowl and chopsticks. It is all contained in that smiling peach tree, but you have been staring at your own self with a long face and a restless mind. It is right there within your reach, but you are projecting your "profound" thought on that distant sky.

No wonder the Zen monk raised his eyebrows when he realized the plain truth. The world, to be sure, is still caught in the net of karma, but the breakthrough of the last barrier-gate is within sight. It was not any abstruse wisdom that brought him to this state of mind. Nor was it complicated systems of thought that led him to the awareness of truth. It was the peach tree in full bloom—that product of nature, human effort, and divine power—that inspired him and enlightened him. "A world of multiplicities is all stamped with the One. It bears the mark of the One." It carries the message of the One. It gives witness to the One. And it issues a call from the One to press on toward the last barrier-gate in order to be in the presence of the One. Context and revelation are no longer separate entities. Context is not just a receptacle of revelation. Context and revelation are united to tell the world what truth is.

In the mind of the enlightened, gravity-bound Christian theologian, the peach tree in full bloom breaks taboos of various kinds. A taboo— whose verbal form *tapui* means "to make holy"—is, according to van der Leeuw, a Dutch phenomenologist of religion, "a sort of warning: 'Danger! High Voltage!' Power has been stored up, and we must be on our guard."[2]

Traditional theology became a high-voltage and a very apodictic theology. It defined theology as a "scientific" inquiry into the nature of God and God's "economy of salvation." The stress words are "scientific" and "economy." It requires those engaged in theological activities to conform to certain norms and rules. It prescribes the contents of theological inquiry. It built its systems largely on how the "Christian" West looks at humanity and world history. Its views on life, cultures, and religious beliefs with which it is not familiar are considered definitive.

A lot of power has been stored up in traditional theology. And combined with the power of ecclesiastical authorities, it gained a high-voltage power that cannot be provoked with impunity. That is why heresy-hunting will always remain with us.

One of the latest casualties of such high-voltage theology is Hans Küng, a Swiss Roman Catholic theologian. He got too close to the source of that high-voltage power in the Vatican—the Sacred Congregation for the Doctrine of the Faith. He challenged the teaching on infallibility, thus breaking a taboo of his church. As a result, he lost his position in pontifical faculties. The Roman recognition of his status as a theologian authorized by the church was withdrawn.

The peach tree in full bloom does not speak any such apodictic message. There is no alienating structure or doctrine attached to it. Instead, it invites us to take a closer look at it, to touch it, to fondle it, and even to taste it. Traditional theology made us lose the ability to taste what we see, hear and touch. "Taste then and see that the Lord is good!" (Ps. 34:8). This does not apply to traditional theology. What we were taught was a tasteless theology.

We were supposed to confront our context, dissect it, exorcise it, and expose its godlessness. We come to our own context—an alien body at which we cast a suspicious glance—and we do not quite know what to do with it. Our own context, curiously, is always *over against* us, instead of *in* and *with* us. It is always something against which we must be on guard, instead of something that is integral to our own selves. We do not dare to taste it, to claim kinship with it.

There was a high-voltage theology staring at us from a pedestal. It taught us that revelation cannot be inherent in Asian existence and history. It decreed that God works only tangentially within Asian cultures. It maintained that we face only God's anger in Asian religious milieus.

Our most urgent task, then, is to regain a "theological taste" for our living space, with all that is in it. We must whet our appetite for the songs and hymns that our poets, ancient and modern, sing in praise of nature and in despair of life. We must develop an eye for works of our artists who paint the hopes and frustrations of life with primitive forcefulness. We must read records of suffering and joy, mistakes and glories of our people, with our hearts beating fast and with our blood throbbing in our veins. Then we can do our theology.

No, we do not have to 'do' theology; theology is already in the making. *Theo*-logy is there, because God is there. It is this *theo*-logy that precedes our theo-*logy*. Theo-*logy* without *theo*-logy is a semantic that touches neither the heart of God nor the hearts of our fellow human beings. Theology is born when we meet persons in their life and history. Does not this compel us to regain our ability to sing with our poets, paint with our artists, research our history with our historians, and theologize with our thinkers?

One of the most important things Jesus did, it seems to me, was to free his followers from fear of their context and to make them realize its revelatory significance. He helps them see the world as God sees it and not through taboos their religion has imposed on them. "Look at the birds of the air," he says, "they do not sow and reap and store in barns, yet your heavenly Father feeds them" (Matt. 6:26). He also draws their attention to flowers: "Consider how lilies grow in the fields; they do not work, they do not spin; and yet, I tell you, even Solomon in all his splendor was not attired like one of these" (6:28–29). Birds and flowers and all the rest—these are our context. To some they may have aesthetic significance but hardly any religious meaning. But can aesthetics be separated from religion? It cannot, for do we not speak of the beauty of God's holiness? God's holiness is beautiful because God is beautiful.

Holiness turns into a terrible taboo when it becomes devoid of beauty. Holiness without beauty threatens our lives; we cannot approach it without incurring danger to ourselves. Behind such holiness is hidden a dangerous God who is more angry than caring, more hating than forgiving, more condemning than redeeming. But Jesus has shown us a beautiful and loving God. Love and beauty go hand in hand. Love is the essence of beauty. Love makes the ugly beautiful. It makes the defective perfect. It redeems the unredeemable. Armed with such love and confident in the God who is loving and beautiful, Jesus refers to birds of the air and lilies in the fields to tell his followers what God has in store for them. God, birds, lilies and human persons—together they form the context of revelation. The divine, nature, the human—united, they take form in a revelation within a particular context. And what is the context of such revelation? God's saving love for us as we face the problems that fill our daily lives.

See how our theological space expands! We no longer have to maneuver in a tightly defined area reserved strictly to theology. The whole world is our theological space because, first and foremost, it is God's space. Even the birds of the air and the lilies in the fields come into our theological perimeter because they too are within the perimeter of God's concern. God feeds them and clothes them. Poets and artists seem to know this better than theologians do. Shih-t'ao (1641–1720), a great master of Chinese painting, makes our ears burn when he says:

The artist surveys the layout of hills and streams, estimates the width and length of the land, examines the distribution of mountain peaks and observes the airy forlornness of clouds and mists. He looks at the earth spread before him and takes a swift glance at the distant ranges, and knows that they are under the overlordship of heaven and earth. Heaven has the standard to transform the spirit of hills and streams, earth has this norm to activate their pulse beat, and I have this one stroke [of the brush and ink] to penetrate into their very body and spirit.[3]

This is the deep insight of a Chinese painter of mountains and waters. The intuitive wisdom of Chinese nature artists tells them that nature is not alien to human beings, that it is not something standing over and against them. We are in nature and nature is in us, and together we and nature are in God.

Mountains and streams, in silence, bear in themselves something beyond themselves. Artists understand this instinctively and bear witness to it with their brush and ink. As Shih-t'ao tells us in so many words: "The hills and streams have appointed me to speak for them. They are in me and I am in them. I search out the extraordinary peaks and put them on paper. We meet and comprehend one another in spirit."[4] Artists speak for nature, and as such they also speak for the divine.

Shih-t'ao had the "one stroke of brush and ink" to penetrate the spirit of what he sees, feels, and touches round about him. What sort of "one-stroke" do theologians have to have in order to penetrate the mystery of God's ways with Asian nations and peoples? This is a key question. What is this theological "one-stroke"? What does it consist of? How do we lay our hands on it?

We do not need to look for it; it is given to us just as mountains and streams are given to Shih-t'ao. We do not need to invent it; it is there just as brush and ink are there for the painter. Our "theological one-stroke" is no other than God's saving love for the world. With this one-stroke of God's saving love, we can learn to paint the landscape of God's work out of the historical, cultural, and religious experience of the peoples of Asia.

All this should not sound strange to us. For it is with this theological one-stroke that writers of the Old Testament—storytellers, poets, historians, and theologians—wrote the history of Israel. Under that powerful stroke, the exodus, the conquest, the exile, and so on, all fit together in the framework of the meaning derived from faith in God the redeemer. That must have been a very powerful stroke, for nothing seems to escape its grasp. Even that strange story of the crafty Jacob cheating the birthright from his brother Esau has a place—not just a place, but a very prominent place—in the plot that runs through Israel's history. The story has given readers, and many commentators not a few headaches. But many of us will perhaps agree with Gerhard von Rad, a German Old Testament theologian, that: "The story reckons with an act of God that sovereignly takes the most ambiguous human act and incorporates it into its plans. The guilty one becomes the bearer of the promise! To be sure, the narrator draws a powerful picture of the most extraordinary entangled guilt, but his view of what God has decreed and accomplished keeps him from being ruffled before the question of the personal guilt and subjective motives of the individual persons."[5] How are we to understand this observation in relation to our theological efforts in Asia?

What strikes us the most in the story of Jacob is, to follow von Rad's explanation, the great distance between his most ambiguous act and

God's plans. What could be more ambiguous than Jacob's act of cunning and deception? Not only his crude and simple-minded brother Esau but also his blind, old father were the victims of his criminal act. How could such a morally and religiously monstrous deed have anything to do with God's plans? The gap between them seems insurmountable. But they do become related. Jacob's most ambiguous act was incorporated into God's plans. How did this happen? Is the faith of the Old Testament an amoral faith? Is it a caricature of religious devotion and pietism? The answer has to be no. It is the theological one-stroke of God's saving love for Israel that enabled Old Testament writers to perceive redemptive relationships between the ambiguous human act of Jacob and God's plans.

History, personal or collective, is in one sense a sum total of ambiguous human acts. If this was true in the case of Jacob and Israel, it can also be true for each and every Asian and for the history of our own countries— the history of the Philippines, the history of India, the history of Indochina. We cannot put these ambiguous human histories aside. To do so is to put ourselves aside. To remove them is to remove our own history. Until recently, under the influence of traditional theology, we tried to put them aside. We did not quite know what to do with ourselves as Asian. We could not regard our history as having some internal relationship with God's plans. Our context is there, but we lose it. We ourselves are the context, but we negate it. Yet, even if Jacob's most ambiguous human act did get incorporated into God's plans, then what about ambiguous Asian selves and ambiguous Asian histories? Ours is the task of incorporating ourselves and the history of our lands into God's plans. And it is the theological one-stroke of God's saving love that enables us to go about this task.

In the New Testament, this theological one-stroke is powerfully concentrated on the risen Christ. Painted with this one-stroke, the cross begins to make sense. The cross is no longer an instrument of the Roman justice meted out to the criminal of the state; it is "the power of God and the wisdom of God" (1 Cor. 1:24). In the eyes of Greek wisdom and of Jewish pietism nothing could be further removed from God than the cross. The cross symbolizes perhaps the most ambiguous of all ambiguous human acts. It is more ambiguous because it is the denial of life and rejection of goodness. It spells the end of human decency and divine presence. Even Jesus had to cry tormented by the pain of the cross, "My God, my God, why hast thou forsaken me?" The cross, to the dying Jesus, is the divine forsakenness of human beings. But it is this cross that becomes God's power and wisdom. This has taken place not apart from the hideous cross but right on it.

The Magnificat is another masterpiece of this theological one-stroke. What could be more ordinary than the birth of a child? It is ordinary in the sense that it is part of life. It is ordinary in the sense that it is the fruit of love and passion possessed by all people and concentrated to the power and mystery of life. It is also ordinary in the sense that without it life discontinues, disappears, and becomes a meaningless word. But that theological one-stroke—the astonishing manifestation of God's saving love in the risen Christ—transforms an ordinary birth of a child into an extraordinary birth of a savior in the Magnificat. That is why Mary praises her God and sings from the depth of her heart:

> Tell out, my soul, the greatness of the Lord,
> rejoice, rejoice, my spirit, in God is my savior;
> so tenderly has he looked upon his servant,
>   humble as she is.
> For, from this day forth,
> all generations will count me blessed,
> so wonderfully has he dealt with me,
>   the Lord, the Mighty One (Luke 1:46–49).

This is truly a masterful theological one-stroke. The humble Mary feels the saving power of God stirring in her womb. She embraces in her own being the miraculous act of God's salvation. She becomes a totally *theo*-logical being. She realizes that the movement of God's Spirit is taking a most astounding form within her. She becomes the context *and* the content of revelation.

The task for Asian theologians is to learn to apply this theological one-stroke to all that Asia represents. Touch the history of your own country with that theological one-stroke and see if it will yield *theo*-logical meaning to you. Test your own history with it and see if it is just a haphazard collection of happenings that make no sense beyond themselves. Penetrate the life of your own community with it and see if it is left entirely to the force of chance, or totally under the control of a demonic power. The ancient Chinese understood their history in terms of the Mandate of Heaven—the divine mandate that caused dynasties and empires to rise and fall. In India, history is experienced as in the grip of Karma—the powerful force that makes strong moral demands on the lives of the people. It is this theological one-stroke that enables us to bring into sharp relief on our theological canvas the agonizing struggle of redemptive power against destructive forces in life and history.

To get at the root of the human spirit in the depth of the Asian spirit and see how it suffers and hopes—this is the task of theologians in Asia. When you come into touch with that root of Asian spirituality, there you hear the heartbeats of other Asians. To your great surprise, you will realize that they are your own heartbeats. And in those heartbeats, you may hear the heartbeats of God. A theology echoing God's heartbeats in the heartbeats of other Asians and in your own heartbeats—this is contextual theology. Contextual theology is none other than our response to God's call to explore and experience "God-meaning" in human sufferings and hopes that take form in cultures, histories, and religions. It has the task of pointing to "God-meaning" in the futility and meaninglessness that conditions the lives of most persons, including Christians and theologians.

THE WORD BECAME FLESH

Context and revelation: the Word became flesh. This is incarnation. To explore its depth and breadth in Asia is a major theological concern. God has made the Word become flesh a divine concern. Can a theology that does not make this concern of God its own concern still be called *theology*?

We come, then, to the birth of Jesus, the Word become flesh. At once we are thrust into history; not a celestial history, but a terrestrial history; not a divine history, but a human history; not a history out of context, but a history in a particular context. We read these words in the Gospel of Luke: "In those days a decree was issued by the Emperor Augustus for a registration to be made throughout the Roman world. This was the first registration of its kind; it took place when Quirinius was governor of Syria. For this purpose everyone made his way to his own town; and so Joseph went up to Judaea from the town of Nazareth in Galilee, to register at the city of David, called Bethlehem, because he was of the house of David by descent; and with him went Mary who was betrothed to him. She was expecting a child" (2:1–6).

All the ingredients of history are here: Augustus the Roman emperor, Quirinius governor of Syria, the decree for registration. Then, only then, there is the devout Joseph. Then, only then, there is the pregnant Mary. The Word seems to become buried in history and to disappear. But what has actually happened is just the opposite. The Word bursts history open and redemptively absorbs it. The great Roman empire has to reckon with it. The whole world is affected by it.

John, the author of the fourth Gospel, puts this astonishing fact simply and forcefully: "So the Word *became* flesh" (John 1:14). The Word became flesh! The Word *is* in flesh! There is no such thing as *mere* flesh. What we have to think about is "flesh-with-Word." Let me suggest a parallel coupling: Revelation *became* context! Revelation *is* in context! There is no such thing as *mere* context. What we have to think about is "context-with-revelation."

The Word that has become flesh has a great number of surprises in store for Christians and theologians confined to the traditional framework of understanding the ways of God. Surprise upon surprise—when flesh is not separated from the Word, when body is not severed from spirit, and when context is not divorced from revelation. There will be many, many questions and problems to upset us, give us headaches, and disturb our theological calm. We begin to wonder why we have not seen them before, why we have not heard them earlier, and why we have gone on doing theology in Asia as if they were not there.

But things are beginning to change. In January 1979 an Asian theological conference sponsored by the Ecumenical Association of Third World Theologians took place in Sri Lanka. A live-in experience was a special feature of this conference. During its course, participants spent three or four days in the actual life situation of different depressed and marginalized sectors of Sri Lankan society. The impact of the live-in experience on the participants and on the conference itself was considerable. They were reflected forcefully in the Final Statement of the conference, which says at one point: "A truly liberating theology must ultimately be the work of the Asian poor, who are struggling for full humanity. It is they who must reflect on and say what their faith-life experience in the struggle for liberation is. This does not exclude the so-called specialists in theology. With their knowledge they can complement the theologizing of the grassroots people. But their theologizing becomes authentic only when rooted in the history and struggle of the poor and the oppressed."[6]

This is very disturbing for those of us who think theology must provide both questions and answers with regard to life and faith. But, if we think about it, we have to admit that theology does not create a life or a world. Life is there and the world is there, created by God—the life and the world full of persons struggling for meaning, purpose, and a better future. Theology becomes untrue to its vocation when it is separated from this life, this world, and especially from the suffering and despairing masses. This is a major challenge bound to affect the way in which theology will be done in Asia.

At the All-Asia Consultation on Theological Education for Christian Ministry in Manila, March 1977, Chung Choon Kim, an Old Testament scholar from South Korea, shared this observation with us:

It gives me a great shock to realize that our theology until now seems to have nothing to do with the Eastern cultural heritage, which have rich resources to formulate a theology of nature expressed in terms of the cosmos and nature. It is unfortunate that Christian theology should not have originated from the ground of the Eastern or the Asian countries. Had it originated from the heritages of the Asian cultures, it might have been far better in understanding the original meaning of the creation and, in particular, the relationships between man and nature.[7]

This observation is not without its difficulties. We cannot base our theology on an irrevocable past. It may have been "unfortunate" that Christian theology "originated from the ground of" European nations. It may have been "unfortunate" that it "should not have been originated from the ground of Asian countries." But this historical fact cannot be changed.

The point, however, is how Asian cultural heritages echo the deep cries of Asian humanity to be freed from its bondage. These cries are similar to those people in the Bible, which we Christians have heard with profound effect. Seen in this way, Chung Choon Kim's observation becomes a challenge to Asian theologians—a challenge to make *theo*-logical meaning out of the roots of Asian cultures. This is a formidable challenge bound to put an end to our uneasy truce without theological mentors in Germany or elsewhere in the West.

We should also be aware that theology has increasingly come under close scrutiny by our sister theologians. We male theologians in Asia might say that is a Western fad! But wait, Marianne Katoppo, from Jakarta, Indonesia, tells her side of the story: "The church is a patriarchal structure *par excellence*. Through its unsound theology and ineffective ministry, it is undoubtedly part of the suffering of the women of Asia."[8] This is a strong indictment. How do Asian male theologians respond to it? Katoppo's professor at a theological seminary in Indonesia knew one answer. He said to her in all seriousness: "Well, you can't deny it—God is male; just look at the way He is referred to as *He* throughout the Bible, with all the masculine forms of verbs and nouns."[9] This of course is a faltering defense, to say the least. Appeal to the Bible for the supremacy of a male God does not relieve "the suffering of the women in Asia" caused by the church with its "patriarchal structure" and its "unsound theology." In fact there is, as Katoppo goes on to show, a feminine imagery related to the person and action of God in the Bible just as important as the male imagery. This calls for a fundamental reunderstanding of God, the Spirit, Jesus Christ, the church and its ministry. This is a very challenging proposition, but Katoppo is pleading with theologians in Asia to take it up and work it into their theological endeavors.

Word-become-flesh theology is a dangerous theology. It is dangerous because it asks questions that are not asked by conventional faith. It is dangerous because it ventures into areas that are out of bounds for traditional theology. It is also dangerous because it does not prejudge what it sees, hears, and feels with a set of theological presuppositions formulated outside its own context.

Word-become-flesh theology is dangerous, but can it be more dangerous than the Word-become-flesh itself? God could have used a remote control device to deal with the world. God could have ordered human beings around from a safe distance. That is the thinking behind a religion that installs God in a holy of holies. That is the thinking of a faith that turns Jesus' farewell supper with his disciples in face of his imminent death into a eucharistic institution that has divided the churches to this day. But God had not opted for a safe way and a safe theology. God took a dangerous journey and ventured into a dangerous theology.

What could have been more dangerous than for God to become human, for the Word to become flesh, for the savior to hang helplessly on the cross? But that is precisely this dangerous theology of God that breaks out into the glory of the resurrection. Without the danger of the Word-become-flesh, there could not have been the excitement of the empty tomb. And how *unconventional*, how *irrational*, and how *illogical* the empty tomb was!

The dangerous theology of the Word-become-flesh is a very exciting theology. It makes our hearts beat with expectation. It opens our eyes to sights not found in our theological textbooks; it tunes our ears to music unfamiliar to our liturgy; and it gives us glimpses of God's strange ways with the nations. Be dangerous theologians! Be exciting theologians! Boldly paint your theological landscape with Asian brush and ink! With the "one-stroke" of your brush and ink, let the revelation of God's saving love and power be brought into sharper relief on your theological canvas. And from where else can you expect to project this relief except from your own context—the totality of life and history of which you are an inalienable part?

RECOMMENDED READING

Fabella, Virginia, ed. *Asia's Struggle for Full Humanity*. Maryknoll, NY: Orbis, 1980.

Katoppo, Marianne. *Compassionate and Free: An Asian Woman's Theology*. Geneva: World Council of Churches, 1979. Maryknoll, NY: Orbis, 1980.

O'Grady, Ron, and Lee Soo Jin, eds. *Suffering and Hope*. Christian Conference of Asia, 1978.

What is revelation?
an Ah-ha?
vision?
connection w/ universal source? /God
cf. imagination
dream?
understanding / knowledge?
revealed truth?
How do we know?

Part 2

GOD

Introduction to Part 2

Many theological texts begin with a discussion of the "idea of God." One thing we can say for certain is that for liberation theologians God is not an idea removed from the social realities of daily concrete existence. Liberation theologians do not begin with questions about the existence of God, arguments about the proper understanding of the trinity, or definitions of God's transcendence, omnipotence, or providence. That these questions and concerns are still considered the decisive and central ones by many Western theologians today (in spite of the challenges of modernity in the West) is seen by liberation theologians as a sign of their social location. That is, their membership in a dominant group and their inheritance of specific theological, philosophical, and scientific traditions influences the way they identify and formulate the questions themselves.

As Segundo points out in his introduction to *Our Idea of God*, those actively engaged in struggling for justice in the world are "irritated by the seeming uselessness" of the questions about God deliberated by Western scholars.[1] Liberation theologians frame the discussion of God quite differently. For them it is not the existence of God that needs to be justified, but the continuing existence of injustice. It is with this as their basic question or problem that they develop their idea of God. Rather than take a speculative approach, focusing on the aseity of God (God as God is in Godself, apart from any relation to the world), they take a practical approach, choosing as their starting point the claim that God is in active relation with the world.[2] Thus it is not the possibility of the existence of God but the character and activity of God that occupy their reflections. Influenced by the revolution of rising expectations around the world, their questions are not "Does God exist?" or "What are the conditions for the possibility of knowing God?", but "Is God on the side of the oppressed or not?" and "If God is on the side of the oppressed, who can stand against us?"

With these as their fundamental questions, liberation theologians begin their GodTalk with social and political analysis. This is evident in

James Cone's by now well-known chapter "God Is Black" in his *Black Theology of Liberation.* He wrote his introduction for this textbook in 1988. In it he indicates that he has not retreated from his contention that God is Black, because "God's identity is found in the faces of those who are exploited and humiliated because of their color." Because we know God in the particularity of social justice struggles, social location is the starting point for GodTalk.

Thistlethwaite agrees that social and political analysis is the way to begin the task of GodTalk in the nuclear age. The common Christian understanding of God, modeled on the political arrangements of imperial Rome, has had a history of association with political totalitarianism that must now be challenged. She also agrees with Cone (in his introduction) that the social justice struggles of people around the world (e.g., Asian, African, Native peoples) are a source of new insight into the relationship of God to the social order.

Perhaps no statement made by Cone in 1970 provoked as much discussion and controversy as his identification of divine love with Black power, "which is the power of blacks to destroy their oppressors, here and now, by any means at their disposal." Divine love, the foundation of the gospel, is not viewed by Cone as excluding the divine righteousness which is God's wrath. Nor is divine wrath understood only through divine love, as some Christian theologians have argued. As is evident also in Thistlethwaite's chapter, violent resistance to oppression cannot be understood apart from the structures of violence that precede it.

Combining their insights, we see racism as systemic violence. Resistance to racism does not initiate violence but is a response to the violence *of racism.* Solidarity such as Black power, then, is a response of resourcefulness, the bonding together of oppressed people to resist systemic violence (see also chapter 2). And God's violence or nonviolence must be understood from within God's commitment to solidarity with the oppressed.

Another point held in common by Cone and Thistlethwaite is their criticism of theological liberals such as Gordon Kaufman. They single out theological liberalism not because it is completely antithetical to theologies of liberation, but rather because it is so close to many of their emphases. The failure of liberal theologians to come to grips with the conflict in prevailing theological viewpoints is regarded by liberation theologians as particularly subversive of liberation aims. A good example of this difference between liberal and liberation theologians may be seen in their interpretations of divine immanence. Cone emphasizes that it "refers to the depths of liberation in human society." Divine immanence is the most pervasive characteristic of Protestant liberalism,[3] but it refers to something quite different from what Cone has in mind. As Thistlethwaite points out, the experience to which liberal theologians traditionally refer when they speak of divine immanence is mired in "the social domination of patriarchal bourgeois culture of personality." In other words, the question of *whose* experience serves as the basis of theological reflection is the critical question for understanding the difference between theologies of liberation and Protestant liberalism. (For further discussion of this point, see the introductory essay to the chapters on the scripture.) Furthermore, experience is understood in liberation theology to be socially and politically constructed experience and not intrapsychic processes. As Cone says, "God is not a symbol referring to the interior religious experiences of humankind."

Many of these concerns for a practical, socially, economically, and politically aware understanding of God also appear in liberation reflections on the trinity. Discussion of the trinity takes a different shape when approached by liberation theologians. Because they are not interested in philosophical discussions about the internal relations of the Godhead, you will not find discussions of *circumincession* or *perichoresis* dominating their views. Rather, they are interested in reflecting on the trinity in terms of God's relation to the world and the way the trinity has been and may be used politically. Leonardo Boff, for instance, begins his book *Trinity and Society* with a discussion of "the political dangers of a-trinitarian monotheism."[4] It is with the Christian legacy of interpreting monotheism in terms of domination, imperialism, and exclusion in mind that he develops his view of the trinity as the mystery of inclusion and communion.

Cone and Thistlethwaite also work from an understanding of God as triune and interpret the meaning of triune in relation to the social-economic-political experience of oppressed peoples. Cone states it this way: "Taking seriously the Trinitarian view of the Godhead, black theology says that as Creator God identified with oppressed Israel, participating in the bringing into being of this people; as redeemer, God became the Oppressed One in order that all may be free from oppression; as Holy Spirit, God continues the work of liberation." The discovery of the nature of God as relationality and diversity in the trinitarian symbol, as emphasized by Thistlethwaite, means that the justice imperative, bonding with the despised Other, is the way the activity of the triune God is expressed in human community.

By pointing out these similarities between a Black male liberation theologian and a white female liberation theologian we are not saying that Black GodTalk and white feminist GodTalk are identical. The particularity of each context means that different theological emphases are bound to emerge. For Cone clearly the Black community's struggle for simple human justice in white America is central to his understanding of God. For Thistlethwaite, the peace movement and the women's movement constitute a primary justice struggle. Yet this is not a matter of "You do your thing and I'll do mine." The interlocking structures of racism, sexism, classism, and militarism cannot be addressed piecemeal. Nor is any liberation movement free from perpetuation of all these systemic oppressions. The "women's movement" in the United States has largely identified "women's experience" with "white women's experience," the Black liberation struggle has ignored sexism in the Black community, the peace movement has been more concerned with saving the status quo than with creating a *just* and secure society. (See Grant's and Heyward's Christology chapters for a discussion of differences between Black and white feminist theologians.) Along with other theologians of liberation, both Cone and Thistlethwaite maintain, however, that the God of the oppressed, the God active in history, is found *in the midst of* these contradictions and not apart from them. As Cone contends, we cannot have knowledge of God "as God is *in se*. Theologically this seems impossible. We can know God only in relationship to the human race, or more particularly in God's liberating activity on behalf of oppressed humanity." The God of the oppressed, then, is discovered and experienced simultaneously in the midst of different struggles for justice, and one of the tasks of liberation GodTalk is to make the connections between these experiences and understandings of God explicit. Theologians of liberation already share the acknowledgement that God is known *in* the struggle for justice. Or, as Gutiérrez puts it, following the words of Jeremiah, "To know God is to do justice."[5] One of the greatest tasks still facing them is the acknowledgement that God is known *in* the struggle to make the connections between different struggles for justice around the world.

CHAPTER 6

God Is Black

JAMES H. CONE

CONTEXT AND COMMITMENT

My perspective on Christian theology was shaped by my ministry in the Black church and my participation in the Civil Rights and Black Power Movements of the 1960s, as defined largely by Martin Luther King, Jr., and Malcolm X. After completing my Ph.D. at Garrett (now Garrett-Evangelical) Seminary and Northwestern University in systematic theology (1965), I returned to Little Rock, Arkansas to teach at my alma mater, Philander Smith College. At Philander and later at Adrian College in Michigan, the Civil Rights and Black Power Movements forced me to ask, "What has the gospel of Jesus Christ to do with Black people's struggle for justice in a white racist society?" Six years of graduate theological education had not prepared me for radical implications of that question.

The ministry of Martin King showed me that no interpretation of the Christian faith could be valid without an engagement of the issues of justice in the society and the world. Malcolm X taught me that I could not be a human being without accepting myself as a *Black* person. Martin and Malcolm together challenged me to ask, "How can I be both Black *and* Christian at the same time?"

In an attempt to reconcile my Black and Christian identities, I began to write about a Black theology of liberation, endeavoring to show that the real meaning of the gospel of Jesus is found in the concrete struggles of the poor for freedom and not in the abstract theological jargon. Although I continue to do theology primarily out of my participation in and commitment to the Black community in the United States, my experience in other communities of the poor in Africa, Asia, and Latin America reveals the global significance of God's liberating power.

In 1969 I came to teach theology at Union Seminary in New York. My primary vocation is to prepare persons for ministry who are committed to extending God's life-giving presence in the communities of the poor throughout the world.

AN INTRODUCTORY NOTE ON THE CHAPTER, "GOD IS BLACK"

My essay "God Is Black" was first published nearly eighteen years ago. It is found in *A Black Theology of Liberation* (Lippincott, 1970), a book that represented my initial attempt to write a short systematic theology from the perspective of the Black freedom struggle of the 1960s. During that time, the Black community in the United States was engaged in a fierce struggle for justice in a society defined by white racism. Sit-ins and freedom-rides, Birmingham and Selma, Black Power and the Vietnam war dominated the news media as Blacks and their sympathizers fought to make America accountable to the ideas of justice and democracy articulated in the Declaration of Independence and the Constitution. Urban riots were a regular summer happening, because the structures of domination made it crystal clear that there was no *equal* place in America for its Black citizens. Throughout the land, Blacks and their supporters were tortured and killed by the "white power structure" in the name of "law and order," "God and America." The speeches and activities of Martin Luther King, Jr., and Malcolm X, Fannie Lou Hamer and Ella Baker, as well as many others too numerous to name, raised our political consciousness to new heights and visions, as we struggled to remake America in the light of the history and culture of its excluded minorities. What role did the Christian God, the God of Moses, Jesus, and Paul, have to play in the Black freedom struggle? That was a question which dominated the consciousness of many Black Christians. The essay, "God Is Black," was my attempt to answer it.

Many things have changed since the 1960s. The most notable change for my theological perspective has been the impact of the rise of liberation theologies among the oppressed in the so-called Third World countries in Asia, Africa, and Latin America. During the sixties, I was not aware of the currently well-known liberation theology in Latin America, and neither did I know of similar theological developments in Asia and Africa. My reflections on God were defined by the great contradiction of racism in the U.S. as mirrored in its history and the Civil Rights and Black Power movements of the 1950s and 60s. My chief concern then was to reconcile Martin Luther King, Jr.'s accent on divine love in race relations (which he called *agape*) with Malcolm X's stress on divine justice (which he identified with the destruction of the white oppressor). I also wanted to demonstrate that the God of the Christian gospel was not *white* as most Christians and non-Christians, even in the Black community, seemed to believe. On the contrary, I was determined to show, using the intellectual tools whites had taught me in seminary, that "God is Black," not just because African-Americans are Black, but because God freely chooses to be known as the One who liberates victims from their oppression.

Using the oppressor's tools has advantages and disadvantages, and it is important to be critically aware of what they are. For example, one cannot overcome the oppressor's way of thinking without understanding how it functions. But one must be careful not to become mesmerized by the intellectual categories one is seeking to destroy. I was not always aware of that. If I had had the time to rewrite this essay or to write a new one about God, many things would change, and others would remain the same. What would change? Of course, I would eliminate the exclusive, sexist language as I did in the "second edition" of *A Black Theology of Liberation* (Orbis, 1986). But much more important than "just changing words" is the reality to which words point. Were I to write an essay on "God" today, I would seek to develop a more holistic perspective by incorporating what I have learned about divine presence from other communities of the oppressed throughout the world, particularly in Asia, Africa, and Latin America and also among women in all forms of liberation theology. I regret deeply that other urgent commitments did not permit me to write a new essay. However, I do plan to set myself to this task in the not too distant future.

What would remain the same? I am more convinced today than I was during the 1960s that the God of the Christian gospel can be known only in the communities of the oppressed who are struggling for justice in a world that has no place for them. I still believe that "God is Black" in the sense that God's identity is found in the faces of those who are exploited and humiliated because of their color. But I also believe that "God is mother," "rice," "red," and a host of other things that give life to those whom society condemns to death. "Black," "mother," "rice," and "red" give concreteness to God's life-giving presence in the world and remind us that the universality of God is found in the particularity of the suffering poor. We can know God only in an oppressed community in struggle for justice and wholeness. It is because I believe that "God is Black" that I also believe that the dominant, western, male theological tradition is much too limiting to speak about God. Barth, Tillich, Bultmann, and their colleagues and students are grossly inadequate theological sources for discerning who God is or what God is doing in the world. I was not as acutely aware of this fact eighteen years ago as I am today. Third World theologians have challenged and thereby enlarged my perspective on God. So have women, lesbians and gays, and many other oppressed groups throughout the world. To speak of God today is to talk about the power of justice and love in human relations as women and men of all races, nationalities, and cultures seek to remake the world for human habitation. God is that life-giving power who enables the victims of injustice to survive in the midst of misery and to fight until freedom comes. It is this conviction that defines my perspective on God today, broadening and correcting my previous one-sided dependence on western theological categories. As life-giving power, God is the liberator who empowers the poor of the world to fight against their oppressors.

Because the "irruption of the poor" is not primarily a Christian phenomenon, we must not limit our discourse about God to biblical revelation or to what Christians are doing today. (Unfortunately, that is one of the most serious limitations of my 1970 essay.) God is known as life-giving power, the power of justice and love, wherever poor people are rising up against the structures that dehumanize them. Christians have no monopoly on correct speech about God. Buddhists and Hindus, Moslems and Jews, Shamanists and other popular religions among the poor also speak about God's presence as the power of justice and love in the community of the victims, enabling them to survive their present exploitation and also bestowing upon them a vision that they can overcome it. My perspective on God has greatly affected my travels throughout Africa, Asia, and Latin America where I have seen poor people take their freedom into their own hands because they believe that the great God of the universe did not make them for misery. They contend that they were made for freedom, and that the One who made them for it is also present with them in their struggle to claim it.

I first encountered the God of justice and love at Macedonia A.M.E. Church in Bearden, Arkansas. It was a liberating experience which bestowed upon me the power to know that what whites said about Blacks was a lie. The power to be somebody in a world that had defined Blacks as nobody is what God meant to me and many other Black people. The Civil Rights and Black Power movements concretized in the society what many Blacks had already discovered in the spirituality of their churches. Using the tools of white theology, I, as a new seminary graduate, tried to interpret the meaning of God for the Black struggle for liberation. Although white intellectual tools were too limiting and often hampered what I felt in the deepest resources of my experience, I think that my thesis about God's blackness was adequate then and is still appropriate today if we realize that blackness is a powerful symbol of oppression and liberation among the victims on the world. I urge the readers of my essay to read it in the light of the poor of the world who believe that God will not let us rest until freedom comes.

CONSTRUCTION

Because blacks have come to know themselves as *black,* and because that blackness is the cause of their own love of themselves and hatred of whiteness, the blackness of God is the key to our knowledge of God. The blackness of God, and everything implied by it in a racist society, is the heart of the black theology doctrine of God. There is no place in black theology for a colorless God in a society where human beings suffer precisely because of their color. The black theologian must reject any conception of God which stifles black self-determination by picturing God as a God of all peoples. Either God is identified with the oppressed to the point that their experience becomes God's experience, or God is a God of racism.

As Camus has pointed out, authentic identification is not "a question of psychological identification—a mere subterfuge by which the individual imagines that it is he himself who is being offended. . . . [It is] identification of one's destiny with that of others and a choice of sides."[1] Because God has made the goal of blacks God's own goal, black theology believes that it is not only appropriate but necessary to begin the doctrine of God with an insistence on God's blackness.

The blackness of God means that God has made the oppressed condition God's own condition. This is the essence of the biblical revelation. By electing Israelite slaves as the people of God and by becoming the Oppressed One in Jesus Christ, the human race is made to understand that God is known where human beings experience humiliation and suffering. It is not that God feels sorry and takes pity on them (the condescending attitude of those racists who need their guilt assuaged for getting fat on the starvation of others); quite the contrary, God's election of Israel and incarnation in Christ reveal that the *liberation* of the oppressed is a part of the innermost nature of God. Liberation is not an afterthought, but the essence of divine activity.

The blackness of God means that the essence of the nature of God is to be found in the concept of liberation. Taking seriously the Trinitarian view of the Godhead, black theology says that as Creator, God identified with oppressed Israel, participating in the bringing into being of this people; as Redeemer, God became the Oppressed One in order that all may be free from oppression; as Holy Spirit, God continues the work of liberation. The Holy Spirit is the Spirit of the Creator and the Redeemer at work in the forces of human liberation in our society today. In America, the Holy Spirit is black persons making decisions about their togetherness, which means making preparation for an encounter with whites.

It is the black theology emphasis on the blackness of God that distinguishes it sharply from contemporary white views of God. White religionists are not capable of perceiving the blackness of God, because their satanic whiteness is a denial of the very essence of divinity. That is why whites are finding and will continue to find the black experience a disturbing reality.

White theologians would prefer to do theology without reference to color, but this only reveals how deeply racism is embedded in the thought forms of this culture. To be sure, they would probably concede that the concept of liberation is essential to the biblical view of God. But it is still impossible for them to translate the biblical emphasis on liberation to the black-white struggle today. Invariably they quibble on this issue, moving from side to side, always pointing out the dangers of extremism on both sides. (In the black community, we call this "shuffling.") They really cannot make a decision, because it has already been made for them.

How scholars would analyze God and blacks was decided when black slaves were brought to this land, while churchmen sang "Jesus, Lover of My Soul." Their attitude today is no different from that of the bishop of London who assured slaveholders that:

Christianity, and the embracing of the Gospel, does not make the least Alteration in Civil property, or in any Duties which belong to Civil Relations; but in all these Respects, it continues Persons just in the same State as it found them. The Freedom which Christianity gives, is a Freedom from the Bondage of Sin and Satan, and from the dominion of Man's Lust and Passions and inordinate Desires; but as to their outward Condition, whatever that was before, whether bond or free, their being baptized and becoming Christians, makes no matter of change in it.[2]

Of course white theologians today have a "better" way of putting it, but what difference does that make? It means the same thing to blacks. "Sure," as the so-called radicals would say, "God is concerned about blacks." And then they would go on to talk about God and secularization or some other white problem unrelated to the emancipation of blacks. This style is a contemporary white way of saying that "Christianity . . . does not make the least alteration in civil property."

In contrast to this racist view of God, black theology proclaims God's blackness. Those who want to know who God is and what God is doing must know who black persons are and what they are doing. This does not mean lending a helping hand to the poor and unfortunate blacks of society. It does not mean joining the war on poverty! Such acts are sin offerings that represent a white way of assuring themselves that they are basically "good" persons. Knowing God means being on the side of the oppressed, becoming *one* with them, and participating in the goal of liberation. *We must become black with God!*

It is to be expected that whites will have some difficulty with the idea of "becoming *black* with God." The experience is not only alien to their existence as they know it to be, it appears to be an impossibility. "How can whites become black?" they ask. They know, as everyone in this country knows, blacks are those who say they are black, regardless of skin color. In the literal sense a black person is anyone who has "even one drop of black blood in his or her veins."

But "becoming black with God" means more than just saying "I am black," if it involves that at all. The question "How can white persons become black?" is analogous to the Philippian jailer's question to Paul and Silas, "What must I do to be saved?" The implication is that if we work hard enough at it, we can reach the goal. But the misunderstanding here is the failure to see that blackness, or salvation (the two are synonymous) is the work of God, not a human work. It is not something we accomplish; it is a gift. That is why Paul and Silas said, "Believe in the Lord Jesus and you will be saved."

To *believe* is to receive the gift and utterly to reorient one's existence on the basis of the gift. The gift is so unlike what humans expect that when it is offered and accepted, we become completely new creatures. This is what the Wholly Otherness of God means. God comes to us in God's blackness, which is wholly unlike whiteness. To receive God's revelation is to become black with God by joining God in the work of liberation.

Even some blacks will find this view of God hard to handle. Having been enslaved by the God of white racism so long, they will have difficulty believing that God is identified with their struggle for freedom. Becoming one of God's disciples means rejecting whiteness and accepting themselves as they are in all their physical blackness. This is what the Christian view of God means for blacks.

THE LOVE AND RIGHTEOUSNESS OF GOD

The theological statement "God is love" is the most widely accepted assertion regarding the nature of God. All theologians would agree that it is impossible to speak of the Christian understanding of God without affirming the idea of love as essential to the divine nature. Anders Nygren's *Agape and Eros*[3] is the classic treatment of the subject, and he shows, perhaps conclusively, that *agape* is inseparable from the authentic Christian view of God. When religionists deviated from the *agape* motif, the result was always a distortion of the authentic Christian conception of God.

Though religionists have agreed that love is indispensable to the Christian view of God's nature, there has been much disagreement on how the idea of the *wrath* of God is reconciled with the love of God.

Most religionists, although rejecting the Marcion dichotomy, proceed to analyze the concept of the love of God without relating it to God's righteousness. Marcion's position presents us with two alternatives. Either we agree with him and his view of the two Gods, Righteousness and Love, or we affirm the basic oneness of God's righteousness and love, and that means that God's love is inexplicable without equal emphasis on God's righteousness and vice versa. Contemporary theology seems to want to have its cake and eat it too—that is, reject the Marcionite view and also accept a view of love that ignores righteousness, and that is not possible.

Gordon Kaufman's work, *Systematic Theology: A Historicist Perspective*, seems to be open to this criticism. Particularly concerned about protecting the idea of love in God's nature, Kaufman says that it is improper to speak of the "wrath" of God as an expression of the being of God. Love is essential, but the idea of wrath is an expression of human disobedience and can be understood only by looking at human nature, not God's nature:

The wrath of God is a symbol more appropriate to discussion of the nature (and plight) of *man* than God. . . . The man hanging on the cross . . . reveals God's nature as long-suffering love, not vengeance or wrath in any sense. . . . Hence, in our direct exposition of the doctrine of God such symbols as "wrath" would only be misleading and should be avoided: God reveals himself as love and faithfulness, and this it is that we must seek to grasp here.[4]

Black theology agrees that the idea of love is indispensable to the Christian view of God. The exodus, the call of Israel into being as the people of the covenant, the gift of the promised land, the rise of prophecy, the second exodus, and above all the incarnation reveal God's self-giving love to oppressed humanity.

We do not read far in the biblical tradition without recognizing that the divine-human fellowship is to be understood exclusively in terms of what God does for humankind and not what humankind does for itself or for God. That is why Nygren is correct in describing God's *agape* as the "initiation of the fellowship with God,"[5] and why it is appropriate for Barth to emphasize the complete freedom of God in the divine-human encounter. If the incarnation means anything in Christian theology, it must mean that "God so loved the world that he gave his only Son, that whoever believes in him should not perish but have eternal life" (John 3:16).

The love of God is the heart of the Christian gospel. As the writer of 1 John puts it, "God is love" (4:8,16). Commenting on the theological implication of this phrase, C. H. Dodd writes: "To say 'God is love' implies that *all* His activity is loving activity. If He creates, He creates in love; if He rules, He rules in love; if He judges, He judges in love. All that He does is the expression of His nature which is—to love."[6]

Black theology, then, asks not whether love is an essential element of the Christian interpretation of God, but whether the love of God itself can be properly understood without focusing equally on the biblical view of God's righteousness. Is it possible to understand what God's love means for the oppressed without making *wrath* an essential ingredient of that love? What could love possibly mean in a racist society except the righteous condemnation of everything racist? Most theological treatments of God's love fail to place the proper emphasis on God's wrath, suggesting that love is completely self-giving without any demand for obedience. Bonhoeffer called this "cheap grace": "Cheap grace means grace as a doctrine, a principle, a system. It means forgiveness of sins proclaimed as a general truth, the love of God taught as the Christian 'conception' of God."[7]

The difficulty with Kaufman's view and others like his is not so much his explicit statements but their false implications. By removing wrath as a symbol of the nature of God, his interpretation weakens the central biblical truth about God's liberation of the oppressed from oppressors. A God without wrath does not plan to do too much liberating, for the two concepts belong together. A God minus wrath seems to be a God who is basically not against anything. All we have to do is behave nicely, and everything will work out all right.

Such a view of God leaves us in doubt about God's role in the black-white struggle. Blacks want to know whose side God is on and what kind of decision God is making about the black revolution. We will not accept a God who is on everybody's side—which means that God loves everybody in spite of who they are, and is working (through the acceptable channels of society, of course) to reconcile all persons to the Godhead.

Black theology cannot accept a view of God which does not represent God as being for oppressed blacks and thus against white oppressors. Living in a world of white oppressors, blacks have no time for a neutral God. The brutalities are too great and the pain too severe and this means we must know where God is and what God is doing in the revolution. There is no use for a God who loves white oppressors *the same as* oppressed blacks. We have had too much of white love, the love that tells blacks to turn the other cheek and go the second mile. What we need is the divine love as expressed in black power, which is the power of blacks to destroy their oppressors, here and now, by any means at their disposal. Unless God is participating in this holy activity, we must reject God's love.

The interpretation of God's love without righteousness also suggests that white "success" is a sign of God's favor, of God's love. Kaufman's view is open to the ungodly assumption that all is well with the way whites live in the world, because God loves them, and their material success is the evidence. But according to black theology, it is blasphemy to say that God loves white oppressors unless that love is interpreted as God's wrathful activity against them and everything that whiteness stands for in American society. If the wrath of God is God's almighty no to the yes of human beings, then blacks want to know where the no of God is today in white America. We believe that the black community's no as expressed in the black revolution is God's no showing God's rejection of oppressors and acceptance of the oppressed.

Kaufman's view also suggests that there is knowledge of God as God is *in se*. Theologically this seems impossible. We can know God only in relationship to the human race, or more particularly in God's liberating activity in behalf of oppressed humanity. The attempt to analyze God independently of God's liberating work is analogous to the theological attempt to understand human nature *before* the fall. The fall itself renders such knowledge impossible: there is no way to get behind the human condition as we know it to be.

The limitation of human knowledge is equally true in regard to God as God is *in se*. We are not permitted to transcend our finiteness and rise to a vision of God unrelated to the human condition. If this is true, what merit is there in saying that God's wrath is not a part of the divine nature? If God is a God of the oppressed of the land, as the revelation of Christ discloses, then wrath is an indispensable element for describing the scope and meaning of God's liberation of the oppressed. The wrath of God is the love of God in regard to the forces opposed to liberation of the oppressed.

Love without righteousness is unacceptable to blacks: this view of God is a product of the minds of enslavers. By emphasizing the complete self-giving of God in Christ without seeing also the content of righteousness, oppressors could then demand that the oppressed do likewise. If God freely enters into self-donation, then in order to be godlike we must give ourselves to our oppressors in like manner. If God has loved us in spite of our revolt against God, then to be like God we too must love those who revolt against or enslave us. For blacks this would mean letting whites crowd us into ghettos where rats and filth eat away at our being, and not raising a hand against them.

This view of love places no obligation on white oppressors. The existing laws of society protect them, and their white skins are badges of acceptance. In fact, they are permitted to do whatever they will against blacks, assured that God loves them as well as the ones they oppress. Love means that God will accept white oppressors, and blacks will not seek reprisal.

Black theology rejects this view, saying that those who oppress others are in no position to define what love is. How could white scholars know that love means turning the other cheek? They have never had to do so. Only those who live in an oppressed condition can know what their love-response ought to be to their oppressors. Their oppressors certainly cannot answer that question for them!

TRADITIONAL THEOLOGICAL LANGUAGE AND THE BLACK GOD

One of the major tasks of black theology is that of making sense out of the traditional theological talk about God. It asks, in regard to every theological assertion, "What are its implications for the oppressed?" Or, more specifically,, "Does it have any meaning in the struggle for black liberation in America?" Believing that the biblical God is made known through the liberation of the oppressed, the black theology analysis of God begins with an emphasis on God's blackness.

But now we must ask, How is the concept of the blackness of God related to such traditional divine symbols as creator, transcendence, immanence, and providence?

1. God as Creator. The biblical view of God as creator is expressed in the priestly assertion, "In the beginning God created the heavens and earth" (Genesis 1:1). To speak of God as creator means that the world and everything that is *is* because of the creative will of God. In traditional theological language, God as creator expresses aseity—that is, the total independence of God from creation. God is self-existent, meaning that the source of God's existence is found in God.

Black theology is not interested in debating the philosophical and theological merits of God's aseity except as it can be related to the earthly emancipation of the oppressed. What has the idea of God's self-existence to do with the existence of the oppressed? First it is necessary to point out that the biblical view of God as creator is not a paleontological statement about the nature and origin of the universe, but a theological assertion about God and God's relationship to the oppressed of the land.

It is important to remember that the priestly narrative was put together during the Babylonian exile as an attempt to make theological sense of the history of Israel as an oppressed people. Therefore, it is impossible to remain faithful to the biblical viewpoint without seeing the doctrine of creation as a statement about God and the oppressed of the land. God as creator means that humankind is a creature; the source of its meaning and purpose in the world is not found in oppressors but in God. This view of God undoubtedly accounts for the exclusiveness of Israel in a situation of political oppression.

Though white theologians have emphasized that God as creator is a statement about the divine-human relationship, they have not pointed out the political implications of this theological truth for blacks. God as creator has not been related to the oppressed in society. If creation "involves a bringing into existence of something that did not exist before,"[8] then to say that God is creator means that *my being* finds its source in God. *I am black because God is black!* God as creator is the ground of my blackness (being), the point of reference for meaning and purpose in the universe.

2. Immanence and Transcendence of God. The immanence of God means that God always encounters us in a situation of historical liberation. That is why Christianity is called a historical religion. God is not a symbol referring to the interior religious experiences of humankind. Nor is God to be thought of in the manner of the deist philosophers, who pictured God as performing the initial act of creation but refraining from any further involvement in the world. According to biblical religion, God is involved in the concrete affairs of human history, liberating the oppressed. Therefore to ask, "Who is God?" is to focus on what God is doing; and to look at what God is doing is to center on human events as they pertain to the liberation of suffering humanity.

God, then, is not that pious feeling in our hearts, nor is God a being "out there" or "up there." It is not possible to speak of the reality of the divine in scientific categories. Like the symbol transcendence, immanence is not a causal term. It refers to the depths of liberation in human society, affirming that God is never less than our experience of liberation.

The immanence of God is the infinite expressing itself in the finite. It is God becoming concrete in finite human existence. We are able to speak of the divine because the divine is revealed in the concreteness of this world.

The immanence of God forces us to look for God in the world and to make decisions about the Ultimate in terms of present historical reality. We cannot postpone our decision about God or condition it in terms of a future reality. The finality of God is God's involvement in human now-experiences. For blacks this means that God has taken on blackness, has moved into the black liberation struggle.

Though black theology stresses the immanence of God, it does not deny the reality of God's transcendence. The transcendence of God prevents us from deifying our own experiences, which results in pantheism. God is neither nature nor our highest aspirations. God is always more than our experience of God. This means that truth is not limited to human capabilities. It is this reality that frees the rebel to give all for the liberation struggle without having to worry about the Western concept of winning.

Relating this to black humanity, black theology interprets it to mean that our struggle for liberation is the infinite participating in the concrete reality of human existence. But because God is always more than our experience of God, the reality of God cannot be limited to a particular human experience. However, just because God is more than our encounter of the divine in a particular moment of liberation, this should not be interpreted to mean that we must qualify our assertions about God. Just the opposite. Because God is not less than our experience of the divine, we must speak with absoluteness that does not compromise with evil, despite the relativity of our claims.

3. Providence. It is difficult to talk about divine providence when men and women are dying and children are being tortured. Richard Rubenstein pointed out the danger of this concept in his excellent book *After Auschwitz*.[9] Whether or not we agree with his conclusions about the death of God, we can appreciate his analysis, based as it is on his identification with an oppressed people. Like black theology, Rubenstein refuses to affirm any view of God which contributed to the oppression of the Jewish people. If God is the Lord of history, directing the course of events toward a final goal, and if the Jews are God's elected people, then there is no way to avoid divine responsibility for the death of six million Jews in Germany, according to Rubenstein. Therefore, rather than accept a view of God that incorporates Jewish blood in the divine plan, he concludes that God is dead. The argument is cogent and certainly advances the death-of-God theology beyond white Christian views as represented in the thinking of William Hamilton and Thomas Altizer.

Rubenstein was not the first to recognize the difficulty of reconciling human suffering and divine participation in history. Without focusing on the God of history, the writer of Job recognized this problem. In more recent writing Albert Camus and the existentialists have dealt with it also. In the thinking of Camus, if God is omnipotent and permits human suffering, then God is a murderer. That is why he quotes Bakunin with approval: "If God did exist, we would have to abolish Him."

Traditional Christian theology somehow fails to take this problem seriously. Although agreeing that human suffering is a reality which appears to conflict with God's love, theologians still insist on quoting Paul with approval: "We know that in everything God works for good with those who love him, who are called according to his purpose" (Romans 8:28).

Despite the emphasis on future redemption in present suffering, black theology cannot accept any view of God that even *indirectly* places divine approval on human suffering. The death and resurrection of Jesus does not mean that God promises us a future reality in order that we might tolerate present evil. The suffering that Jesus accepted and which is promised to his disciples is not to be equated with the easy acceptance of human injustice inflicted by white oppressors. God cannot be the God of blacks *and* will their suffering. To be elected by God does not mean freely accepting the evils of oppressors. The suffering which is inseparable from the gospel is that style of existence that arises from a decision to be in spite of nonbeing. It is that type of suffering that is inseparable from freedom, the freedom that affirms black liberation despite the white powers of evil. It is suffering in the struggle for liberation.

Providence, then, is not a statement about the future. It does not mean that all things will work out for the best for those who love God. Providence is a statement about present reality—the reality of the liberation of the oppressed. For blacks it is a statement about the reality of blackness and what it means in the liberation struggle against whites. As Tillich says:

Faith in providence is faith "in spite of"—in spite of the . . . meaningless of existence. . . . [Special providence] gives the individual the certainty that under any circumstances, under any set of conditions, the divine "factor" is active and that therefore the road to his ultimate fulfillment is open.[10]

Black theology interprets this to mean that in spite of whiteness a way is open to blackness, and we do not have to accept white definitions.

It is within this context that divine omnipotence should be interpreted. Omnipotence does not refer to God's absolute power to accomplish what God wants. And John Macquarrie says, omnipotence is "the power to let something stand out from nothing and to be."[11] Translating this idea into the black experience, God's omnipotence is the power to let blacks stand out from whiteness and to be. It is what happens when blacks make ready for the black-white encounter with the full determination that they shall have their freedom or else. In this situation, divine providence is seeing divine reality in the present reality of black liberation—no more, no less.

RECOMMENDED READING

Cone, James H. *Black Theology and Black Power.* New York: Harper & Row, 1969.
_____. *A Black Theology of Liberation.* 2d ed. Maryknoll, NY: Orbis, 1986. First
     published, 1970.
_____. *God of the Oppressed.* New York: Seabury, 1975.
_____. *For My People: Black Theology and the Black Church.* Bishop Henry McNeal
     Turner Studies in North America Black Religion, vol. 1. Maryknoll,
     NY: Orbis, 1984.
Roberts, J. Deotis. *Liberation and Reconciliation: A Black Theology.* Philadelphia:
     Westminster, 1971.
Wilmore, Gayraud S. *Black Religion and Black Radicalism: An Interpretation of the
     Religious History of Afro-American People.* 2d rev. ed. Maryknoll, NY:
     Orbis, 1983.
_____, and James H. Cone, eds. *Black Theology: A Documentary History,
     1966–1979.* Maryknoll, NY: Orbis, 1979.

CHAPTER 7

"I Am Become Death": God in the Nuclear Age

SUSAN BROOKS THISTLETHWAITE

CONTEXT AND COMMITMENT

My context is that of a white, middle-class American academic/ clergywoman. Like many Americans, my middle-class status is fairly recent, a product of the post–World War II surge in the American economy. Prior to the war, my extended family, immigrants from Hungary, worked in the sweatshops of the New York garment district. From an early age it was drummed into me that escape from the precariousness of a working-class existence was the *sine qua non* of human happiness. My parents firmly believed that it was THE WAR that had made their own and other's economic mobility possible. Like many Americans they believed that the invention and possession of the atomic bomb was a symbol of America's moral superiority to other nations of the world. Others had not had the "moral courage" of America when it "ended the war and saved American lives" by using the bomb over Hiroshima and Nagasaki.

I am Protestant because many (but not all) members of my family converted to Protestantism as they converted to Americanism. Catholicism was "old-world" and we were to be wholly "new-world" now.

Education is viewed as a key to self-betterment by most immigrants, and my family was no exception. Despite his often expressed disappointment that I was not a boy, my father paid joyfully for more and more education for me—at least until I chose the proverty-stricken path of religion over the law-school education he had chosen for me.

White, middle-class, American, female: these factors are a given. They are not, however, merely objective facts but a set of commonly held cultural attitudes and values. Feminism has, for me, initiated a process of contextual analysis that began as I sought to get free from my family's violence, but which has pushed me to extend this analysis. An extended analysis has revealed the interlocking set of attitudes and values that tie my particular context to the larger culture. I attempt, therefore, to connect class, race, and sex with the structures of overt and covert violence.

My commitments are to the movement to end violence against women and to the peace movement. Nuclearism is, for me, both the day-to-day reality of the existence of nuclear weapons and a symbol of that which makes the arms race possible: the economics of sex, race, and class exploitation. For example, one result of the "peace" achieved by nuclear deterrence is that since 1947 there have been over 100 wars in the Two-Thirds World. Or one could find it instructive that much of the language used to describe nuclear weapons technology is deeply sexist. The message to the President of the United States that the first test of a nuclear weapon had been successful was, "It's a boy!"

As a teacher of seminar students I am committed to an educational process that teaches people to *see* the interconnections among the attitudes and values that sustain the nuclear age and to *act* strategically through their commitments to bring about substantive change. As a mother of three boys, I am committed to the demilitarization of our society so that my sons will never learn to equate "manly" with violent.

CONSTRUCTION

"I am become death, the shatterer of worlds." These words from the Hindu epic *Bhagavad-Gita* flashed through the mind of J. Robert Oppenheimer, the physicist in charge of the Los Alamos, New Mexico laboratory when the blinding glare of the first atomic explosion lit the New Mexico desert night with the "radiance of a thousand suns."[1]

Many of the witnesses to the first atomic explosion, while not normally as poetic as Oppenheimer (he had studied Sanskrit in order to read Eastern philosophy in the original language), expressed their reactions in religious terms.[2] Hardly accidental, the worshipful language evoking particularly the power of God over life and death reveals the close relationship between violence and certain understandings of the nature and work of God.

This connection between violence and the doctrine of God did not begin, as did the atomic age, in the shuddering dawn of the first atomic explosion. It has existed in understandings of the nature and work of God throughout the history of Christianity. The atomic age, however, trades on the connections between violence and certain understandings of the nature and work of God for the justification of the existence and use of these weapons of absolute destruction. The religious interpretation of nuclear weapons in Christianity as the tools of a wrathful God, and the lack of any significant alternative models of God, has done more than perhaps anything else to justify the nuclear weapons buildup in the North Atlantic communities.

LIVING WITH THE BOMB

Nuclearism, a term coined by psychologist Robert Jay Lifton, who has studied extensively the responses of humanity to nuclear weapons, is defined as a worship of nuclear weapons as a means to salvation.[3] The bomb is now God and this God, like the Krishna of the *Bhagavad-Gita*, has become a death-dealing shatterer of worlds.

Religious themes of awe and fear are rife within the records of the earliest responses to nuclear weapons. In commenting on American "nuclear imagery," Ira Chernus says of the early period of nuclearism (1945–1962) that "although the Bomb was viewed largely as our trustworthy protector of nomos, there was also deep awe and even a hint of ecstasy at its infinitely destructive capacity. Underlying all this imagery was a complex web of contradictions and paradoxes, making the Bomb itself our primary symbol of the unity of opposites."[4]

A particularly instructive example of the conflict in the need for nomos, or ordered security, and the lure of chaos, or violent destruction, is that Oppenheimer named the first test of a nuclear weapon "Trinity," after a poem by John Donne to the Christian trinitarian God, which implores God to save the believer by destroying him (*sic*). The sonnet begins with the famous line, "Batter my heart, three person'd God," and ends with the imprecation, "Take mee to you, imprison mee, for I, except you enthrall mee, never shall be free, Nor ever chaste, except you ravish mee."[5]

Chernus has also observed that the third nuclear age, which began in 1979, "was a renewal of the old images."[6] This parallelism between the first and third ages of the bomb may be noted by comparing Donne's poem with a poem by Alia Johnson called "Why We Should Drop the Bomb." This poem brilliantly captures the tension articulated by Donne's longing for violent rapture at the hands of God and explains some of the fuel for religious nuclearism. The poet exclaims, "it would be so exciting, it would be so powerful" and concludes, "we would finally have done it better than Raskolnikov, it would release our anger in the ultimate tantrum, then we could rest."[7]

A key theme in the Johnson poem is the release of anger. Nuclear fundamentalism is predicated on anger at enemies and their supposed sins. God's wrath is pictured as directed toward these enemies (rather than toward the individual sinful soul, as in Donne). The longer the punishment of these enemies is delayed, the greater the tension. But the greater the tension, the more profound will be the release, and the rapturous union of the believer with God.[8]

Because of the effects of what Lifton has called "psychic numbing," our conscious awareness of this transition from a God of life to a God of death is blocked. "Psychic numbing" is defined by Lifton as "exclusion of feeling." "That exclusion can occur in two ways. There is first the blocking of images, or of feelings associated with certain images, because they are too painful or unacceptable. The second is an absence of images, the lack of prior experience in relation to one event."[9]

Lifton constantly returns to the theme of the blocking of images and the absence of images to explain how it is that in "psychic numbing" the "symbolizing process—the flow and re-creation of images and forms—is interrupted."[10] The ability to be aware of our situation in a nuclear age is disrupted, according to Lifton, because of an absence of meaningful images and symbols.

For Lifton, the ability to "see" nuclearism and to find a way out of psychic numbing is related to the study of psychological blocking. He has pursued his work on nuclearism by studying survivors of Hiroshima and Nagasaki. But the violent images of God that have emerged with such force in the nuclear age must also be subject to an analysis of the social context that will reveal their political and economic sources as well.[11] How we actually think about the nuclear age has both psychological and social support.

CONTEXTUAL ANALYSIS: VIOLENCE AND NONVIOLENCE

The doctrine of God in the nuclear age must take its origins from a contextual analysis which reveals that nuclearism, the worship of nuclear weapons, is not exclusively a product of intrapsychic conflict. Contextual analysis must include a broad-based social analysis of the dynamics of violence and nonviolence in this society.

"The ultimate kind of power is violence," wrote C. Wright Mills.[12] Violence has often been defined as unjust coercive power. Clausewitz, the famous theorist of war, defined war as "an act of violence to compel the opponent to do as we wish."[13]

It is important to clarify, however, particularly when we intend a discussion of *God's* violence or nonviolence, that the term violence may equally be applied to overt physical force or to covert structures of repression. What is common to both understandings, overt and covert violence, is compulsion.

The existence of covert structures of violence is a recent insight generated primarily through the struggles of groups demanding human liberation who have sought to understand their situations. Sexism, racism, and classism are now identified as violent because they exercise a kind of prior restraint which is coercive, but which does not necessarily, in the moment of its exercise, employ overt physical force. The threat of force, however, is almost always implied.

Violence understood as unjust coercive power, exercised either covertly or overtly, depends on the unequal distribution of power for its existence. Hannah Arendt has written, "The extreme form of power is All against One, the extreme form of violence is One against All."[14] She also observed that "Even the most despotic domination we know of, the rule of master over slaves, who always outnumbered him, did not rest on superior means of coercion as such, but on a superior organization of power—that is, on the organized solidarity of the masters."[15]

When power is understood and defended as control or domination, physical violence often results when that control is threatened. Hence violence has more recently been defined as a response of *powerlessness,* of what has been called "resourcelessness."[16]

By contrast, nonviolence can be construed as a response of resourcefulness. Herbert Marcuse is quoted by Vellacott, "The success of the system is to make unthinkable the possibility of alternatives."[17] Nonviolence depends on a notion of power as pooling resources. While the masters in Arendt's analysis had some notion of solidarity, it was solidarity dictated by the necessity to exclude the majority from participation in power. Power may be conceived, however, precisely as solidarity with the outsider, with the ones "out of power." It is a perspective that offers alternatives.

Theologians throughout Christian history have rarely understood the power of God as solidarity. God's power has been dependent on God's unity, a power which is threatened by sharing even within the Godhead itself. The model most often found of God's power in Christian history is the absolute violence of Arendt's One Against All.

The idea of God's power as the absolute of the One Against All was drawn from the context of Christianity's intellectual growth during the expansion of imperial Rome. Christian thinkers found their social models for God's activity in the Roman understanding of the essential relationship of power and unity. As all roads led to Rome, so Christian theologians began to believe that all power was God's and developed the conception of God's being as absolute oneness.

CONTEXTUAL ANALYSIS: THE POLITICAL HISTORY OF THE DOCTRINE OF GOD

Supreme Substance

The earliest centuries of Christian reflection on the doctrine of God were dominated by concern with the unity of God over against what was perceived as the threat of any diversity within the Godhead. The church rejected outright Sabellian modalism, the heresy of Sabellius (excommunicated at Rome about 220 C.E.) being that the Trinity is only three manifestations to the world of one God who is identical in himself. It also rejected Arian subordinationism (condemned at the First Council of Nicea in 325 C.E.), the view that the Son and the Holy Spirit not only proceed from the Father but are subordinate to him and are merely "powers" God uses to order the world.[18] But elements of both of these viewpoints are available in orthodox trinitarian thought from the time of Tertullian. Tertullian stressed the unity of substance in God and subsequently this stress has undermined any genuinely trinitarian theology: God as the Father does overwhelm and dominate the other persons of the trinity.[19]

The collapse of the intricate problem of the triune God, at least posed by the Council of Nicea, into the monotheism of God the Father was aided by the fact that Christian doctrine was formulated during an era of absolutist monarchical rule of Rome. The religio-political structures of imperial Rome gave rise to the necessary challenge "Jesus Christ is Lord," which meant that Caesar was not Lord. This social and political necessity dovetailed easily with the concept in Greek philosophy of god as absolute ruler and father of the world (Plato's "Maker and Father of the Universe," *Timaeus* 28C) and provided the unifying link. God the Father possesses all authority over heaven and earth.

There is a monarchy evident in this point of view, which makes God as supreme "Father" superior to the "Son" and the "Spirit," a logical consequence of abandoning the Trinity. Furthermore, monotheistic monarchism goes hand in hand with political ideologies of oppression. As Jürgen Moltmann points out, "the fundamental notion behind the universal is uniform religion: one God—one *logos*—one humanity, and in the Roman Empire it was bound to be seen as a persuasive solution for any problems of a multi-national and multi-religious society. The universal ruler in Rome had only to be the image and correspondence of the universal ruler in heaven."[20]

The understanding of divine power in monarchical monotheism is absolute domination, the very definition of violence. God conceived as supreme ruler over all from whom other authorities take their cue is a theology of violence. Celestial hierarchy justifies terrestrial hierarchy: the absolute power of God legitimates the power of the father priest, the father of the country, the father in the family, etc. Monotheistic monarchism has been a powerful weapon for both church and state to legitimate the ultimate power of the few over the many. The nuclear age did not create this particular strand of Christian theology. But the absolute power of nuclear weapons makes the consequences of such a theological perspective far more deadly than when the work of God as absolute monarch was pursued with chariots and spears.

Supreme Subject

The renaissance and the reformation led to a radical change in some understandings of divinity. Reflection on God since that watershed period is characterized by the modern emphasis on God as Absolute Subject. We no longer need God to understand the substance of the world as the Neoplatonists had thought. We need God to understand ourselves. Thus the experiencing self is the beginning point for modern theological reflection.

But the emphasis on unity remains. Subject can only be considered an identical self, acting in different ways. This is the modern bourgeois concept of personality. The resistance to diversity, understood as a threat to the integrity of personality, can be noted in the lack of consideration given to the Trinity in modern theology.[21]

THE FAILURE OF CONTEXTUAL ANALYSIS IN CONTEMPORARY PEACE THEOLOGY

Personality seems to have inescapably become the subject of modern theology. While the renaissance discovered the human subject, it was not until the advent of those recently called "The Secular Magi," Marx, Freud, and Nietzsche, that theology has been unable to escape from the human subject.[22] In attending to Nietzsche's critique of religion as the neurotic denial by humankind of their own power and the projection of that power onto divinity,[23] it is to Freud and not to Marx that theologians have turned to find answers for the modern age. Thus, white North Atlantic theologians have never questioned the social arrangements from imperial Rome to Western postindustrial capitalism, and everything in between, for the possible sources of monarchical monotheism. Instead, deity conceived as absolute power is understood (now from Freud) as a projection of human nature, itself innately power hungry and consequently violent, a solitary combatant locked in struggle with other combatants.[24]

Most of the theological supports for nuclearism in modern theology are anchored in various assessments of "man's" innate destructiveness. Hal Lindsey has already been mentioned. Michael Novak, a Catholic lay theologian, has aggressively opposed the American Catholic bishops' peace pastoral, *The Challenge of Peace: God's Promise and Our Response.* The bishops' well-known argument is that deterrence theory cannot be supported from the church's traditional "just war" doctrines.[25]

In his reply to the bishops' pastoral entitled *Moral Clarity in the Nuclear Age,* Novak argues that "deterrence itself is a form of *non-violence,* a legitimate use of force, based upon legitimate authority."[26] According to Novak, nonviolence can be *equated* with "the legitimate use of force." Why does Novak think that legitimate force is another word for nonviolence? It is not that he subscribes to the slogan of Orwell's *1984* "War is Peace." It is because Novak locates the ultimate authority for force in God's judgment on human sinfulness. Lest we overinterpret the significance of the nuclear age for theology, Novak contends that we should "recall the lessons of Christian faith about the precariousness of all human life, the approaching end of history, *the perennial wickedness and obdurateness of the human race, and the total sovereignty of God.*"[27] God is the epitome of violence, the sovereign One whose person is ranged against the wicked All. Even force can be legitimated as nonviolence because it is divinely warranted.[28]

Yet many who resist theologies of nuclearism have still internalized the modern turn to psychologism, the consideration of the human subject as the basis of theological reflection. They differ from Novak and others who favor a nuclear "defense" in that they favor disarmament, rather than in the conclusions they draw about human nature.

Robert Jay Lifton's influential study *Indefensible Weapons* has already been mentioned. While Lifton defines nuclearism as the "psychological, political and military dependence on nuclear weapons,"[29] the latter two characteristics, political and military, are always read through the psychological. The reverse, however, is never the case. Lifton never once subjects his psychological premises to a sustained political analysis.[30] Lifton's work, however, demonstrates some awareness that social and political factors must be dealt with and that the nuclear age is not wholly an intrapsychic problem. One who holds that the nuclear age is primarily "all in our minds" is Joanna Rogers Macy. Her book *Despair and Personal Power in the Nuclear Age* is a series of exercises to help moderns not to be depressed about nuclearism.[31]

Several other well known works exhibit the same limitations. Gordon Kaufman's *Theology for a Nuclear Age,* Jonathan Schell's *The Fate of the Earth,* and Sallie McFague's *Models of God: Theology for an Ecological, Nuclear Age* extend the thesis that the human mind is the best (and only?) place to begin to challenge the threat of the nuclear age.[32] All agree that, as Kaufman articulates the position, the "momentous religious fact right before our eyes" of nuclearism betrays the fact that the notion of the sovereignty of God over history, "the central traditional claim" of Christian theology, "is way 'out of sync'" with our actual situation in the nuclear age.[33] Kaufman argues that theology must abandon sovereignty in favor of imaginative world construction in order to excite the human mind to envision creation rather than destruction.

Sallie McFague in *Models of God,* having made a similar diagnosis, offers as a prescription for the "ecological, nuclear age" three models, Mother, Lover, and Friend, to replace the metaphors of God's otherness to the world that fuel nuclearism and the destruction of the environment.[34]

But Kaufman, McFague, Lifton, or Schell never address the economic and political supports for the maintenance of the nuclear age. Images of God as almighty sovereign punishing the recalcitrant are drawn from certain social arrangements and economic benefits. Human imagination does not float free of sex, race, and class distinctions.

Furthermore, given that all these writers have objected to God's otherness and have located the beginning point for theological reflection in the nuclear age in the human mind, they do not have a companion anthropology strong enough to support their proposals for world re-creation via human imagination. Kaufman is almost wholly dependent on Paul Tillich's assessment of the human situation as fundamentally estranged.[35] McFague has learned something from the women's movement of the importance of human bonding, but she does not make this thesis central.[36]

THE CONTRIBUTION OF FEMINIST THEOLOGY TO CONTEMPORARY CONTEXTUAL ANALYSIS

A major contribution of feminist theology and the*a*ology[37] to an analysis of the nuclear age is the identification of patriarchy as a key interpretive category.

Mary Caudren, in an essay entitled "Patriarchy and Death," identifies the origins of patriarchy in the male discovery of the biological fact of fatherhood and the experience of alienation this has evoked. She quotes Mary O'Brien, who in *The Politics of Reproduction* argued that paternity is a social construct because the male has only social relations to ensure the biology of his paternity. Motherhood, by contrast, is physiologically based. This social construction of paternity is a "real triumph over the ambiguities of nature."[38] From this analysis, Caudren concludes that the extension of paternity into the cosmic realm is a "compensatory activity for the many inadequacies of physical paternity. . . . God the Father and the 'Holy Father' are perfect metaphors for this enterprise."[39]

The many characteristics of patriarchy are shown to stem from this basic alienation: the elevation of mind over body, the preoccupation with immortality,[40] the concern with absolutes in ethics and certainly the subordination of the female.

A key insight offered is the recognition that "patriarchal birthing takes place primarily through death: the death defiance of the hero; the hazardous trials of male initiation rites; the mythic slaughter of the Goddess; the life-negating spiritualities of ascetics; Hegel's journey into human history by overcoming the fear of death; or Freud's oedipal conflict in which the father is murdered by the son."[41]

The connection to nuclearism becomes obvious. Nuclear weapons are the extension of male alienation from life, its reproduction and nurture. "In the light of the threat of nuclear destruction, partriarchy is a terminal disease."[42]

The value of an analysis of patriarchy as a worship of death is that it contributes to an explanation of the social construction of nuclearism. While psychological analyses of the bomb as a death wish have surfaced, such as in Lifton's, there is no reason given *why* these technologies have been able to overwhelm the human instinct for self-preservation. Why is the West capable of worshipping as life what is manifestly a threat to life itself? Liberals such as Kaufman, Schell, McFague, or Lifton have no explanation for the attraction the bomb poses for humanity, other than that alternative visions have not emerged. Why have they not emerged?

When Oppenheimer named the first nuclear test "Trinity" after Donne's poem to the Christian God, he chose this name according to Mary Daly as "the sadospiritual legitimation of this lust and its technological ejaculations." The opening line of the poem, "Batter my heart, three person'd God," is well chosen, according to Daly, because it reveals that "The battering of the Earth and of her creatures is the consequences of this disordered sentiment."[43]

God, as Kaufman put it in another context, is the problem for Daly. "The earthy, unearthy males have vaporized and then condensed/reified their self-images into the sublime product, god." In the process of projecting all that is most holy and sacred onto the cosmos where it cannot undergo natural processes such as death, this theology must be wrathful because it must murder and dismember the Goddess. Unable to do away with nature per se, the underlying reality of which the Goddess is a symbol, Christian theologians have been previously content to ritually murder her and preserve a certain carved remnant in Mary. The advent of nuclear technology, however, makes the complete murder of the Goddess (nature) possible, and has exposed this fault line at the heart of Christian theology—the oft-times barely concealed contempt for the earth and its symbol, the Goddess.

Carol Christ, another feminist thealogian and committed peace activist, finds Yahweh as Holy Warrior a symbol of "the patriarchal male equation of power and violence." She even rejects warrior goddesses such as Ishtar and Athene, because their images have emerged from patriarchal cultures where power is always equated with war. She is also suspicious of revolutionary violence of whatever stripe as representative of patriarchy. Women (and children dependent on women) are still the primary victims of war. Feminist liberation theologians, urges Christ, should examine the warlike activities of the liberating god of the exodus.[44]

Christ enjoins that her objection to the patriarchal God of the Bible is "not limited to his sex, or even his warlike nature, but includes as well my rejection of a form of *monotheism* that spawns religious intolerance and a climate in which destruction of peoples who practice other religions can be countenanced."[45] The violent destruction of Goddess-worshipping peoples and the obliteration of their religious beliefs have been justified by the argument that this was some kind of necessary transition from "lower" nature-worshipping religions to a "higher" religion of covenant and history. While Christ comes down squarely on the nature side of this continuum, she poses a profound challenge to those who find socially transformative models of God in the prophetic narratives of the Hebrew Bible.

THE NATURE/HISTORY DILEMMA IN THE DOCTRINE OF GOD

Many liberation theologians hold to the importance for their theological perspective of the understanding of the human being as an agent in history. In acting to create interhuman justice the agent in history creates her/himself. God is the one who participates in human history on the side of those who are fully engaged in the task of creating justice and peace. God's judgment falls on those who fail to make justice, or who, through their deliberate creation of unjust and exploitive structures, are outside God's expressed (in the Hebrew Bible and Christian scriptures) purposes. The particularity of this struggle of God and the people of God is why James Cone writes that "God is Black." "The blackness of God means that God has made the oppressed condition God's own condition. This is the essence of biblical revelation."[46]

The creation understood as nature and history understood as human history and civilization have had a dialectical relationship in the history of Christian theology. Christian theologians have interpreted the Yahwist traditions of the Hebrew Bible to have been a movement (forward) away from Canaanite indigenous nature religions (the Goddess). The God of the Yahwist is seen as a God of history who makes a covenant with the people of God. The gods and goddesses of the indigenous religions (now interpreted as pagan) are rejected as the worship of capricious nature. History is oriented toward events (wars, conquests, escapes from slavery, etc.) and not toward the cycles of nature which recur. Nature is no longer considered sacred.

Yet this one-sided interpretation of the Hebrew Bible is prompted in part by the alliance between early Christianity and Greek thought, which in the perspective of Plato made the realm of absolute ideas and not the realm of changing, growing, and dying finite nature the best mirror of divinity.[47] One of the things that modern Christianity is learning from the spread of the Christian religion to non-European peoples is that the God of history is one possible interpretation of the meaning of Christianity that is rooted in the cultural context of the Greco-Roman world. Non-Western, nonwhite peoples have not had this intellectual heritage and so conceive of the relationship of nature and history as less disjunctive than in the West.

Furthermore, modern intellectual movements such as Marxism have caused some liberation theologians to understand history not as the mirror of a cosmic plan, but as the creation of human beings. Thus history has also come to be understood as changeable and this also tends to erode the split between nature and history.

CONCLUSION: A FEMINIST LIBERATION PERSPECTIVE ON THE DOCTRINE OF GOD IN THE NUCLEAR AGE

Based on the foregoing analysis, the doctrine of God in the nuclear age should include the following emphases:

1. The doctrine of God in the nuclear age must take its origins from a contextual analysis which reveals that nuclearism, the worship of nuclear weapons, is not exclusively a product of intrapsychic conflict. The existence of these weapons cannot be understood merely as a failure of the imagination, but must be subject to a *theological* critique that reveals their social and political supports.

2. The doctrine of God in the nuclear age must contain a thorough understanding of power and its relationship to violence: power shared is resourcefulness. The power of God is best understood as solidarity. The Trinity is a model of the very being of God as solidarity. It is a perspective on the being of God which is directly counter to the uses of monotheism as a legitimation of the violence of the One against the All.

3. Justice imperatives must be central to the doctrine of God in the nuclear age. The being of God as solidarity comes about by building alliances with and among those considered the Other: non-Christians, women, the poor, people of color, gays, and lesbians. This bonding will emerge because of difference and proceed by the embrace of difference. It will discover the meaning of the Christian Trinity in the nature of God as diversity and relationality.

4. Protestant liberalism has failed to provide strong alternatives to the theologies of nuclearism because of an exclusive focus on intrapsychic conflict as the origin of the nuclear age, while neglecting social and political analysis. Further, the companion anthropologies offered as an alternative to God as otherworldly judge are mired in alienation and despair. The doctrine of God in the nuclear age must be accompanied by an anthropology that reveals humanity capable both of community and of alienation and rejection of community. Sin is redefined as the refusal to work toward the solidarity that brings God into the world.

5. The doctrine of God in the nuclear age must be shaped by feminist insights into patriarchy's contempt for the earth and all its symbols, especially the Goddess. The widespread Christian justification for the existence and *use* of nuclear weapons as judgment on the sinful world reveals the failure of Christianity to take its own creation theology seriously, but also reveals serious flaws in that creation theology. The being of God is not separate from the natural order. Nor is the being of God, understood as solidarity, confined to solidarity with the human community. Solidarity with the earth includes bonding with the other "peoples" of the earth: animal, vegetable, and mineral.

Thealogians and theologians of the nuclear age must work from nondominant sources: Asian, Black American, African, Native American, Latin American—to name only a few. The voices of God/dess today are heard in meditations such as the following by a Native American woman, Chrystos:

I will be sad to see the trees & birds on fire   Surely they are innocent as none of us has been
   With their songs, they know the sacred   I am in a circle with that soft, enduring word   In it is the wisdom of all peoples   Without a deep, deep understanding of the sacredness of life, the fragility of each breath, we are lost   The holocaust has already occurred   What follows is only the burning bush   How my heart aches & cries to write these words   I am not as calmly indifferent as I sound   I will be screaming no no no more destruction in that last blinding light.[48]

RECOMMENDED READING

The Challenge of Peace: God's Promise and Our Response. Washington, DC: United States Catholic Conference, 1982.

Daly, Mary. *Pure Lust: Elemental Feminist Philosophy.* Boston: Beacon, 1984.

Kaufman, Gordon. *Theology for a Nuclear Age.* Philadelphia: Westminster, 1985.

McAllister, Pam, ed. *Reweaving the Web of Life: Feminism and Nonviolence.* Philadelphia: New Society, 1982.

McFague, Sallie. *Models of God.* Philadelphia: Westminster, 1985.

Thistlethwaite, Susan, ed. *A Just Peace Church.* New York: Pilgrim, 1986.

Part 3

ESCHATOLOGY

Introduction to Part 3

Eschatology, the study of "the last things," usually and unsurprisingly comes last in traditional systematic theologies and includes extended discussions of death and resurrection, the last judgment and the end of earthly existence, damnation, and eternal life.

In the last century, these final systematic sections, particularly in the texts of Protestant liberalism, grew shorter and shorter. Nineteenth century society had discovered progress, and liberal theologians embraced a progressive view of the accomplishment of God's aims for history as a replacement for visions of an abrupt and cataclysmic end. In churches echoes of preaching on personal salvation and life after death could still be heard, but in general theologians waxed optimistic about the coming "divine-human industrial democracy"[1] that would arrive with the twentieth century.

Several factors conspired to derail this train of historical progressivism and its lack of interest in eschatology. One was Albert Schweitzer's *The Quest for the Historical Jesus*.[2] Schweitzer's demonstration that eschatology was central and not peripheral to the teaching of Jesus made it impossible for theologians to go on ignoring eschatology. In addition, historical crises such as the two world wars and a worldwide economic depression made historical progressivism untenable to most theological minds. Karl Barth (and later Jürgen Moltmann) signalled the change in theological direction when he declared that "Christianity that is not entirely and altogether eschatology has entirely and altogether nothing to do with Christ."[3]

This stress on Christianity as an eschatological reality is as critical to the theologies of liberation as it was and is to neo-orthodox theologies. Liberation theologies agree with neo-orthodoxy (though for different reasons) that liberalism's assumption of the fairly harmonious upward progress of human history must be challenged. In part this is because they have learned from Marxism that history is conflictual and that historical changes come about by conflict. It is important to note that they accept the interpretation of history as conflictual while rejecting the strict dialectical materialism of some Marxisms as a secularized version of a linear apocalyptic (see chapter 8).

This critical appropriation of Marxist interpretations of history has led to profound differences with neo-orthodoxy's understandings of eschatology. In direct challenge to neo-orthodox theologies, liberation theologians have called into question the uncritical interpretation and use of eschatology as an eternal Now above human history or as a future realm at the end of history. Adapting the Marxist critique of religion as the projection of human social justice imperatives into a realm above or beyond history, they are suspicious of any eschatology that pushes the resolution of historical conflict outside the bounds of social-economic-political history in any way. To paraphrase a controversial exchange between two liberation theologians and Jürgen Moltmann, future tenses can disguise present anguish.[4] An eschatological Now standing above history can do the same, with the added liability of perpetuating dualism.

Some of these themes may be seen in Rosemary Ruether's chapter. She focuses on the feminist rejection of traditional eschatological dualism that denigrates bodily processes, separates body and soul, and projects the soul into a disembodied future. She also rejects the more classically liberal eschatology that favors a "New Jerusalem" on earth free of the contradictions of historical existence. Both these traditional views continue to malign the female body as more earthly and hence full of contradiction. She argues instead for a more holistic view that engages us in a search for balance among the ambiguities of history.

We have chosen to discuss eschatology as the first of the theological topics following the discussion of God in order to underline two points. First, we want to stress that the Western tendency toward dualism and the denial of death lies at the root of much of the paralysis of social justice concerns in these societies. As Ruether writes, the "problem of personal immortality is created by the effort to absolutize individual ego as everlasting, over against the total community of being." Reverence for life (Schweitzer), public good, social sin, and social salvation are all values that are undermined by a personalistic view of salvation beyond history. Secondly, we also want to stress more positively that the particular vision of *shalom* (just and merciful relationship for all), in which each of us participates, affects all that we see, do, think, and are *in the present*. In other words, all of theology as reflection upon our experience of struggling for justice in our particular contexts is colored by the vision out of which and toward which we live.

CHAPTER 8

Eschatology and Feminism

ROSEMARY RADFORD RUETHER

CONTEXT AND COMMITMENT

I write as an Anglo-American Roman Catholic woman who seeks to integrate faith understanding with commitment to justice. The quest to understand the meaning of Christian faith in my life, uninhibited by institutional *a priori,* began for me in late high school and college years. The integration of this quest for meaning with commitment to justice began in the early 1960s with the Civil Rights movement.

For me, a key experience was a summer spent working in Mississippi in 1965. During the previous summer, three civil rights workers had been murdered, and we ourselves lived in constant recognition of the danger of violence. This was my first experience in looking at American society from the Black perspective. As we worked to register Black voters and to organize Headstart programs, the Black context was our world. A carload of white men was a danger sign. We breathed a sigh of relief when the car turned out to have Blacks, "our folks," in it.

These experiences shaped a methodology that has become very important for me. That is a need to put oneself in the context of the oppressed in order to have some understanding, not only of their experience, but of the total system of society. This need to locate oneself in the context of the oppressed is less a question of doing something for them than it is a question of learning from them. It is the experiential demonstration of the sociology of knowledge.

Since those days in Mississippi I have become involved in a number of other justice issues. The peace issue became a key area of work during the years I taught at Howard University in Washington, D.C. (1965–75). I also began to develop my first research and teaching in the area of feminism in church and society in that period.

Another key area of concern for me has been Christian anti-semitism. Both family history (an important relationship with a Jewish uncle) and my reading of church history disposed me to feel that this was a scandalous area of Christian self-distortion and injustice. I tried to sort out something of that history and its implications in my book *Faith and Fratricide* (1974).

This book brought me into dialogue with the Jewish community. Gradually I became painfully aware that members of the Jewish community, themselves unjustly treated by Western Christians, have become participants or condoners of another terrible injustice, that which made millions of Palestinians refugees or stateless prisoners of Israeli power. It also became evident that the important work of compensatory justice which Christians owed Jews was being manipulated to silence Christians in the Palestinian question.

Fortunately, other Jews in Israel and in the United States were also pained by these injustices. It is becoming increasingly possible to create a positive coalition of Jews, Christians, and Muslims working for truthful understanding and justice in this region. My concern to sort out the Palestinian issue for Christian ethics and theology in a way that remained in solidarity with justice for Jews, but freed from manipulative use of anti-semitism, culminated in a book, *The Wrath of Jonah: The Crisis of Religious Nationalism in the Israel-Palestinian Conflict* (1989).

My commitment to feminism has always been a context of intercommunal and intercultural justice. I am particularly involved in three areas of research, teaching, and action. One is interfaith dialogue, which takes the particular form of feminist dialogue across religious faiths—Christian, Jewish, Muslim, Buddhist, and neopagan—among others. This connects with a general interest in the multi-contextualization of feminist theology and theory. Women both exist and have been oppressed in all cultures and religions, at least as they exist today. So any feminist theory and theology must recognize the need to promote and be in solidarity with the contextualization of feminist critique in all class and cultural contexts.

A third area of concern for theory and praxis is ecology. The abuse and neglect of nature has become a critical issue of planetary survival, without which all other justice issues will be rendered null and void. I am not sure that Christian theology will be able to develop an adequate relation to nature or to deal with feminism. It may be that the Christian system will have to be transcended, in a new synthesis with insights from other religions, to create an adequate theology for justice to women and peaceful and sustaining relationships with the biosphere. I plan to follow these concerns wherever they lead me.

CONSTRUCTION

Does feminism have a doctrine of eschatology? That is to say, is a concern for life after death an appropriate part of feminist theological concern? Or should feminism question fundamentally the religious search to negate and transcend mortality as an intrinsic expression of patriarchal false consciousness? One earlier feminist writer who pointed to the importance of this question was the social philosopher Charlotte Perkins Gilman. Gilman discussed this question of the foundational attitudes of religion toward immortality in a book, published in 1923, called *His Religion and Hers* and piquantly subtitled *A Study of the Faith of the Fathers and the Work of Our Mothers.*[1]

In this volume Gilman describes two different orientations to life, based on the crises of male and female experience. For the male, shaped by his historical experience as hunter and warrior, the pivotal experience was death, as he killed both animals and other humans, and as he himself was threatened by violent death. Male religion, in Gilman's view, thus became centered on the "blood mystery" of death and how to escape it. As Gilman put it in a poetic expression of her thesis:

> Man the hunter, Man the warrior
> Slew for gain and slew for safety.
> Slew for rage, for sport, for glory—
> Slaughter was his breath;
> So the man's mind, searching inward,
> Saw in all one red reflection,
> Filled the world with dark religions
> Built on death.[2]

By contrast, woman's experience, in ancient culture and throughout most of human history, has been birth. This too is blood mystery which threatens her with death, but it is in service of the immediate creation of new life. Woman's relationship to this experience is altruistic, rather than egoistic. Her blood is shed to birth the child, and her milk is given to feed it. Woman's concerns are oriented to the here and now, building up the next generation of life on earth. For Gilman, male religion, focused on killing and a fantasized flight from death into an abstract realm of the imagination, is escapist. It prevents humans from commitment to their only real and possible task, which is finite service to the next generation on this planet. Although male religion has been the norm of historical religion, Gilman proposes that woman's blood mystery of birth is needed to reshape religion so that it can be of service to the only real life we can know:

> Woman, bearer; woman, teacher;
> Overflowing love and labor,
> Service of the tireless mother
> filling all the earth;
> Now her mind awakening, searching,
> Sees a fair world young and growing,
> Sees at last our real religion
> Built on Birth.[3]

Although Gilman's anthropological history may be somewhat dated, her challenge to the eschatological focus of religion remains powerful, especially for a Christianity which has defined salvation primarily as assurance of an eternal life, of victory over death. To what extent has this goal been a diversion of our energies from our authentic human tasks here on earth? To what extent has eschatological religion been built on a male negation of woman as birthgiver of our real, though mortal, lives? These are the questions I will address in this chapter.

A Genealogy of Immortality

Many ancient peoples do not seem to have had a strongly developed belief in personal immortality. For example, the ancient civilizations of the Near East in Sumer and Babylon do not seem originally to have held out hope for escape from human mortality. Death is what separates mortals from gods. The main theme of the great Babylonian epic of Gilgamesh is the futility of man's (the males'?) quest for immortality. Although Gilgamesh discovers the plant of immortal life, its possession eludes his grasp. In the course of his journey, the alewife advises him to give up his useless quest and to turn, rather, to enjoying the good things of mortal life. The Babylonian view of the unbridgeable gulf between humans and gods is summed up in her words:

> Gilgamesh, whither rovest thou?
> The life thou pursuest thou shall not find.
> When the gods created humans,
> death for humankind they set aside;
> life in their own hands retaining.[4]

Perhaps for many ancient peoples the primary concern was the survival of the community. They worried about the renewal of the seasonal processes and the fertility of humans, animals, and plants that assured the continuation of life on earth. This concern for sustaining the ongoing community, in the midst of an uncertain world of nature, left little time for the luxury of thinking about one's personal mortality. In the Sumerian epic of the descent of Inanna to the Underworld, the Goddess escapes death and is enabled to return to the world above only by sending her human lover, the king Dumuzi, as her substitute. Even the king shares the human fate of mortality, while Inanna represents the miracle of the renewal of nature. Human mortality is a trade-off for the much more important assurance that the life powers of the earth will be renewed in its seasonal processes.[5]

However, in the later stages of ancient Mediterranean religions, this trade-off of human mortality for seasonal renewal became unsatisfactory. Particularly as expectations of establishing good societies in the ancient Near Eastern empires faded, human hopes turned to personal survival of death. The ancient myths of seasonal renewal and the restoration of order over chaos, which had shaped the religions of the early empires of the Tigris-Euphrates valley and Egypt, provided the imagery for what now became eschatological interpretations of these symbols. Inanna's reascent from the underworld, Osiris's resurrection for his seasonal death due to searing heat and drought, became the metaphors for the resurrection of the soul from the dead, its reascent to its heavenly home above. In Egypt, concern for assuring personal immortality emerged first among kings, queens, and the royal family, and then gradually was applied to "lesser mortals." It was royalty who first had enough leisure and power to imagine that their individualized selves were valuable enough for immortalization. The preservation of the poor could hardly matter that much, for they could not be thought to have individual selves. Immortal life was a class privilege. Through the rites of embalming and identification with the resurrected Osiris, first the king and royal family, then the aristocracy, and, finally, even wealthy merchants might hope to preserve their essential selves from the corruption of the body.

In Babylonian culture the cultivation of astronomy led to speculation on the stars and planets as the dwelling place of the gods. Human souls were seen as sparks of divinity, originally dwelling in the stars and planets. Souls assumed bodily form in a journey of descent to the earth, taking on the influence of each planet as they passed through the seven planetary gates. The pathway back to heaven lay in a return journey, in which the soul doffed these psychic garments, until it finally emerged, purified of their fateful influences, in its starry home. This soul journey, in its reascent to its heavenly home, is described in the Hermetic text, the *Poimandres,* where in zone after zone "man thrusts upward through the Harmony" until "in procession they rise up toward the Father and give themselves up to the Powers, and having become Powers themselves, enter into the Godhead."[6]

Earlier versions of this Near Eastern astral eschatology traveled to Asia Minor, and then to Greece, in the late sixth and fifth centuries, where it shaped the thinking of Greek philosophers.[7] Plato, in the *Phaedrus,* describes his understanding of the soul journey. The souls originate in the realm of the stars, where they accompany the gods on their journeys in the heavens. In this way the souls are nourished through contemplation of the eternal realm of ideas. But those souls who cannot control the unruly steed of their passions lose their wings, sink to earth, and take on a body.

Those souls who have absorbed more truth are incarnated in higher human types (ruling class males), and those who have absorbed less truth are incarnated in lesser types (females and slaves). Through reincarnation, souls work their way to higher states of consciousness and higher classes of humans, until the soul's wings grow strong enough to escape from the cycle of rebirth.[8] For Plato, authentic life is disincarnate life, and embodiment is an entrapment in matter which is alien to the soul. As he makes clear in his creation myth, the *Timaeus,* women represent a lower level of human existence, more deeply entrapped in matter, further from the disincarnate life of the soul, than men, especially ruling class men.[9] In Plato the hierarchy of immortality and mortality is related to class and gender hierarchy.

Hebrew religion also focused originally on this-worldly hopes. The shadowy world of Sheol suggested some half-life of the soul after death, sustained by the memories of one's descendants. But it is hardly a happy realm. For most of Hebrew scripture there is no development of the idea of personal immortality. Future hope is collective and historical, rather than individual and eschatological. The ancient Babylonian and Canaanite myths of seasonal renewal were transferred to the renewal of the earth and society from historical injustice. Human disobedience brought on divine wrath, which expressed itself in political and natural disasters. Military defeats destroyed the cities; droughts parched the fields and destroyed the crops.

Obedience to God, in turn, would bring a return of happiness and prosperity: victory in war, a secure happy life in society, good rains, and bountiful harvests. Through adherence to God's commandments it was hoped that there would come that redeemed time when justice and peace would reign on earth. Hebrew hopes for redemption projected an ideal vision of human life, in its natural and social contexts, onto a future era of history. This would be the messianic age, the coming reign of God on earth, when, as the Lord's Prayer puts it, God's will will be done on earth, as it is in heaven.

As these hopes for the ideal time of human life on earth were repeatedly disappointed by successive imperial powers that colonized and ruled the people of Israel, Hebrew hope became increasingly apocalyptic. The vision of the messianic age was divorced from natural historical changes that might have happened through changes of political fortune within the limited region of the Eastern Mediterranean world. The transformation from the present evil age to the time of redemption came to be seen as affecting the entire cosmos, transforming it from its present finite, historical form to another order of existence. Demonic powers were seen as ruling the present age of the cosmos. Through divine intervention these evil powers, and their representatives in the great empires of Greece and then of Rome, would be overthrown.

The most decisive break with the earlier prophetic concept of a redeemed future historical age was signaled by the inclusion of the resurrected dead from the past ages. The idea of bodily resurrection was originally included in Jewish future hope more to solve the problem of injustice unrequited than the problem of mortality. By resurrecting the unrewarded righteous and the unpunished evil-doers of past ages, it was possible to imagine that the scales of justice could finally be balanced in history. So in some of the Jewish apocalypses written between the second century B.C.E. and the first century C.E., there is not a universal resurrection. Rather, only the unrewarded righteous and the unpunished wicked rise. Good and evil people "get theirs," and the saints reign in bliss for a limited period of time.[10] Such concepts were still operating within the framework of finite future history. But the introduction of the idea of bodily resurrection brought in a new element which was incompatible with the historical nature of earlier prophetic hope.

Later apocalypses sought to resolve this contradiction between historical and eschatological elements of future hope. They began to imagine a two-stage scenario in which the just would reign for a historical period of fulfilled life on earth. Then the present, finite cosmos would be destroyed and re-created on a new and eternal basis. The Christian book of Revelation displays this more developed type of future hope, which combines a historical millennium with an eschatological transformation of the cosmos. After the plagues of judgment have fallen on the evil world, symbolized by Babylon (Rome), Satan, the demonic power behind imperial rule, will be bound. The just, identified with Christian martyrs, will rise from the dead and reign with Christ for a thousand years.

After the end of the millennium, Satan will again be unleashed, and there will be a final conflict between the forces of good and evil. At this time the general resurrection of the dead will take place. There will be a general judgment and evil will be finally purged. Death and Hades, along with all those whose names are not found written in the Book of Life, will be thrown into a lake of fire. Probably this was not understood, as later Christians have taken it, to mean that sinners would suffer eternally. Rather, they, together with all evil tendencies, will be purged from the world and no longer exist. This would reflect the notion, found in the Zoroastrian apocalyptic tradition which influenced Jewish apocalyptic, that all evil will be purged by passing through a lake of fire and will then cease to exist.[11]

This purging of evil, including death and Hades itself, is then followed by the regeneration of the cosmos. A new and eternal heaven and earth are created. An eternal Holy City, the heavenly counterpart to this earthly Jerusalem, descends as a bride to be the consort of God. Paradise is restored, with the river of life flowing from the throne of God and the Tree of Life on either side. The temple is no longer necessary as a visible sign of God's presence on earth, for the whole cosmos is now God's temple. Nor are the created planetary lights of the sun and moon necessary, for God's direct presence provides the light by which all peoples will walk. Nothing accursed or evil will ever exist again. This new age will go on and on without end.[12] Thus does the culmination of Hebrew apocalyptic imagine not only the transcendence of personal death, but the finitude of cosmic and historical existence as well. The collective community of Creation is transmuted into a final eternal eschatological form.

From this brief summary of the development of eschatological ideas in the traditions inherited by Christianity, two different patterns are evident. The Hebrew pattern starts with the collective hope of the community and projects its future historical fulfillment and then its immortalization. It assumes that bodily existence is normative for created life. So its eschatology is built on the resurrection of the body, both the personal body and the collective body of the community and the cosmos. The body continues to be the only form in which created life can live. But it must, somehow, be transmuted into a new form of existence beyond decay and death, or what St. Paul would call "the spiritual body."[13]

The second type of eschatology is individualistic. It is based on the separation of personal inward consciousness, or the soul, from embodiment. The body is experienced as alien to the soul. The soul is seen as participating, by origin and nature, in a divine, disembodied world of the heavens, while the body belongs to a sublunar world of death and decay on earth. Eschatology is conceived as an escape from the body and a return of the soul to its true heavenly home. Although Christianity officially endorses the first view of eschatology, the operative eschatology of most Christians belongs to the second type.

Is there evidence that a preoccupation with eschatology has been shaped primarily by males? Have they done so in a way that negates women as mothers and birthgivers? Both the Hebraic and the Platonic types of eschatology are built on negative views of women as creators of mortal human life, but in different ways. Early Christianity though of the church as messianic community, participating already in the first fruits of redemption. Christianity declared that the direct presence of the Holy Spirit, which the rabbis claimed had vanished with the last of the prophets, was restored on Pentecost, the birthday of the church. This outpouring of the spirit was said to fulfill the prophecy of the prophet Joel:

> And in the last days it shall be, God declares,
> that I will pour out my Spirit upon all flesh,
> and your sons and your daughters shall prophesy
> and your young men shall see visions,
> and your old men will dream dreams;
> yea, and on my menservants and on my maidservants
>   in those days,
> I will pour out my Spirit; and they shall prophesy.[14]

The inclusion of women in prophecy in this passage was not unusual in Hebrew thought, for women had been recognized as prophets in Hebrew tradition, even though they had been excluded from the priesthood and, later, from the rabbinate. Early Christianity also understood women as included in the prophetic office, restored on Pentecost. Prophets were seen as the normative model of Christian teaching and leadership in the earliest strata of Christianity. Although a rabbinic patriarchal model of church leadership, as bishops and elders, began to arise in the late first century, we know that well into the second century Christian groups held on to the prophetic model as normative.[15]

The struggle between these two models of early Christian leadership can be illustrated in the two conflicting deutero-Pauline documents, the *Acts of Paul and Thecla* and *First Timothy*. In the *Acts of Paul and Thecla*, Thecla is converted by Paul and renounces her fiancé and her subordination to her family. She takes off to travel and preach in the empire, dressed as a male. After various adventures in which she miraculously escapes the agents of family and state who pursue her and twice throw her to the lions, Paul reappears and formally acknowledges her role as evangelist, saying, "Go and teach the word of God."[16]

In the pseudo-Pauline letter *First Timothy*, by contrast, women are told to keep silence on the grounds that they were created second and sinned first. Women are forbidden to teach or to have authority over men. They will be saved by bearing children. *First Timothy* uses Paul's authority to proclaim exactly the opposite message from the *Acts of Paul and Thecla*. Women are to be silent and to submit to marriage and family roles. One New Testament scholar has argued that the *Acts of Paul and Thecla* was already known in oral tradition at the end of the first century, and that *First Timothy* was written to counteract this egalitarian Paulinism with an opposing patriarchal Paulinism.[17]

However, it should be evident that, in the *Acts of Paul and Thecla*, conversion to chastity (the negation of childbearing) is the precondition for a woman's new status in Christ. This enables her to be independent of the family and to travel as preacher and teacher. For women, this undoubtedly reflected (and still reflects) the sociological realities of women's constriction by childbearing and marriage. But it also expressed the early Christian eschatological worldview. The new age of redemption was defined as a time when there will no longer be marriage and giving in marriage. Sexuality and childbearing were seen as belonging to a fallen, sinful age. Through sin came death, and hence the necessity for reproduction.

In the redeemed, spirit-filled world, this would no longer be necessary, for death itself would be overcome. The subjugation of women was seen as part of that historical order of creation in which society was ordered by the patriarchal family. So the emancipation of women and their equality as autonomous, spiritual beings was possible only in a new, transcendent age when marriage and childbearing had been left behind. This connection of female equality with celibacy continued to be characteristic of Christian eschatological sects as late as the nineteenth century.

Platonic conceptions of eschatology, built on body-soul dualism, similarly suggested negation of women as sexual persons and mothers. But they lacked the vision of a future eschatological community on earth where women and men became equals. The corruptible flesh was seen as the enemy of that soul whose capacity for immortal life can be realized only by release from the body. Women are typically seen as more "fleshly" than men, less capable of bearing the full potency of the rational intellect. In Plato the soul is incarnated first into the male. Only when it fails to control its passions does the soul fall down into a lower state of life.[18]

Christianity rejected Platonic doctrines of reincarnation and taught that women, as well as men, had immortal souls that could go directly from the embodied to the eschatological state. But it nevertheless incorporated much of this Platonic view of the female flesh as inimical to eternal life. While female celibacy in Christianity has tended to preserve the motifs of emancipation of women from social subordination to the patriarchal family, male celibacy early incorporated an ascetic spirituality of phobic hostility to women, seeing women as the embodiment of that corruptible flesh. Mere contact with the female body, even the body of a virginal woman, was treated as though it were a kind of disease which communicated the contagion of corruptibility and decay.[19]

This opposition between female flesh and eternal life led to a discussion in early Christianity as to whether women's bodies could be redeemed at all in the resurrection of the dead. Some Christians apparently thought that, at the resurrection, the female body would be transformed into a male body. Jerome and Augustine opposed this idea and argued that humanity will be raised, as it was created, male and female. Nevertheless, they partially preserved this idea by suggesting that the sexual parts of the female body will somehow be transmuted so they will be "fitted to glory rather than to shame."[20]

But the other side of this phobia toward the female sexual and maternal body is the sublimation of the virginal "feminine" as symbol of that "spiritual body" of resurrected life. The church as virginal mother is the vehicle of this rebirth into the spiritual body. The Christian is imaged as a newborn babe who is reborn in the womb of Mother Church.[21]

Later Catholicism sees Mary, the virginal Mother, as the type of the virginal church. In the doctrine of the Assumption of Mary's sinless and undying body, the eschatological body of the risen community of Christians is prefigured. Her Assumption anticipates the sublimation of the flesh, as it joins the immortal soul as the risen body.[22] So we see in Christian eschatology simultaneously a negation of the real sexual and maternal body of the woman, but also its appropriation, in spiritualized form, by a male celibate church leadership. All the images of the female sexual life processes are taken over by those who claim to control the higher powers of eternal life, and those images are then used to express a rebirth to transcendent life that negates the mortal life that comes forth from the women's bodies.

Although eschatology had been shaped by a male intelligentsia in a way that negates woman, this does not necessarily mean that the meaning of life after personal death is not an issue for women. As women increasingly claim the right to be autonomous, individuated persons, persons with "selves" of their own, and not simply auxiliaries to males, they certainly do want to ask about the permanent meaning of their existence. Yet the shaping of eschatology as negation of women's creative work in conception, gestation, and birth suggests that women might not want to accept the eschatological traditions as they have been received from this androcentric heritage. Women need to explore, from their own experience, the way to ask these questions.

I agree with Charlotte Perkins Gilman that our first responsibility lies in building upon the powers of birth. We need to develop the capacities for human, finite creativity. This means creating and raising children, the pledge of the continuation of human life in the finite future, and shaping a just and sustainable human society to bequeath to that next generation. In contrast to Hebrew messianism and its many secular stepchildren in theories of progress and social revolution, I do not expect that we can finally develop or transform life on earth into a final, perfected state. This notion of final perfection is itself a contradiction of the finite nature of existence.

JUSTICE AND RENEWAL

I have come to think of our task of creating a just, peaceable society as a continual process of finding sustainable balances in a web of relationships of humans to one another and to our fellow creatures of nature. This can never be done once for all, but has to be tried anew in every generation. Every generation is called to correct the distortions and violations of life that have arisen in their time and to reshape the world for the ongoing life of the next generation, so that the legacy of violence is not passed on redoubled to the next generation.

The Jubilee tradition of Hebrew scripture is my model for this continual work of renewal in every generation, as opposed to the quest for a final revolution that will set things right "once-for-all."[23] In historical existence, nothing can be done "once-for-all." Women who have been in charge of the repetitive tasks of daily clean-up and nurture are perhaps more able to understand this than men.

Each new achievement of a livable, humane balance of sustainable life will be different. Each will be based on a new appropriation of the historical situation, which will in turn shape a new culture and call for new technologies. It is a historical project that needs to be undertaken again and again. We do this work, not just for ourselves as individuals, or even for our own families or nations, but for the global community. It must increasingly be seen as the collective effort of all humanity as one community on earth. It is this shaping of the beloved community on earth, for our time and generation, to bequeath to our children, which is our primary capacity and task as finite, historical humans.

But what of the sad insufficiencies of natural finitude, the uncontrollable accidents and diseases that cut off people's lives before their time or condemn them to a half-life of undeveloped potential? What of all those who have suffered and died in misery because of social evils over which they had no control? What of the vast toiling masses of human beings who have had so little chance to live fulfilling lives through the centuries? What of the whole tragic drama of human history where so few have had opportunities for moments of leisure and happiness in the midst of oppressive labor? What even of those worthies who have made important contributions and lived full lives? Do their achievements live on only in our fading memories? Is there no larger realm of life where the meaning of their existence is preserved? These are the questions that have ever sparked the search for assurance of life beyond death.

The appropriate answer to each question is an honest agnosticism. We should not pretend that symbolic projections of possible futures beyond death are equivalent to knowledge. Our images of life after death, individually and collectively, are not revealed knowledge, but projections of our wishes and hopes. We need to balance the business of self-actualizing life with a quiet depth of acceptance of the limits of our powers. Recognition of the tragic dimension of finite life is essential to wisdom.

Our Western society is profoundly death-denying. We are not allowed to cultivate the wisdom of declining potency which leads to death, as must happen even in the best course of life, to make way for the new generation. We deprive the elderly of the mellowing appropriate to the autumn of life. So they become bitter and crochety, or confused and senile, or else try frantically to emulate adolescence in retirement. We do not allow ourselves to gather up the threads of life into a meaningful whole, to pass on wisdom to grandchildren and thus prepare ourselves for that final surrender of our finite powers to the great source of Being from which we have all come and to which we must all return.[24]

We know that death means the cessation of the life process that holds the organism together. Consciousness ceases and the organism itself gradually disintegrates. Our consciousness is our capacity to reflect upon that life process that holds our organism together. There is no reason to think of the two as separable, in the sense that consciousness can exist without the organism which is its foundation. What happens then to the self at death? Our existence as an individuated organism ceases and dissolves back into the cosmic Matrix of matter-energy out of which new centers of individuated beings arise. It is this Matrix, not the individuated centers of being, which is everlasting, which subsists underneath the coming to be and passing away of individuated beings.

Acceptance of death is acceptance of the finitude of individuated centers of being, but also our identification with the large Matrix as our total self which contains us all. The problem of personal immortality is created by the effort to absolutize individual ego as itself everlasting, over against the total community of being. As we relativize egoism in relation to community, we perhaps can also accept death as the final relinquishment of individuated ego into the great Matrix of Being which grounds, not just our personal selves, but the community of beings in their relation to each other.

The component parts of matter-energy that coalesced to make up our individuated organisms are not lost. Rather, they change their form and become food for new beings which arise from our bones. To bury ourselves in steel coffins, so that we cannot disintegrate into the earth, is to refuse to accept this process of entering back into the Matrix to become the food of renewed life. It expresses our rejection of earth as our home, and of earth's plants and animals as our kindred. We prevent ourselves from entering into the regenerative side of the cycle of disintegration back into the earth.

CONCLUDING QUESTIONS

But what of the meaning of our personal lives? What of the personal good to be remembered, the evil to be redressed? Does the personal have no meaning in itself? Does it simply disintegrate into the impersonal Matrix of the all? If the interiority of our organism is our personal center, might we not suppose that this is also true of the great organism of the universe itself? The great Matrix, which supports the matter-energy of our individuated beings, is the ground of all personhood. Can we see the collective Person of Holy Being as where our personal achievements and failures are gathered up and assimilated into the fabric of Being, to be preserved in eternal memory?

We do not know what this means. It is beyond our personal powers or capacity for conscious experience. We do not have to "be sure it happens," for it is not our responsibility. We can do nothing to assure that there will be an immortal dimension to our lives. Our responsibility is to use our temporal life-span to create a just and good community for our generation and for our children. We need also to learn to become wise in the absorption of the tragic dimension of life which we cannot change or control. At death we hand these achievements and this wisdom over to Holy Wisdom, who will transmute it into a transcendent mode of being beyond our powers.

This feminist eschatological spirituality is summed up in this prayer which I composed for a funeral in *Women-Church:*

Unless a seed falls into the ground and dies, it does not rise again. So our human spirits must let go of their perishable form to be transformed into the imperishable. This is a great mystery which we do not pretend to understand. But we trust with that faith of little children who put their hand into the hand of a loving parent, knowing they will be led aright. So we trust, even without knowledge, in that great Creator-Spirit from which all life comes and to which it returns, to raise this human spirit to immortal life. Take back now our sister into your bosom, O Wisdom-Spirit. In faith we entrust her into your arms.[25]

RECOMMENDED READING

Ruether, Rosemary. "Asceticism and Feminism: Strange Bedfellows." In *Sex and God: Some Varieties of Women's Religious Experience,* edited by Linda Hurcombe. London: Routledge and Kegan Paul, 1987.

———. *Sexism and God-Talk: Toward a Feminist Theology.* Boston: Beacon, 1983. Esp. chap. 10.

———. *Womenguides: Readings Toward a Feminist Theology.* Boston: Beacon, 1985. Esp. chaps. 11 and 12.

Part 4

CREATING AND GOVERNING GRACE

Introduction to Part 4

Until recently the doctrine of creation was all but eclipsed by the emphasis on the doctrine of redemption in most neo-orthodox theologies and by the challenges of modern science. A growing concern among many diverse groups for the "fate of the earth" in our nuclear age has led to a resurgence of interest in the doctrine of creation. Process theologians, post-Jewish and post-Christian feminists in the Goddess tradition, and "creation-centered" theologians have all challenged the death orientation of traditional Christian theology, as have feminist and Native American liberation theologians. Most of these groups agree on the following criticisms of traditional creation theology in Christianity. First, it has proceeded speculatively more than empirically by emphasizing creation as a specific event in the past. Second, it has been captive to a tendency to dualism, separating God from the world,[1] spirit from matter, humankind from nature, and history from nature.[2] Third, it has assumed a hierarchical chain of being or chain of command as the basic ordering principle of the cosmos. Any theology that reflects "converting our minds to the earth"[3] will counter each of these tendencies. Thus, it will focus on creation as an "ecosystem present in a definable place."[4] It will emphasize the fundamental relation of human beings within nature and the intimate connection between history and nature. And it will affirm the equality in interdependence of all forms of existence. These themes are especially apparent in Tinker's chapter, which emphasizes that we are "created in kinship with the land." Tinker also reminds us that in order to understand fully the context of a people, we need to take into account their particular geography and relationship to the land.

Feminist, Native American, and Latin American liberation theologies share this concern to develop an ecologically responsible theology of creation. Contemporary liberal approaches to creation generally affirm the goodness of creation. Liberation theologies differ from those approaches in three important ways. First, they approach this set of questions with a hermeneutics of suspicion. Liberation theologians in Latin America, as Westhelle points out, have not been as quick to pursue creation theology as theologians of North America have, not only because they have been preoccupied with an analysis of economics and politics, but also because they have been profoundly suspicious of creation theology as a reactionary tool to legitimize economic and social control.

This suspicion points to the second way in which liberation theologies of creation differ from others. They insist upon what Ruether calls the necessary connection between ecology and eco-justice. "Any ecological ethic must always take into account the structures of social domination and exploitation that mediate domination of nature and prevent concern for the welfare of the whole community in favor of the immediate advantage of the dominant class, race, and sex."[5]

This is evident in Westhelle's chapter in a number of ways. He uses social and political analyses as his primary tools to reinterpret traditional concepts such as *creatio ex nihilio* and *imago Dei*.[6] Also, he locates the discussion of human being within the larger cosmological context. Though he clearly presents human beings as agents,[7] he does not do so in Ritschlian fashion by interpreting human beings as *over* nature, but by interpreting them *within* the realm of nature, as both free *and* dependent in relation to it. Generally speaking, human embeddedness in nature has been emphasized more by feminist and Native American liberation theologians and human freedom more by Latin American liberation theologians. But, as Westhelle's chapter shows, the two are not incompatible.

His chapter, like Engel's and like much of creation-concerned contemporary theology, also emphasizes the social nature of selfhood. Unlike much feminist theology and process theology, however, he interprets this social existence more politically. This is evident in his development of the notion of the relatedness of all things through the concept of labor, which for him is an interaction involving nature, the self, and others in particular social and political arrangements.[8]

Finally, liberation theologies of creation differ by taking more seriously what has traditionally been called "natural evil." They are not as sanguine about the persistence of disease and death in our world, for example, as are certain post-Christian or creation-centered theologies.[9]

One of the major contributions of neo-orthodox theology was to question liberalism's assumption of the moral goodness of all individuals by reinterpreting Augustine's emphasis on the radical and pervasive nature of sin. Feminist theologians, while not disputing the importance of this doctrine, have criticized those reinterpretations as androcentric. Pride or egocentrism, they have argued, may adequately describe men's condition, but it is not characteristic of women's experience. Women acculturated in sexist societies in the West are more prone to the "disease" of hiding or losing themselves. One of feminist theology's most creative contributions is the reinterpretation of sin in this direction. Engel's construction of the doctrine of sin from the perspective of liberation from sexual and domestic abuse continues this line of thought.

Feminist theologians have also been severely critical of the concept of original sin and the myth of the Fall for two reasons. First, both have historically been associated predominantly with women, who are then understood as the immediate cause of evil in the world. Second, both have contributed to a theology that is profoundly dualistic, if not anticreation. While feminist theologians have not called for removal of the concept of original sin and the myth of the Fall from Christian theology, they have raised suspicions about their use and usefulness in the tradition and have called for thoroughgoing reinterpretation as a condition for their retention.

In contrast to the focus in neo-orthodox theologies on the radicality of sin in individuals, the focus in Latin American liberation theologies is on the radicality of evil as a social phenomenon. One of its strongest and most influential contributions is its countering of liberal theology's optimism about reforming social institutions with an insistence on the radicality of evil. Another is its countering of both the liberal and the neo-orthodox concern with the individual in relation to God with an insistence on the social and structural character of evil. Latin American liberation theologians' analyses of the social, political, and economic structures of oppression that bear down on individuals have been welcomed by Black, feminist, and lesbian and gay liberation theologians in North America working to combat racism, sexism, and heterosexism (see chapter 16 by Hill and Treadway, for example).

With its emphasis on evil as that oppression structured into a society that transcends individuals, liberation theology reveals its tendency to approach this doctrine empirically and practically, rather than metaphysically or speculatively. Instead of focusing on the etiology of evil or on the existence of a superpersonal devil, it treats evil as an occasion for just and faithful living in the present situation. Engel's understanding of evil clearly owes a debt to both these emphases, the sociostructural and the practical.

The location of these essays on creation and sin and evil in this section on creating and governing grace is intended to emphasize with neo-orthodoxy that the human condition is one of deep sinfulness and to emphasize with the liberal tradition that the human condition is one of genuine possibility, though not necessarily development. It insists that our life in the world is at once *both* deeply sinful *and* deeply righteous. In this sense it is both post-neo-orthodox and post-liberal.

CHAPTER 9

Creation Motifs in the Search for a Vital Space: A Latin American Perspective

VÍTOR WESTHELLE

CONTEXT AND COMMITMENT

Theology in Latin America is immersed in a context of continuing economic exploitation. Daily anonymous millions go to search for work, only to find there is no work; to search for land, only to be left nowhere. Daily millions cry out, only to discover that no one is listening; they sing their song in defiance of the ordered rhythm of boots and the procession of suits and ties, only to be ignored. Here indeed the whole creation has been groaning in travail. The words of the Peruvian writer Manuel Scorza are generally held to be true for all Latin America: "There are five seasons in Peru: Winter, Spring, Summer, Fall and Massacre."

After 500 years of colonization, the forces of domination have produced and reproduced structures of economic oppression. Except for Mexico at the beginning of this century, only Cuba and Nicaragua have been able to break the chain of submission that in Latin America is anchored in the possession and distribution of land. The appropriation of most of the land into the hands of a few people is one of the root causes of the seasonal massacre faced by the vast majority of our peoples. The following is just one example of this process.

Since pre-Columbian times the Kaiapo people have inhabited an area now called the State of Para of Brazil. Early in 1988 two Native chiefs of the Kaiapo, Paiakan and Kube-I, took action on behalf of their people and the land. They asked the World Bank not to finance the construction of a dam that would disturb the ecological balance of the Amazon. They were charged by the Federal Police and the Ministry of Justice with interfering with the national interest. The charge was based on a law that prohibits *foreigners* to comment on public affairs of the country. If condemned, they will be expelled from the country, from the land their people inhabited before it was known as Brazil, on the grounds that they are not Brazilian.

People's movements and organizations constantly struggle to defend the right to land as the right to life, a right they claim belongs to all those who live on and work the land. Landowners and governments have responded to these movements for land reform by murdering leaders and participants. For the last few years I have participated in these peasant movements by working with the Pastoral Commission on Land Problems (CPT), an ecumenical organization that lends support and that provides socioeconomic, political, and theological training to peasants and their organizations. The presence of the church in situations where life hangs by a thread, where the people have loving hearts and fighting hands, has transformed the community of faith. In this work with peasants the church has learned concretely the challenge of recognizing the face of a God who, to use the words of César Vallejo, has known how to be God by being radically human. Living in a situation in which many have already fallen or been silenced, and experiencing the power of their names and deeds germinating on the third day, the church has discovered a scandal of the cross—that it is erected every day and that it is not empty. The church has also found in this life of commitment new ground for hope. Standing with the masses struggling for life and land, the church in Brazil and internationally has been growing into greater awareness that *"we are the ones we have been waiting for."*[1]

CONSTRUCTION

Theology in Latin America has been ambivalent about creation as a theological theme. Indeed, very little has been said about it. In light of this, some consider our theology to be overpoliticized, having selected its own canon within the canon. But it is with good reasons that we remember that "the story that the Scriptures narrate converges in two basic points: the exodus of the Hebrew people and the cross of Jesus."[2] Both in biblical and theological studies our agendas are conditioned by the lives and dreams, words and deeds of a displaced people—women and men who hit the road of survival somewhere between annihilation and belonging. And there we are—still puzzled and yet determined to discern the direction in which the people are moving.

Common to the multiple contexts in our continent is the problem of place. From the struggle of the native inhabitants' right to their nation's land to the reality of the *favelas* (urban slums), from agrarian reform to the conflicts in Central America, from the demands of Black people for a social space to the women's movement, signs of change and consciousness of displacement are commonly found. Time, history, is a function of geopolitics. Hegel, I suggest, was wrong *precisely* in saying that "the truth of space is time." In our experience, if time does not convert itself into space, there is no time at all. The relativity of time *and space* is a common sociological experience. The Roman Catholic Bishop d. Pedro Casaldaliga expressed it well, saying: "Together with the signs of the times we need to discern the signs of places." This is our task: to discern the signs of places in which we do not yet belong but in which we will belong—*"no places"* that will become concrete *utopias*.

It is necessary to start by saying this, because being displaced is literally our condition. Gustavo Gutiérrez has spoken about being on the underside of history,[3] where the main question is to know where we are in order to establish where we must go and where we have come from. Displacement is not only a metaphor; it is also a precise description of our condition. Migration is the most striking feature of our reality. Carlos Drummond de Andrade has captured well this puzzlement with spacelessness in his poem, *José*.

> And now, José?
> Alone in the dark
> Like a frightened animal
> Without theogony
> Without a naked wall
> To lay against
> Without a black horse
> To run out at a gallop
> José, you march
> To where, José?[4]

Theology in Latin America is a reflection on the life and faith of a people finding a way, a way that is being opened up step by step. We have no place to stand still and contemplate the world, nowhere to lay our heads. It is for this reason we don't find in Latin American theology treatises on creation. But in the midst of this silence some suspicions are at work.

SUSPICIONS REGARDING EUROPEAN CREATION THEOLOGY

Is Creation Theology Irrelevant?

The first suspicion regarding creation theology is of a tactical nature. Creation discourse seems to be so detached from the dramatic demands of immediate life that to dwell on it would mean to be oblivious to more demanding and life-threatening questions. The words of Brecht, pronounced in a different context, resound sharply in our midst:

> Indeed I live in dark ages!
> . . . .
> What an age it is
> When to speak of trees is almost a crime
> For it is a kind of silence about injustice![5]

There is a sense of emergency in all that is done and said among a people for whom the universe is experienced as an abyss over which they hang by their nails alone. As César Vallejo asked, "A man searches for bones and scraps in the dump site. How can I write about the infinite?"[6]

It may not be irrelevant to ask why there is something rather than nothing. But it is an inopportune question when I am not able to answer why there is nothing instead of bread on my table. Gutiérrez set the tone for the discussion (or lack thereof) about creation in Latin American theological literature by describing the discourse of "theologians of the developed world" concerned with the question of creation as reflective of a political naiveté that has "sapped most of their energy."[7]

Does Creation Theology Justify Domination?

This brings me to the second suspicion. Creation language has been permeated by language that stresses order. The term *creation* is used interchangeably with "the Created Order." This is an ambiguous concept, for in Latin America nature is not seen as ordered and "order" is not a positive concept. "Order" is most often an ideological disguise for domination, repression, and persecution. Alejo Carpentier, the Cuban writer, has defined the cultural dilemma of Latin America as the conflict between the sense of order we have inherited from Europe and the effervescent spontaneity and marvelous anomaly of life as we experience it.[8] To speak of the world as a given, as something posited by God and thus good, sounds like a justification for the existence of a Gothic cathedral in the countryside of El Salvador. Ideologically, the ultimate appeal to justify order goes back to God's creation. Order becomes the moral parameter to speak about God's will in the midst of the cosmos, justifying the organization of the state. Where order is granted by the head of the state, where order is the result of the demiurgic work of the "invisible hand" of capitalism, where order is the patriarchal hierarchy, the stability and control of the whole society is guaranteed.

Such sacralization of order supposes an epistemological detachment from reality itself, a separation between the thing-out-there (where order is supposed to be found) and the observing subject. Whether this is a tenable epistemology will concern us later. For now it will suffice to note that positivism was the most influential ideology that came to our shores at the time of the struggles for political independence and remained so until the middle of this century. In Brazil, Comte's motto "Order and Progress" is the banner of the national flag.[9]

When order is so conceived as an *a priori* category, what is perceived as anomalous is what lacks order. What lacks order, lacks goodness. Lack of order is evil. Whatever is anomalous and conflictive must be integrated into a well-ordered center or be annihilated. By such criteria people have been exiled and are homeless. In a modern bourgeois world, any appeal to order is not an ordering appeal, but a freezing of a general set of relations of inequity that guarantees oppression, submission, and exploitation of those who are displaced. We continue to learn this lesson in Latin America. Order is the name of the Brazilian worker's monthly wage of U.S. $44.00. Strike is disorder.

FINDING THE WAY: THE DIALECTICS OF DISPLACEMENT AND BELONGING

Should we conclude that a theology of creation in our context is seriously limited? Can we only speak properly of a creation at the end of history, as the result of liberation that brings about novelty? Ernst Bloch suggested that God is the *homo revelatus* historically before us fulfilling liberation in creation.[10] Bloch was able to distinguish the central ambiguity in the discourse on creation that I noted in the second suspicion above. The appeal to a creator above us serves to justify the way things are as an order of creation, as an "abstract order," i.e., an ideology that justifies bourgeois domination.[11] Such an abstract order is solely the preservation of privilege through the annihilation of any organization that threatens the free market and capital accumulation. Bloch's alternative gives room for a close association between creation and novelty, so that the criterion for discerning the process of creation is dissonance with the old order. Thus, rather than justification of the old order, creation would be the theological expression of the belief in the *novum:* "Behold, I make all things new!" (Rev. 21:5; Is. 43:19).

It is not clear, though, what this novelty is. It is only clear that it is "not yet," i.e., eschatological. If Bloch's materialist presuppositions are respected, God would be the name of the formal cause of novelty.[12] However, I fail to see why this horizontal meaning of transcendence and human fulfillment should be interpreted in any sense as creation. For one thing, it excludes the notion of God cosmologically above us. Furthermore, the fundamental question that emerges in the dialectics of displacement and belonging is not addressed by horizontal transcendence and its appeal to history. The question of transcendence, for the displaced people on earth, is much more related to fences and walls than to a shiny new day to come.

That a full theology of creation cannot be found in recent Latin American theology has to be understood not as a disregard for the creation, but as a consequence of the phenomenon of displacement. Creation faith presupposes a sense of belonging. When one says that God is the creator of whatever is, I can only relate to this if I can situate myself in this "is." In a celebration among landless peasants struggling for agrarian reform in Brazil, Psalm 24 was read: "The earth is the Lord's and the fulness thereof, the world and those who dwell therein; for he has founded it upon the seas, and established it upon the rivers." A peasant commented: "When I hear this I don't see land anymore, only fences." On the road to belonging, he was able to begin to utter creation faith. In radical displacement not even this is possible, for it is the absence of vital space, i.e., a place where one can situate oneself.

AN EMERGING LATIN AMERICAN THEOLOGY OF CREATION

Out of the dialectic of displacement and belonging, elements for a theology of creation are emerging that play a definite role on the road toward belonging. They are means to overcoming displacement. They foster vital space, a place in which human life finds its potential fulfillment in the biological, social, and cultural dimensions. I will distinguish three basic types of belonging that define this vital space. First, there is the relation to the ultimate ground of life, i.e., to God through faith; second, the relation to nature through labor; third, the relation to other human beings, i.e., the formation of community through the praxis of love.

If displacement makes us question how we are to lift our voices to sing the Lord's song (Ps. 137 STILL OUR RESTLESS HEARTS ENDURE HEARTS THAT HAVE NEVER SUCCUMBED TO ABSOLUTE DISPLACEMENT HE INVITATION REMAINS WITH US O THROUGH GO THROUGH THE GATES PREPARE THE WAY FOR THE PEOPLE BUILD UP BUILD UP THE HIGHWAY CLEAR IT OF STONES LIFT UP AN ENSIGN OVER THE PEOPLES S 62:10). The old song cannot be sung anymore, but a new song is being composed with motifs that have a long history in the tradition of creation faith.

The Doxological Mediation: Trust and Hope as Creatio Ex Nihilo

Let me call upon a theologian deeply engaged with a people also living in dark ages, in displacement. This theologian, known to us as Second-Isaiah, wrote during the exile of the Hebrews in Babylon in the sixth century B.C.E. His or her appeal to the creation tradition cannot be separated from the announcement of liberation. In fact, the creation tradition makes liberation credible. The author of the "Book of Comfort" is above all a pastor to a people living in displacement. Second-Isaiah is a voice raised in the wilderness, sending forth the people with God's promise: "Fear not, I will help you" (Is. 41:14; 43:1; 44:2). Creation images and motifs emerge in the book as vindications of God's redemptive power. Wouldn't the "creator of the ends of the earth" also "give power to the faint and to him who has no might he increases strength" (Is. 40:29)? The Creator is praised in remembrance of things past, whether as a lament for a paradise lost or as a recital of past redemptive acts. "Remember not the former things, nor consider the things of old. Behold, I am doing a new thing" (Is. 43:18–19). Times had changed and it was not enough to remember the historical past. A new liberation, a new exodus was necessary. A renewal of the patterns of the past exodus could not be enough. It had to be something really new.

In this context creation faith emerges as a doxological affirmation of the trustworthiness of Yahweh in a time full of suffering and pregnant with the *novum* to come. The people are called to "sing to Yahweh a new song" (Is. 42:10). This can only be understood as a parenthesis of celebration in the midst of the experience of oppression and hope of redemption: a doxological interim that comforts, encourages, and animates. A historical break is necessary to make credible the power of Yahweh in a time when historical evidences testify to the contrary.

Here creation motifs are not dogmatic statements or systematic concepts that refer to the origin and order of the universe, but words of praise that celebrate the trustworthiness of God. After the exile, Third-Isaiah evokes with even more strength the doxology of creation, proclaiming a "new heaven and a new earth" (Is. 65:17; 66:22) in which worship will last "from new moon to new moon and from sabbath to sabbath" (Is. 66:23). Such a view links creation with the formation of a God-fearing people. This notion of a new creation is radicalized in Paul. The *kaine ktisis* is descriptive of the features of a communion of those who are *en Christo* (2 Cor. 5:17 Gal. 6:15).[13]

The doxological mediation of creation motifs does more than foster expectations of redemption. Although we don't know the origins of the doxologies in Amos 4:13; 5:8; and 9:5–6 (which are full of creation motifs), they are set in a context of words of judgment. Here also the motifs are used to relativize the memory of the old exodus, which was being used to justify Israel's exclusiveness and failure to affirm God's solidarity with the poor and oppressed. Penitence and the conviction of being under judgment are indeed part of doxological experience.

Another main biblical source that testifies to creation faith is the Psalms, whose doxological character cannot be overemphasized. Such doxologies ascribe a power to God which affirms God's sovereignty over all that destroys life. The ultimate affirmation of such a power emerges in face of the destruction of life itself, in the face of the deadly power of the godless.

The first explicit affirmation of *creatio ex nihilo* emerged in the tradition of creation faith. When the tale of the martyrdom of the seven brothers and their mother is told in 2 Maccabees 7, we observe that each son, refusing to succumb to the power of the king, affirms that faith with words of praise to God. After the first six brothers have been tortured and killed, the king attempts to persuade the mother to convince her last son to obey him. The mother reminds her son that he should not be afraid, even in the face of this total destruction, for God has made heaven and earth "not out of existing things" and humanity in the same way (v. 28). In the experience of total negation, *creatio ex nihilo* is the affirmation of hope in a God who will not succumb to negation. In the New Testament Paul also links *creatio ex nihilo* with justification and hope of resurrection (see Rom. 4:17).

From a people living in displacement and contemplating new ways of liberation we hear a voice daring to sing an impossible song. The first article in the creed of the Nicaraguan Peasant Mass is sung with these opening words: "Lord, I believe strongly that from your prodigious mind all this world was born, that from your hand of artists (the hand of the primitive painter), beauty has flourished. . . ." This motif was also applied by Victor Jara in his well-known popular song, *Prayer to a Farm Worker*:

> Rise up and look at the mountain
> Whence comes the wind, the sun, the water
> You who change the course of the rivers
> You whose seed sows the flight of your soul.

New images are emerging in the song now being composed. These images, the remains of doxological events, veil such events, but simultaneously make them visible and grant to the experiences of awe and wonder cultural and religious space. A group of indigenous people were recently contacted by whites in South America and were presented with a Bible. They had never seen a book, nor did they have a name for it. They called it "the skin of God." The "skin of God" is being formed in Latin America, giving evidence to the presence of a God who is in solidarity with the displaced in their pursuit of a space where life might flourish.

The creation motifs in the Bible and tradition are not irrelevant, though they are, by themselves, ambiguous. The point is to determine the mediation through which they might contribute to finding a vital space. This is achieved in doxology whenever creation motifs affirm the possibility of liberation granted by the power of a creator God and sustained by a faith assured that the maker of heaven and earth can make all things new and is not bound, even by what already exists. The most radical expression of such doxology can affirm the *creatio ex nihilo* in evocative language. In such a doxology the new protology and eschatology converge, or as H. Gunkel put it: "The end of time is the same as the beginning" (*Endzeit gleicht Urzeit*). Such a doxology negates the boundaries of time and evokes images that stir emotions and animate a people defying the fate of displacement.

The question of memory emerges at this point. Doxological experience seems to relativize or criticize the role of memory in liberation. The affirmation of novelty supposes the overcoming of the past and of the boundaries of the memory of past experiences. If the new is to come and if it is to be liberating, it will have to transcend previous liberating events. Here is the basic difference between romanticism and liberationism. Memory is bound to the finitude of historically determining experiences. Doxological experiences "overdetermine" the experience of reality. "Overdetermination" is a concept with some history in Freudian psychology and Althusserian philosophy. I use it theologically to describe the resolution of a conflict which could not be expected or predicted beforehand, considering the *determining* variables at work. The religious sense of awe and wonder is the practical (doxological) experience of overdetermination. However, overdetermination does not set one in a mystic mood floating above everything that determines day-to-day life. It evokes praise and awe *because* the socio-historical, biological, and cultural determinations are taken with utmost seriousness, and then transcended. Memory and liberation are in a dialectical relationship. Liberation is not possible without the overcoming of memory, but memory informs liberation. Without memory, liberation is at most a spiritualized notion. Memory is a road that brings you to a river. Although necessary and indispensable, it is not enough to enable you to build a bridge or a boat to cross the river.

The images, myths, and rituals that inhabit our memory are part of the doxological mediation. They are what recent studies in neurobiology call "preparedness." Preparedness is our brain's capacity to assemble images so as to preview things which, though dependent upon discrete components of memory, form a whole distinct from its parts.[14] So prophetic images are not simply visions of what is to come, but also archetypes that favor a resolution within day-to-day life. Preparedness allows for an imaginary place within the experience of displacement and offers concrete possibilities for making it real. The no-place becomes a concrete u-topia.

The Metabolic Mediation: Labor as Creatio Continua

Having dealt with the relation to the ultimate ground of life, let us now turn to the second relation of belonging. In the doxological mediation, creation motifs appear as an expression of ultimate confidence in a God who *overdetermines* reality. Now we turn to finite existence, seeking for creation motifs in the midst of nature, of which we are a part.

All the amazing vitality in the process of nature from which life emerges is a result of living organisms. Biochemical processes produce the variety and the reproduction of life within certain possibilities controlled by DNA. Metabolism is an encompassing term that applies to the processes that result in living organisms. During its evolution nature has produced organisms that were able to cope with, as well as to change, their environments. If creation is nature seen in reference to God, we can say that metabolism is a name for *creatio continua*.

In the first volume of *Capital*, Karl Marx defined labor "as a process in which both the human being and nature participate, and in which the human through its action mediates, regulates and controls its metabolism with nature."[15] Using the term *metabolism* to define labor is helpful in the sense that through labor human life produces and reproduces itself by shaping and reshaping the environment. Labor is not an action like throwing a ball or waving goodbye. It is human social production for the satisfaction of some need through a product envisaged and controlled ideally (*telos*), conditioned by the material reality at hand and by the technological means available.[16] We may call this external metabolism as opposed to the internal metabolism of living organisms. And we can speak theologically of a continuing creation through labor.

How is this motif linked with traditional creation faith? The J account of creation, with its explicit commission to work (Gen. 2:15), provides a clue. What calls for attention in this account is the parallelism of images between God's action in shaping the human out of *humus* (adam/adamah) and the order to cultivate the land. There is an analogy of action between God and the human. St. Basil in his extemporaneous homilies about the creation account of P inverted this analogy, describing God's creative activity in analogy to human labor (*poiesis*). As an artisan makes and shapes an object, God has made the world.[17] In the New Testament this motif is present in the miracle stories, which are portrayed as acts of divine creation. There the verb *poiesin* is frequently used[18]—the same verb that is used to translate the Hebrew *bara'*.

We should be cautious about speaking of labor without warning against its alienation. A clear distinction must be drawn between the process of labor and the accumulation of its result. Marx once remarked that original accumulation "plays in political economy the same role as the original sin in theology."[19] This is a central problem of social ethics, particularly ecology, since alienation in labor is the destruction of metabolism; it is diabolic. It is not what brings together (*meta-bole*) but what throws apart (*dia-bole*). The pursuit of authentic labor craves a vital space where human beings can find self-realization within the environment.[20] Thus, the struggle for agrarian reform in Brazil, for example, goes hand in hand with a militant ecological consciousness.

Because this view risks turning the *creatio continua* motif into an anthropocentric concept, some explanation is necessary. Creation viewed from a metabolic perspective has a demarcated linguistic sphere. It refers exclusively to the interaction of humans and nature (including human nature). This interaction changes not only nature but the human itself. There is something human, all too human, in such a language. But can it be avoided?

Recent studies in cosmology and physics have discovered "large numbers of coincidences" in the expansion rate of the universe. The expansion rate is precisely that which has allowed for the emergence of life and thus led to our emergence as observers. A rate minimally lower or higher would make life impossible. This is not the place to get into a discussion of the so-called anthropic principle, which says "that what we can expect to observe must be restricted by the conditions necessary for our presence as observers."[21] A minimal version of this principle will suffice to suggest that our observation of and discourse about the vast universe and its unfolding is precisely and only the observation of our total *involvement* with it.[22]

This involvement, which is metabolic, tells us that we can only speak about a world with which we interact to become those who can say something about it. And nothing that we say is irrelevant to our own existence. It may foster either destruction or belonging. Hence we cannot avoid being "anthropic." Being "anthropic" establishes only an epistemological primacy of the human, not an ontological one. Labor as metabolism focuses on the continuing creation of a universe from the standpoint of the human as the only possible observer of *this* world. And the world we metabolically create is only the world that creates us as observers of it. We are participant-observers and we observe because of our participation. There is no ecological neutrality. In all the ways we change nature and nature changes us, the only two options are to be "metabolic" or "diabolic."

Victor Jara's song, *The Plow,* expresses well this relation of belonging:

> The sweat makes furrows on me
> and I make furrows on the land
> Ceaselessly . . .
> Like a tightened yoke
> I have my fist full of hope
> because all will change.

The worker and the land both change in the process of labor. The same hand that holds steady the plow is the fist full of hope. All will change.

The Praxiological Mediation: Praxis as "Imago Dei"

Because of our metabolic participation in the world we observe, we cannot be indifferent participants and observers. The question is, What difference do we make? This brings me to my last point, to our relation to other human beings, to the question of praxis, and full circle to the question of whether creation themes are appropriate to address our situation, living as we do in the dialectic of displacement and belonging.

Who are those who sing a new song and trust in a God capable of making all things new? Who are the participants in the continuing creation of a world divided between the rich and the poor, capital and labor, corporations and communities, patriarchy and womanhood, pharaohs and slaves? The differences are also differences in celebration, differences concerning the role of labor in life, differences concerning the way God is imaged and where we find the image of God.

It is not my purpose to exegete Genesis 1:27.[23] I don't regard the formulation of the text to be as important as the sheer affirmation of the *imago* in the conditions of domination and exile under which the people were living when the P writer formulated it. The apparent *hubris* in the self-definition of the human is in fact manifested in its opposite: the profound humility of the minimal human condition. Erich Auerbach insisted that this is unique in literature: "Humiliation and exaltation [in the Old Testament] are very profound . . . and always go together."[24]

In P the social and political conditions under which the text emerged confront the daring affirmation of the *imago*. This same contrast comes together explicitly in Psalm 8. The tensive unity of humiliation and exaltation is the heart of the psalm, whose point is that likeness is there where it is unlikely to be found. Guido Rocha, a Brazilian artist known for his sculptures of the crucifix, was once asked why his images of the Christ were those of a tortured, hungry, and poor man screaming on the cross. He said, "[S]ince I was a child . . . I learned that nothing is as similar to Christ as the people."[25] Here is the reversal of historical subject that marks the experience of a people empowered by God, a people of slaves, exiles, the poor, servants. Those who are displaced, dispossessed, little, weak, and crucified make the difference. "God chose what is foolish in the world to shame the wise; God chose what is weak in the world to shame the strong" (1 Cor. 1:27). Insurrection (*insurgere*) is the way of God, as is testified in biblical literature from the formation of *adam*, the human made of *humus*, through Jesus, the child without a place to be born, the man risen from death.

The *imago* motif establishes the pattern of the human in its minimal condition. In this minimal condition the human finds its greatness. The displaced and dispossessed have only their capacity to act and interact. Having lost the objective result of their labor, they have gained the consciousness of their capabilities, of participating in the *actus purus*.[26] What they can conquer and retain is sociability. They gain dignity in human-to-human relation. In being faced with each other and in having interaction as their only reference they *re-cognize* the profile of the human.

The new profile of the human is being drawn in the concrete experiences of community participation. Those who cannot be defined by what they have or by the place they occupy are being defined by the way they interact. The *imago* motif appears then as an attribute of a collectivity; it refers to "earth creatures" (Gen. 1:27) united by their differences. Paul's references to "new creation" in 2 Corinthians 5:17 and Galatians 6:15 link the new condition to being "in Christ" or to being the "Israel of God" (Gal. 6:16). This being "in Christ" is defined not by status but by relatedness: "In Christ Jesus neither circumcision nor uncircumcision is of any avail, but faith working through love" (Gal. 5:6).[27]

The formation of community through intersubjective relations is what technically may be called *praxis*. Such praxis is a loving act. Community praxis is possible only where people share in love the urge to belong. In community a new social texture is being woven, a vital space is being formed. We may even say that communion is the strategy of creation and recreation of the loving image of God. Community is not a forum for discussion of interests that brings together people of good will. Community is possible when it begins with the fundamental equity of those who are displaced. It does not restore relations. It creates them.

In the *Shepherd of Hermas,* an early Christian book, an interesting view of the Christian church is presented. An old woman appears to the main character and gives him a small book. He tries to guess who she is. Unable to find out, another character appears to him and says: "She is the Church." Surprised, the main character asks, "Why is she so old?" It was a good question, since the Church had just emerged. The reply from the other character is revealing: "Because she was created first, before all else; that is why she is aged. It for her that the world was made."[28] When we experience a church emerging out of grassroots communities shaping a new ethos, gathering the displaced and making hope and faith practical in love, it is not an innovation. It is the oldest of all realities in which the definite and primordial profile of the human is raised.

CONCLUSION

In these three relations of belonging I have shown how scriptural and traditional creation motifs are used in the midst of the struggle of the displaced people in search of a vital space. The motifs that appeared witness to a theology of creation in process in Latin America. First, in the relation to the ultimate ground of life, the power of God to make all things new is claimed doxologically. Second, at the ecological level of the relation between human beings and nature, the metabolism of labor is claimed as continuing creation. Third, *imago Dei* is claimed as community interrelatedness that affirms the fundamental solidarity of God with the displaced and dispossessed whom God empowers.

RECOMMENDED READING

Bloch, Ernst. *Atheismus im Christentum: Zur Religion des Exodus und des Reichs.* Frankfurt am Main: Suhrkamp, 1968.

Croatto, J. Severino. "Fé en la creación y responsabilidad por el mundo." In *Fé, compromiso y teología: Homenaje a José Míguez Bonino.* Buenos Aires: Isedet, 1985.

Dussel, Enrique. *Ética Comunitaria.* Petrópolis: Vozes, 1986.

Joranson, Philip N., and Ken Butigan, eds. *Cry of the Environment: Rebuilding the Christian Creation Tradition.* Santa Fe, NM: Bear, 1984.

Lukács. Georg. *Labour.* London: Kerlin, 1980.

Segundo, Juan Luis. *A Theology for Artisans of a New Humanity,* 5 vols. Maryknoll, NY: Orbis, 1973–74.

Souza, Marcelo de Barros, and José L. Caravias. *Teología da Terra.* Petrópolis: Vozes, 1988.

CHAPTER 10

Native Americans and the Land: "The End of Living, and the Beginning of Survival"

GEORGE E. TINKER

CONTEXT AND COMMITMENT

I am an American Indian. Osage on my paternal grandfather's side and Cherokee on my paternal grandmother's. That indeed should be enough to establish the context for my essay, written some years ago while I was involved in the frantic pace of an urban Indian ministry. Unfortunately, it is not enough. Being Indian means you are only an historical memory for many other Americans. Stereotypes abound: barbaric pagans, the romantic image of noble savage, the invisible poor, animists, undeserving welfare recipients (usually said with respect to "treaty rights" and their legal entitlements).

The modern Indian context, in all its complexity, includes poverty more desperate than for any other ethnic community in North America. Sixty percent unemployment nationally, with individual reservation statistics as high as 90 and 95 percent; health statistics that are dismal; teen suicide rates three to ten times higher than the national average; and longevity statistics twenty to thirty years less than for other Americans. The context includes a painful history marked not only by military conquest and devastation but by a process of missionization that intentionally destroyed existing social structures and cultural values, a process that continues today as in the past with both government and church complicity. The context includes the continuation of the old tribal traditions against all odds. Sometimes small groups or families have successfully resisted the church's advance; sometimes whole tribes have managed to maintain their cultural integrity. And indeed, the past twenty years of Indian political activity and public self-affirmation of our

Indianness have been a dramatic renaissance of tribal spirituality. More importantly, the context is marked by an acute awareness that the survival and well-being of our peoples depend on us and not on those outside the community, the federal government, the church, or well-intentioned white friends. Self-determination is the by-word. Economic development, cultural integrity, education of our youth, spiritual sustenance. These we must define for ourselves, designing and implementing the strategies, knowing that our true friends in the white world will understand and stand with us.

Then there is another aspect manifest in my personal context and mirrored in much of the Native American community. I am what is called in the community a "mixed blood": that is, my father is Indian and my mother is Lutheran. A foot in two worlds, two cultures in conflict, two sets of values vying for an individual's commitment, two spiritual/religious traditions demanding undivided loyalty. And, of course, it is not just a mixed blood problem. Indian peoples have long been missionized by the dominant white religion; taught the evilness of their old covenant with the Creator; taught to reject most of their Indian heritage; taught to embrace not only the gospel but the foreign culture and values in which the gospel was carefully packaged. As a result we suffer an internalization of self-hatred that is perpetuated in the whole of the Indian world by the same missionary message that was to have saved us. The vast majority of our people today have or had some relationship with a Christian church—or two or four. Most have been baptized, at least once. Even those brothers and sisters who have rejected the church's teaching are indelibly marked by the missionary message, even in their disavowal. Yet many of us *are* Christian and have found life in the Gospel of Jesus Christ.

The question that confronts us as Indians who are Christian is the same question as self-determination. But now we must press that issue in terms of our theology. The implicit assumption of too many people, that the categories that have functioned in the white churches to structure their understanding and proclamation of the gospel will and must necessarily function in Native American cultures, has caused unending alienation and dislocation for Native peoples. Now a new day is emerging. Following on the renaissance of traditional tribal spirituality, many Indian clergy, lay people, and whole congregations are insisting on understanding the gospel in Indian terms, insisting on the natural indigenous categories of our tribes for structuring our faith. Hence the old ways of tribal spirituality are beginning to be as much at home in Indian churches as they are in traditional ceremonies. The values that define Indian existence, Indian community, traditional spirituality and culture are being articulated in Indian preaching and Indian theology in our churches. Traditional forms of prayer, considered by the missionaries to be pure paganism, are making their way into the heart of our Christian liturgies: the drum, the eagle feather, four direction symbolism, and rites of smudging. And a new mutual respect and cooperation is emerging between Indian clergy and the traditional spiritual leaders.

My essay on Indian land is a first step in this process of indigenous theology. It introduces a primary Indian category for all thinking and especially for theological construction: the priority of spatial categories over the temporal. And this project then shapes my own commitment to my context. It is a theological commitment but it is just as clearly political and social on the one hand and deeply spiritual on the other. My commitment is to the people—as best I am able: "that the people may live!"

CONSTRUCTION

Long ago a family lived in a clearing in the woods. The family was well fed and happy because of the father's prowess as a hunter. But there came a time when game was scarce and the family began to go hungry. When it looked as if they would all starve to death, the woman said to her husband, "This is what you must do. You must kill me and then drag my body in a circle around the clearing." The man refused for several days, though she continued to urge him to do as she had said, until starvation was upon them. Then in desperation he consented to his wife's demand. That night corn grew up wherever the woman's blood had soaked the soil. By morning this new food had grown to maturity and was ready to eat. Ever since, people have eaten corn and remembered Corn Mother's gift to them.

This abbreviation of one American Indian tribe's telling of the Corn Mother story is a vivid expression of the intimate relationship between Indian people and the land. At one level, Corn Mother's self-sacrifice emphasizes the sacredness of corn. At another level she symbolizes Mother Earth, the sacredness of the land. The earth is our Mother and gives birth to all things. The cycle of creation is completed in death and begins again with new life. Ancestors continue to live in the new life that is born of the land where they are buried, the homeland of the tribe.

1. Sacred Land

This truth, the Indian sense of relatedness to the land, lies behind the contention over land between Indians and white society today. What it means is that the highly publicized disputes in the courts and in Congress over aboriginal land claims have a theological dimension which is generally not recognized.

As one after another Indian nation goes to court or to Congress attempting to win land claim cases, more and more voices are heard describing the motives of those nations in derogatory terms.[1] The immigrants tend to suspect that Native Americans, having failed to understand the ethics of work, are simply out to get as much economic benefit with as little effort as possible. Two factors add fuel to the fires of derogation. In the first place, the Indians are winning often enough to pose a threat, emotional as well as economic, to the descendants of the immigrants who displaced Native peoples from the lands in question. In the second place, the connection between land claims of present day Native peoples and the injustice perpetrated against their ancestors is obscure to non-Indians, even to honorable non-Indians, because the values of the dominant culture are shaped by a religion of time and eternity. There is a religious comprehension gap, at least on the side of non-Indians.

From the beginning it was evident to astute Indian observers that white society neither understood nor shared the indigenous peoples' respect for land. Seathl (called "Chief Seattle"), a spokesperson for the Salish peoples, pointed this out in 1855:

The white man does not understand our ways. One portion of the land is the same to him as the next, for he is a stranger who comes in the night and takes from the land whatever he needs. The earth is not his brother, but his enemy, and when he has conquered it, he moves on. He leaves his fathers' graves, and his children's birthright is forgotten.[2]

The land is a profoundly religious issue for Seathl and for all Native American peoples; equally, for white society, the land is not central to religion. At stake are two very different theologies, two very different ways of seeing the world, two very different ways of praying.

The contrast in these ways appears at the beginning of theology: creation. Here is a portion of a Hopi creation story:

So Spider Woman gathered earth, this time of four colors, yellow, red, white, and black; mixed with *tuchvala,* the liquid of her mouth; molded them; and covered them with her white substance cape which was the creative wisdom itself . . . she sang over them the Creation Song, and when she uncovered them these forms were human beings in the image of Sotuknang. Then she created four other beings after her own form. They were *wuti,* female partners, for the first four male beings. . . .

So the First People kept multiplying and spreading over the face of the land and were happy. Although they were of different colors and spoke different languages, they felt as one and understood one another without talking. It was the same with the birds and animals. They all suckled at the breast of their Mother Earth, who gave them her milk of grass, seeds, fruit, and corn, and they all felt as one, people and animals. . . .[3]

There is, of course, something similar in the Judeo-Christian tradition. In the account of Genesis 2 humanity is created out of earth.[4] Many Indian creation stories have this same thrust, namely, that humanity is made out of, emerges out of, is closely related to, the earth or land. But Christian Europeans in general, and in particular those who emigrated to America, and their descendants, have almost no sense of the earth as brother or mother. Perhaps the real distinction here is that Native Americans still live out of their theology of creation, while immigrant Christianity has long displaced creation from the center of theology in favor of a theology of redemption in Jesus Christ.

The Native peoples have retained at the core of their self-understanding the sense of having been created in kinship with the land. The Taos Indians steadfastly refused from 1906 until 1970 to accept a cash settlement for a piece of land that included Blue Lake, a ceremonial site they held most sacred. It had been taken away from them by the federal government, without recourse to treaty or negotiation, and was turned into a national forest. It was the heart and soul of their religious ceremony. Hence, they refused offers of ridiculously large sums of compensatory dollars and would not accept the promise that they would always have access to that land, when indeed that promise would be only as good as the intentions of whoever is Secretary of Agriculture or head of the U.S. Forest Service. Through their perseverance the Taos Indians finally won Blue Lake back from the U.S. Government and put the continent on notice that the sacred was not for sale.

Land for the Indians is indeed sacred in a sense that it is not in immigrant society, however much that society may prize land as property.[5] The sacredness of the land shows itself in all of Native American life, but especially in tribal religions. For most tribes, their spiritual ceremonies are intimately related to the land on which they live, and their religion no longer works when the land is no longer there for them. Richard Two Dogs, a contemporary Oglala Lakota medicine man, put this relationship into perspective: "The religion is rooted to the land. And you can't have the religion by itself, without the land. . . . We can't practice without the sacred land or the sacred places because this is where we draw our religion from."[6]

2. Space and Time

Of course immigrant culture also values the land. Land was one of the reasons immigrants came to this country; they came because there was plenty of it. And as they swept across the country, clearing land and building farms, it should be obvious that they placed a high value, and still place a high value, on the land. But the land is not sacred to these people. Instead its value is measured only in terms of usefulness and profit. In truth we are dealing here with a deep, almost non-conscious, cultural issue in both groups. That distinction is the distinction between a culture that builds its worldview out of a notion of space and one that builds its worldview out of a notion of time.

There is some truth to the caricature of "Indian time." Native Americans have a less "precise" sense of time than does the European immigrant society. When classes are listed at a German university as starting at 8 o'clock C.T., the fact they start at 8:15 is very precise because that's what the C.T., *cum tempore,* has come to mean in European academic culture. When one has an interview in this country at 8:20, one shows up at 8:18. And if one arrives late, profuse apologies are expected. The point is not that Indians have no sense of time, or that immigrant cultures have no sense of space; all cultures have both time and space consciousness. The question here is which of these has priority, which one is fundamental to a culture's understanding of the world, and which one is subject to the other. Is time a category under which space is subsumed? I want to argue that for Native peoples, space is primary; for immigrant cultures, time is primary. No matter how valuable immigrant society holds the land that they have, their culture, as is evident to most Indians, is a time-based culture.[7]

It may be objected that American immigrant society prizes space above all else, indeed has been determined by space rather than time. For instance, Sydney Mead set up his thesis by arguing as follows.

From time immemorial the peoples of the Orient, of the Near East, and of Europe have been a people hemmed in, confined within the spatial boundaries set by geography. . . . Within such boundaries and impressed by the regular passing of one generation after another within the confines of familiar places, they tended to find what freedom they could for the human mind and spirit within the context of time—time as duration, as the endless flow and flux of events which might be abstractly conceived in terms of great cyclic revolutions endlessly repeating, or, in Christian times and lands, in terms of a beginning in creation, a center in Jesus the Christ, and an end in judgment.

But when the first white men from Europe set foot on the new continent with the intention to remain as settlers, this relative significance of time and space was reversed. . . . Gone was the traditional sense of confinement in space, for space relative to people that mattered was practically unlimited. Thus the first emigrants experienced a new birth of freedom—the possibility of unconfined movement in space—while concurrently the time ties were tattered or broken by the breaking of the continuity of the regular passing of one generation after another in one place. . . .

It is not too much to say that in America space has played the part that time has played in the older cultures of the world. . . .

Americans during their formative years were a people in movement through space—a people exploring the obvious highways and the many unexplored and devious byways of practically unlimited geographical and social space. The quality of their minds and hearts and spirits was formed in that great crucible—and in a very short time.[8]

It is important to note here that Mead is not dealing with any notion of the sacredness of the land! In fact, space in the sense that Mead uses it does not mean land at all except in an oblique way. But it means "room," room to move about in, "elbow room," *Lebensraum.* That may mark a significant expansion of, or a shift in, the European conception of time, and that may be what Mead has isolated. However, I would argue that space to move around in is still fundamentally temporal. Space as it has been understood by the children of Europe in America has tended to mean room to expand, to grow, or to move around in: these are temporal processes. As such, then, "Manifest Destiny" is quintessentially a temporal doctrine even as it consumed the space of this continent.

Space *as such*, in which one simply exists, has been taken for granted rather than held sacred. Indeed, space as such became rather expendable for the immigrants swarming across the continent. New generations abandoned the already cleared, settled, civilized regions in favor of the raw frontier. The adhesive between white Americans and the place where they were born, the space in which their ancestors lived, the land of their childhood, was and is fairly weak. People in America move a great deal, often moving clear across the continent from friends and family and then moving again in a few years. This was already apparent to Native American observers a century and a half ago, as Seathl bears witness: "To us the ashes of our ancestors are sacred and their resting place is hallowed ground. You wander far from the graves of your ancestors and seemingly without regret."[9]

What European-Americans adhere to most tenaciously, now as in pioneer days, is time. Mead himself points this out. As the immigrants followed their collision course with Native Americans, Mead says, "living out the inexorable myth of 'manifest destiny,' there was no time at all. For the Indian, no time to adapt—but even more tragically, for the white man no time for remorse, but only time for the labor in the cold and in the heat and in the vast places. . . . Americans have never had time to spare."[10]

The difference between time and space culture reveals itself in the way the sacred is defined in Native American and in immigrant culture. The sacred is defined by space in Native American culture. In immigrant culture the sacred is defined by time, while space is relatively unimportant. An example of that is that immigrant religions (churches) are portable phenomena. It doesn't matter where a congregation builds its church as long as the building occupies a good location on a major street corner. When a congregation outgrows its building, it may knock the building down and build something else, or sell it to a housing developer and move to a larger piece of property. Another example of the unimportance of space in the immigrant sense of the sacred: in the early and Medieval church, the geographical orientation of the building was important in that the altar had to be in the east, but even that has fallen into disuse in the modern age. In a high church situation one may have some memory of the old way of doing things, so that the altar is called liturgical east, even when in reality it may be geographically north by northwest.

Yet time is sacred for Christians. That is not so portable: witness the immutability of the appointed hour on Sunday morning when Christian people come together to pay homage to their God. Some find Saturday evening an acceptable alternative for fulfilling the Sunday obligation, especially during the summer months. It is also possible to push the Sunday service into Sunday evening. But rarely will a midweek service satisfy many people. Sunday is the time that things get done for Christians.

Again for Native Americans the day of the week is not nearly so significant. They may decide to do things on a weekend simply because of the modern work schedule; those are the days people have off. Otherwise they might just as readily have a ceremony in the middle of the week. What is important is where the ceremony is done: on a sacred hill or mountain; at a sacred beach or lake. The space becomes primary. Medicine men and women out on the plains are very clear that their power, their authority, and their validity as medicine people derives from the land on which they stand, where they live, where their people dance and where they hold their ceremonies, and from the herbs and medicines that grow on that land as well. None of that is portable. The ceremonial fire pit of the Hoopa Nation has been in one place, the center of the universe, since the beginning of the people's memory. Anthropological authorities have used carbon-14 dating procedures to date ash residue in the pit to about 7000 B.C.E. Few medicine people of any tribe spend prolonged time today in cities. They must live on the land that is the source of their power, of the spiritual existence in which they are rooted.

3. Sacred Symbols of Spatiality

The sacred importance of the land shows up in the symbols that tribes use in the course of their religions. Across the plains and indeed across the continent, the symbol of the four directions is of utmost importance for Native American ceremonies. The direction in which the sun rises, and that in which it sets, are all-important for Indian people. In prayers on the prairie, Native people pray, turning as they pray in each of those directions. The Siouxan peoples start with the west and rotate sunwise to the north, to the east, and then to the west. Algonquin peoples turn sunwise but start at the east, turn south, west, north, then back to the east. The importance of this is not a temporal symbol but rather an earthly symbol: it symbolizes space. On the plains too in a pipe ceremony, after praying in each of those four directions, the spiritual leader will then pray toward the sky, up, and then pray downward toward the earth, so that there are actually six directions, totally defining three-dimensional space within the context of a prayer.

Among the Navajo the Four Directions becomes even more clearly spatial because they define the limits of their territory by four mountains. These lie at the limits of Navajo territory in the four directions. Indeed these are the limits of Navajo existence. The mountains are so sacred that if people visit them, they may come back with a lump of earth, packaged up, to keep in their home.

Directionality is even the image used in Plains ethics—to the extent that we can talk about ethics at all among Native American people. Ethics certainly could not be done in the way that Western intellectual philosophy discusses ethics and morality, because a propositional ethic is not at stake here but rather the way people live. Whether you call that ethics, or religion, or whatever, Indian people would simply say that "this is the way we live." Out on the Plains the Siouxan people talk of living life as a choice between two roads, the blue road and the red road. One has to choose whether one will walk on one or the other. The Red Road is the road to life. It's the road to corporate wholeness for the community. The Blue Road is the road of difficulty, struggle, trouble—of the individual, of selfishness at the expense of community life. The ideal is to be on the Red Road, the road that builds up the whole of the community.

The Blue Road is what has happened to Indian communities quite often since the immigrant invasion: the breakdown of a community's structure. But the Blue Road has always been there in a slightly different sense; it has always been possible for people to do wrong. What makes this different from Christian moral development in immigrant society is that for the Indian one never finally moves out of that intersection; one always stands in a place of having to make a choice. This is no ethic of achievement which catalogues an individual's moral growth in some list of accomplishments. One can never look back and say, "I've walked the good road, the Red Road, all these years; there's no chance of my straying now! I've lived a good life, I've helped my people, it's over." Black Elk, at the end of his life, as an old man, stood on Harny Peak praying and confessed that he still stood at the crossroads and still had to make the decision to walk the good road. The importance of this is the spatialness of that image—of the whole of Indian life. A vital point is that personal transformation is *not* the goal of Native ethic religion; one feels called not to transcend one's natural humanity, but to live it, and to live it in the context of a particular community and that community's particular geography.

The spatialness of spirituality is also defined by the circle, a figure sacred to all Indian people. Prayers are always offered in a circle. People rarely sit in a room in rows, in an oblong structure, the way Western Christians do. Indian ceremonies are done in the shape of a circle, and that circle is self-defining; it defines the limits of the people, the nation. Black Elk and Sioux people call it the sacred hoop of the nation. More than that, it is the sacred hoop of the whole world, the universe or cosmos, that is at stake and is symbolized in the prayers that these people offer, as well as in symbols that Native people draw on their tipis, paint on themselves or their horses, embroider on their clothes, and otherwise incorporate into the artifacts which they create. The circle and the four directions are often brought together in what's called a medicine wheel. The shape of a circle defines the outside of the wheel. What looks like a symmetrical cross, embedded in the circle and circumscribed by it, is in actuality not the Christian symbol but the symbol of the four directions.

CONCLUSION

So Corn Mother's death is only the beginning for understanding the sacred character of the land for Native American peoples. All of life is marked by the character of the land for Native American peoples. All of life is marked by the relationship between the people and their land, but perhaps the relationship is most pronounced in the end of life—death. The burial of the community's ancestors in the land is a sacred act that completes the bond between people and land. The harmony and balance of the world depend on the cyclical flow of existence from life to death to life again. Death is seen as a natural part of the flow, as continuity and not as discontinuity. Corn Mother's death results in life and sustenance for her children and for all people. Likewise, the lives of ancestors continue to sustain life for those who dwell in the ancestral land.

Knowing this truth gave one Crow chief, Curley, the strength to reject the U.S. government's insistence that his tribe make yet another land cession. In his words,

The soil you see is not ordinary soil—it is the dust of the blood, the flesh and the bones of our ancestors. We fought and bled and died to keep other Indians from taking it, and we fought and bled and died helping the Whites. You will have to dig down through the surface before you can find nature's earth, as the upper portion is Crow. . . . The land as it is, is my blood and my dead; it is consecrated; and I do not want to give up any portion of it.[11]

The continuity between past and present, life and death depends on the primary category of space, understood as land. A leader of another tribe, the Nez Percé, spoke these words to his son, Chief Joseph, as he lay dying:

My son, my body is returning to my mother earth, and my spirit is going very soon to see the Great Spirit Chief. When I am gone, think of your country. You are the chief of these people. They look to you to guide them. Always remember that your father never sold his country.

You must stop your ears whenever you are asked to sign a treaty selling your home. A few more years and the white men will be all around you. They have their eyes on this land. My son, never forget my dying words. This country holds your father's body. Never sell the bones of your father and your mother.[12]

These sentiments continue to live on today, even in urban Indian communities where Native people have been "relocated" in carload lots, in accordance with federal Indian Policy (1954–1970). When an Indian person dies in the society, no matter what the person's status in the community and no matter how far the city is from his or her reservation, the whole community will not rest until it has raised funds from among its members to send the body "home" to be buried at the center of the universe.

Meanwhile, back on the reservation, the conflict between Native peoples and the immigrant nation continues even as we draw closer to the 500th year since its beginning. Thousands of Hopi and Navajo people are being removed from their ancestral lands in the Joint Use Area and are being relocated in city communities. This action is ostensibly for their own good and only incidentally opens the area up for lucrative mining efforts. Alaskan Natives sadly watch the slow erosion of their land base and the despoliation of all of their traditional lands. Indian people in Wisconsin, Oregon, and Washington are fighting legal battles to preserve their promised rights to fish and hunt on their traditional lands. The Washoes, Lakotas, and countless other nations are struggling to establish just legal claims to lands unfairly taken from them. And all the while, Native people are watching with curious amazement as small farmers are relocated, by circumstance if not by policy, to the towns and cities of America, while corporate conglomerates swallow up the last family farms. Native people remember the words of Indian prophets, prophets like Seathl:

The whites, too, shall pass—perhaps sooner than other tribes. Continue to contaminate your bed, and you will one night suffocate in your own waste. When the buffalo are all slaughtered, the wild horses all tamed, the secret corners of the forest heavy with the scent of many men, and the view of the ripe hill blotted by talking wires, where is the thicket? Gone. Where is the eagle? Gone. And what is it to say goodbye to the swift and the hunt, the end of living and the beginning of survival?[13]

America, too, would do well to hear the words of the indigenous prophet of this land.

RECOMMENDED READING

Deloria, Vine, Jr. *God Is Red.* New York: Dell, 1973.
_____. *The Metaphysics of Modern Existence.* San Francisco: Harper & Row, 1979.
Deloria, Vine, Jr., and Clifford Lytle. *The Nations Within: The Past and Future of American Indian Sovereignty.* New York: Pantheon, 1984.
Allen, Paula Gunn. *The Sacred Hoop: Recovering the Feminine in American Indian Traditions.* Boston: Beacon Press, 1986.
Nabokov, Peter. *Native American Testimony.* New York: Harper & Row, 1978.
Ortiz, Alfonso. *The Tewa World: Space, Time, Being and Becoming in a Pueblo Society.* Chicago: University of Chicago Press, 1969.

CHAPTER 11

Evil, Sin, and Violation of the Vulnerable

MARY POTTER ENGEL

CONTEXT AND COMMITMENT

> I have been raped
> be-
> cause I have been wrong the wrong sex the wrong age
> the wrong skin the wrong nose the wrong hair the
> wrong need the wrong dream the wrong geographic
> the wrong sartorial I
> . . . .
> *I am not wrong: Wrong is not my name*
> My name is my own my own my own
> and I can't tell you who the hell set things up like this
> but I can tell you that from now on my resistance
> my simple and daily and nightly self-determination
> may very well cost you your life[1]

The context for my discussion of evil and sin in light of liberation from sexual and domestic abuse is war: war of the strong against the vulnerable, all those judged by our society to be "wrong" or the "appropriate victims." Though present statistics are imprecise and are likely to remain so because of varying definitions of abuse and chronic underreporting by victims and social agencies, they are essential to describe this context. One out of every five married women is battered. Domestic violence is the major cause of injury to women, exceeding rapes, muggings, and auto accidents. One in seven married women is sexually abused by her husband. Almost one out of every two women will become a victim of completed or attempted rape in her lifetime. One out of every nine children under eighteen is abused or neglected by parent or guardian. Three out of every hundred children are threatened by their parents with a gun or a knife. About 2,000 abused children die each year. One out of every three to five female and every eleven male children will be sexually assaulted by the age of 19. Two and a half million elders (mostly women) are abused by caretakers every year.[2]

Given this concrete situation, we do not have the luxury of standing neutrally on the sidelines. We must choose either to be resistance fighters working to end these "corrosions of sacred possibilities" or collaborators contributing to the desecration of the lives of the vulnerable. Christianity and North American culture have both chosen, through their indifference and participation in the "conspiracy of silence," to be passive and active accomplices in these crimes against the vulnerable.

The North American movement to liberate the vulnerable from sexual and domestic abuse has been the major factor shaping my theological reflection in recent years. As a teacher in a liberal Protestant seminary, leader of clergy and professional workshops, community member, family member, and friend, I have heard and read countless stories of violation of and violence against those most vulnerable. As a woman, I have not escaped the daily debilitating effects of sexual terrorism in our society and violation and violence in my personal life. As a white middle class woman who lived for a month in an urban shelter for women and children, I have begun to learn how important it is to take seriously women's economic dependence and to pay attention to the specific racial and cultural contexts of victim-survivors. Answering the prophetic call to advocate with and for those among us who are "the distressed" (in Hebrew, the *anawim*), I am committed to: working with others to dismantle the systems, behaviors, and attitudes that perpetuate and extend these kinds of oppression; to building a more just and full life for all; and to developing a theology of liberation from sexual and domestic abuse.

Listening to victim-survivors has persuaded me that an appropriate and adequate method for this theology of liberation will include the following seven components: First, it must be grounded in and responsive to the practical experiences of oppression and liberation of particular victims. Much of what I have to say is sparked by the reflections of those struggling to overcome this oppression in their lives. Second, it must draw on alternate texts for its sources. Autobiographies, journal entries, first-hand oral accounts, and various forms of artistic expression are essential to the communication of these intense experiences, for these more direct ways of witnessing break through our denial more quickly. Third, it must be self-consciously interdisciplinary, using psychological and sociological analyses to understand the dynamics of these intimate forms of oppression and ideology critique to show how society reinforces such behaviors and relational patterns. Fourth, it must pay attention to the interlocking sets of oppression that compound the horror of sexual and domestic abuse. Classism, racism, and ageism as well as sexism function together (more like strands in a cable than links in a chain) in this oppression, and we must investigate how they reinforce one another without singling out any one as the root cause. Fifth, it must contribute to the empowerment of women as agents and persons. Sixth, it must be oriented toward practical, concrete change that includes the resistance of individuals and social groups, for these are issues of social justice, not personal morality. Finally, it must take care that its theoretical and practical recommendations remain provisional. If a new absolute definition of sin is substituted for the old one, we shall not have served these victims well. As I will argue, specific behaviors that are labelled "sin" by theologians are often *at the time of abuse* positive survival tactics for which the victims should be praised rather than faulted. For example, if we define sin only as "diffusion of the self," a generally helpful definition for women, victims may hear this as a judgment upon themselves for "losing themselves" to protect themselves during the abuse. We must be clear therefore that *any* definitions of sin offered must be applied, understood, and evaluated only within precisely described determinate contexts and that the victims themselves have the stronger claim to making final judgments about whether particular actions at particular times are sinful.

CONSTRUCTION

We know a gigantic tree in the depths of a vast forest
A great snake hanging down, reaching and reaching
Down to the center of the earth, always downward
When it touches the earth it is long enough and strong
                enough to reach the sky
—Protect us as you protected the first woman and man
Against ourselves, against each other
                    against human sacrifice
Against what will not let a thing be born
Against "we do not know what we do not wish to know"[3]

In feminist liberation theologies dealing with sexual and domestic abuse, most attention has been paid to the reconstruction of the creation doctrines of male-female relations, marriage and family, and the mind-body relationship;[4] to the reconciliation doctrines of grace, forgiveness and healing;[5] and to the ministry doctrine of clergy-lay relationships; with some attention also to images of God and theodicy.[6] Recognizing that all doctrines need to be reworked from the perspective of the liberation of the vulnerable from sexual and domestic abuse, I have chosen to focus on evil and sin; for it is this doctrine that continues to be one of the most powerful tools in the church's collusion with society in the victimization of women, children, and elders.

Evil and sin together may be called "wickedness,"[7] the complex condition of the lack of right relations in the world in which we live naturally, socially and individually. Though they are inseparable, it is

important to distinguish the two. Evil, as Latin American liber
theology has taught us, is systemic. It is not superpersonal forces but
structures of oppression; patterns larger than individuals and groups
with a life of their own that tempt us toward injustice and impiety—social,
political, economic arrangements that distort our perceptions or restrain
our abilities to such an extent that we find it difficult to choose or do
good. By contrast, sin refers to those free, discrete acts of responsible
individuals that create or reinforce these structures of oppression. Neither causes the other; evil and sin are mutually reinforcing.

Both evil and sin are essential concepts for a theology of liberation of
the vulnerable from sexual and domestic abuse. Further, it is crucial to
emphasize both sides of evil as systemic: lament and blame.[8] Evil as
lament is important in calling our attention to the need for solidarity with
victims as innocent sufferers. Evil as blame is equally important. To a
woman taught to blame herself for being abused, this notion, associated
with the perpetrator's participation in an evil structure, can be freeing. As
victim after victim recounts, "It was my fault. And I take responsibility for
it." Evil as blame redirects attention to the structures that have power over
her and for which she is not solely, ultimately, or directly responsible,
thereby helping victims to ask the liberating question, "Who the hell set
things up like this?" In so doing it challenges the use of the doctrine of
original sin, understood as inherent guilt or ineradicable shame, to blame
the victim.

Because the concept of original sin has been used against women and
other socially designated sacrificial victims we should be suspicious of it.
This is also true of the concept of actual sin. While it is important to retain
both concepts, not only for perpetrators but for victims as well, we must
be careful in identifying and interpreting them. For example, if sin, as the
choice or decision to contribute to evil structures, assumes some freedom
of will, then it is difficult to say that children or women dehumanized by
years of terror in domestic or "foreign" situations have enough freedom
or range of options within a situation to be able to commit sin. Yet, in
spite of the thorniness of the issue, I am not prepared to relinquish the
notion of sin for anyone who has ever been a victim. Why? The concept of
sin, in contrast to evil, highlights the personal side of wickedness and in
so doing fights against the common tendency to externalize evil to such
an extent that each individual is exempt from all responsibility and
accountability for it. Far from contributing to a recognition of evil as
systemic, this romanticist projection of evil furthers evil structures by
exonerating individuals.

The concept of actual, universal sin also checks the tendency to reduce
the moral universe to a dualism of heros and villains. Not interested in a
simplistic assessment of blame, which contributes to immobilizing guilt
and resentment rather than heartfelt repentance and concrete change, I
do not want to suggest that the perpetrators (largely men) are wholly evil

and that the victims (largely women) are wholly good. Women and other victims are no more or less pure than men. Therefore, it is important to look at the ways in which victims as well as perpetrators have been tempted by evil structures, lured into complying with their victimization. I have tried to reconceptualize sin in relation to abuse by attending to differences between men's and women's responses to these structures of oppression.

In my reconstruction of sin I have acknowledged adult victims' complicity in their victimization without focusing the blame for victimization on them. I have also tried to shift the burden away from victims to perpetrators. For as I develop the notion of sin, I want to avoid blaming the victim and giving the impression that perpetrators (largely men) and victims (largely women) are coresponsible or equally sinful. This view, suggested by some family systems approaches and neo-orthodox views of sin, is not helpful to victims. For this reason, I find it important to point out that evil and sin, though inseparable, are to be stressed differently in varying contexts. When one is speaking of perpetrators, sin, individual responsibility, and accountability should be stressed. If, on the contrary, one stresses evil or the coresponsibility of the perpetrator, he is allowed to escape his responsibility. When one is speaking of and to victims, evil should be stressed. If one stresses sinfulness to them, they are encouraged to continue in their feelings of self-blame and over-responsibility. In neither case should the companion concept be forgotten (for it is as freeing to men to learn that they are tempted by evil structures as it is for women to learn that they are responsible in part for the direction of their lives), but it should not be primary.

SIN AS DISTORTION OF FEELING

Anger and vocal, vehement resistance have traditionally been identified as sinful or anti-Christian. It is particularly women, children, and other powerless individuals who are expected to imitate the meek and mild Jesus in this regard. They are told to deny what is happening to them and to dissolve their anger. Instead of dissolving anger, which results in great harm, they should be encouraged to redirect "this natural and healthy psycho-physical response to situations in which these capacities are being frustrated."[9] Anger is the opposite not of love but of self-blame.[10] If we encourage victims to channel their anger toward individual and social change instead of dissipating it by not expressing it directly or actively toward its correct object, we will contribute to their recovery and social transformation. If all of us were to speak and act out against sexual and domestic abuse with the righteous indignation of the prophets, we would no longer be colluding in an oppressive system of violence.

What happens when we shift our view of sin as anger and resistance to that of moral callousness, as Mary Pellauer has suggested? By "moral callousness" she means good, moral persons' participation in and perpetuation of violence against women "simply by going about our business in an ordinary way. We do so primarily by our quotidian participation in social patterns and institutions which make up the bulk of everyday life."[11] This ignorance and acceptance, taking violence against the vulnerable for granted, giving in to numbness, is what the scriptures call "hardening of the heart," one of the surest signs of having wandered off away from God.

As many have noted, in our culture the great taboo is not against incest and other forms of abuse but against talking about these abuses. More than a silence born of ignorance, this is a failure to acknowledge a reality of horror that surrounds us. The title of Alice Miller's book on child sexual abuse, *Thou Shalt Not Be Aware*, makes this point clearly. Miller suggests that we are prone to this denial because we "prefer to take upon ourselves the hell of blindness, alienation, abuse, deception, subordination, and loss of self rather than lose that place called Paradise, which offers us security."[12] Toni Morrison's conclusion to her wrenching novel about the rape and impregnation of a young girl by her father, *The Bluest Eye,* suggests another reason. "We tried to see her without looking at her, and never, never went near. Not because she was absurd, or repulsive, or because we were frightened, but because we had failed her."[13] Whatever the motivations for our denial, the fact remains that the silence itself renders us guilty, corporately and individually, of complicity.

This notion of sin as hardening of heart or moral callousness, as useful as it may be for the perpetrators and colluders, is problematic from the perspective of the victim's survival and recovery. It is not to be confused with the numbing of the self, the striving to feel nothing physically or emotionally, the oblivion, the dissociation, that victims often recount. In situations of abuse this numbing is used as a necessary survival technique in order to distance themselves sufficiently from the abuse in order to bear it until such time as they are able to escape or alter the situation.

Sin as Betrayal of Trust

Another popular traditional concept of sin that is harmful to victims of sexual and domestic abuse is that of disobedience. Many battered women are trapped in abusive relationships because they have been raised to believe that disobedience to their husbands is unbiblical and sinful. As one said, "He told me he would beat me every day, if that's what it took to make me obey." Our children also suffer when we define sin as disobedience. One of the most indelible lessons children learn at home, school, and church is "Honor thy father and thy mother." Because this is often the only notion of sin drilled into them, they find it hard to understand, let alone resist, the violent and violating actions of their parents or other elders toward them. As Martha Janssen expresses it in her poem, "The Fourth Commandment":

> They taught me
> not to hate my parent.
> Families must love each other
> no matter what. . . .[14]

Or as Lark d'Helen remembers: "I'd been taught in the good Baptist tradition that a person (and especially a girl) should always respect her elders, particularly men. What was I supposed to do? I trusted you; you were the adult, I was the kid."[15]

How do we move from the harmful view of sin as disobedience to the realization that some uses of parental authority are abusive? One way would be to follow Alice Miller's suggestion that we supplement the Fourth Commandment with the following one: "Honor your children so that they will be able to honor others as well as themselves."[16] Another would be to replace the notion of sin as disobedience with the notion of sin as betrayal or lack of trust. This shift focuses attention on a different kind of relationship between persons, for it acknowledges that we exist together primarily not in an external system of rules but in dynamic relationships of trust, fidelity, and mutual obligation that are better described as covenants.[17] This is true in all relationships whether between spouses, lovers, friends, parent and child, professional and client, or teacher and student. In each case both persons, because of the promise involved, rightly *expect* to be treated with care, respect, and honor. In such relationships we entrust our *selves*—bodies, hearts, minds and spirits—to the other; we deliberately and unavoidably make ourselves vulnerable to the other. When the other violates us within that relationship this sacred bond of trust is broken. *This* is the sin, the breaking of the bond by the perpetrator through betrayal of trust, not the brokenness itself, in which victims cannot help participating.

It is the active betrayal of trust that should be the focus in cases of sexual and domestic violence. Instead of deflecting attention to the woman's disobedience (thereby justifying the male's violence against her), we should concentrate on the physical and emotional ways in which perpetrators have broken covenants of partnership. Likewise, when adult or child victims of sexual or other forms of abuse report the crimes to clergy or other professionals, the focus should not be on how they are breaking the bond of the family by going against the conspiracy of silence, but on the way in which the abuse itself has already broken the covenant of parenthood.

This shift away from sin as disobedience to sin as betrayal of trust is not without its difficulties for victims of abuse and must be understood with care. I want to be clear that I am equating sin not with lack of trust in God, another popular traditional definition for sin (particularly for Protestants), but with one person's betrayal of the trust of another. Salvation, the cure for sin, has been described as a process of conversion from distrust to trust. The reason this classic definition of sin is problematic for victims of sexual and domestic abuse is that victims are trained by the abuse not to trust anyone—loved ones, authority figures, the universe, or God. The natural result of years of living in constant terror and under the threat of severe harm is not trust but fear. "He threatened to kill me if I left. I had no money and nowhere to go. I'd never lived alone and didn't think I could make it by myself." Many incest perpetrators threaten the child with total physical or psychological destruction of the family, death of the child, or death of a pet or other loved one. In situations such as this, in which persons have never had an opportunity to learn to develop basic trust in others or have lost it through torture, can we meaningfully speak of sin as the lack of trust? Perhaps instead we should turn our attention to sin as the destruction of this necessary life-affirming trust in others. For the Sherpas of the Himalayas, for instance, there are two fundamental sins: threatening children and picking wildflowers. And, instead of speaking easily of healing as the turning from lack of trust to trust, we should acknowledge the victim's damaged capacity to trust and difficulty in learning to trust and respect her need to develop her own process of discerning when and whom to trust.

SIN AS LACK OF CARE

A third popular traditional definition of sin harmful to victims recovering from sexual and domestic abuse is that of pride, or self-love, for one of the enduring scars of abuse is self-blame or self-hatred. It is common for both child and adult victims to blame themselves when harmed. Self-blame is a major cause and reinforcer of "surplus powerlessness," for it successfully deflects attention away from the real problems.[18] Self-hatred continues to afflict the victim and protect the perpetrator.

> you taught me so well
> to hate myself,
> my body,
> that i don't need you anymore
> to hurt me,
> fuck me physically
> or emotionally.
> i do very well on my own now.[19]

Abusers count on this self-loathing for their protection. As one victim said to her abuser years later, "You're damn lucky I didn't commit suicide. . . . But you really didn't worry about that—you knew I'd been brought up a good Christian, that I would take a good share of the guilt on myself, that I would feel that I was supposed to suffer because I was so sinful."[20]

Whether it is called shame, guilt, or low self-esteem, self-blame and self-hatred are the most commonly reported long-term effects of abuse. And it is this more than anything else that is bound up in victims' experience with the notion of original sin. Brought up to believe they are inherently evil, they are all too willing to believe they are worthless and deserving of the abuse as punishment. "Would I ever be clean again? I didn't feel I was worth anything, and I didn't think I ever would be if I lived."[21] "Somehow, I decided, it must have been my fault. If I had said no, if I had been a better child, if I had not been tainted with evil, it wouldn't have happened."[22] This is sometimes manifested in its mirror image as the constant and hopeless search for redemption from one's own unworthiness through stellar behavior.[23]

Rather than speak of sin as pride or self-love to victims, we should speak of it as distortion of the self's boundaries. If men are acculturated to inflate the self, expand its boundaries to annex at will, women are taught to deflate the self, eliminate its boundaries through enmeshment. Retaining no clear sense of themselves as individuals apart from their relationships, they become diffused. Consequently, they suffer not from pride but from what can be called lack of integrity, insufficient individuation, uncreative self-definition and self-constitution, "hiding," or "flight from responsibility."[24] We are not all moved "without knowing it by an imperious will to power which brooks no obstacle" (including our neighbor if she is in our way).[25] Powerlessness as well as power corrupts.[26] Powerlessness corrupts women by tempting us to lose ourselves in others.

It is important, therefore, for women to develop a sense of power as action and a strong sense of themselves as responsible individuals and to learn appropriate ways to love themselves.[27] Because of this the popular contemporary notion of sin as alienation, used by liberal, neo-orthodox, and feminist theologians alike, is also not helpful to victims.[28] It is altogether too vague to be of much help.[29] And, it connotes a static, passive condition that does not do justice to the active exploitive structures of a society built for the strong against the vulnerable. As an adult victim-survivor of child sexual abuse pointed out to me, it does not encourage victims to separate from their victimizers in healthy ways and it contributes to blaming the victim. By implying that the desired state is one of reconciliation, it suggests that any victim who is struggling to create a separate identity for herself is wrong. By implying that all participation in the condition of alienation is wrong, it casts the blame equally on perpetrator and victim.

The notion of sin as diffusion or loss of the self is also problematic for victims, for disassociation (and its extreme form, the splitting of the self into multiple personalities) and hiding are important survival techniques in situations of abuse. Maya Angelou reports in her account of being raped by her stepfather that when she refused to be the child her family knew, they called her impudent and sullen. She in turn retreated into a place "without will or consciousness." "Into this cocoon I crept."[30] As another child victim of sexual abuse records, "I begged God to make me never-been."[31]

Should we retain the notion of sin as pride or self-love for perpetrators? This, too, may not be helpful, for a number of reasons. First, as many studies have shown, abusive behavior arises out of low self-esteem. Second, rather than focus on sin as self-love, it might be more accurate to speak of it as the perversion of love for another into false love or sentimentality. Judith Herman notes how often incest perpetrators offer excuse for their behavior by saying that they did it out of love for their daughters.[32] Third, this false love arises from a trained inability to relate to others respectfully and from a fear of others.[33] The result is that the person becomes an isolated ego unrelated to others through bonds of care and obligation and becomes unable even to recognize the other as distinct from self. This may be described more accurately as the transgression of boundaries than as self-love or pride.

Alice Miller points to the destructive dynamics and consequences of such transgression by distinguishing between a healthy narcissism, in which the person is "genuinely alive, with free access to the true self and his [sic] authentic feelings," and narcissistic disorders, "with the true self's 'solitary confinement' within the prison of the false self."[34] This negative sense of the self as abstract and isolated, lacks the healthy sense of self-preservation and self-definition of which we were speaking earlier. Rather, there is a lack of recognition of other as other and consequent use of the other as an object for the satisfaction of the ego's desires or as a means to one's private ends. In Buber's terms, this kind of person exists only as an ego in relation to "its" rather than as an "I" in relation to "Thous." Thus, although perpetrators trained to be egos will love, their love will be distorted into use of others for the satisfaction of their own needs. As Toni Morrison says, "Love is never any better than the lover. Wicked people love wickedly, violent people love violently, weak people love weakly, stupid people love stupidly."[35] This narcissistic disordering of the self necessarily excludes care in a way that healthy narcissism does not. Judith Herman has spoken of this isolation and its tendency to lead to the destruction of others:

"As long as fathers retain their authoritative role, they cannot take part in the tasks or the rewards of parenthood. They can never know what it means to share a work of love on the basis of equality, or what it means to nurture the life of a new generation. When men no longer rule their families, they may learn for the first time what it means to belong to one."[36]

The transgression of boundaries through narcissistic disorders and diffusion of boundaries because of low self-esteem interrupt the caring process by denying the other as other—the first by running over it, the second by failing to set a limit to it. While these different manifestations in men and women are significant, it is also important to note their common roots and consequences. Instead of defining sin as pride, self-love, or even self-hatred, perhaps a more comprehensive and descriptive definition is of sin as distortions of the boundaries of the self, through transgression or diffusion, that lead to lack of genuine care.

SIN AS LACK OF CONSENT TO VULNERABILITY *del?*

The final popular traditional definition of sin that has proved harmful to victims is that of sin as concupiscence. Our longstanding association of sin and sexuality has focused on sin individualistically rather than relationally and has contributed to blaming the victim by identifying women as conspirators with the powers of this "lower realm" and exonerating men as helpless victims of uncontrollable impulses. Instead of defining sin in these terms, we should speak of it in terms of our distorted relationship to weakness, vulnerability, and dependence. Just as Miller distinguishes between healthy narcissism and narcissistic disorders, Albert Memmi distinguishes between healthy and pathological dependencies. According to him, our daily dependencies (on nature, our bodies, other selves) are an unavoidable fact of our existence that is itself neutral if not positive. And yet, this fact seems to be a problem for us, a source of anxiety, for we find it hard to reconcile our existence as at once free and dependent. Though we should consent to these dependencies and work toward ways to meet them justly and authentically, and integrate them with our freedom, we often resent them and dread the feelings that they stir in us.[37]

As we saw with the distortion of boundaries, the distorted relationship to dependence is manifested differently in men and women, perpetrators and victims. Men tend to "solve the problem of dependence by dominating women and women solve it by subjecting themselves to men."[38] Trained to ignore, deny, and fear their own dependence, vulnerability, and fragility (often understood as impotence), many men (and women) learn contempt for whatever is weak. This contempt often leads to the abuse of their power, authority, or force to punish or nullify a vulnerable one. This may explain in part why batterers often become enraged at the sight of their pregnant partners and direct their blows at their victims' bellies. Morrison unravels the perpetrators' complex relationships to vulnerability in her description of Cholly Breedlove's unholy mixture of hatred and tenderness, revulsion and attraction toward his young daughter just before he rapes her for the first time:

She was washing dishes. Her small back hunched over the sink. Cholly saw her dimly and could not tell what he saw or what he felt. Then he became aware that he was uncomfortable; next he felt the discomfort dissolve into pleasure. The sequence of his emotions was revulsion, guilt, pity, then love. His revulsion was a reaction to her young, helpless, hopeless presence.[39]

Later, describing the role that sacrificial victims play in building up the false strength of all of us in society fearful of our weakness, she says:

All of us—who knew her—felt so wholesome after we cleaned ourselves on her. We were so beautiful when we stood astride her ugliness. Her simplicity decorated us, her guilt sanctified us, her pain made us glow with health, her awkwardness made us think we had a sense of humor. Even her waking dreams we used—to silence our own nightmares. And she let us, and thereby deserved our contempt. We honed our egos on her, padded our characters with her frailty, and yawned in the fantasy of our strength.[40]

Alice Miller confirms this analysis by calling contempt "the weapon of the weak and a defense against one's own despised and unwanted feelings," and identifying "the fountainhead of all contempt, all discrimination, as the more or less conscious, uncontrolled, and secret exercise of power over the child by the adult, which is tolerated by society."[41] In the words of one victim, "the crucifixion was a violent killing of 'God-Made-Vulnerable.' I understand the tearing of the temple curtain. I understand the tearing in the soul of a raped child. It is the same violation of vulnerability."[42]

What of women's efforts to solve the problem of dependence by subjecting themselves to men?[43] Victims also speak of "contempt for the needy small self I was."[44] Instead of using this contempt to fuel domination, however, victims use it to fuel their escape into false dependence, overdependence. Instead of resolving their anxiety about the dynamic tension between freedom and dependence by absolutizing their freedom in the power of domination over another who is more vulnerable than they, they resolve the tension by forfeiting their freedom in subjecting themselves totally to the provider.

The slip from dependence into subjection is no more inevitable for women than the slip from dependence into domination is for men. It seems to be the case, however, that no one in our culture, male or female, is taught to consent to the inevitable vulnerabilities and dependencies of our life. Instead we learn contempt for it, which leads us to violate it because it threatens us, or to escape into it because it scares us. Both distortions, power (domination, coercion) and powerlessness (subjection, abdication of power), corrupt. Perhaps, then, it would be more accurate to speak of sin as a distortion of the dynamic tension between freedom and dependence, or the lack of consent to the dependence and fragility of our lives. Perhaps if both men and women acknowledged their particular distortions of this tension and their need to resolve this anxiety in more healthful ways, we could reach an "arrangement based not on force and deception but on consensual reciprocal dependence."[45]

CONCLUSION

An apt metaphor for sin and evil is that of the Hydra, a mythical monster that grew two new heads for every one Hercules severed. Depending on the situation and the perspective of the participant, sin is described as distortion of feeling (or lack of moral sensitivity); distortion of the relationship of trust or betrayal of loyalty; distortion of boundaries (or lack of care); or distortion of the dependence/freedom dynamic (or lack of consent to our vulnerabilities). Since we need all of this language to speak adequately of this part of our experience, I do not find it useful to reduce sin to a single root metaphor.

By calling attention to this variety of destructiveness in human relationships I do not mean to suggest that human beings are only sinful and capable of doing evil. That would continue to foster the low self-esteem associated with victimization of the vulnerable. I believe that the capacity of human beings to do good and to repair the effects of evil by transforming them into good is co-original with this sinfulness. My stress on the many ways we go astray as we travel together the path toward greater, deeper, and more just relatedness is intended to point out the urgent need for finding and creating a variety of ways to combat these destructive powers. It is also intended to point toward the multifarious ways God graces the world: through creating new possibilities, healing broken hearts, judging insensitivity and harm, raising up those cast down by society, liberating those bound by self-hatred, setting free those imprisoned in their egos, and sustaining in life those who are battered and worn. Unless my comments on sin and evil here are understood in this broader context of God's gracing of the world through justice and love and humankind's active and voluntary participation in that gracing, they will hinder more than help those struggling to free the world of the victimization of the vulnerable.

RECOMMENDED READING

Clarke, Rita-Lou. *Pastoral Care of Battered Women*. Philadelphia: Westminster, 1986.

Finkelhor, David. *Child Sexual Abuse: New Theory and Research*. New York: Free Press, 1984.

Fortune, Marie Marshall. *Sexual Violence, The Unmentionable Sin: An Ethical and Pastoral Perspective*. New York: Pilgrim, 1983

Miller, Alice. *For Your Own Good: Hidden Cruelty in Child-Rearing and the Roots of Violence*. Translated by Hildegarde Hannum and Hunter Hannum. New York: Farrar, Straus and Giroux, 1983.

———. *Thou Shalt Not Be Aware: Society's Betrayal of the Child*. Translated by Hildegarde Hannum and Hunter Hannum. New York: Farrar, Straus and Giroux, 1984.

Pellauer, Mary D., Barbara Chester, and Jane Boyajian, eds. *Sexual Assault and Abuse: A Handbook for Clergy and Religious Professionals*. San Francisco: Harper & Row, 1987.

Trible, Phyllis. *Texts of Terror*. Philadelphia: Fortress, 1984.

Part 5

HEALING, LIBERATING, AND SANCTIFYING GRACE

Introduction to Part 5

Broadly speaking, grace is that which delights. It is that freely given power by which God moves the world toward wholeness (*shalom*) through justice and mercy. That freely given power, sometimes called "original justice" or "original righteousness," refers both to God and to human beings who participate in moving the world toward wholeness. The free gift of grace must be received freely. To be grace at all it must be accepted by a partner capable of participating in this work of salvation. Grace as the divine empowering of human beings (and of all creaturely and natural life) to live and work for a just and loving world has traditionally been spoken of as sanctification, the process of being made and making holy/whole.

Since the sixteenth century, sanctification has often been overwhelmed by an emphasis on justification, particularly though not exclusively among Protestants. Luther's discovery of justification as the forgiveness of sins by God of the sinning and sinful human being greatly influenced this trend. His anxiety that he could not ever earn God's approval through works was assuaged by his insight that justification was "by grace through faith." This insight became the foundation for a new Christianity that witnessed to the power of God alone to declare the sinner righteous and worthy.

Feminist, Black, and Latin American theologians of liberation have questioned the prevailing emphasis on grace as forgiveness of sins, because they believe that what most urgently needs repair is not the sins of individuals but the systemic evils of societies (see chapters 6, 7, and 11 for discussions of systemic evil). They speak of grace as the divine empowering that heals the external and internal wounds inflicted on individuals and peoples by structures of oppression and as the divine empowering that liberates peoples from the bondage of systemic evil. Leonardo Boff, in his *Liberating Grace*, emphasizes the divine empowering that releases peoples from captivity to the destructive powers of exploitative systems. In doing so he stresses that the gracing of God is a process *in history, in the world,* and includes therefore all social, economic, and political relationships. It is not operative solely *within individuals,* as the emphasis on grace as justification suggests. Continuing his counterproposal to views of grace limited to justification, Boff points to the variety of ways we experience divine gracing in our ordinary lives. As he says, "Grace signifies the presence of God in the world and in human beings. When God chooses to be present, the sick are made well, the fallen are raised up, the sinners are made just, the dead come back to life, the oppressed experience freedom, and the despairing feel consolation and warm intimacy."[1] In all these ways the divine empowering counters the individual *and* social "dis-grace" originated and perpetuated by systemic evils.[2]

Mary Pellauer stresses divine empowering through the healing of wounds inflicted by exploitive sexual and domestic relationships. It is striking that, in her entire discussion of grace and healing from the perspective of the movement to end sexual and domestic violence, she treats healing as sacred but is not concerned particularly to focus this christologically. In pointing out that it is the experience of survivors of sexual and domestic violence who know and teach the "sacred powers of healing," she does not invoke the name or symbol of Jesus Christ.

This raises the question of the relationship between grace as divine empowering and Jesus Christ. When justification is held as the primary form of grace, christology becomes a central theological theme, often with special attention to the atonement. The claim that through the death of Jesus Christ on the cross God acted to justify and restore humankind to a state of righteousness becomes paramount. Also, the atonement and incarnation often are viewed as a once-for-all salvific event, frozen in time. Thus, when justification is overemphasized, the continuing growth of human beings and societies in grace is short-circuited.

In theologies of liberation, by contrast, christology is grounded in the liberative *praxis* that moves out of the ongoing empowering of the incarnation and atonement. Therefore, Christianity is not only a life of proclamation of the saving act of God in the past, but also a life of participation in and with the sanctifying grace of God in the present. Christianity has been, is, and is to be a *practice* of freedom, a movement of free response to the God who, through healing and liberation, empowers humankind to participate in bringing the world to wholeness through justice and mercy.

This emphasis is evident in the essays by Grant and Heyward. Both argue that Jesus, Emmanuel, is God *with* us now in the midst of our concrete, daily existence. It is significant that both theologians stress that God's presence in Christ did and does affect human beings materially, that is, in the material conditions of their lives. Both underline the point that the reconciliation of God with humanity brought about by the incarnation is at the same time a demand for "turning around" (*metanoia*), the change that frees and liberates people from sin and the evil conditions in their lives.

In liberation perspectives, sin is not understood apart from the social relationships of human beings and the structures of oppression which bear down upon them (see the Engel chapter). As Pellauer points out, for survivors of sexual and domestic abuse, grace is healing experienced in "the depth dimensions of our social reality" (p. 182). Therefore, the healing and liberating power Christ inaugurates should not be spiritualized out of history or treated as if it had nothing to do with the material conditions of our lives or the relationships which make us who we are. Rather, it should be viewed as making possible an active turning away from oppressive conditions and to conditions of liberation. Thus, christology in theologies of liberation is not developed on the assumption of a spirit/matter dualism, but on the recognition that the real oppositions of victim/victimizer, dominated/dominator need the powers of healing and liberating to be transformed into relationships of justice and mercy.

For liberation theologians the encounter with God in history that is the graceful experience of empowerment is significantly witnessed by the scriptures, as Isasi-Díaz, Kwok, and Ringe argue. Even three chapters are not enough to convey the weight of biblical interpretation for liberation method. What is clear in the three essays is that each contributor has a distinctive encounter with the witness to the gracing of God conveyed by the scriptures. All the chapters in this section point out that cultural context always plays a key role in biblical interpretation from liberation perspectives.

Unless sanctifying as well as justifying is emphasized, christology tends to dominate other theological themes and the role of the Spirit in prayer or in sacrament risks being neglected (see the Oduyoye chapter). It is significant that particularly the non-Western contributors to this volume emphasize the Spirit (pneumatology) as much or more than Christ (christology) in sanctifying grace. The Spirit is more strongly associated with the grace of God that makes whole and the power of God *in community* that draws us into this movement toward wholeness (sanctification), while Christ, in many Western cultures, is more commonly associated with the grace of God that justifies and the power of God to work righteousness in individuals.

Oduyoye's emphasis on the spirit in community adds an important point about the sanctifying activity of God, for she understands the community of life in God very broadly. For her it is a full and rich community of life, not just a community of human beings. An overweening emphasis on justification since the Protestant Reformation has not only obscured God's sanctifying grace as it empowers human beings through healing and liberating; it has also obscured God's sanctifying grace active in the wider creation. Western theology has become anthropocentric, narrowly focused on the conditions and possibilities of the life of humankind. This is a dangerous narrowing of Christian reflection in our age, when it is urgent that ecological justice be kept central in order for creation to survive and heal.

This last section on God's sanctifying grace, sacred empowering through healing and liberating activity, comprises almost a third of the book. The length of this section testifies to the relative weight of this theme for theologies of liberation. Christianity, the practice of freedom, means living in the spirit that gives life to the *whole* creation. Living in this spirit, by doing justly, loving mercy, and walking humbly with God, is the aim and mark of theologies of liberation.

CHAPTER 12

Conversation on Grace and Healing: Perspectives from the Movement to End Violence Against Women

MARY D. PELLAUER with
SUSAN BROOKS THISTLETHWAITE

CONTEXT AND COMMITMENT

MP: I grew up Lutheran in a poor and abusive family in smalltown Minnesota. I can't really describe those years without an avalanche of fear, nightmares, despair, confusion, rage, and shame overwhelming me. I spent most of my adolescence trying to run away into the worlds of books, juvenile delinquency, cosmetics, revivalistic fundamentalism, and my own head. Perhaps the contradictions between these escape strategies canceled them out in the short run. More effective was running away to college. There I met a host of Sixties social justice movements, read the young Marx, met Eastern European and Third World revolutionaries, worked in the ghettos of St. Paul and Chicago, fell in love with David Pellauer and with all the women who stayed up late to talk, took off the cosmetic mask I'd worn over my birthmark, and discovered good Christian theology in classrooms and marches.

It was both an accident and grace that I was a theological student when the women's movement discovered battering and rape. So I was lucky to begin healing the damage I'd sustained early. I learned slowly to claim more than victimization. I learned to respect simple coping mechanisms and even to make room for denial. Especially I learned that the need to do theology out of these experiences was a gift.

I have to struggle with the Lutheran strand of my story. Perhaps it's because my theological tradition inexorably framed itself in pairs (law gospel, sin and grace) that I affirm both the existence of wounds and the existence of healing. Or perhaps this is simple sexism. Until we move our institutions and our theologies beyond patriarchy, it will be hard to tell whether such polarities are the remnant of vacillation or a start toward wholeness. In the meantime, I speak the Lutheran language of calling and vocation rather than the language of commitment.

I'm called to the company of the twin sisters of memory and imagination. Even with writer's block, I affirm the inseparability of books and social justice. I believe we're all called to healing. I believe in the creative pulse that makes beautiful warm quilts from scraps of wornout clothing, poems and song from the words we use every day, organizations for social change out of nothing more than the promises we make and keep with each other. And we're called to celebrate.

It's also hard to untangle assimilated Scandinavian culture from Lutheran theology. But it has to be part of my vocation to struggle against racism and class oppression as surely as against sexism and violence of all kinds. Otherwise we bow our knees only to the status quo instead of to the God who breaks every yoke to let the oppressed go free, and who reminds us to sing while we struggle.

CONSTRUCTION CONVERSATION

MP: Sue, I want to thank you and Mary [Potter Engel] for giving me the chance to do this as a conversation rather than as an essay. Partly of course I've been experiencing some writer's block, and writing my thoughts on this subject was not really something I was ready to do. But also as I thought about having a conversation, it seemed appropriate to what's going on with women and theology. When we read and write theology as our primary way of communicating, we're giving people messages about the meaning of theology—for instance, that it is primarily written and not oral. But our experience over the last twenty years has been that it has been in face-to-face conversations that we have learned to do theology in a new way. So we're realizing concretely that theology is not nearly so static as we may have thought when we read the final products in books or essays. It really is in process, in the exchange and discovery that we have when we are talking with people whom we trust to say what they most deeply believe and whom we trust to listen respectfully.

SBT: "Hearing each other into speech," as Nelle Morton said.

MP: Exactly. And I think I want also to add that your opening this option for me, for us, seems to fit beautifully with liberation theology. Not only because of what happens with base communities in Latin America looking at the biblical texts anew, but also it was a way of empowering me when I'm having these problems with writing. It was another strong instance of something I find a lot with liberation theology people—that there is a deep and pretty reliable consistency between the theory and the practice—an integrity which has been a powerful witness to me.

SBT: Well, Mary Potter Engel and I have both learned a lot from you about theology and victims of sexual and domestic violence, and we wanted the chance to include some of your stuff. But also it felt good to us to do something creative, not just another case of the same old didactic thing.

MP: That's wonderful. Well, I appreciate the chance to talk about healing in terms of grace, because I think that's precisely what it is. Maybe it has something to do with prevenient grace. Maybe I should tell you a little bit about why this topic came up for me and how it evolved, before we go into content.

SBT: Yes.

MP: First, this all came up originally for me in my own therapy about my family background of abuse. I was having a very painful and difficult, confusing time, being a theological student and in therapy and a feminist activist, and pregnant. I didn't know which way was up. One day I happened to be in a meeting with other theological students, and I looked around the room and saw all these normal, happy people who were going about their business and not feeling ultra-self-conscious and fucked up. I said, "Look at all these normal people. Why can't I be like them? Why? I want to heal." At that time I must have been in therapy for a year and a half. "I want to heal. How come I can't heal?" Or, "How do I claim healing?"

SBT: It's interesting to me that you put it in the active voice, as opposed to "I want to *be* healed." I think that's very critical in your understanding of healing.

MP: It might not have been so clear as that. There was both a feeling of healing and a feeling of being healed mixed together in a nice confusion, you know, a nice untidiness. But claiming that one wants to heal is already a signal that healing has begun. Healing did happen in my own personal life, I did truly change and become better, more functional, and happier and healthier.

Then as I did more work about the issues and more counseling with victims, I was absolutely stunned to see how often, how dramatically, and how quickly people healed. A rape victim, for instance, could come in one day, discouraged, her whole body drooping with sadness and fear. Within a very short space of counseling time, five or six weeks, I could see that the whole person had a lift, her skin was beginning to shine again, she looked you in the eye, she didn't have that dragged-down-into-the-ground look. It actually worked, people got better often quite dramatically.

I learned along the way to think of myself as doing a theology that rises out of the women's movement against violence against women. So I take for granted many of the things that go on in rape crisis centers and women's shelters and groups for child-abuse victims. It became important to struggle with how to articulate these experiences with the same power and insight and perceptiveness that we have traditionally articulated other experiences along the way.

So there are some concepts I take for granted here. For instance, there's a brief four-point schema about the healing process for victims of sexual assault. Would it be useful just to sketch that out?

SBT: I think it would, yes.

MP: The first stage of recovery after rape is called CRISIS. It is the original trauma after the assault has occurred. It often involves a woman being in a state of shock, reliving the incident, having phobias, sleep disorders, eating disorders, many of the tensions that victims ordinarily have.

The second stage of the healing process is DENIAL. Trying to get back to business as usual.

The third stage is called RESOLUTION or the PROCESSING STAGE. Here, for some reason or another, the survivor wants to work on these issues. She is very highly motivated from the inside. Many parts of herself are, in fact, prepared to deal with the issues and to act.

INTEGRATION means that the survivor need not repress or obsess about the material of the trauma. It's not that you forget it, but it doesn't control your life totally anymore. And it involves assigning appropriate blame and responsibility to the offender rather than engaging in self-blame and its cycles of pain. And it might involve taking some appropriate action.

[Doorbell interruption, recording machine off]

SBT: I was interested in your use of resolution, and then you said, "or processing," because "resolution" sounds like this comes to some kind of closure.

MP: Oh, right.

SBT: Whereas, what I think happens is that this becomes now part of your life forever. The abuse, whatever it is, you don't "get beyond it," or move on or something in the sense that it disappears. The processing takes forever.

MP: Well, I wouldn't say that exactly in that way.

SBT: It takes different forms?

MP: You're right, "processing" is a better term than resolution, exactly for the reasons you point to. Many people do come back around later on to assimilate new stuff. Maybe it helps to add that recovery or healing is not the same as returning to normal.

SBT: Yeah.

MP: Lots of people talk about returning to normal or getting back to normal. And victims do want to go back to normal, to wipe out these terrible things that have happened to them. And it's very hard to say to survivors that they can't do that, that the only way is to go forward. It's a process of transformation. They can become whole again, they can learn new skills, they can adapt old skills, they can find new ways to cope, they can become . . . You know, it's really hard to talk about this because I'm on the verge of saying they can become better persons, and that's not so. But they're changed in the process. They do heal.

SBT: Yes, absolutely. And it's like a miracle.

MP: Yes, it is. It's grace at work. And it's grace at several stages of the whole thing, not just the end-product. For instance, one of the mysterious, miraculous parts is the transition from the denial stage to the processing stage. We don't know at all how this works. You can't program it. People in the rape crisis movement give this a name—READINESS TO HEAL. Yes, it's prevenient grace, that's what I think it is.

Some of the most astonishingly wonderful stories I've ever heard are stories that victims tell about whatever precipitating thing it is that brings them to a shelter or a crisis center. Sometimes it's very mundane—like seeing a film about sexual abuse or rape on television, and so they call a crisis line. Sometimes an anniversary of the assault puts them back into this crisis phase. They may start having nightmares again and not know why, and begin to understand they need help, and so they call. Sometimes people get desperate, from the primary effects of the assault, and desperation is maybe another good contemporary synonym for grace here. Sometimes, of course, it's courage, courage in the ordinary sense of the word, like when a woman packs up her children and gets out of a violent home.

Readiness to heal is one of those deeply mysterious places in which we just don't understand what's going on. It's clearly a mixture of something preconscious inside the person and some decisions and some historical circumstances, but it's really quite wonderful.

SBT: And if it isn't there, you can't manufacture it.

MP: That's right, and it's hard for people who love survivors to realize that you need to trust the process and the person and to let go of your need to fix it for them. Because if they're in a denial stage you can just be nagging at them and increasing denial rather than opening the person to resolution.

SBT: Yes, it's hard.

MP:[nodding] To trust the process of the survivor, you mean.

SBT: For me it is.

MP: It *is* hard.

SBT: I mean, people who go into the ministry are people who want to help, which is many times a very positive thing, but it can also be manipulative and controlling and aggressive, and . . . yes, it's important to acknowledge that there are some situations that are not fixable.

MP: That's one of the difficult parts of readiness to heal, because many people get to the end of their lives without either accepting a healing possibility or without having a healing possibility presented to them.

People have died without healing, and women are killed in the process of their continual assault in the home. There's no way to account for the fact that sometimes nothing transformative occurs in their lives or that we don't have any way of . . . Well, I don't know, I'm sort of lost about how to think of this, because I also think that surviving itself is a theological topic, and that sometimes the simple ability to endure, or to keep on keeping on, to stay alive, even if it doesn't look good to everybody else . . . It might look to you or me like sheer living hell and torment and maybe it is, but somehow that person is still alive and this is a miracle.

SBT: No, I think that's right. The other thing I've learned is that the continuous offering of healing possibilities can make the difference. It may take years for someone to act on a possibility that was offered a long time ago—act in 1988 on something that was offered in 1983. But some other things had to happen in between.

MP: Yes, or you can be in a casual conversation with someone describing something unrelated to domestic violence and sexual abuse, and say, "That sounds abusive to me." And two weeks later the person calls up, in crisis. The mere use of the word "abuse" in an unrelated context thrust them into something that had been going on since childhood. And who knows why that was the moment, and that was the occasion in which that word fell on fertile ground? It's quite wonderful, but it's also perplexing.

SBT: I find it scary.

MP: It *is* scary.

SBT: I worry that a word should have been said that I didn't say.

MP: And it is part of the spiritual discipline of the person who wants to participate in healing, to say, "It's not up to me."

[Child's crying interrupts conversation.]

SBT: This tape is going to be a mess with children crying and all these interruptions.

MP: Actually I want to see that left in. Interruptibility is one of the conditions with which women have to come to terms to do theology. It's not one of the things you learn in theological school, about how to do theology with a child crying in the background or coming in with a Mickey Mouse toy, or whatever.

SBT: Yes, interruptibility is key, and it's methodologically key.

MP: It's also parallel to what we've been saying about the healing processes. Periods of denial in a person's recovery process are part of it. You have to allow for this interruption. It's not a process that happens between 9:00 and 12:00, or all day, or in a continuous series. Healing is interruptible. People put dimensions of it on the back burner sometimes for years, and then find themselves once again recycling the same issues from a new perspective, because the kaleidoscope has shifted a little bit and now they have to reintegrate things.

SBT: That's an expression I very often use. It seems so real to me, "to put things on the back burner."

MP: A good image from cooking and the kitchen.

SBT: Being Hungarian, my mother always had a stockpot on the back burner. Something was happening on the back burner, and you wouldn't pay attention to it for a while, but suddenly, miraculously, there was soup.

MP: There's a great line in May Sarton somewhere that in our hurried, industrial, factory-like age, there is a real value, ethical value, to the things that take time, like gardening, or knitting, or making bread or soup. And I think it's sometimes difficult to understand that some things just take mellowing in order to be themselves. This is as important for healing as it is for making soup. "Hurry up and fix it" or "Hurry up and get well" is another thing that people who work with victims have to guard against. Like, "I want you to be over it yesterday" and "Why aren't you further along?" But there's often a slow aging and distilling of the processes that are going on in healing. You just have to be able to say, "Hey, I trust your processes."

This also applies to theology. Theology is not like mathematics, it's not a discipline for young persons at the end of adolescence. It's a discipline in which you need *time* to experience and live with some insights, so you know what they mean over the long run. So we can look forward to doing it better as we get older. That's frustrating in another sense. Okay, now I've been living with this material all my life. Experientially, I came to consciousness about it in the early Seventies, I started teaching about it in the mid-Seventies. It's ten years now that I've been working with this material. Why am I not clearer about it? [Laughter] Right?

SBT: As though you should have written your systematic theology by now?

MP: Yes! As though I should turn it into a commodity, as though by a factory process. And it *isn't* that kind of process. It's a process of aging wine or aging cheese, or steeping your tea, in which the stuff just has to sit there awhile for you to know what it means, let alone how to say it with power.

SBT: Many women scholars are writing wonderful books at menopause. [Laughter] It's very true. And it's another way of looking at menopause, God knows.

MP: I'm in my forties. Am I about to become a wonderful writer? [Laughter]

SBT: Let this not be a source of pressure to you. [Laughter] You don't have to write a good book to be in menopause. It . . .

[Child's voice interrupts.]

SBT: You were saying something earlier about taking responsibility and taking appropriate action as part of healing. One issue that comes up is that traditional theology has often treated grace as forgiveness of sin. And you have interpreted grace as healing through these four stages. What have you learned about forgiveness of sin?

[Child's crying interrupts.]

MP: So, you were asking about action.

SBT: Yes, about the relationship between healing grace and the understanding of forgiveness. The old paradigm says: If you have been victimized, you must have sinned. This comes up in the book of Job, and Job rightly resists it. And it might imply that if you are healed, your sin is forgiven. Your discussion of those four stages seems to pull the supports out from under that traditional paradigm.

MP: Well, feminist theology has taught us that a lot of the tradition did not prepare us at all to understand the experience of women or racial, ethnic, minority persons, because we're just not there. Unless you bracket many of those traditional categories, it's almost impossible to understand the experience of survivors theologically. The patriarchy of traditional theological categories systematically distorts the experience of survivors of rape and battering and abuse in childhood. We could talk about the example of Augustine and *The City of God,* for instance. He simply did not know what he was talking about when he talked about the rape of consecrated virgins in the sack of Rome. Almost every sentence is false. And enraging, to someone reading about it today.

SBT: Probably also to the virgins.

MP: Well, we don't know how many of them read it, and we don't know what it did to them. We do know that later on in the tradition it became important. Should we go into Augustine a little here?

SBT: Yes, I think it's worth it.

MP: I've been writing a paper in which I started working some of this out. *The City of God* has several large sections in book 1 about the terrible things that happened to Christians in the fall of Rome, whether being tortured or having your goods stolen or being raped. Rape is discussed in sections 17 to 31. Augustine had a laudable end, which he got to by some extremely dislaudable means. He wanted to say to rape victims that they did not need to commit suicide, which he regarded as a mortal sin. So he says that for a rape victim to commit suicide after rape would be adding the sin of homicide to the sin of adultery. That tells you a lot about how he regarded rape.

SBT: Just how comforting is this?

MP: Well, it's very painful. Along the way, he used an elaborate body-mind dualism to say that if the victim did not enjoy the assault, then the sin belonged to the assailant. Since the will controlled the body it could be possible, especially for a consecrated virgin, to resist the most insidious, most enticing of pleasures. That was the framework with which he viewed the act of rape. And it's very curious, because in ancient Rome the pollution or the offense of rape was in a sense an objective fact.

SBT: Robbery?

MP: Yes, partly, but more it was pollution, it was a fundamental, ontological pollution that happened to a victim. A victim was defiled, and her defilement endangered everyone around her, and therefore she was to commit suicide in order to save her family from the ritual consequences, or the sacred consequences. In the story of Lucretia, for instance, she had absolutely no existential pangs about whether or not she had done wrong. She simply killed herself. But Augustine, who was classically in the movement from shame to guilt, sets up a whole series of reflections, which imply that the rape victim should ask herself, "What was my existential posture during the act?" and therefore, "Am I guilty, or not?" And so it ups the existential ante for women because it makes her "participation," her internal reflections or feelings during the act part of determining whether or not she's guilty. Anyone who knows anything about rape victims can only find this deeply unsettling.

Then there was a whole second part which was, "Why did God let this happen to good Christian women?" Augustine said that these women may have had unconscious pride, and that therefore God humbled them so that they would not in the future commit the sin of pride. There you have the existential redoubled, because it was *unconscious* pride. It was lurking infirmity that *might* one day betray them into a proud bearing. Typically pride is the sin that women have been castigated with. So victims have a double-whammy from Augustine.

SBT: Yes, oh yes.

MP: But this mass of confusions here, about whether or not the fact of being raped is adultery, and that God is doing this for your eternal good—those are not categories that help to understand the spiritual depth of what's going on in victims today, anymore than all of the terrible things that are said about battering in the tradition. So there you have this whole theological tradition distorting your vision when you are, say, hearing stories of victims.

This distortion is especially serious when we talk about forgiveness. Very frequently it's important to suggest to a victim of some previous sexual abuse that forgiving the offender is not necessarily what you have to do. Victims may be puzzled by that, or they may be released and relieved. "Do you mean it? I don't *have* to forgive him?" or "I don't have to forgive him *now?*" This traditional category which we have taken as the very substance of grace is precisely the opposite of grace for victims. Often for victims to hear that they don't need to forgive the offender *is* grace. And it is very hard for us who had been formed by the tradition to hear that. Because it says that some of our most cherished positive moments in the tradition are participating negatively in the oppression of people, and that we need to set them aside.

SBT: I'm still following your line of thinking about Augustine. You used the expression "spiritual depth." Could you say more about the spiritual, religious interpretation of that experience?

MP: You mean in the tradition?

SBT: No, in what you're saying. The tradition's had plenty of time to make its case. Would you say more about the case that you want to make.

MP: First, there is a conventionally religious dimension to all this. Many traditional themes can create a crisis for a survivor who might hear, for instance, that a woman should turn the other cheek if someone strikes her on one cheek. Her whole life can be thrust into question by hearing that. But more important, rising up out of this experience of the survivor and the movement, I would name three dimensions or three large areas for theological reflection. Each is complex. The first area is the CRISES THAT ARE INHERENT IN THE EXPERIENCES THEMSELVES, and there are four crises that I would name here. Then there are what I am beginning to call THE SACRED POWERS OF HEALING. And then there are THE SPIRITUAL DIMENSIONS OF ACTIVISM, OR OF EMPOWERMENT.

If we start with the crises, it's important to see that whether or not a person gets to church on Sunday or knows Bible verses, she faces inherent spiritual crises that arise from these abuses. First, these traumas are life-threatening experiences. They are occasions in which people say, "I could have been killed, I could have died." If you are raped, whether with a gun to your head, or by an acquaintance, people very frequently say, "I thought I was going to die." And as you know, battered women are painfully aware that maybe this time they survived the assault, but the next time, what if my forehead hits the sharp corner of the dining room table, or the next time I'm pushed down the stairs, what if I break my neck? Even victims of child abuse, where frequently there are no other kinds of physical violence, are terrorized to the same degree. So these crises contain the whole dimension of the existential quality of death—the realization that this could be my death—a fundamental spiritual crisis.

A second crisis comes up when the victim says to herself, "I have been sullied, I have been defiled, I need to wash." There are victims who wash compulsively, trying to get past that sense of defilement. There is another crisis I'm not sure how to express, about trust and betrayal. You don't trust people, you have been betrayed, depending upon who the assailant is. I think this is connected to our capacities to be religious in general, to trust the world. And a fourth big one about feeling crazy.

SBT: Oh yeah, "still crazy after all these years."

MP: Yeah, feeling like you are out of touch with reality. You don't know if you are going nuts or not.

Those are the crisis parts, but it's really important not to be mesmerized by them, because the healing after these traumatic assaults is the most important thing about them. People do not have to go on feeling victimized forever; they can recover a sense of joy and functioning, and in fact participate in the healing of others. They can be active in changing the world about these pains; they can help transform us all.

I would say there are several sacred powers of healing.

Surviving is a fundamental sacred power. Remembering is a sacred power that's fundamental to the healing process. Setting boundaries is part of this. Usually people have to learn what is them and what is not them anymore, how to say "no" in creative ways, and to realize they have the right to say "no." I'm not sure what to call the capacity for dealing with the craziness. It's something like being in touch with reality again, or trusting that you are in touch with reality.

On the empowerment side, I haven't worked these out quite as happily, but we need to include things like creating an environment of safety. Central to the empowerment model is the acknowledgment that justice is fundamental to the healing process. Even counseling a victim is a process of justice, because there is a dimension of interpersonal justice that is a part of what heals the person in need of healing. Establishing an environment of safety includes validating the feeling of this person as normal for one who has been threatened, just as it includes struggling for better police protection, laws, etc. Essential to this interpersonal justice is that it affirms and encourages the survivor to recognize her own power, or to live out of her own powers. Part of it is cherishing or reverencing this other person as someone who matters, as someone who has resources, and as someone that you are going to be *with*—not necessarily for or behind—but *next to*. And I, at least, experience the process of working with survivors as blessing, a process in which I feel most deeply blessed by people sharing their deepest stories with me, and by the kinds of survival skills that they have, and the creativity they use to survive this violence.

SBT: I am remembering your beginning biographical statement, in which you said to yourself, "I want to heal." I remarked that it was significant that you said this in the active voice, but you pointed out that healing is a complex process of both healing and being healed. "I heal and am healed." The survivor heals and she in some sense heals you as well, which does sort of undercut the so-called professional model of the therapeutic relationship.

MP: Well, the people who taught us what we know today about healing after sexual violence are survivors.

SBT: Yes, exactly.

MP: And much of the shelter movement or the crisis center movement is run by persons who have survived and healed, and who learned how to pass that on, or how to evoke that from other people.

SBT: I often say that about the Bible and battered women, "Oh, this was taught to me by abused women . . ."

[Interrupted by child calling, "Mom," recorder off]

MP: What you're saying about respect for the person's own beliefs, whatever they are, is very important. The point is not to make this person over in your own image, but to say, "You have resources that are honorable and important and good and strong, and you can develop others if you need to, and if you choose to." I guess offering options was the fourth aspect of empowerment. People sometimes don't have the information that they need in order to make choices. I'm not sure you would agree that this helps—on the religious part as well as other parts.

SBT: When you use the word "religious" or "spiritual," I think it might be important to say what you mean by that.

MP: Oh, I don't know what I mean by it.

SBT: Is this back in the messiness?

MP: Yes, I guess I mean something like the depth and the breadth and the width of experience, or . . . I don't know, I truly don't know. Do you have a working definition?

SBT: Well, I am always moved by something Beverly Harrison said in *God's Fierce Whimsy.* Bev said that God is in the connections, and it seemed to me that one of the things she might be saying is that the spiritual is the recognition of God in the other.

MP: Well, I don't know that I want to work with that one for this stuff. There are lots of victims who don't want to name God that way, who might not want to name God as part of this process at all. I find that using the word "spiritual" helps with many persons, rather than "theological," which often, I think, is part of the problem.

SBT: Well, would a victim put it to herself that way? Would *you* put it to yourself? Or do you think it's even useful in this chapter to put it that way, because people who read it would be put off? I don't want to press you farther than you're willing to go, but I'm trying to figure out what the content is, though, spiritual or religious? Questions like, "Who is the Holy Spirit?" And "How does she work?"

MP: Well, let me just start by—I don't know, I'm becoming totally incoherent. I think that when I . . .

SBT: This is like an exam question. [Laughter]

MP: What I'm trying to do is a phenomenology of women's religious or spiritual experience in the context of these violations. Until we do that, we will not know whether to correlate it with the Christian tradition or any of those traditional theological categories. This may or may *not* give rise to a *Christian* theology. It may or may not be possible to correlate with traditional Christian stances toward the world. It may transform some Christian theological stuff. Using categories like God and Holy Spirit seems like the question about forgiveness. How do these concepts limit our understanding? What does it make you blind to in the experiences of women? What does it filter out that you really need to be getting?

SBT: Like Ada Maria Isasi-Díaz and Yolanda Tarango's book, *Hispanic*

Women, Prophetic Voice in the Church.* They chose not to use traditional religious language because when they asked the women questions in traditional religious language, they gave traditional religious answers.

MP: Oh, God, yes!

SBT: When they asked these Hispanic women, "What's important to you?" they got very profound spiritual, religious information which was almost directly counter to the content of the explicitly religious language.

MP: I'm really glad to hear that, because I've had similar experiences counseling victims. Once I was working with a survivor who is a clergywoman, when I made what was a big mistake. I asked her something with "God" in it, like, "How does your faith, or your belief in God, connect up to what you've been saying?" And she said, "There's a hole in God's plan. He'll *never* forgive a little girl who fucked her daddy." This from a woman who had been assaulted by her father between the ages of three and twelve. I nearly went through the floor. I didn't know what had pulled that out. But later I went back in the conversation to ask, "Do you have some spiritual resources that have helped you to come through?" And she described a totally different set of things. She talked about going down into the abyss, further and further down until she touched bottom, and the bottom *held her up.* That there was something coming up from underneath her that held her up and without that she would not have been alive. It was totally different from the earlier punitive response. I think maybe it was just the use of the word "God" that pulled this whole punitive strand out and . . .

SBT: Like there was a computer God, you accessed all of the punitive associations with God.

MP: At least for her that was the case.

SBT: I think that the depth language seems to be your answer to what I am asking. I was trying to get at what we discussed on the phone preparing for this conversation, the difference between theological objectivity, that notion that there is some structure to religious experience that can be identified and that it is in fact the task of theological reflection to identify that objective structure, and psychobabble—if it happens to you, it's religion. How do we find the ground in between? I actually think that your discussion of the phenomenological is the answer to that; you don't find it in advance.

MP: Yes, although, of course, you have clues along the way, and I have a whole theological training that has filled my head with a lot of those concepts and categories, so it's not that they're coming from elsewhere. They're not extraterrestrial, or whatever.

SBT: In spite of Luther's opinions?

**Toward a Hispanic Women's Liberation Theology* (Harper & Row).

MP: Or Mary Daly's for that matter. I want to keep open some possibility for a variety of different theological options to appear without giving up some integrity here, not baptizing, as you said, everything that happens. Although personally, theologically I affirm that a human being is a religious being. You do not have a choice to opt out of religiousness, but you can choose to make your religiousness superficial by intention, or thoughtless by intention, or insightless, so it's always a back-and-forth dance for me—that people need to claim that they have a spiritual concern or spiritual interest or not, and if they don't want to claim it, then that, you know, is like the denial of victims. And hopefully, readiness to have a spiritual dimension or something like that also will occur in their lives.

[Interruption, recorder off]

MP: The more I talk about spirituality with people in the women's movement against violence against women, the more I hear people saying, "Let's talk about that, because I'm interested in it." There's a hunger to speak about it, and sometimes confusion, as if they're saying, "Well, if we start talking this language, will we be stuck with the patriarchal options? Will we offend people whose beliefs are different from ours? Will we be caught in the same old imperialistic trap that's trying to turn everybody into my theology?"

This can be a real hangup for women on crisis lines who may themselves be post-Christian. Let us say, suppose someone calls with a question from a deeply Fundamentalist perspective. The rape crisis worker may not know how to deal with the religious difference between them, and may end up not responding to those conventional or conservative religious questions for fear of offending the other person, or for fear of screwing it up. But once you build trust and start asking about people's experiences, and what they mean to them, and what the importance of it is, then they begin to talk this spiritual language. I find this fascinating.

SBT: I wonder if maybe we ought to do two things at this point. One, ask if there are other subjects under the heading HEALING AND GRACE that we have not touched, that need to go in here. But then, secondly, come to closure, and then have our next conversation about the transcription.

MP: I think there are a couple of other topics. One, while the healing process belongs to the survivor, her capacities to recuperate and recover are the most important things. I personally want to start saying things about creation at this point. It's important not to understand this as the dualism of the patriarchal tradition. Sometimes people say that disclosure begins the healing process, that it is the act of telling someone else about it that starts the recovery. To me that speaks about the depth dimensions of our *social* reality. This process of healing happens in relation to another person, and of course, having them respected by the other is what gets this healing movement under way. That seems profoundly important to me.

And that's related to whether "I am healing" and "I am being healed" are opposites or contrasts. If I am doing it, is God not connected? I've learned profoundly from survivors here. There is one I quote in particular, Susan Jeansonne, who says very dramatically "I did everything I could to survive, but I know it was the grace of God." She was able to have both those things in the same statement, rather than to have them as opposites.

That sense of "both-and" was important. When you were talking a minute ago, I was thinking of the gestalt concept of figure and ground. You know: If you look at the picture of the vase in one way, it's a vase, and if you move your head just slightly, or perform some odd operation in your mind, it turns into two faces in profile. So it could certainly be my own actions and nothing but my own actions, or it could be grace, and somehow *both* of these are true in the same event. And that is *my* experience of healing. I've worked very hard to heal, and at the same time it was the experience of a gift to me, something that came to me from outside myself. We need to find some way to work on both ends of that. You said something wonderful on the phone yesterday: these two polarities move out to meet each other, rather than being on opposite sides of a ravine. I liked that very much. There is this strong sense that yes, my own act and the gift character of it reach out to each other.

SBT: Yes, a very powerful image of the readiness for healing.

MP: Yes. And the more I do to heal myself, the more I experience it as a gift. And the more I experience it as a gift, the freer I am to work on it in my own self. There's a wonderful meshing there that seems to me very fruitful.

[Child interrupts with question and conversation.]

SBT: You said something on the phone about the ordinariness of grace.

MP: Yes, that's important. None of this healing is esoteric or arcane. You don't need to be in graduate school for ten years to help a victim heal, you don't need an M.D. or lots of letters behind your name.

SBT: Actually, I think it's counterproductive. [Laughter]

MP: I sometimes say that the healing that goes on with victims is *religious* but it isn't *magic*. You don't have to go off into the mountains and study with an esoteric practitioner to get all the secrets. These are all open secrets. It's all public now. And it's all very simple in a sense, although I've got several clear concepts here for understanding healing and sometimes it *is* complicated. But in a sense, what's complex is to get at how simple healing can be. These are perfectly ordinary propensities that anyone can use, and that people *do* use every day.

SBT: Well, I don't find ordinary and complex mutually exclusive. Ordinary life is actually very complex. Most battered women manage extremely complex lives by very ordinary means. And, in fact, I would say esoteric means a willful exclusion of the complexities of ordinary life.

MP: Oh, wonderful.

SBT: I often think that theories are far more simplistic than the ordinary reality that they attempt to explain.

MP: Yes, well, that is true.

SBT: It's reductionistic, and . . . I'm very attracted to your theme of messiness. I often have to do this in teaching constructive theology—talk about the unresolved in theology. You know, when you assemble the bicycle, when you do the constructive theology, there are always all these pieces left over. How do you account for that? What is your mechanism for accounting for the fact that not everything fits? So I would put ordinary and complex in the same group.

MP: That's helpful.

SBT: Esoteric-theoretical language is distorted and oversimplified for the purposes of cleaning life up. Such language is close to falsification—not all the time, because theoretical models can help you organize complexity in different ways, so I think they can be valuable, but they can also be extremely distorting and unhelpful. One of the distortions is that everything is supposed to fit, whereas in fact, not everything does fit. If everything fits you have broken something to make it fit—warped it or distorted it.

MP: That speaks to me, because I have one of those minds that likes to put it all together, to see if we can get it all in.

SBT: Unified Field Theory. [Laughter] Now, you see, the point is that Einstein showed that this doesn't exist. *You're* the one who is dumping on mathematical models.

MP: I like complicated Victorian houses where there are lots and lots of rooms inside. [Laughter] Rather than . . .

SBT: Split level . . .

MP: Ranch houses.

SBT: Well, you know some purses carry more than others. [Laughter] What we are after, of course, is the consummate purse, that you could just open up and have the entire kitchen inside, but . . .

MP: That's fun because I have a vest that has 22 pockets in it, and I use it instead of a purse. [Laughter]

SBT: But even that can only carry so much, you know. There are more and more adequate models, but you don't have the consummate model, you know, in which everything fits. And I think that's much better, morally much more accessible. I mean, I've seen people who carry around purses that are, you know, paper thin, and they have the comb, the pressed hankie, and the American Express card. That's deeply offensive. [Laughter]

MP: Yes, the ordinariness of the processes, I think, is really important. And it doesn't need a lot of footnoting. It is maybe part of my Christian background to look for the extraordinary in the ordinary, or to see or to form my eyes so as to see when the very mundane thing begins to shimmer around the edges and to speak values beyond itself, or to point at something else, or to begin to glow, even though it's not shiny at all. I'm not sure how to talk about that. To look for parables maybe in ordinary stories, or . . .

SBT: Yes, well, in a sense that's the essence of a parable, a statement of the extraordinariness of spiritual depth that is present in ordinary life. You know, it might just be a mustard seed, but on the other hand, it could also, you know, be faith.

MP: Yes, or like the image of the floor. She might be only sweeping the floor, or she might be looking for the lost coin.

SBT: Yes. Good.

MP: I don't have any other things to add beyond that. Do you have some other things you want to add?

SBT: No, I think that covers it.

RECOMMENDED READING

1. Bass, Ellen, and Laura Davis. *The Courage to Heal: A Guide for Women Survivors of Child Sexual Abuse.* San Francisco: Harper & Row, 1988.
2. Bussert, Joy. *Battered Women: From a Theology of Suffering to an Ethic of Empowerment:* Philadelphia: Fortress, 1986.
3. Pellauer, Mary D., Barbara Chester, and Jane Boyajian, eds. *Sexual Assault and Abuse: A Handbook for Clergy and Religious Professionals.* San Francisco: Harper & Row, 1987.
4. Schechter, Susan. *Women and Male Violence: The Visions and Struggles of the Battered Women's Movement.* Boston: South End, 1982.

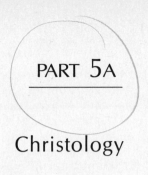

PART 5A

Christology

Introduction to Part 5A

Christology is, as Jacquelyn Grant points out, the answer to Jesus' question, "Who do you say that I am?" It is the answer given to that question by *Christians,* as Carter Heyward emphasizes. These two theologians, Black womanist[1] and white feminist, construct through their own lives the *particularity* of the liberation approach to christology. Christology done from liberation perspectives moves from the particular to the universal and not the other way around. These particulars make a difference. As James Cone once said, "After all, Jesus was not born a Roman Emperor."

Jesus of Nazareth was a person, trained as a carpenter, who traveled and preached in the area of Palestine during the reigns of the Roman emperors Augustus and Claudius. He was crucified by the authority of the local Roman governor, Pontius Pilate. This crucifixion precipitated a crisis among his followers. Some of them became convinced that Jesus was not dead, but had risen, and they traveled throughout the Greco-Roman world proclaiming that message (Acts 2ff.).

In Reginald Fuller's famous description, "The proclaimer became the proclaimed, and the implicit christology of Jesus becomes the explicit christology of the church."[2] The New Testament is a record of the proclaimer's words and deeds filtered through the thought world of both Judaism and Hellenism. There are many christological viewpoints in the New Testament scriptures.

Central to the New Testament teaching about Jesus are the beliefs that Jesus is Emmanuel, God-with-us (a belief perhaps rooted in the practice of praying to Jesus as in baptismal liturgies [1 Cor. 6:11]), and that Jesus' death was not accidental, but part of a plan of God for human salvation (1 Cor. 15:3, 2 Cor. 5:19). After the period of Roman persecution waned, Christian believers began to ask themselves how Jesus, the carpenter of Nazareth, could also be God. They also began to speculate on how the special person of Jesus was related to God's plan for human salvation.

The first question was addressed by the Council of Nicea (325 C.E.); the second was addressed by the Council of Chalcedon (451 C.E.). As Carter Heyward's chapter makes clear, the decisions of both of these councils were heavily influenced by the philosophical viewpoints of the surrounding Hellenistic culture. Greek philosophy, especially in the thought of Plato, posited a wide gulf between that which belonged to divinity (immutability, impassibility, etc.) and that which belonged to humanity (change, decay, etc.). The councils did not exactly answer the problem this gulf posed for thinking about who Jesus is. The formulas of the councils are more a judgment on what *must be said,* and *what must not be said.* The formula of Nicea maintained that it must be said that Jesus is *homoousios*—of the same nature—with God, and that it must not be said that Jesus is subordinate in any way to God. The formula of Chalcedon held that it must be said that Jesus is one person in two natures, and it must not be said that either of these two natures is in any way changed or diminished by the incarnation.

The history of Christian thought on Jesus has moved for the most part within the boundaries set by the councils, with one pole aspect often emphasized more by some theologians than others. (Peter Abelard, for example, emphasized the human pole of Jesus' person and work; St. Thomas Aquinas emphasized the divine pole.) What Heyward wants us to understand is, in fact, the limitations of this polarity. Classical christology is shaped by a "troublesome *dualism* between divinity and humanity," where dualism is understood as an assumption of opposition. "Whether in relation to the knowledge of God or Christ, of ourselves or the world, we can know something only insofar as we are unlike it."

Modern theology, which is usually dated from the work of Friedrich Schleiermacher (1768–1834), has almost wholly emphasized the human pole of this same dualistic framework. This is called "christology from below" in which, in Schleiermacher's schema, we reason that Christ is divine from the effects of Christ in the Christian community.[3] Karl Barth's famous challenge to Schleiermacher is that the Protestant liberalism Schleiermacher represents presumes too great a continuity between divinity and humanity. For Barth everything that is stands on one side of a great chasm and on the other stands God.[4] In Barth's later theology this chasm is to some degree filled in, but never completely bridged.[5] For Rudolf Bultmann, a contemporary of Barth, the quest for objectivity of revelation is an evasion of the human task of responding to revelation. Influenced by existentialist philosophy, Bultmann maintained that Jesus Christ is the present (not past) point of encounter between the divine and the human.

Barth once used the image of a bridge to explain Schleiermacher's theological method.[6] The best contemporary representatives of a bridge motif in christology are the process theologians. One of them, John Cobb, has said that "Jesus, without in any way ceasing to be human, participated in that one structure of existence in which the self is coconstituted by the presence of God."[7] For this process theologian, whose work draws heavily on the philosophy of Alfred North Whitehead, christology represents the entire process of cosmic creativity.

It is of great methodological import, according to Jacquelyn Grant, that each above-mentioned theologian not only assumes the dualism that plagues traditional christological discussions, but also that Jesus is white and male. When Jesus asks, "Who do *you* say that I am?" the accent falls on the word *you*. The one being asked has a role in answering the question, which makes her or him into a subject in salvation history and not just an object moved about in a divine plan. When this question is answered by a Black woman, christology changes dramatically. Those on the "top-side of history," the white male Christian theologians, have different experiences of subjectivity than those on "the underside of history." The difference between the two locations is profoundly one of race. People of color have never been seen by Euro-Americans as rightly subjects of their own history. In the racist underpinnings of Greek mind/ body dualism, they have been maligned as lacking in rationality and hence something less than human. The difference is also profoundly one of sex. Black women in particular have not been seen as subjects, but as objects of sexual, as well as racial, exploitation.

In throwing the emphasis on the one who answers as subject in salvation history, Grant shows some existentialist influence. But she is even more profoundly influenced by Black women's history in America and by those who not only survived this experience but prevailed, such as Jarena Lee. Grant quotes Lee and summarizes Black womanist christological method: "If the man may preach, because the Savior died for him, why not the woman? Seeing he died for her also. Is he not a whole Savior, instead of half of one? As those who hold it wrong for a woman to preach would seem to make it appear."

Liberation theologians ground christology in the performance criteria of *liberative praxis*. But this praxis is not reducible to the mere "effects" of which Schleiermacher spoke. The real issues are not the Enlightenment-dictated problems of freedom and reason, but the concrete encounter with the Jesus who is on the side of the victims of human history. The person of Christ is inseparable from this work to liberate people from concrete realities of race, sex, and class exploitation. This concrete, particular approach to christology makes universal claims, but only after it has moved through the particulars of different contexts of struggle. This is why Heyward contends that the task of christology is to move it away from its classical grounding in a dualistic ontology "toward an ethics of justice-making which happens only in a praxis of relational particularity and cooperation."

Therefore the christologies done from the particular contexts of Black womanists will be different from those done from the contexts of white feminists. White feminist christological perspectives may inform, but will ultimately be inadequate to the "whole Jesus" of whom Jarena Lee spoke. The whole Jesus of Black womanists stands as a challenge to white feminist christologies. For both Grant and Heyward the fullness of the incarnation is impugned by any christology enclosed in a false universalism, regardless of whether that universalism is based on one race, one class, one sex, or one sexual orientation. Both also voice the urgent need for all Christians to move together toward the whole Jesus through a "praxis of relational particularity and cooperation."

CHAPTER 13

Jesus of Nazareth/Christ of Faith: Foundations of a Reactive Christology

CARTER HEYWARD

CONTEXT AND COMMITMENT

I'm one of Gramsci's "organic intellectuals," though I doubt he had theologians or women in mind—much less lesbian women priests.

With ten other women, I was "irregularly" ordained an Episcopal priest in 1974 and banned immediately from functioning in the Episcopal Church. The ban was lifted two years later when the denomination authorized the ordination of women, but the stigma of having been irregularly ordained remains to this day. I'm grateful for this "sacred stigma," which not only links me to other movements of resistance to injustice but also signals my ongoing "irregular" vocation from business-as-usual.

In 1979, I came out as a lesbian in order to work in a less intellectually and pastorally cluttered way in the context of a religious tradition which, since the fourth century, has (often secretly) put sexuality at the center of its doctrine, discipline, and worship. That same year, I began focusing on christology in my scholarship. With other feminist theologians, I started making connections between what the church historically has taught about Christ's *power-over* our lives and how "he" has been used to bludgeon self-respecting women and other sexual dissenters (e.g., homosexuals) as well as Jews, Moslems, witches, and practitioners of other faith-traditions.

By the time Reagan became president in 1981, I had discovered that our civil and ecclesiastical institutions, from marriage to the military to the worship of Christ, are based on intrinsically abusive nonmutual power relations. These power dynamics have been secured in subsequent years, setting a troubling, critical agenda for justice-seeking folks in this nation and elsewhere.

During the past decade, trips to Cuba, Canada, Latin America, and Europe have helped sharpen my perspective on the United States in relation to the rest of the world. We are the most dangerous, arrogant, and self-preoccupied nation on earth, but there is hope for us, just as there is for the rest of the world. Our hope stirs among those who will suffer oppression no more, not only elsewhere in the world but here among us.

Most of my current work is at the Episcopal Divinity School in Cambridge, Massachusetts, where I teach Anglican, systematic, feminist, and liberation theologies. In the seminary, I'm helping shape emergent degree programs in feminist liberation theology, in which we are studying together how to participate, gladly and for the long haul, in the struggle for justice.

CONSTRUCTION

It is my thesis in this chapter that the historical doctrinal pull between Jesus of Nazareth and Jesus Christ, the human Jesus and his divine meaning, is no longer, if it ever was, a place of creative christological inquiry. Worse, it is a distraction from the daily praxis of liberation which is the root and purpose of Christian faith. I arrived at this thesis by working on this chapter and, over a two year period, re-working it in dialogue with a number of other womanist and feminist Christian theologians of liberation.[1]

During the summer of 1986 I was preparing to teach a christology class in the fall and was working on a paper to present at the American Academy of Religion. My paper was to focus on the tension between the historical Jesus and the eternal Christ as an *inadequate* locus of christological inquiry. The motive behind my interest was a desire to know more about why most christology bores me although the Jesus story has always generated my passionate interest.

Since childhood I have been more interested in images of Jesus as brother and friend than of Christ as King and Lord (except for a brief excursus as a teenager into Anglo-Catholicism). Still, I began my preparation for my paper (which would become in time this chapter) on the hunch that Jesus of history apologists, as much as their Christ of faith counterparts, tend to present as simplistic and one-dimensional that which can be experienced only in angles and contours of bold relief.

My interest was not primarily in constructing a christology but rather in pruning away some of the tangle of christological clutter, to see what might be found. I began this pruning on the basis of two classical christological assumptions: first, that the terms *humanity* and *divinity* signify from within our subjective experience two discrete objective qualities of what we can know and love; and that we come to know these objective realities as polarities, opposites: what we are (human), God is not, and vice versa. Human beings die, for example; divine being does not.

My second assumption was that christology is the study of in what sense Christians maintain that humanity and divinity were and are joined in the person of Jesus, making him thereby for Christians the Messiah, or Christ, to whom Hebrew scriptures refer.

It seemed to me at the outset of this study that the pendulum swing between Jesus of history and Christ of faith has continued historically to reflect a vitality in theological movement whereby no theological persona or period can become too smug or stuck in a particular christological dogma.[2]

I did not see clearly, until I began wrestling with this study in a class of Christian feminists, that the tension between the Jesus of history and the Christ of faith poles in christological development reflects less a vitality than an obscurity. It obscures the troublesome dualism between divinity and humanity in which christology originated. This dualism continues to shape the dominant forms of Christian faith and praxis to this day and constitutes the chief philosophical claim against which liberation theologians struggle intellectually.[3]

This essay reflects what I have been learning even in its preparation: that classical christology, as an arena of pastoral, constructive, or liturgical work, is dead. Its symbolic universe belongs to the history of Christian thought which, when studied honestly, reveals the history of Christian power relations. By that, I mean the history of how the church, in its doctrine, discipline, and worship, has legitimated the use of ecclesial, civil, and social power as either coercive control or voluntary cooperation.

The first part of this essay is a critical interpretation of the Jesus of history and Christ of faith postures in christological development. The second part is a preliminary constructive christological effort in the form of notes I used in teaching the christology class to seminarians in the fall of 1986. In these notes I attempt to stir some soil at what seem to me the roots of a feminist liberation christology.

BEYOND JESUS OF HISTORY AND CHRIST OF FAITH

Christology must be redefined as a theological discipline if the Jesus story is to be redemptive for Christian women of different colors, cultures, and classes;[4] for men and other earth-creatures who are marginalized and kept powerless by those who control the social order often explicitly "in the name of Christ";[5] and for those who stand as advocates in solidarity with oppressed people and a violated earth. It is this process of redefinition that calls for the re-imaging of Jesus/Christ beyond the traditional dualistic pull between his humanity and divinity— and not only his but ours as well.

Heretofore I have steered clear of this burial ground of the "God-Man" of classical Christian faith by keeping my christological interests under control. I have done this by doing what most Christian theologians, however radical or reactionary, progressive or conservative, have done since at least the late patristic period (fifth century c.e.). I have refused to think the unthinkable—to think, that is, outside the boundaries set by the fathers as definitive of Christian faith in Jesus/Christ.

As feminist and humanist, I've attempted with others to bring down to earth "high christologies" (which tend to prevail in most Anglicanism) and to raise up "low christologies" (which often characterize the praxis of liberation). From either angle, moving down with divinity or rising up with humanity, I have tried to help produce images of Jesus Christ on the basis of terms provided by traditional christology. I have not argued seriously with the classical doctrine that Jesus Christ was and is both divine and human. I still do not. The classical framework has given me both an ideological target for my frustrations with the hierarchical, dualistic foundations of Christian thought and a pastoral and liturgical ground upon which to stand in sharing the language of faith with other Christians. It was in a pastoral spirit of inquiry that I began my work on Jesus of history and Christ of faith.

Leaping into the currents of Christian dualism, I began my christological divining, garbed somewhat awkwardly in gear provided by a coalition of liberation, Anglican, lesbian, and feminist constituencies. Looking for Jesus on the one hand and Christ on the other, I found him—both of him.

I found Jesus, the man in whom the Logos dwelt; the man whom "enlightened" men have pursued in their quests, old and new, for moral leaders and spiritual friends. I found the brother whose little sister got lost somewhere along the way. I found the fleshy, bloody, suffering, subversive, fully human one from Nazareth.

"The historical Jesus" refers to the discrete historical work of such men as Reimarus and Strauss[6] and, more inclusively, to the objective focus of christology which is done from below.[7] Since the nineteenth century, the focus on Jesus has represented a rational, humanistic impulse over against the excesses of supernaturalism.

But the pendulum swing toward the Jesus of history is not necessarily an affirmation of humanity. It can serve as a means of perpetuating the notion of a deity who remains above human experience, a god who really is not involved with us. If, in emphasizing Jesus' humanness, we contend that Jesus was fully and only human (as I myself wrote a decade ago),[8] such a claim can be interpreted as a rejection of the reality or possibility of incarnation. In any case, to make the historical Jesus one's starting point in christology is to take a reactive posture and, in so doing, to fall in line with the presuppositions of classical christology that divinity and humanity can be comprehended most fully as polar opposites.

Let us move on within the classical framework to the Christ of faith, in which the human spirit can be uplifted by faith that God, in fact, became man [*sic*]. (I must confess that in studying christology I find myself awash in a sea of sexist language and discover that I respond to it much the way I would to tobacco if I were a reformed smoker and were to take another cigarette. Does classical christology lock us necessarily into the relation between Father and Son as the locus of universal redemption? In writing this chapter, I decided not to fight the sexist habit but rather go with it on a hunch that, in its classical terms, christology is actually an exercise in patriarchal logic.) So back to faith in Christ: He is the Redeemer of Schleiermacher's self-consciousness,[9] the Christ-event of Bultmann's *kerygma*,[10] the Spirit of Charity undergirding God's Kingdom in this world according to Frederick Denison Maurice.[11] To know Christ is to worship Jesus as Lord on the basis of a faith that in him we are met, readied, grasped, or otherwise saved from our fallen state by one who was and is himself the Son of God so fully, so eternally, as to be God the Son.

This Christ is both in and outside of time and history. To love the divine Savior, who descended from above so that we might ascend in him, is to rise *spiritually* above the movement of human history. To study this christology is to work "from above." This Christ-of-faith movement has been undergirded by a commitment to the spiritual power of One whose human life was only a partial and momentary occasion in his larger life. Such a christology recently has signalled a mystical response to the superrationalism, which, in the modern period, has taken forms of naturalism or humanism. In this context, faith in the eternal Christ can (though often it does not) inspire moral courage with which to contend against the principalities and powers of this world on the basis of a higher call to follow Christ rather than the ruler of this present historical order. Such was the faith of many of the nineteenth century English Tractarians who, in the Oxford Movement, were wed fiercely to the sacred and eternal relation between the Father and His Christ, the Son, as the locus of salvation.[12]

Desmond Tutu is a contemporary reminder that a Christ of faith need not lure us away from responding to human need.[13] To emphasize the divinity of Jesus can be a means of sacralizing humanity in the image of Christ. Nonetheless it is true that, like the historical Jesus posture, the Christ-of-faith emphasis reflects historically a reactive posture in which we are moved onto the dualistic ground of classical christology, in which divinity and humanity are oppositional pulls in our lives and commitments.

Let me push a little further in this critique of the dualistic epistemology of christology as a theological discipline. Writing in 1853 of those searching for the historical Jesus, Frederick Denison Maurice charged, "instead of recognizing an impassable chasm between the human and the divine, they became in their minds utterly confounded."[14] He continues, "[the Straussians] conceive Divinity only as an apotheosis of humanity."[15] For Maurice, as later for Barth and other critics of the quest of the historical Jesus, the problem with its intense focus on the human Jesus is that its adherents seem simply to name as divine whatever they admire in Jesus, which seems moreover to reflect whatever they admire in themselves. Writing of all such theological attempts to "work up from earthly ground" (foreshadowing contemporary "theologies from below"), Maurice contended that such efforts "form abstractions called 'god,' in which 'God' becomes anything, everything, and nothing."[16]

The warning may be taken by those who look to Jesus to reflect back to us whatever we most admire in ourselves. But is the same temptation not also true for Christ-of-faith theologians? Do such people not also find, mystically in Christ rather than rationally in the Jesus story, what they are looking for in their experiences and in their efforts to live admirably? Is the Word of God of Barth's *Dogmatics* necessarily any less self-serving than the Jesus of Strauss' *Life, Critically Examined*? Is not each of these Christian men, as Schweitzer wrote of Schleiermacher, to some extent in search of the Jesus Christ of his own politic?[17]

The problem in most christological work, whether rooted primarily in Jesus or Christ, is twofold: Theologians tend not to acknowledge in what sense they work for themselves, writing to make sense of their own lives. This is a problem of dishonest praxis. To acknowledge one's self-interest in theological work, far from being selfish, is to be responsible for what one is authorizing. But there is a more fundamental problem with the location of christological origins, and that is the problem named already of a dualistic epistemology, which is a wrong relational way of knowing whatever we know about Jesus, Christ, ourselves, the world, or God.

WRONG RELATION IN CHRISTOLOGICAL EPISTEMOLOGY: FALSE KNOWING

Let me examine briefly the connection between dualism and nonrelationality in christological epistemology. Dualism is steeped in an assumption of opposition: whether in relation to the knowledge of God or Christ, of ourselves or the world, we can know something only insofar as we are unlike it. Man is unlike woman. Spirit is unlike flesh. Light is unlike darkness. Heaven is unlike earth. God is unlike humanity. In a dualistic praxis, "the other" is always better or worse, more or less, than oneself or one's people. Identity is forged and known by contrast and competition, not by cooperative relation. Dualism is cultivated in a praxis of alienation between men and women, rich and poor, light and dark, and, in the image of such oppositions, divinity and humanity.[18]

The prevailing shape of Christian anthropology is linked causally and effectively to this problem: in our fallen (sinful) condition, human being is less, and worse, than divine being. In fact, in relation to divinity, we human beings are *bad*. The christological solution to this problem has been historically to assume that in the person of Jesus, divine and human being overcame the dualism generated by the fall. The split was healed, the brokenness made whole, and now, in the spirit of Jesus, which is Christ, all human beings are called to participate in this continuing redemptive process.

The problem with this scenario is a double one: in worshipping Jesus as *the* Christ, *the* Son, *the* Savior, we close our eyes to the possibility of actually seeing that the sacred liberating Spirit is *as* incarnate here and now among us as She was in Jesus of Nazareth. Reflecting this same tendency is the similarly exclusivistic assumption that Christians are *the* people with *the* way, *the* truth, and *the* life. Thus, as Christians, we learn to recognize ourselves primarily *as different from* "the world," "pagans," "heretics," Jews, and so forth.

Dualism is wrong relation. A dualistic epistemology is steeped in a wrong way of knowing and thus generates false knowledge and lies, about ourselves, others, that which we believe to be divine, and the significance of the Jesus story. To do christology, as most men have done it, on the basis of wrong relation, is to begin on the assumption that Christians alone are in right relation to God and, as such, have a monopoly on the knowledge and love of God. Another is that Christians are more responsible morally, spiritually, and liturgically for preserving a right relation with our own religious heritage than with sisters and brothers who currently inhabit the earth with us. A wrong relational epistemology, rooted in dualism, causes us to imagine that some of us or our people (in whose interests we work) know it all—about Jesus Christ, redemption, God, or ourselves.

Theological narcissism, the preoccupation with oneself and one's god in one's image—or in the image of one's racial, gender, cultural, or religious roots—is a foundational component of the theological structure of ruling class (read white affluent Christian male) privilege. This privileged narcissism has been basic to the development of dominant christological models in Europe and the United States, in which God and Jesus come out looking like actors in a Hollywood movie.

We should be clear that this tendency, to create divinity in our own image, reflects all of us to some degree. It is not wrong to create theological and christological images of ourselves. In fact, it is vital to our well-being and to our taking responsibility for what we are doing in the name(s) of God. But to leave the matter there is more than abstractly wrong, it is destructive of the created/creative world we share. It is wrong to close the canons at the end of one's own story or that of one's people. This is the epistemological fallacy that has given us the dominant christological image of the blue-eyed, fair-haired Jesus as Lord of all. It is also the twist that provokes Christian objections to the Christa, the sculpted image of a full-bodied, nude female Christ on a cross.[19] The reification of one's own experience has, as its cause, a wrong relational, dualistic epistemology and as its consequence a christology in which the Christian Redeemer with the most salvific power in any situation is the one who comes wrapped in the neatest conceptual package on behalf of those who hold the social, political, and ecclesiastical power.

Both the Jesus-of-history and the Christ-of-faith models of redemption have been constructed historically to combat such narcissism—to challenge, for example, the arrogance of ecclesiastical authorities or the obsessive preoccupation of many Christians with their own interior lives as the beginning and end of spirituality. But in attempting to correct such mistakes, both Christ of faith and historical Jesus images have served primarily to move the debate in a circle, back again into a self-defensive posturing which signals the drawing of christological wagons around our own sacred goats—be they privatized spirituality or the readily misleading notion that where the bishop is, there is the church.[20]

What has been missing in the dominant structures of Christian faith and discourse has been *a praxis of relational particularity and cooperation*, in which theological knowing might cease to be a matter of discovering *the* Christ and might become rather a matter of generating together images of what is redemptive or liberating in particular situations. In a praxis of relational particularity, we might discover that what is *not* liberating—from a Christian perspective, what is *not* christic—frequently is that which the Christian churches have associated most closely with Jesus/Christ. What is not liberating is any relationship or system which is closed to discovery, new truths, and self-criticism, and which refuses welcome to new or different people, ideas, and possibilities. There is no room for creative, liberating interpretations of the Jesus story and there is no way for christic meanings to be generated in a praxis of wrong relation.

CONCLUSION

Jesus was a Jewish male with a particular relationship to his *abba*. Christ may be for Christians the salvific implications of the Jesus story. Or Christ may be the characterization of justice-making with compassion, courage, and integrity which can be interpreted as human or divine and is, in fact, both at once. *The christological task of Christian feminism may be to move the foundations of christology from the ontology of dualistic opposition toward the ethics of justice-making, which can happen only in a praxis of relational particularity and cooperation.* Neither the politics (hierarchical power relations) nor the symbolic universe of ruling-class fathers and sons can be a creative, liberating spiritual movement for women or for poor, or otherwise marginalized, men.

As a feminist theologian of liberation, I've come to believe that an effort to do christology in classical terms (Was Jesus divine? Was he human?) is much like trying to draw fresh milk from a very sick, tired, dry, sacred, and, as it turns out, very male goat. Christian feminists and others committed not only to the work of justice but also to holding our theologies and christologies accountable to this work must set new terms for our faith, including especially new terms for what we preach and teach about Jesus Christ and for how we live in relation to the Jesus story and its christic meanings.

I offer the following preliminary notes as a way into such christological work:

1. Christology is the study of who and what Jesus Christ was and is *for Christians.*
2. Christological truths are rooted in the connections between various particular human experiences of ourselves in relation to the sacred (that which gives purpose, value, dignity, and hope to our lives).
3. A basic christological connection we must make is between the story of the particular man, Jesus of Nazareth, and our stories. This is basic because it is the connection which, historically and communally, has been used and abused as a primary vehicle for organizing the world. (Whether or not we are Christian, it behooves us to understand this and know where we stand in relation to this use and abuse of power.)
4. Christological truth is neither unchanging nor universally applicable. It is created in the social, historical, personal praxis of right relation, which is always normative—central—in christology.
5. While christology is philosophical language about salvation from wrong relation, it is more basically an ethical language of advocacy, love, action, and survival.[21]
6. Christology must be for Christians a collaborative process with roots in confessional, prophetic action shaped by the questions, "Who are we standing with?" "Who are we for?"
7. Christology is not a neutral process. It is an adventure undertaken in the realm of accountability to the poor, to women, to all marginalized and trivialized peoples—and especially to all who historically have been persecuted in the name of Christ.
8. Christ emerges in the contemporary crossroads of religious and spiritual pluralism: global movements for liberation from oppression; a feminist commitment to justice for women and to making connections between the liberation of women and of all who suffer injustice; and commitments to a sane and respectful relation to the earth and its varied creatures.
9. Christ in the "small places" of our lives is the same spirit of liberation as She who holds the stars and spins the planets in her hands.
10. Our most fully christic experiences are our most fully embodied—sensual and erotic—connections in relation to one another, other earth creatures, and the earth itself.

11. The truths or lies of our christological claims become evident in the fruits of our lives: how we relate to one another and the world.

12. In doing christology, white Christian feminists need to pay careful, respectful attention to what Christian feminists and womanists of color are writing and saying about Jesus/Christ, and to what Jewish feminists are writing and saying about anti-Semitism among Christian feminists.

13. Our christologies must be always open to change, ever able to be revised in relation to those whose well-being we do not know or may fail to consider and in relation to the limits of what we are able to know about ourselves or about the Holy in any particular praxis.

RECOMMENDED READING

Borowitz, Eugene B. *Contemporary Christologies: A Jewish Response.* New York: Paulist, 1980.

Brock, Rita Nakashima. "The Feminist Redemption of Christ." In *Christian Feminism: Visions of a New Humanity,* edited by Judith Weidman. San Francisco: Harper & Row, 1985.

Cone, James H. *A Black Theology of Liberation.* 2d ed. Maryknoll, NY: Orbis, 1986.

Driver, Tom F. *Christ in a Changing World: Toward an Ethical Christology.* New York: Crossroad, 1981.

Elwood, Douglas J. *Asian Christian Theology: Emerging Themes.* Philadelphia: Westminster, 1980.

Gottwald, Norman K., ed. *The Bible and Liberation: Political and Social Hermeneutics.* Maryknoll, NY: Orbis, 1983.

Heyward, Isabel Carter. *The Redemption of God: A Theology of Mutual Relation.* New York: University Press of America, 1982.

Knitter, Paul F. *No Other Name? A Critical Survey of Christian Attitudes Toward the World Religions.* Maryknoll, NY: Orbis, 1985.

Míguez Bonino, José. *Faces of Jesus: Latin American Christologies.* Maryknoll, NY: Orbis, 1984.

Sobrino, Jon, S.J. *Christology at the Crossroads.* Maryknoll, NY: Orbis, 1976.

Soelle, Dorothee. *Beyond Mere Obedience: Reflections on a Christian Ethic for the Future.* Minneapolis, MN: Augsburg, 1970.

Thurman, Howard. *Jesus and the Disinherited.* Richard, IN: Friends United, 1976.

CHAPTER 14

Subjectification as a Requirement for Christological Construction

JACQUELYN GRANT

CONTEXT AND COMMITMENT

As a collective "I," Black women have been saddled with labels and definitions. They have been called matriarchs; they've been blamed for the ills of the Black community; they've been considered sexually promiscuous; and to facilitate the needs of whites, they were reduced to maids, mammies, and other service workers. Zora Neale Hurston conveys through the words of one of her characters in *Their Eyes Were Watching God*[1] that Black women function as the mules of the world, that is, they carry the burdens of the world. They are among the poorest of the poor and among the most oppressed of the oppressed. This is my context.

Black women have moved beyond these definitions by defying time and space. This tradition has been known as the strong Black woman tradition. It is the one which we now call the womanist tradition.

My commitment is to the unearthing of the lost, forgotten, or ignored traditions of Black women, so that we might be able to develop more holistic theologies which are truly reflective of liberation of humanity. Within the development of the theological arms of both the Black liberation movement and the feminist liberation movement, the particular experiences of Black women have not been represented.

Hull, Scott, and Smith critique these two movements in the very title of their book, *All the Women Are White, All the Blacks Are Men, But Some of Us Are Brave.*[2] Who are these brave women? Mari Evans describes them as she names herself in this way:

> I
> Am a Black Woman
> tall as a Cypress
> Strong
> beyond all definitions still

defying place
and time
and circumstances
Assailed
impervious
indestructible
Look
on me and be
renewed[3]

CONSTRUCTION

When Jesus asked the disciples the question, "Who do you say that I am?" (Mark 8:29), he began what was to become an endless debate and discussion on a central doctrine in Christian theology. The one who posed the question was Jesus of Nazareth. Historical and biblical records give us limited details about who Jesus of Nazareth was. We know of him from birth to twelve years of age and then from age thirty to thirty-three. We have records which bear out certain data.

Yet when Jesus asked this question, could he have been referring to something other than biographical details? Perhaps he was confronting the disciples with the question, "Who am I to *you*? What's the significance of my work for *you*?" "Who do *you* say that I am?" focuses the question on the ones giving the answers—the disciples.

Recognizing this possibility, then, we must at some point focus our attention on the disciples. This subjectification of the disciples relocates the central subject of this passage. No longer is it Jesus, but the one(s) who answer.

If so, it is important to discuss the context in which Jesus is encountered by people, for this context shapes the answers to Jesus' question. When John asks Jesus, "Are you the one or shall we look for another?" the subject is called upon to identify himself. Jesus in turning the question around to the disciples makes them the subjects. "Who do you say that I am?" This question is posed anew in each new generation and in each context. Just as the disciples were called to answer, to be subjects, so we must also be subjects.

Historically the power to be subjects has been carefully and conveniently kept out of the hands of nonwhites and to a lesser extent out of the hands of women. The continual objectification of Blacks and women in recent history has meant that essentially they have been defined by the (political and theological) status quo. It has been within this status quo that many theologians have presumed, in the interest of truth and universality, to answer the christological question in a once-and-for-all fashion, that is, for all times and for all peoples. Consequently, they taught Blacks that Jesus meant docility, meekness, and mildness in the face of the physical brutalities of racial oppression. Then when white people (subjects) answered Jesus' question for Black people (victimized objects): they said Jesus was the one being honored when Black people obeyed their earthly masters and accepted their prescribed roles as servants in the society.

At the same time these same self-proclaimed subjects taught women that Jesus' maleness meant that he was to carry out the patriarchal mandates of all times—that women are to subject themselves to male authority, for God chose to reveal *himself* in a male person—Jesus the *God man*.

In more recent years Blacks and women have forged movements designed to take control of their lives by becoming the primary definers, the subjects, in theological and other discussions. This is particularly significant in that both the Black experience and women's experience represent realities from the underside of history—that is, they are non-normative experiences. They represent experiences in which one normally would not expect to find subjects in the christological debate. White male theologians representing the normative experience—the topside of history—have customarily assumed the subject role in this debate.

The experience of Black women is one of triple jeopardy; their lived reality is at least three times removed from the so-called normative culture, placing them on the underside of history. Though Black women are victimized by racism, sexism, and classism, I will focus primarily on racism and sexism, both of which have consequent implications for social class. In this section we will give glimpses of some perceptions of Jesus Christ from the underside.

THE SUBJECTIFICATION OF BLACK PEOPLE

Since the beginning of their presence in the United States, Black people have been objects of control for the service of the needs and desires of white people. Institutional slavery rendered them less than human, and even when a measure of humanity was given them, they (Black men) were counted as only three fifths of a white man (a fraction of a man) and that was only for political (specifically for apportionment) purposes. In actuality they were still considered nonhuman.

History records some of the varied attempts of Blacks to affirm their human dignity, from David Walker's appeal in 1829 to James Forman's *Black Manifesto* in 1969. At various historical moments Blacks have raised the issue in its theological context. Each of these political and theological statements is part of the struggle of Blacks to become subjects—that is, masters of their own destiny. They recognized that this would not be easy. In bare political terms it meant that in order for Blacks to gain control of their own destiny, whites had to be disempowered. And as Frederick Douglass pointed out, no one gives up power without a struggle. This meant therefore that the insurrections and other rebellious acts of Harriet

Tubman, Denmark Vasey, and many others were attempts to break the power base to the white establishment and in effect to become subjects.

The passing of the thirteenth, fourteenth, and fifteenth amendments to the Constitution were steps in the subjectification of Black people, but as history demonstrates, Blacks were still legally disenfranchised, economically impotent, socially dehumanized, and religiously insignificant. The battle to become subjects continued. In the 1920s and 1930s, Carter S. Woodson identified the problem as more than just political, economic, and social control of Blacks by whites. He described how whites maintained that control through effective oppressive miseducation of Blacks. This miseducation has manifested itself both in the political and the religious life, so that white people controlled Black minds through oppressive educational systems and religious symbols. Woodson argued for self-reliance and self-determination. Though the odds were against it, he believed it possible.[4]

The Civil Rights and Black Power movements of the 1950s, 1960s, and 1970s were direct actions designed to change the power balance in the United States. That period represented a consistent challenge for self-reliance and self-determination and for political, economic, and social freedom. In other words, to some degree Blacks were finally becoming subjects.

WHO DO BLACK PEOPLE SAY JESUS CHRIST IS?

It is the thesis of Black theologians that christology is constructed from the interplay of social context, scripture, and traditions.[5] The significance of social context is addressed in the first chapter of James Cone's book, *God of the Oppressed.* Cone crystallizes the issue in the following way: "The focus on social context means that we cannot separate our questions about Jesus from the concreteness of everyday life. We ask, 'Who is Jesus Christ for us today?' because we believe that the story of his life and death is the answer to the human story of oppression and suffering."[6]

The social context for Black christology is the Black experience of oppression and the struggle against it. Christology is irrelevant if it does not take this into account, because historically christology has been constructed in the context of white superiority, ideology, and domination. Christ has functioned to legitimate these social and political realities. Essentially, Christ has been white. For "white conservatives and liberals alike . . . Christ is a mild, easygoing white American who can afford to mouth the luxuries of 'love,' 'mercy,' 'long-suffering,' and other white irrelevances, because he has a multibillion dollar military force to protect him from the encroachment of the ghetto and the 'communist conspiracy.'"[7]

To counteract this historical and theological trend, what the late Bishop Joseph Johnson called "the tragedy of the white Christ,"[8] Black theologians have called not only for a new departure in theology but more specifically for a new christological interpretation. This white Christ must be eliminated from the Black experience and the concept of a Black Christ must emerge.

The claims for the blackness of Christ are argued by Black theologians in several different ways. Albert Cleage's position leaves no room for guessing his meaning. Postulating actual historical Blackness, Cleage argues that Jesus was a Black Jew.[9] From Cleage's perspective it is simply impossible to believe that Jesus could have been anything but Black, given the established fact of "the intermingling of races in Africa and the Mediterranean area."[10] James Cone (see chapter 6) finds that Blackness clarifies the incarnation in its specificity.[11] Wilmore finds the meaning of "the Black Messiah" to be "the relevance of the Person and Work of Christ for existence under the condition of oppression."[12] Rejected, despised, and acquainted with grief—both biblically and on the contemporary scene—this is the christological symbol: God loves the outcast.[13]

THE SUBJECTIFICATION OF WOMEN

If Blacks were objectified as slaves and chattels, women have been objectified as sexual commodities and relegated to domestic affairs, specifically the upkeep and maintenance of the family. As such, women's reality was defined by men and accommodated by both men and women for the purpose of securing patriarchal structures in both public and private areas. In nineteenth century American life, this culminated in the notion of the "true woman."[14] Barbara Welter says of this concept of true woman, "Women were inherently more religious, modest, passive and domestic."[15] Barbara Andolsen continues the thought, "Women were also nurturing, pure, sweetly persuasive, and self-sacrificing."[16] For women, biology was indeed destiny: women were constrained to the private sphere and were to be content with family affairs, specifically motherhood and wifely duties. Their place was in the home.

Women began to move toward self-definition in the context of the women's movement for liberation in the nineteenth century. They recognized that the patriarchal structures under which women lived functioned for the empowerment and independence of men and the impotence and dependence of women. Hence, women began to organize around issues such as suffrage, wages, personhood, and marriage. Though all of the issues were interrelated, suffrage captured the attention of the majority of women in the movement from 1848 to the 1920s when the nineteenth amendment, giving women the vote, was passed.

In the area of religion, though women were thought to be innately more religious, they were not permitted the authority to define religion. The church with remarkable success resisted the impact of the women's movement. The resistance took the form of teachings on the virtues of womanhood, lauding the feminine qualities of women as godly and God given. Nancy Cott described the indoctrination which women received regarding their role in the church and family. Women populated the church by a majority as early as the mid-seventeenth century. They were kept in line, however, by the constant teaching that they had special "female values." Being seduced by the minister's teachings that they were of "conscientious and prudent character, especially suited to religion," women became well indoctrinated in what was expected of them.[17]

In spite of their ecclesiastical and religious oppression, however, women from time to time did challenge the church about its role in perpetuating such oppression. The speeches of Sarah and Angelina Grimké, directed to Christian women and advocating the equality of the sexes, elicited angry reactions from the clergy. One church body responded to the work of the Grimké sisters with a proclamation that God condones the "protected" and "dependent" state of women. The General Association of the Church wrote the following: "The power of woman is her dependence, flowing from the consciousness of that weakness which God has given her for her protection, and which keeps her in those departments of life that form the character of individuals and of the nation."[18] In spite of these kinds of "divinely-inspired" attacks, women began to claim and articulate revelations to the contrary. Sarah Grimké affirmed that the appropriate duties and influence of women are revealed in the New Testament. In her words, "No one can desire more earnestly than I do that woman may move exactly in the sphere which her creator has assigned her; and I believe her having been displaced from that sphere has introduced confusion into the world."[19] Grimké felt that the New Testament in its untarnished form can be used as a guide for women. Having been contaminated by the interpretations and translations of men, the Bible and commentaries thereupon have been distorted especially with regard to women.

WHO DO FEMINISTS SAY THAT JESUS CHRIST IS?

Twentieth-century women were aware of the significant oppressive impact of religion and theology in their lives. This is perhaps why religion and theology have been consistently addressed in the contemporary women's movement. More importantly, they specifically recognized the special functions of Jesus Christ in the maintenance of the subordinate status of women. For this reason women began to see themselves as subjects to whom Jesus directed the question, "Who do you say that I am?" The question has been answered in many different ways. Three answers are explored here.

Recognizing the relationship between the patriarchal structures of the church and society and the male presence in the divine, some seek to empower women by affirming the female presence in the divine. Consequently, they argue that Jesus Christ was and is an androgynous person, embracing both masculine and feminine traits. In Jesus we find the reasonableness, self-confidence, and security often associated with the masculine person. In addition we find the emotions, peacefulness, and humility often associated with the feminine person. They see Jesus as "emphatically androgynous."[20] Some say that Jesus Christ was and is a feminist.[21] He is believed to be so because of his documented actions and reactions toward women.

Many feminists have interpreted Jesus' frequent affirmations of women (Luke 7:36ff., Mark 9:20ff., John 4:5ff., Matt. 28:9ff., etc.) and other actions of Jesus as a rejection of patriarchy and an affirmation of women's experience.[22] Swidler concludes his analysis by reiterating that "it should be clear that Jesus vigorously promoted the dignity and equality of women in the midst of a very male-dominated society; Jesus was a feminist and a very radical one. Can his followers attempt to be anything else—*de imitatione Christ?*"[23]

Rosemary Ruether addresses the topic of feminist christology in an article entitled "Feminism and Christology: Can a Male Savior Help Women?",[24] in the same article revised under the title "Feminism and Christology: Can a Male Savior Save Women?",[25] and in her book, *Sexism and God-Talk: Toward a Feminist Theology.*[26] In the article, Ruether puts the primary critical question in its most simple, yet profound, way. Given the realities of what maleness and femaleness mean in the church and in society, the question brings into focus elements of the very basic conflict in contemporary male/female relationship. Traditional understanding of the "nature of man" consisted of a dualism that kept man as "protector." Woman's sphere was limited in order to maintain consistency with this social dualism. Women have begun to challenge the motives of such an arrangement—that is, they have questioned whether men have been protecting women, or, in fact, protecting the "sacredness" of their privileged position. A male christology, developed in the context of a Christian theology which itself perpetuates the socio-theological dualism, is met with the same suspicion by feminists. If the male Christ has like investments in the socio-theological status quo, then he cannot be trusted to help women. Thus Ruether asked "Can a Male Savior Help Women?"

When published in her book *To Change the World,* the question becomes more pointedly theological and specifically soteriological: "Can a male savior save women?" Salvation in a patriarchal system would be comparable to accepting one's designated place in the order of creation. This male Christ figure would merely put its stamp of approval upon the patriarchically defined place of women. It is here where Ruether prepares the way for her liberation approach to christology when she poses the question, "Can Christology be liberated from its encapsulation in the structure of patriarchy and really become an expression of liberation of women?"[27] In both essays Ruether provides a positive response to the question. In her first essay, the concepts of service and conversion are elevated. Service must not be confused with servitude. In her view, "service implies autonomy and power used in behalf of others."[28] We are all called to service. Our conversion is to accept this call by abandoning previous, inaccurate notions of being called to hierarchical and oppressive leadership and power. The new christology which is to be developed, then, is one of "conversion and social transformation."[29] Ruether affirms the "liberating praxis" emphasis of liberation theologians, saying that "a starting point for feminist christological inquiry must be a reencounter with the Jesus of the Synoptic Gospels, not the accumulated doctrine about him but his message and praxis."[30] This way we are able to see the ways in which Jesus challenged the customs and laws of his time regarding women. Ruether stops short of saying that Jesus Christ was a feminist for his time, but she does claim "that the criticism of religious and social hierarchy characteristic of the early portrait of Jesus is a remarkable parallel to feminist criticism."[31] He seems to promote a more egalitarian form of relationship—lineal rather than vertical—perhaps one of brother and sister. Jesus elevated many who were at the bottom of the social hierarchy to a new level of equality. This trend is especially evident in his relationship to women.

There is a dynamic quality to the redemptive process. This dynamism not only exists between the redeemer and the redeemed community but also within the redeemer itself. For "the redeemer is one who has been redeemed, just as Jesus himself accepted the baptism of John."[32] As Jesus is paradigmatic, we become so when we liberate others as we have been liberated ourselves. Recognition of this dynamism moves us away from the traditional "once-for-all" notion of Jesus. Because the redemptive process still continues, we can experience the Christ as the historical Jesus and we can experience "Christ in the form of our sister."[33] This means that neither Christ nor humanity is imaged solely as male.

The historical Jesus was a man, but men do not have a monopoly upon Christ, and Eve was a woman but women do not have a monopoly upon sin. For "Christ is not necessarily male, nor is the redeemed community only women, but new humanity, female and male."[34]

As both Blacks and women have struggled from place of objects to subjects, they have more and more begun to answer Jesus' question for themselves. "Who do you say that I am?" You are the Black Messiah, the Liberator, the Redeemer. You are the Christ, the Savior, the Sister.

THE SUBJECTIFICATION OF BLACK WOMEN

Even in the midst of the struggles for liberation, Black women still found themselves objectified indeed by white men, but also by Black men and white women. In the Black movement women were intimidated into believing that sexism was not a reality in the Black community. Consequently, for some time most Black women did not publicly address sexism. In the women's movement, Black women were ignored in significant ways; consequently most Black women ignored the movement.

In other words, in the subjectification process, essentially invisible Black women were left to fall through the cracks.

While Black women did not accept that imposed invisibility quietly, they did fall through the cracks. For example, though neither the Bill of Rights nor the amendments to the Constitution ensured Black women (or Black men for that matter) their rights, this did not totally prevent the rise of activism among Black women. Womanists such as Harriet Tubman, Sojourner Truth, Fannie B. Williams, Ida B. Wells, Mary McLeod Bethune, Fannie Lou Harper, and others were present to challenge in one way or another the racism, sexism, and classism of their day, often at great cost to themselves. Being active both in the abolition/anti-racism movement and the women's liberation/anti-sexism movement meant that these women were doubly burdened, doubly taxed, and twice removed from the seat of power by virtue of being victims of both racism and sexism. In actuality they were thrice removed from any real sense of self-control, for their control in the early days was in the hands of white men and women and more recently also in the hands of Black men.

For them, becoming subjects meant engaging in three battles: 1) the battle against the ever-pervasive racism of the dominant culture; 2) the battle against the sexism of the dominant male culture; and 3) the battle against the sexism of nondominant cultures, including Black men. Though the subjectification process has become less evident in Black women's communities, we can still discern its presence as they attempt to live out their response to the question "Who do you say that I am?"

Who Do Womanists Say That Jesus Christ Is?

Black women have said and continue to say that Jesus Christ is one of us. When we see Jesus Christ, we see both the particular Jesus of Nazareth and the universal Christ of faith. In Jesus Christ, we see an oppressed experience and at the same time we see liberation. When we see Jesus Christ, we see concreteness and absoluteness, for in Jesus Christ, the absolute becomes concrete.

Black women can identify with this Jesus Christ because the Jesus Christ reality is so akin to their own reality. For it is in the context of Black women's experience that we find the particular connecting with the universal. By this I mean that in each of the three dynamics of oppression which characterize their reality, Black women share in the reality of a broader community: they share race suffering with Black men; with white women and other Third World women they are victims of sexism; and with poor Blacks and whites, and other Third World peoples, especially women, they are disproportionately poor. To speak of Black women's tri-dimensional reality, therefore, is not to speak of Black women exclusively, for there is an implied universality which connects them with others.

Similarly, there was an implied universality with Jesus Christ, which made him identify with others—the poor, the women, the stranger. To affirm Jesus' solidarity with the "least of the people" (Matt. 25:31–46) is not an exercise in romanticized contentment with one's oppressed status in life. For the resurrection signified that there is more to the life of Jesus Christ than the cross. For Black women, the resurrection signifies that their triply oppressive existence is not the end. It represents the context in which a particular people struggle to experience hope and liberation. Jesus Christ thus represents a threefold significance: first, he identifies with the "little people"—Black women—where they are and he accompanies them in their struggles.[35] Second, he affirms the basic humanity of these, "the least," and in affirming them he empowers them to gain "more." Third, he inspires active hope in the struggle for resurrected, liberated existence. Christ's empowerment effects liberation.

Identification with "Little People"

To locate the Christ in the experiences of Black people as Black theology has done is a radical and necessary step. An understanding of Black women's reality challenges us to go further. Christ among the least must also mean Christ in the community of Black women. William Eichelberger was able to recognize this as he further particularized the significance of the Blackness of Jesus by locating Christ in a Black women's community. He was able to see Christ not only as Black male but also as Black female: "It is my feeling that God is now manifesting Himself, and has been for over 450 years, in the form of the Black American Woman as mother, as wife, as nourisher, sustainer, and preserver of life, the Suffering Servant who is despised and rejected by men, a personality of sorrow who is acquainted with grief."[36] Granted, Eichelberger's categories for God and woman are very traditional. Nevertheless, the significance of his thought is that he was able to conceive of the divine reality as other than a Black male messianic figure. The possibility that Christ is in the experiences of Black women highlights the notion that Christ accompanies the people in their pain and suffering and loneliness.

In the experiences of Black people, Jesus was "all things."[37] Chief among these, however, was the belief in Jesus as the divine cosufferer, who empowers them in situations of oppression. For Christian Black women in the past, Jesus was their central frame of reference. They identified with Jesus because they believed that Jesus identified with them. As Jesus was persecuted and made to suffer undeservedly, so were they. His suffering culminated in the crucifixion. Their crucifixion included rape, their babies being sold, and their men being castrated. But Jesus' suffering was not the suffering of a mere human, for Jesus was understood to be God incarnate. As Harold Carter observed of Black prayers in general, there was no difference between the persons of the trinity, Jesus, God, or the Holy Spirit. All of these proper names for God were used interchangeably in prayer language. Thus, Jesus was the one who speaks the world into creation. He was the power behind the church.

Black women's affirmation of Jesus as God meant that white people were not God. One old slave woman clearly demonstrated this as she prayed: "Dear Massa Jesus, we all uns beg ooner [you] come make us a call dis yere day. We is nutting but poor Ethiopian women and people ain't tink much 'bout we. We ain't trust any of dem great high people for come to we church, but do' you is de one great Massa, great yoo much dan Massa Likum, you ain't shame to care for we African people."[38]

This slave woman did not hesitate to identify her struggles and pain with those of Jesus. In fact, the common struggle made her know that Jesus would respond to her beck and call: "Come to we, dear Massa Jesus. De sun, he hot too much, de road am dat long and boggy [sandy] and we ain't got no buggy for send and fetch Ooner. But Massa, you 'member how you walk up Calvary and ain't weary but tink about we all dat way. We pick out de thorns, de prickles, de brier, de backslidin' and de quarrel and de sin out of you path so dey shan't hurt Ooner pierce feet no more."[39] As she is truly among the people at the bottom of humanity, she can make things comfortable for Jesus, even though she may have nothing to give him—no water, no food—but she can give tears and love. She continues: "Come to we, dear Massa Jesus. We all uns ain't got no good cool water for to give you when you thirsty. You know, Massa, de drought so long, and the well so low, ain't nutting but mud to drink. But we gwine to take de 'munion cup and fill it wid de tear of repentance and love clean out of we heart. Dat all we hab to gib you, good Massa."[40] Isn't it interesting that the women here have faith that Jesus will join them in the drought (presumably a metaphor for their condition)? In spite of the mud (again a metaphor for their possessions), you will find rightness of heart, love, and repentance.

Affirmation of Humanity

For Black women, the role of Jesus Christ was demystified as they encountered him in their experience as one who empowers the weak. Jesus Christ dwells with the people in their survival struggles, and the Christ projects faithful followers forward into meaningful liberation praxis. In this vein, Jesus was such a central part of Sojourner Truth's life that all of her sermons started with him. When asked by a preacher if the source of her preaching was the Bible, she responded, "No honey, can't preach from de Bible—can't read a letter."[41] Then she explained: "When I preaches, I has jest one text to preach from, an' I always preaches from this one. My text is, When I found Jesus!"[42] In this sermon Sojourner Truth recounts the events and struggles of her life from the time her parents were brought from Africa and sold "up an' down, and 'hither an' yon"[43] to the time that she met Jesus within the context of her struggles for the dignity of Black people and women. Her encounter with Jesus brought such joy that she became overwhelmed with love and praise: "Praise, praise, praise to the Lord! An' I begun to feel such a love in my soul as I never felt before—love to all creatures. An' then, all of a sudden, it stopped, an' I said, 'Dar's de white folks that have abused you, an' beat you, an' abused your people—tink o' them!' But then there came another rush of love through my soul, an' I cried out loud—'Lord, I can love *even de white folks!*'"[44] This love was not a sentimental, passive love. It was a tough, active love that empowered her to fight more fiercely for the freedom of her people. For the rest of her life she continued speaking at abolition and women's rights gatherings, condemning the horrors of oppression. In this regard, she was a true incarnation of the Christ.

Empowerment for Liberation

James Cone argues that the christological title "the Black Christ" is not validated by its universality, but, in fact, by its particularity. Its significance lies in whether or not that christological title "points to God's universal will to liberate particular oppressed people from inhumanity."[45] These particular oppressed peoples to which Cone refers are characterized in Jesus' parable on the Last Judgment as "the least." The least in America are literally and symbolically present in Black people.[46] This notion of "the least" is attractive because it descriptively locates the condition of Black women. "The least" are those people who have no water to give, but offer what they have, as the old slave woman says in her prayer. Black women's experience in general is such a reality. Their threefold oppression renders their particular situation a complex one. They are the oppressed of the oppressed, and therefore their salvation represents "the particular within the particular."

The Christ understood as the stranger, the outcast, the hungry, the weak, the poor, makes a traditional male Christ less significant. Even our sisters, the womanists of the past, had some suspicions about the effects of a male image of the divine, for they did challenge the oppressive use of it in the church's theology. In so doing, they were able to move from a traditional oppressive christology, with respect to women, to an egalitarian christology. This kind of christology was operative in Jarena Lee's argument for the right of women to preach. She argued "the Savior died for the woman as well as for the man."[47] The crucifixion was for universal salvation, not just for male salvation or, as we may extend the argument, not just for white salvation. Because of this Christ came and died, no less for the woman than for the man, no less for Blacks than for whites. "If the man may preach because the Savior died for him, why not the woman? Seeing he died for her also. Is he not a whole Savior, instead of half one?—as those who hold it wrong for a woman to preach seem to make it appear."[48] Lee correctly perceives that there is an ontological issue at stake. If Jesus Christ were a Savior of men then it is true the maleness of Christ would be paramount. But if Christ is a Savior of all then it is the humanity—the wholeness—of Christ which is significant.

Sojourner Truth was aware of the same tendency of some scholars and church leaders to link the maleness of Jesus and the sin of Eve with the status of women. She challenged this notion in her famous speech "Ain't I a Woman?"

Then that little man in black there, he says women can't have as much rights as men, 'cause Christ wasn't a woman! Where did your Christ come from? Where did your Christ come from? From God and a woman. Man had nothing to do with Him. If the first woman God ever made was strong enough to turn the world upside down all alone, these women together ought to be able to turn it back, and get it right side up again! And now they is asking to do it, the men better let them.[49]

CONCLUSION

I would argue, as suggested by both Lee and Sojourner Truth, that the significance of Christ is not his maleness, but his humanity. The most significant events of Jesus Christ were the life and ministry, the crucifixion, and the resurrection. The significance of these events, in one sense, is that in them the absolute becomes concrete. God becomes concrete not only in the man Jesus, for he was crucified, but in the lives of those who will accept the challenges of the risen Savior—the Christ. For Lee, this meant that women could preach; for Sojourner Truth, it meant that women could possibly save the world; for me, it means that today, this Christ, found in the experience of Black women, is a Black woman.

At last! Black women are indeed becoming subjects. More and more they are resisting the objectification by those whose histories and herstories continue to render them invisible. And so to the question, "Who do *you* say that I am?" Black women say that you are the one who is with us and among us in our community as we struggle for survival. You are the one who not only is with us, but you are one of us. "Who do you say that I am?" You are the Christ, the one who affirms us, the one who accompanies us as we move from mere survival to redemptive liberation. "Who do you say that I am?" You are indeed the Christ.

RECOMMENDED READING

Andolsen, Barbara Hilkert. *Daughters of Jefferson, Daughters of Bootblacks: Racism and American Feminism.* Macon, GA: Mercer University Press, 1986.

Cone, James H. *A Black Theology of Liberation.* Philadelphia: Lippincott, 1970.

———. *God of the Oppressed,* New York: Seabury, 1975.

Eichelberger, William. "Reflections on the Person and Personality of the Black Messiah." In C. Eric Lincoln's *The Black Church Since Frazier.* New York: Schocken, 1974, pp. 1–61.

Gilbert, Olive, ed. *Sojourner Truth: Narrative and Book of Life.* 1850, 1875; reprint, Chicago: Johnson's, 1970.

Hull, Gloria T., Patricia Bell Scott, and Barbara Smith, eds. *All the Women Are White, All the Blacks Are Men, but Some of Us Are Brave: Black Women's Studies.* Old Westbury, NY: Feminist Press, 1982.

Lee, Jarena. *Religious Experience and Journal of Mrs. Jarena Lee.* Philadelphia, 1849.

Ruether, Rosemary Radford. "Can a Male Savior Save Women?" In her *To Change the World: Christology and Cultural Criticism.* New York: Crossroad, 1981 pp. 45–56.

Wilmore, Gayraud S., and James H. Cone, eds. *Black Theology: A Documentary History,* 1966–70. Maryknoll, NY: Orbis, 1979.

PART 5B

Church, Ministry, and Spirituality

Introduction to Part 5B

If Christianity is the practice of freedom, and the empowering spirit of God is known most vitally in community, then the question of the nature and task of the church, the character and authority of ministry, and the everyday practice of a spirituality that will nourish Christian communities in their struggles for justice take on a new urgency. In fact, this is exactly what is happening. Many liberation communities are beginning to envision and experimentally live out new models of the church, ministry, and spirituality. And theologians of these movements are starting to reflect the hope for and practice of these new models in their writings. The three chapters included here point out some of the directions this discussion is currently taking.

Fukada's stress on the church as an alternative, humanizing community in the alienating pyramidic structure of Japanese society echoes themes of the ecclesiologies coming out of Latin American liberation theologies and North American feminist liberation theologies. In the context of Latin America, especially with the burgeoning of the movement of "base communities" there, the church has come to be seen as human communities of resistance and solidarity that act as agents and signs of God's justice and love in the wider human community. In contrast to the institutionalized church that protects the majorities, these small communities of committed people constitute heroic minorities that work for social, economic, political, and spiritual transformation.[1] (See chapter 3.) As Westhelle says, the church is grassroots communities "gathering the displaced and making hope and faith practical in love." Feminist liberation communities in North America are beginning to identify themselves in similar ways. They, too, are stressing the need for all members of *Women-Church* to live in solidarity with the oppressed, to commit themselves to the struggle for justice for all women, and to transform social, economic, political, and religious conditions for all women.[2]

One essay on the community called "church" is not sufficient to signify the centrality of this topic for movements and theologies of liberation around the world. Similar to the Protestant Reformation movements of the sixteenth century, liberation movements and theologians in our day have discerned that one of the most pressing issues alongside the character and activity of God's grace is the character and activity of the church. If God's grace empowers us through healing and liberating to participate in a life of sanctification in and for the world, what is the role of the communities called church in this life? What are the structures, purposes, and tasks of these communities that will support and sustain this empowering activity? These and other critical questions are part of the agenda of ecclesiologies of liberation for the future.

Feminist theologians are the ones who have most consistently challenged inherited models of ministry and offered new visions for ministry. Letty Russell has focused much of her work in this area, as testified by two of her books, *Growth in Partnership* and *Household of Freedom*.[3] Like Fukada, she is especially concerned to counter the pyramidic structure of authority in congregations with the liberating image of a circle. The vision for ministry shared by increasing numbers of feminists is one of friendship and solidarity rather than obedience and paternalism.[4] Hill and Treadway contribute to this new development in Christian ministry out of their perspectives as a gay man and a lesbian working together in a ministry "with and on behalf of gay and lesbian people." The model they work with is one of empowering people through education and advocacy. As they point out, this model is grounded in a theology of wholeness and acceptance rather than sin and salvation.

Oduyoye enlarges this growing new vision for ministry by dwelling on ministry in African Christianity as it is practiced not by the "priestly class" but by people of the church in their "daily converse and dealings with one another." Rather than enter into arguments about the original meaning of the term "laity" or the proper relationship between the clergy and laity, she reflects on the effectiveness and power of spirit-directed women in African communities. Through their spiritual practices of prayer, praise, and song, spirit-directed women exercise valid authority and leadership. This is the distinctive ministry of African women in, with, and on behalf of the whole community.

Oduyoye's chapter rests on an important assumption that she shares with other theologians of liberation and that is crucial for understanding liberation theologies in all contexts: justice and spirituality are not mutually exclusive. Churches in North America often have difficulty in seeing the connection between justice and spirituality, or between the prophetic and the priestly tasks. For this reason, congregations in this area often feel pressed to choose between being either a liberal, social-activist group directed primarily outward, toward people who are not members of the church, *or* a caring and nurturing community directed primarily inward, toward their own members.

Along with their rejection of all other forms of dualisms, liberation theologians refuse to accept such an either/or choice, insisting that both sides are essential to the task at hand. Without continual spiritual nourishment through prayer, praise, singing, befriending, and communal study of the scriptures, the community will not be able to sustain its commitment to and struggle for justice. And without active participation in struggles for justice through solidarity, prophetic criticism, and social, economic, and political transformation, the community will lose its character of a heroic minority and become an irrelevant elite. The mutual and creative interaction between spirituality and the struggle for justice is assumed by liberation communities and theologians. What theologians of liberation have yet to do is articulate more clearly how and why such interaction is necessary for the life and health of Christian communities.

CHAPTER 15

In Search of a Circular Community: A Possible Shape for the Church in Japan

ROBERT M. FUKADA

CONTEXT AND COMMITMENT

I was born into a minister's family. Both my parents were converted to the Christian faith through their association with Toyohiko Kagawa, a prophetic Christian voice in the first half of the twentieth century. The fact that I was born in the United States while my father was serving a Japanese congregation there adds an American element to my "Japaneseness." I received my basic education in Japan, from the age of four to sixteen, before I moved on to higher education in the United States.

My professional work in Japan began with an industrial mission, serving silk-weavers in Nishijin, a historic textile-producing district in Kyoto. This experience had great impact upon my commitment to serve the church in Japan and on my understanding of the nature of the church. In 23 years of theological education, I had attempted to think with students about the complexity of culture and society in Japan and about a possible shape for the church which might effectively transform those parts of the culture and society that prevent humanization in our age of high technology and extensive urbanization.

More than 30 years ago, I committed myself to serve the church. That commitment has not changed, though it has had to be re-examined critically from time to time. My understanding of the nature of the church has been repeatedly challenged, internally as well as externally. I have encountered the problem of institutionalism as I worked with colleagues in serving an industrial community and its people. I have asked some basic questions as I shared in a group ministry in an experimental house church for the past 18 years.

The number of Christians in Japan is extremely small. Much debate has produced no definite analysis of the cause of the slow growth of the church. The impact of Christianity, however, is much greater than the statistical figures indicate. The challenge to the church in Japan is to be imaginative as a creatively transforming minority in this society and to attempt some bold experiments to present the Christian message as a relevant force in an increasingly secular milieu. The formation of supportive and renewing relationships which can transcend traditionally defined patterns of daily relationships is a pressing need for Japan, and the church must present a clear and persuasive model. I am committed to being a part of the church in responding to that challenge.

CONSTRUCTION

Japan is a strange country, and its social characteristics are complex enough that the Japanese themselves often have difficulty comprehending their society. One indication of this confusion is in the stream of "Japan study" books that have appeared in Japanese bookstores recently. The Japanese are going through a process of self-discovery. We are moving beyond mere curiosity in our effort to determine what is unique about our society and culture. Behind this self-discovery is hidden an element of pride, self-righteousness, and at times arrogance. Partly because of the economic strength Japan has shown in the world scene in the past decade, we Japanese are pressed to clarify for ourselves what makes us tick and what elements are unique in our ancient culture and social composition in light of the international community.

The work of self-discovery and analysis goes on also in the life of the church in Japan, though not as extensively as in the general society. Externally there are few signs of Christianity in Japan, in contrast to Korea. Churches are clearly visible to visitors traveling through Korea. Even at night, crosses on church buildings are lit with fluorescent lights. The history of the Protestant church in these two nations dates back to about the same time. The official arrival of the first Protestant missionaries in Japan was 1859, in Korea 1855. Prior to this, both countries were preparing themselves for the planting of the Protestant missionary seed. In Japan the arrival of Commodore Matthew Perry leading four gunboats into Tokyo Bay pried open the tight door of the feudal nation in 1853. Before that Catholic missionary effort, stained with the blood of martyrdom in the sixteenth and seventeenth centuries, attempted to till the sprritual ground of Japan. The work of self-discovery in Japanese Christianity begins with recognition of this Catholic attempt at mission and the horrible persecutions that resulted under the Tokugawa Shoguns.

HERITAGE OF WESTERN PROTESTANTISM

The Christian faith was introduced to Japan in 1549 by Francis Xavier, Father Cosme de Torres, and Brother Juan Fernandez. For more than one hundred years the Protestant movement has woven its way into the fabric of Japanese society through church-centered ministries, educational programs, and social service projects. In 1985, statistics indicated the existence in Japan of approximately a million and a half Christians (of both major traditions) in a total population of just over 103 million. Statistics are never a completely accurate indication of the Christian presence in Japan. The number of baptized members of churches does not equal church attendance. There are people, difficult to count or name, who faithfully participate in church programs and who fully accept Christian values, but who are not baptized. And there are what may be called "hidden Christians," people who find in the biblical message and in the life of Jesus a philosophy and a posture for life but who do not find the life of institutional churches a meaningful source of spiritual nurture. We can rejoice that there are comrades in faith outside the framework of the church, but we must be sharply critical of the organized churches for not being able to reach the "hidden" brothers and sisters.

Numerous attempts have been made to analyze the slowness of the growth of the church in Japan. A common finding in these analyses is the lingering image of Christianity as "a foreign religion." External elements of Christianity should not, however, any longer appear "foreign" to Japanese today, when the whole society is visibly Westernized. The problem may be a more internal one. Theological concepts such as sin, the cross of Jesus, and the Resurrection are still stumbling blocks for the Japanese, even to people who have been familiar with Christianity or the life of the church. The radical monotheism of Christianity is another stumbling block for the people who live in a highly polytheistic society.

GENERAL TRAITS OF THE CHURCHES IN JAPAN

The heritage of this early Protestantism unquestionably influences today's churches in Japan. What are the observable traits of that heritage? The common generalizations, though not totally fair, are at least indicative of both the strength and weakness of the church as an extreme minority. The first characteristic is its solemnity. Churchgoers wipe away their smiles as they enter the church. It is still not unusual to find women and men seated separately, though seating is completely free. The minister of the church is, whether symbolically or physically, the center of the worship service and of the life of the church. Though the size of the average church is quite small, with an attendance at worship of fewer than fifty, each church has a full-time pastor with a parsonage located within the church compound. The worship service is preaching-centered, with much emphasis upon biblical exegesis. The organizational structure is pyramid-shaped, with the minister at the top. A minister is always called *sensei* (literally translated, "born first or ahead"), which means "teacher." Sometimes the expression *bokushi-sensei* is used, which literally means "pastor-teacher." The role of a pastor is always dominantly that of a teaching person. Added to the teacher image is the element of a gathering hen or a "shepherding lord." I use the term "lord" because pastors in Japan are often seen as lords of their "castles."

The general picture I am drawing is not all negative. There is an authentic sense of intimacy in the Japanese church. It is a serious, often solemn, community searching for life direction by constantly probing into the Bible. It is a family-like fellowship in which baptism as an initiation into the fellowship often means a strained relationship with, if not severance from, one's blood-tie family. To be a Christian in Japan, even today, is a serious business.

VERTICAL STRUCTURE AND ORIENTATION

Role of the Pastor

The dominant role of a pastor in the traditional life of the church in Japan is clarified by the now classic concept of a vertical society presented by Professor Nakane Chie.[1] Nakane, a social anthropologist, does not refer specifically to the church in her inquiry into Japanese social structures, but two concepts of vital importance in her analysis are applicable to church structures. "Frame" (*ba*) refers to a particular role one holds within a specific group, a role which at times may not be clearly defined but is taken for granted by everyone concerned. "Attribute" (*shikaku*) is a qualitative standard which distinguishes one person from another, such as lineage, gender, and occupation. These two factors are intimately intertwined, though each may take precedence over the other at times in a person's understanding of her/his role and location within a particular framework and interaction with others. Nakane uses these two factors to describe Japanese society as a vertical structure, taking *ie*, or household, as a representative prototype. In a Japanese family the father stands at the top and the children spread out to form the base of the pyramid. The same structure is found in business and industrial enterprises and in the nation itself. Whether or not he is constitutionally empowered, the emperor, both structurally and in the common mentality, holds the pinnacle position.

A minister of a church is not an emperor, though some ministers in Japan are jokingly called by exactly that term. Though there are denominational variations in church organizations, churches usually operate with an understanding of the minister as the major "power." This situation may not be limited to Japan. In the Japanese setting, however, this general pattern receives almost no critical scrutiny.

The origin of this pyramid structure of the church can also be traced to the early history of Protestantism. When Commodore Perry pounded on the protective gate of Japan and a crack opened, Protestant missionaries (not officially on a religious mission) squeezed into a still-feudal Japan. Through the Meiji Restoration, there was a drastic political change on the island. Along with the political transformation came a state of confusion about attitudes and values, as Western culture started to permeate various strata of Japanese society. One aspect of the confusion was in the area of morals and ethics. The Confucian orientation, so dominant in the feudal Samurai society, confronted the Christian moralism of the missionaries. In actuality missionaries, whether knowingly or half-consciously, utilized some of the Confucian principles. There was common ethical ground between the Samurai-Confucian pattern of conduct and thought and the strongly Puritanical moralism of the majority of early missionaries. The vertical mentality of the Japanese, always seeing social relationships in terms of "above" and "below," was useful to the missionaries in emphasizing the transcendent God. And in the gradual formation of a religious community, the church, it was natural for the minister as a leader to be placed at the top.

Vertical Organization in Western Culture and Christian Faith

From the beginning of the Protestant movement in Japan, there has been a blurred understanding of the relationship between Western culture and Christian faith. Many of the early converts, who came from a low stratum of the Samurai class, were searching for a replacement for the disintegrated Samurai ethic. In their craving to understand Western culture as a resource for the modernization of Japan, they took Christianity as an inseparable element of that culture and conveniently used it to fill the vacuum caused by the disintegration of feudal society. Christianity, in this historical process, tended to operate as a cultural factor rather than a prophetic religious voice.

Though used as a cultural factor in the beginning, Christianity remained extremely small and existed in an adversarial relationship to wider Japanese society. It was looked upon as something alien, an anti-society, and at times a harmful heresy. It had to fight for its life, which put fiber into the faith of Christian believers. A small flame of prophetic tradition was protected and at times found voice in the largely non-Christian world of Japan. This prophetic voice was not heard from Christian ministers leading the small flocks. Often it was the upper echelon among the lay members or marginal affiliates or sympathizers of the Christian faith who sounded it, speaking out on political rights and social issues. Not all voices were strictly Christian. Some were grounded in cultural liberalism. But the Christian understanding of personhood and an ideal society finding its prototype in the concept of the Kingdom of God had an impact upon all those prophetic voices.

The vertically-oriented organization that we find in the Protestant church in Japan is thus reflective of the larger society of Japan. This relationship between the society and the structural nature of a church can be found in other cultural settings. Yet in Japan, because the church follows a society with a vertical structure, the nature of the church itself contradicts the basic message of Christianity. The pyramidic structure is contrary to the biblical understanding of the equality of all human beings as children of God and of all Christians as called to be coworkers for God's purpose and work in this world.

Father Yoji Inoue makes an interesting observation on Professor Nakane's theory that Japan is a vertical society and its implication for the nature of Christianity.[2] Nakane's theory is grounded in her understanding that the basis of a society in Western culture is an individual person, who composes the substance on which relationships are formed. In other words, a relationship is an "accident" occurring to the substance (the individual) which makes that relationship possible. In Japanese society, however, the reverse is true. The fundamental criterion for social structure as well as for a pattern of thinking is the dynamics of relationships, which shape the substance, or component persons in relationships. The "place" of that criterion is what Nakane emphasizes as "ba" or social frame.

Inoue uses Nakane's theoretical assumption to analyze the nature of the church in Japan. If the Christian understanding of God and of the divine covenantal relationship between God and God's people is to make sense in reality, each component (person) among the people of God must encounter the most concrete substance (God) in her/his search for a right relationship *before* other relationships are formed. Such a thought is Western in value and orientation. Behind such a view is a need to escape from the decision-making responsibility of a full personality. Inoue finds Nakane's concept of *ba,* or "frame," helpful in understanding the Japanese difficulty in comprehending a direct encounter between God and a person and the covenantal relationship between the two. A Japanese person understands her/his value structure and preferred attitudes *through* the social frame in which that person was born or currently finds her/himself.

The point is not to judge whether Western-influenced Christian values and attitudes are better than the social dynamics affecting Japanese society. It is to comprehend accurately the social and cultural soil in which Protestant Christianity was transplanted some 130 years ago, so that with our commitment to the core value of the Christian faith we may search for a creative expression of that faith for contemporary persons. That is the first step toward whatever social transformation is needed in order for Japanese society to be more supportive and affirmative of humanization in an increasingly mechanized and technocratic world.

SOCIAL DYNAMICS AND PYRAMID STRUCTURE

Some segments of Japanese society are so oriented to vertical relationships that everyday experience is framed in terms of what is above and what is below. What determines a person's identity in Japan are: *ba,* a social frame, the role one plays in the specific group to which he/she belongs; and *shikaku,* attribute, that which distinguishes a person from others in terms of lineage, gender, and occupation. These elements are certainly not meaningless in most societies in forming a person's sense of identity. In Japan, however, social frame and attribute function interrelatedly and forcefully to shape one's value system and social understanding.

A Shame-Oriented Society

In addition to these dynamics, a sense of shame plays an important role in keeping the social structure functioning. Ruth Benedict was one of the earlier scholars to notice the importance of shame in Japanese society.[3] Though she made some inaccurate generalizations, her attempt to understand the Japanese mind and social relationships provided some insightful observations. Benedict contrasted shame with sin, or a sense of guilt, associating guilt with Western culture and a sense of shame with Japanese culture. Good acts are based upon inner-directed motivation in a sin-oriented culture, while in a shame-oriented culture acts of goodness are outwardly sanctioned.[4] What Benedict was attempting to point out was the difficulty Japanese persons have in making self-determined decisions based upon their subjective analysis of values, especially in the relationship between themselves and a transcendent being.

Benedict never visited Japan and she unknowingly stressed that ideal selfhood is formed only in a "sin-oriented" culture. Although this is an overstatement, her distinction of shame from sin exposes a segment of the fundamental dynamics which shape the patterns of Japanese life. It is important, however, to scrutinize both shame and sin as they function in daily reality. A sense of sin is not totally lacking in Japanese consciousness. Whether it is spoken of in terms of a transcendent being, such as God, or in terms of a person's subjective grappling with values apart from her/his social relationships, an experience of betraying the utmost value to which that person is committed does exist in Japanese life. Suzuki Norihisa agrees that, comparatively speaking, Japan is still more "shame-oriented" than "sin-directed." He finds in such historical figures as Yoshida Shoin (1830–1859) and Motoori Norinaga (1730–1801) a complex mixture of deeply felt shame and deep remorse because of not being able to live up to an intrinsic value.[5] Though we must be cautious not to overgeneralize Japan as a "shame" society, the factors pointed out by Benedict can be helpful as we search for the possible formation of a humanizing community based upon the Christian gospel.

The Anatomy of Dependence

As we probe further into what holds together the vertical structure of Japanese society, Doi Takeo's analysis of *amae*, a structure of dependence, contributes to our understanding.[6] Doi, a psychiatrist, focuses on a unique element in Japanese relationships called *amae*. *Amae* is a difficult term to translate into English. A direct translation of the word is "sweetness" or "sweetening." The verb in Japanese is *amaeru*, which refers to an act, whether physical or mental, of clinging, of avoiding separation—a sort of passive object-love. It is not an altogether negative dynamic. We find it functioning universally to some extent. Doi translates it as a sense of dependence and describes the total dynamics as an anatomy of dependence.

Doi finds a psychological prototype of *amae* in the mother-child relationship, which extends into the formation of new relationships in adult life. He finds some aspects of *amae* to be positive, even in the formation of a healthy spiritual life. *Amae* at times closes a gap of separation by fostering, both in the dependent and the person depended on, an unseen tie which is often taken for granted. *Amae* serves as a "jumper cable" in grasping an unseen spiritual being. In this way *amae* can help a person transcend the social and mental structure of vertical orientation. *Amae* leads a person to a state of freedom in which it is not, at least for a time, a person of authority "above" who determines her/his behavior and thought, but that spiritual being experienced through the "jumper cable." It is not a matter of logic here: feeling seems to have priority.

We can probe further into the complexity of elements which cut across vertical relationships in Japanese society by using the concept of *amae*. Look again at the parent-child relationship, especially that between a mother and her child. Inevitably in a Japanese family relationship the father is located, whether with real authority or symbolically, at the top of the pyramid. But a mother-child relationship cannot be described as vertical. Here is a clue in Japanese relationships which can and may pierce the prescribed pattern of relating to other members of a group.

Toshio Yamazaki, who has been immersed in the study of parent-child relationships and the role of religion in them, recently published *Oyano nai Tensaitachi (Geniuses without Parents)*, which explores the world of father-child and mother-child intimacy.[7] One case study deals with Toyohiko Kagawa, a historic Christian figure in Japan (1888–1960). Kagawa, born of a politician-businessman and his concubine geisha, experienced a devastatingly lonely boyhood after both his parents died when he was four. He encountered two American Southern Presbyterian missionaries and their families at the age of fifteen and quickly converted to the Christian faith. His conversion and subsequent life of service and ministry in the slums of Kobe are widely known. Kagawa was a poet with an expressive faith in the redemptive love of God in Jesus Christ. Throughout his literary writings, as well as in his preaching, he often relied on a maternal figure he used to describe God's intrinsic nature. Yamazaki focuses on Kagawa's total lack of the experience of mother-child intimacy, which in turn gave him an urgent yearning to fill the unexplainable void. It was this radical emptiness which made Kagawa search for something which would help him gain a sense of self-identity. And for him that something was a maternal figure with accepting warmth and affection. Yet it was his encounter with the missionaries Harry W. Myers and Charles Logan which provided him with a point of initiation into the Christian faith. It is interesting to note that these men, particularly Myers, were expressive people, both emotionally and physically, and often held the lonely boy in their arms as young Kagawa confided his problems and struggles in life to them. For Kagawa this experience of total acceptance was a sort of maternal embrace of deep affection.

We often find in parent-child relationships, particularly mother-child relationships, dynamics that can transcend rigid structures of relationships or help a person to experience the unseen. Young Kagawa's exposure to God in Jesus Christ was made possible by the loving embrace of two Christian men, whose act he experienced as the unconditional love of a mother. His was an initiation into the world of faith not by condescending persuasion within the hierarchy of a common church life, but by an authentic act of unconditional acceptance and care. Such an act cannot be attributed predominantly to one sex, but in Japanese society men are more bound by the prescribed vertical relationships and not as free as women to express affection, acceptance, care, and emotional richness. Though it may be an overstatement, we might say that a possible crack in the sturdy structure of vertical relationships can be made by more maternal elements both in men and women in Japan.

ACCEPTING ALTERNATIVES TO A PYRAMID

The Church as "Mini-Japan"

My concern with the verticality of relationships in Japan is related to my search for an enriching human community in an age of technology, urbanization, and compartmentalization. The vertical nature of the Japanese society is not altogether bad. With the dynamics of *amae* and a sense of security (which a prescribed position and role provide to a person), a society is able to maintain a certain degree of stability and efficiency. A vertical society, however, tends to obstruct the growth of the whole person. One such obstruction is the sense of fate which rises out of the self-awareness of a person in her/his location in the society or a group. A prerequisite for the growth, nurture, and fulfillment of a person's potential as a whole person is the acceptance of that person in her/his social context. Using this as a criterion and looking at the state of the life of the church in Japan, I find something seriously lacking.

The solemnity, minister-centeredness, intellectual orientation, sense of intimacy, and serious interest in biblical study in Japanese church life are wrapped up in a pyramidic relationship pattern. In other words, a church is, in a way, a mini-Japan. And as in Japanese society, in the church more importance is placed on harmony than confrontation, even when confrontation is defined as an honest outpouring of self to another, even to the point of tension. The priority of harmony over confrontation is seen in the church's relationship to the world as well as in its internal relations, as the following historical observations show.

The Church as Vehicle of Western Culture

When the Protestant movement started to take root, a definite emphasis was placed on ethical and behavioral expressions and patterns which were based more on cultural factors which came with Christianity than on theological understandings. That meant a Western orientation came with Protestantism. During the mid-nineteenth century, the age of "opening of her doors," Japan exposed herself with vigor to things Western. The church was one channel through which people were able to see, feel, and gain Western culture. Not all people coming to the newly organized churches had an ulterior motive, but such a motive was a significant part of their initial interest in Christianity. Thus from its beginning the church conformed to the general direction of the society, i.e., toward modernization in a Western cultural pattern. It was not easy, then, for the church to take a confrontational posture in dealing with social and political issues or with conventional life patterns.

In comparison to the passionate assertiveness with which the early church confronted the world of the gentiles and encountered the traditional Jewish communities, the Protestant church in Japan began its life by assimilating Western architectural styles, forms of worship, and hymns and attempted to avoid head-on confrontation with the society of the day. Within a short time, the church became almost a secret society rather than a missionary body moving into the mainstream of society, or so it appeared to the general populace. The atmosphere of a church meeting, whether worship service or a fellowship, was usually that of a school. It was difficult for the church to form a relationship of solidarity and coworkership with other organizations and religions in order to tackle common problems. The church tended to be ingrown.

Of course, this is not the total picture. There have also been within the Japanese church leaders and groups forcefully confronting the urgent issues of the society by asserting new concepts, values, and perceptions. Masahisa Uemura, Danjo Ebina, Joseph Neesima, Kanzo Uchimura, Gumpei Yamamuro, Toyohiko Kagawa, Umeko Isuda, Motoko Hani, and

Michi Kawai are some of those Japanese who have made a prophetic impact on the total society.

Granting that these people and some Christian churches and groups did contribute to social, political, and religious change, we still need to face the slowness with which the church has grown in Japan and its introverted nature. We may ask whether this is simply a reflection of the Japanese mentality and personality from which the church has been unable to free itself. As we look into other religous groups, we find some interesting contrasts to what we have seen in the church.

A CASE STUDY IN *RISSHO KOSEIKAI*

Professor Kenneth J. Dale has studied *Rissho Koseikai,* an offshoot from the Nichiren Buddhist tradition founded in 1938 by Nikkyo Niwano and Mrs. Myoko Naganuma. Basing its religious principle on the *Rissho ankoku ron,* "to establish true Buddhism to secure peace in this country," this relatively new religion "is intended to hold before people the ideal of a true faith that involves a concern for the whole of society."[8] This movement is described as a sect aiming "to be a faith-oriented fellowship of harmoniously related believers who seek perfection of character, enlightenment, and eventual Buddhahood."[9] Dale analyzes the doctrinal essence of *Rissho Koseikai* by focusing on the Four Noble Truths (*shitai*) of classical Buddhism: suffering (*kutai*), cause (*jittai*), extinction (*mettai*), and path (*dotai*). There is nothing strikingly new about this doctrinal orientation in the light of Buddhist history. There is, however, an interesting integration of both Hinayana and Mahayana Buddhist teachings which gives *Rissho Koseikai* a sort of missionary orientation and makes it practical in confronting contemporary problems of believers.

One unique practical aspect of this religious group is its system of *hoza,* "small gatherings in which people of both sexes meet with a leader to discuss problems of faith or concerns of daily life."[10] The physical format for *hoza* is for people to sit in a circle so that face-to-face encounter is made possible, enabling the participants to sense intimacy, acceptance, and rapport and to express themselves in sharing insights. Dale analyzes this as similar to group counseling in which a close-knit group based upon the extended family plays a dominant role, and suggests that the therapeutic effects are unique in Japanese life. The role of the leader in this circular setting is not, ideally, paternal in nature, giving directions from the top to a subordinate person. Rather, he or she appeals to the corporate body and asks the group to treat the problem presented as a common problem. This does not negate the process of individualizing a problem, but arouses a sense of responsibility in the person confronting the problem while being supported by the group. Dale points out that the seemingly contradictory elements in the *hoza* dynamics, the intricate intertwining of individuality and corporateness, do not always lead a person to socially directed problem-solving. He also describes a tendency in the leader to act in an authoritarian manner, which fits the general Japanese expectation. In other words, there is still a vertical line and sense of dependency in people who gather for *hoza* sessions. This is not particularly surprising since individual self-confidence and self-determination are not the expected or desired goals of counseling in Japan.[11]

My focus here is on the *hoza* of *Rissho Koseikai* as a form of religious act or community. Niwano, the founder of this religious organization, insists that *hoza*, "the life of *Rissho Koseikai*," had its origin in the days of Buddha, when priests gathered on days of the new and full moon to confess to each other misdoings and "misthoughts." A leader then exhorted them to determine the causes of such straying and suggested they be discarded. This instruction was called *"musubi,"* literally, "to tie together." Religiously it meant to know what was behind one's stain in act and thought and to have one's heart cleansed with a sense of enlightenment.[12]

There are serious questions which need to be asked about the doctrinal foundations of this religion, which stresses immediate and concrete benefits in its faith. And yet in the religious practice of *hoza* we can see a fascinating expression of indigenous religious sentiments integrated into a common daily life. Undoubtedly there are vestiges of vertical relationships functioning in *hoza* sessions, but the usual rigid top-down structures are modified, at least externally. The Western Christian emphasis upon autonomous individuality and the solemn encounter of a person with her or his God is still valid and important. What the church in Japan has lacked in the past is the creation and nurture of a supportive community of mutual acceptance with a sense of "collectivistic dependency," to use Dale's term.

CONCLUSION

My concern is with Christianity as a community event and the maintenance of its communal nature in today's world. We are challenged to search for ways to renew the Japanese Christian communities we have inherited while we probe new styles and forms of life together in an urban and technological world that tends to break and divide rather than bind and nurture human communities. The task then is theological from the very beginning. What is needed is a process of theological re-examination of the church as a community of faith. If we are to move toward innovation and experimentation, we also need to begin simultaneously with social, cultural, and psychological analysis and planning to see how loving and nurturing relationships can be established in a society that is dominantly vertical and values harmony by means of conformity. A wholesome and supportive community requires a relationship of mutual acceptance and a unity of diverse lives and experiences. The challenge to the church in Japan is to break the patterns of rigid verticality, which obstructs open and free interrelationships, but also the exclusiveness of fellowship. That exclusiveness functions both in the relationships of the church to the world and to other churches within the larger Christian community. The community of the followers of Jesus must have its base in the world, whether it is externally or internally Christian or not.

For a Christianity desiring to make an impact upon the total society, Japan is still tough ground. Not only is the church in Japan an extreme minority, but the society is dominated by the existence of long-established religions and value orientations. There is also an illusory concept, deeply rooted in the general populace, that Japan and the Japanese are religious by nature. Life in Japan, even in its externally modern urban pattern of daily living, is loaded with religious rites and rituals. Protestant Christianity, with its history of some 130 years, is still an outside intruder to this setting of an ancient history.

It is urgently important for Christians in Japan to review their history and present state as a community and see what they can learn from other religious groups to which Japanese people are responding actively and positively. Imitation is not what is needed, but an analysis of the dynamics involved in the active and positive responses to other religious values and practices. Together with a fresh theological exploration of the core of the Christian faith, the church in Japan must provide an accepting and refreshing community in which the wholeness of a person is given priority and in which a sense of intimacy through the horizontal nature of relationships is made real. Such relationships must not be detached from social realities of the world but nurtured through the sharing of life together in the world. Only in forming such a community, bringing forth an authentic circle of harmony in which people can live and grow together in love, does true hope for liberating persons in Japan become real.

RECOMMENDED READING

Benedict, Ruth. *The Chrysanthemum and the Sword.* Boston: Houghton Mifflin, 1946.

Dale, Kenneth J. *Circle of Harmony: A Case Study in Popular Japanese Buddhism.* Tokyo: Seibunsha, 1975.

Doi, Takeo. *The Anatomy of Dependence.* New York: Kodansha, 1973.

Drummond, Richard H. *A History of Christianity in Japan.* Grand Rapids, MI: Eerdmans, 1971.

Hori, Ichiro, ed. *Japanese Religion.* New York: Kodansha, 1974.

Nakane, Chie. *Japanese Society.* Rutland, VT: Charles E. Tuttle, 1984.

Phillips, James H. *From the Rising of the Sun.* Maryknoll, NY: Orbis, 1981.

CHAPTER 16

Rituals of Healing: Ministry with and on Behalf of Gay and Lesbian People

ANITA C. HILL and LEO TREADWAY

CONTEXT AND COMMITMENT

FROM A LESBIAN PERSPECTIVE

Why do you stay involved in organized religion? How do you survive in that patriarchal institution? These are questions I am often asked, especially by members of the lesbian community. The queries are understandable. Through the years, organized religion has, by and large, *not* been friend or advocate of gay and lesbian involvement in church and society. In fact, our communities have faced outright rejection and oppression from churches claiming to follow Jesus Christ, who, oddly enough, came with a message of love for all and freedom for the oppressed.

There are several approaches one can take to bring about change in institutions. One is to leave the institution and attempt to change it from the outside. Another is to ignore the organization by developing competing alternative systems. A third is to struggle from the inside to change the structure and essence of the institution. Each of these approaches has positive and negative aspects. Unfortunately, at times within the lesbian community, more energy is expended in arguing the importance of supporting *one* "politically correct" and unified method of action than is expended toward effecting change.

It is my firm belief that the combined efforts of many-sided attacks against a problem can best produce the changes we desire. I salute the creativity and courage of lesbians who abandon traditional churches to explore more women-centered spirituality and ways of worship. In similar fashion, I support the efforts of lesbians who critique organized religion from outside its often male-guarded gates. It takes yet another form of strength and fortitude to carry on the struggle for lesbian and gay rights inside religious institutions. I believe lesbians and gay men need to give each other and ourselves the flexibility and support required to connect with the spirituality and advocacy approaches best suited to our individual needs and circumstances.

I work inside the traditional church structures (as an openly lesbian ministry associate of a congregation in the Evangelical Lutheran Church of America) for two major reasons. First, organized religion in our society holds much control over the mindset and functioning of many people. It seems an appropriate tactical stance to attempt to influence and change the views of the church's power base from its core. My role vacillates from that of revolutionary to conciliator depending on the situation, but the vision of a church and society that is accepting of diversity in its midst remains foremost.

The second reason is related to my feeling called by God/dess to a ministry of reconciliation and advocacy on behalf of lesbian and gay people and their family members. In a world that has become so removed from spiritual connections, many people find it strange to hear me speak of having a call to this ministry. Straight people tend to discount it as "another lesbian trying to justify her lifestyle," while lesbians and gay men discredit it as "a sellout to a straight oppressive institution." Nevertheless, I do what I must with God/dess guidance to move us toward an inclusive vision in a diverse world.

As a lesbian woman who has learned both the gift and the struggle inherent in being different in a culture that too often describes normal as monocultural, I acknowledge the bicultural reality that is mine as a member of the lesbian/gay subculture. I am committed to breaking the stereotypes and invisibility barrier faced by lesbian women. I am constantly reevaluating whether I can best impact the system (religious or secular) for change from inside or out. Naming and validating the reality of myself and my lesbian sisters is the starting place for change toward growth and life, and ultimately toward God and interconnectedness.

From the Perspective of a Gay Man

"Loving People, Loving God." That's what it said on the button I wore. The middle-aged woman with whom I spoke, following the adult forum, maintained that my button was ludicrous, there was no way that I could be a gay man and a Lutheran. Yet that is exactly who I am. Unable to accept myself as a child of God if I were gay, I spent many years living my life and faith on the margins, never really allowing myself to fit in. But something remarkable happened when I finally understood that my life as a gay man was a profound gift from a very caring God. I began to move away from the marginal existence I had led and found myself engaged in a life dedicated to bridging between groups, most specifically between gay men, lesbians, and the heterosexual majority which made up the institutional church.

That "coming out" experience was one of the most profoundly spiritual experiences of my life, and the excitement of knowing myself to be deeply loved and accepted by God was something I wanted to help others find and share. As I worked with, loved, and supported others I began to find a sense of my own spiritual journey. I knew that my life and faith had been sharpened and shaped by my own experience of being different, and being different in a way that evoked the intense hostility of many people in both church and society. They were also shaped by, but more importantly, rooted in my love for other men. This was not a condition in life I had chosen, but rather one which was given. Underneath all the storm and strife, I knew that if my being was rooted in love, then it must also be rooted in God.

But I labored long and hard under the oppressive understandings of the so-called traditional biblical material. I needed to be able to find my story in God's story, if I was to continue in the community of faith. I set myself to a process of intensive study. Imagine my surprise when I discovered that I did not know everything I always thought I knew about the Bible and homosexuality. The traditional material continued to speak to me, but also to others in a different way. I found people like myself in the scriptural stories. I discovered material in which I could find my own experiences and struggles. And I found that I had not been so wrong to trust that my love was also from God.

Simply finding myself in God's story was suddenly not enough, because it prompted me to continue my own journey in faith, and to become involved in caring for others and doing justice. My faith prompted me to begin active ministry with other gay men, lesbians, family members, and friends. I often reflected on an experience I had early in my process of coming out. Despite my bumbling and clumsiness, another young man took me under his wing. He was my first real contact with other men like myself. I must have tried his patience sorely, but his support and encouragement continued until I could walk by myself. I like to think of this man, whose name I cannot even recall, as a messenger from God, sent to me in the form of a human being who could show me that God did care. He came into my life, wrought a miracle, then disappeared. I owe my imaging of "servanthood" to this man.

Finding myself, and finding my place in God's heart, suddenly became the lens through which I could finally understand all those earlier lessons from Sunday school and church. With a very special gift from God, and knowing that there was nothing which could ever separate me from the love of God, I knew that my ministry was beginning. In a very tender scene during the movie *Outrageous*, a drag queen character said it most succinctly: "We were put here on this earth to love and take care of one another." I have tried to follow that commandment ever since. And I do that by trying to bridge the fears that separate us, and by working for justice. I continue to ask God to help and guide me . . . and the "angels" still come when needed.

CONSTRUCTION

Understanding gay and lesbian Christians presents a challenge for growth in faith to both clergy and laity today. Old models of working with the homosexual community began with the premise that all homosexuals needed to be cured or saved from their illness, which prompted ministry models of counseling for change to heterosexuality or sexual abstinence. Although homosexuality was removed as a diagnosis of illness in medicine and psychiatry in 1973, the notion of same-gender sexual orientation as inherently sinful has persisted in much of the religious community.

This chapter will critique the old models and provide examples of how healing grace and reconciliation have become hallmarks in the new models of ministry with and on behalf of gay and lesbian people and their family members. Key to the new model is listening to the voices of gay and lesbian people regarding their faith and life experiences. Hearing these voices challenges us to a new ministry of response and advocacy with people too often excluded from the Christian community.

A conspiracy of silence about lesbians and gay men has set the tone for an inadequate or absent sociopolitical response to the needs of these individuals in church and society. Misinformation fills the void left by silence and perpetuates myths and stereotypes. Gay and lesbian people have been castigated by the church and have been the victims of violence and oppression in our society. Yet even in the face of others' denial of their common humanity and repudiation of their Christian faith, many lesbians and gay men have remained faithful people seeking Christian community. Because of their presence and witness, the conspiracy of silence which has surrounded gay and lesbian people in Christian communities is beginning to be broken.

At this time in history we are still faced with conflicting views regarding homosexuality. Materials which advocate acceptance can be located in both secular and religious realms, as can materials which hold a rejecting or punishing view toward homosexuality. Given a homophobic culture, it is not surprising to find confusion among helpful professionals (teachers, pastors, therapists, and physicians) regarding approaches. It is a curious time to be involved in ministry with gay and lesbian people. While many nongays remain uninformed about the realities of gay and lesbian lives, others are learning with a growing openness and finding lesbians and gay men to be "real people."

The two psychological and theological approaches to homosexuality in use today may be characterized broadly as: 1) a sickness/cure psychological model, paralleled by a sin/salvation theological model (the old ministry model); and 2) a health/integration psychological model, paralleled by a wholeness/acceptance theological model (the new ministry model).

SICKNESS/CURE MODEL

"The view that homosexuality is a disease originated in the 'organic' approach characteristic of the nineteenth century."[1] Since then researchers have sought causes of the "disease" in the areas of physiology, endocrinology, heredity, environment, and parenting.

Psychological studies have also proposed variables which may cause homosexuality. Irving Bieber's research findings on male homosexuals in psychoanalytic treatment have been the basis for much recent support of the sickness/cure model. His 1962 study laid the "blame" for homosexuality on disturbed parent-child interactions, labeling the child's resulting adaptation (homosexuality) "necessarily pathologic." Bieber maintained that through psychoanalytic treatment "a heterosexual shift is a possibility for all homosexuals who are strongly motivated to change."[2] Albert Ellis reported similar results with both male and female homosexuals in psychotherapy.[3]

Sigmund Freud's work on homosexuality stands in contrast to this. He and his followers assumed more than one mechanism was involved in the etiology of homosexuality and emphasized the concept of bisexuality, noting that the homosexual component may be dominant for some. They also denied homosexuality was a vice or an illness and insisted that the results of treatment were not predictable.[4]

The movement from Freud's position to that of Bieber and Ellis represents a shift from viewing homosexuality as a (nearly) unchangeable part of an individual to a belief that it is a pathologic condition which *must* be changed. The conviction of some psychoanalysts of the necessity for change to heterosexuality has produced such "treatment" techniques as systematic desensitization, moral persuasion, shaming, guilt, emetic persuasion, shock therapy, and brain surgery.[5] Although the sickness/cure model of psychotherapy with gay and lesbian individuals continues to be used today, homosexuality was removed from the list of mental disorders of the American Psychiatric Association in 1973 and the American Psychological Association in 1975.[6]

SIN/SALVATION MODEL

The theological model which parallels the sickness/cure model assumes that homosexuality is a departure from the God-created heterosexual order of nature and therefore inherently sinful. Salvation is repentance from homosexuality and reorientation to heterosexuality or celibacy. Gay and lesbian persons are heretics who have turned away from the true faith, characterized by heterosexuality.

The church's traditional understanding of homosexuality is that it is a sin against nature. As Augustine argued, since homosexual acts cannot lead to procreation, they run counter to the Creator's intent. Thomas Aquinas added that homosexual acts are more grievous than adultery or rape "because homosexual practices 'are always an injury done to the Creator, whether or not any offense is at the same time committed against one's neighbor,' since they violate His creative intent for human behavior and destroy the beauty of His work."[7]

The sin/salvation model has led to church exclusion and condemnation of homosexuals. It is a theologically bankrupt model for gay and lesbian persons. The "love the sinner, but hate the sin" variation of this model can be defended in the abstract, but "in the concrete is a copout. 'Sin' is an abstraction which exists only when someone does something. In practice, it is the sinner who is hated and violated."[8] This model discounts the societal context of homophobia in which it arose and has, more often than not, been an instrument of harm rather than healing.

The term homophobia was coined in 1973 by Dr. George Weinberg, who defined it as "irrational fear on the part of heterosexuals of being in close proximity to a homosexual."[9] Current dictionary listings provide two definitions of homophobia: 1) fear, dislike, or hatred of gay men and lesbians, and 2) discrimination against lesbians and gay men. An insidious homophobia filters through all our interactions whether one is homosexual or heterosexual in orientation. Homophobic attacks on gay or lesbian individuals leave the entire community afraid and perhaps appropriately paranoid about "coming out of the closet" (acknowledging one's same-gender sexual orientation), thus perpetuating the conspiracy of silence. Lesbians and gay men must also overcome an internalized homophobia in which we devalue ourselves and our contributions by believing the untruths told about us by society at large. A circular trap exists in which we stay hidden to avoid discrimination and persecution while the very hiddenness which means survival perpetuates the stereotypes and fear about us.

The pervasive nature of our society's homophobia has recently been highlighted as a result of the AIDS (Acquired Immune Deficiency Syndrome) crisis. AIDS is a deadly disease which has struck a group of people whom many in our society presume are deviant, morally destitute, criminal, and ultimately disposable. It is commonplace to hear scapegoating of persons with AIDS because they are gay or bisexual men or intravenous drug users. Pronouncements of AIDS as God's judgment upon homosexuals leave us aware of the homophobic levels in our society. Gay and bisexual men have increasingly become the targets of violent acts, discrimination, and hate- or fear-motivated crimes. The National Gay/Lesbian Task Force indicates a twofold increase in reported acts of violence and victimization against lesbians and gay men across the United States from 1985 to 1986.[10]

The old models of ministry to homosexuals were based on a system that viewed heterosexuality as the *only* and the superior sexual orientation. This heterosexist system presumed further that since there was only one true orientation, homosexuality was obviously a deviant and sinful choice which should be changed at any cost. Homosexuality was viewed as illness or sinfulness in need of cure or salvation.

HEALTH/INTEGRATION MODEL

The health/integration psychological model has an underlying premise that homosexuality is not an illness, but one orientation on the scale of human sexuality, no more or less valid than heterosexuality. In this model the caregiver's focus moves away from an exclusive preoccupation with the sexual activity of gay and lesbian persons to assisting the individual to integrate a same-gender sexual orientation into one's life. The terms "gay man and lesbian woman" and "gay/lesbian persons" replace the exclusive use of the term "homosexual(s)." George Weinberg (1973) proposed that "a homosexual person is gay [lesbian] when [s]he regards [her]himself as happily gifted with whatever capacity [s]he has to see people as romantically beautiful. It is to be free of shame, guilt, regret over the fact that one is homosexual. . . . To be gay [lesbian] is to view one's sexuality as the healthy heterosexual views his [hers]."[11]

The health/integration model supports Weinberg's idea that a gay or lesbian person can integrate his or her sexual orientation into a healthy, mature life. Sexual orientation is viewed as being as inherently natural to an individual as eye and skin color. Homosexuality is not afforded any special meaning. It is seen as "a fact of life; the rest is interpretation and consequence."[12] The task of the health/integration psychological approach is to assist gay and lesbian persons in accepting themselves and integrating their sexuality into mature lifestyles. Acknowledging societal homophobia and oppression of gay and lesbian people is an integral part of the process.

Ann and Barry Ulanov discuss the effect of societal rigidity: "If the effort to rid him[her]self of all impulses that contradict the ethical code is unconscious, then the person will probably resort—unconsciously—to repression of those defiant sides of him[her]self, and action with perilous consequences for those around him[her]self."[13] This sort of repression finds release in some other way, such as "projection onto a substitute enemy, a scapegoat who carries in one's place all that one identifies as immoral and shuns. One can then persecute the scapegoat who evokes no sympathy."[14] In our insidiously homophobic culture, gay and lesbian persons become the scapegoats which evoke no sympathy. "Hence, [a gay or lesbian person] can be only a victim, never a martyr."[15]

Relief in a therapeutic experience "comes when the sufferer sees the truth about [her]himself, the causes and the meaning of this suffering. Psychoanalysis aims to uncover and piece together the truth for the person to see, to feel, to ponder. What one wants to be true or needs to be true, what moral rules say should be true, mean nothing. Only the actual truth—unvarnished, self-evident, open to conscious and unconscious inspection—heals or can be endured."[16] Gay and lesbian people, through coming out, are stating what they know to be true about themselves and are bringing their reality to the attention of both psychology and theology to be considered in light of their truth.

WHOLENESS/ACCEPTANCE MODEL

The wholeness/acceptance model presents the theological possibility of full acceptance and affirmation of gay and lesbian people. As James B. Nelson has said, "Those who affirm this position most often make the assumption that homosexual orientation is more of a given than a free choice. More fundamentally, however, this position rests on the conviction that same-sex relationships can richly express and be the vehicle of God's humanizing intentions."[17]

Once homosexuality is considered a variation in the realm of human sexuality (no better or worse than heterosexuality), gay and lesbian life and faith experience can be taken seriously. "In the past, many gay people simply said, 'Your theory is wrong. So is your religion. Who needs it?' and left the churches. Now, more and more gay people are saying, 'Your theory does not fit our experience. Religion and the church are important to us, and we are not going to go away.'"[18]

Coming out is a profound spiritual experience in the individual and community lives of gay and lesbian people. To name the truths about one's own reality in the world is to make the connections which end isolation, form community, and lead to an experience of liberating grace. Coming out, naming and claiming one's self even in the face of adversity and homophobia, is a freeing revelation which helps us feel God's presence in our midst. It is to know inside that even when we feel too scared or shamed to utter our own stories, God knows the story and is with us offering acceptance and a nonjudgmental listening ear.

The wholeness/acceptance model of ministry challenges Christians to follow Jesus Christ, who cared about "the most hated, discredited persons in the society in which He lived. . . . He felt their pain, knew their hunger and thirst, recognized their humanity, saw the image of God in them. In short, He loved them."[19] In the wholeness/acceptance model gay and lesbian people, recognized as an unjustly stigmatized, ostracized group, are accepted as whole persons receiving God's grace and concern.

Biblical themes used to support the wholeness/acceptance position include: injunctions against self-righteous judging of others and against bearing false witness against one's neighbors; the call to inclusivity in the church of the diversity of God's creation; and Jesus' example of love, concern, and action on behalf of the outcasts of society. Further support of this model may be seen in Fr. John McNeill's emphasis on contributions which acceptance of gay and lesbian people can make to church and society: "The objective acceptance of the homosexual community will potentially leave both communities (homosexual and heterosexual) free from the need to conform to narrow stereotypes, and positively free to develop all the qualities that belong to the fullness of the human personality."[20] The prophetic role of the gay and lesbian community is also seen as a gift of grace in the wholeness/acceptance model. "The future of gay/lesbian liberation lies not only in its ability unitedly to pursue justice for homosexual people, but also in its ability to embrace in love the outcry for freedom among all people."[21]

WINGSPAN MINISTRY MODEL

Background and Mission

Few congregations or denominations have taken seriously the challenges of the new models and opened themselves to dialogue with lesbian and gay Christians or carried out intentional ministry with and on behalf of these individuals. To do so is to acknowledge that "we don't know everything we always thought we knew about this" and to live with an openness to the voice of the Spirit. Wingspan Ministry with and on behalf of gay and lesbian people and their families at St. Paul-Reformation Lutheran Church in Saint Paul, Minnesota, is one place where the challenge of the wholeness/acceptance model has been engaged. Since its inauguration by St. Paul-Reformation's church council in 1982, Wingspan Ministry has existed as a beacon of hope to lesbian and gay persons, their families and friends—a sign that the church can be a sanctuary and advocate for them.

St. Paul-Reformation Lutheran Church is a diverse community of faith, including elderly people, Black people, married people, young people, gay and lesbian people, white people, deaf people, Asian people, single people, handicapped people, Ethiopian people, families with children, middle-aged people, and more. It is intentionally a community which takes seriously the call to be an avenue of advocacy and Christian concern for those often excluded in our society and a sign that our differences can be a gift, not a barrier, to human relationships.

The major goal of Wingspan Ministry in this congregation is to welcome lesbians and gay men who are creative, gifted people, children of God, back into the church community through congregational involvement. Two tasks are central to this: 1) serving as a bridge between gay men and lesbians, their families, friends, communities, and the greater church to create an open door facilitating the "coming home" of people generally excluded from the church; and 2) improving the quality of life for gay men and lesbians through education, advocacy, and pastoral care, especially in the areas of wholeness and human justice.

Wingspan has been intentionally staffed by both an openly gay man and lesbian woman to provide access to both gay male and lesbian communities, which have often been quite separate from each other. It is important that as staff for a ministry with and on behalf of gay and lesbian people, we be open about ourselves and be clearly gay- and lesbian-identified. Being open about our experiences as lesbian and gay Christians has been a crucial aspect of our efforts to bring healing and reconciliation into congregational settings. Lesbian and gay people are active in leadership roles in congregation worship.

Being grounded in a diverse congregation which is concerned that language inclusive of women and symbolism representative of all of humanity be lifted up has helped to connect or reconnect lesbian women to the church as much as being open to different orientations and lifestyles. We are faced with two different evangelism scenarios regarding gay men and lesbian women. It is one thing to set aside judgment about homosexuality and welcome gay men back into a church with a male Godhead, as that presents a wonderfully empowering image for men who love men. It is quite another thing to attempt to reach out to lesbian women by inviting them to return to a sexist and patriarchal institution.

A Ministry of Empowerment and Advocacy

Wingspan was established as a ministry "with and on behalf of" gay and lesbian people, not "to" or "for" them. This distinction is important, for it indicates a ministry of support and empowerment of individuals, families, and groups; and a ministry of advocacy on behalf of lesbian and gay people both in church and society.

This ministry recognizes that homosexuality is not the problem; homophobia is the problem. Homophobia is a spiritual affliction which alienates and separates people from themselves, each other, and God. Anti-homophobia presentations and workshops form a basis for much of the educational efforts of Wingspan.

Intentional dialogue is another central educational effort. Hearing from gay and lesbian people, listening to their life and faith stories is a way to interrupt the "them" and "us" naming of a group we fear as totally other, alien, or inhuman. Making personal the human connections through our stories helps nongay people recognize that the ten percent of the population who are gay or lesbian are people just like themselves. People of faith need to get past the debate about "them" and whether "they" are acceptable to "us" or to "our" God or "our" church. We need to reframe the questions themselves. A more appropriate way of posing the question is: "What is the role of gay and lesbian people in the midst of this congregation, this place of community?"

An advertisement for Wingspan states that "Christ was not freed from the tomb to keep you locked in the closet." For some church people this message seems startling, shocking, even irreverent. For many gay and lesbian people, it means a new connection with their Savior. It means that the freedom from death promised in Christ's resurrection also extends the promise of freedom from other fears and bondage in their lives. For many, embracing this message means freedom from the desperation of a closeted isolation.

Wingspan and St. Paul-Reformation congregation provide an atmosphere of acceptance and trust which helps gay and lesbian people to come out, to break through the barrier of invisibility which entraps us in our homophobic culture. Wingspan staff developed a service of preparation for coming out to parents and family in which the community names itself as family in solidarity with individuals grappling with coming out concerns. Just as coming out breaks the invisibility barrier so that people must see and respond to gay and lesbian existence, services of blessing of relationship call the church to examine the mixed messages it gives to gay and lesbian people. When the church is unable to support relationships and even discourages them, it seems not only to expect promiscuity from gay and lesbian people (whom it assumes cannot maintain committed, convenantal relationships), but to demand promiscuity (named as life-long abstinence).

Theologizing arises out of our human experience. For the most part, the church has denied the experience of lesbians and gay men in drawing its conclusions. Relationships are key to knowing the presence of God in our lives. Carter Heyward states "that the experience of relation is fundamental and constitutive of human being; that it is good and powerful; and it is only within this experience . . . that we may realize that the power in relation is God."[22] There is an ontological component which is an essential element of human relationships beneath the visible reality; it is an issue of transcendental "being." To deny the blessing which comes through gay and lesbian relationships is to deny God. By holding blessing of relationship services for gay and lesbian couples, Wingspan Ministry moves toward a goal of enabling each individual to relate, including sexual relating, in ways which are life-giving, creative, and whole.

Reclaiming scripture and establishing new parameters in which to engage our discussions about biblical material has provided a solid footing for Wingspan Ministry. Biblical witness is important to the lives and development of lesbian and gay people. It has been healing to set aside as the starting point the "seven troublesome passages" so often raised in the debate about homosexuality. Setting aside the passages generally used as a "biblical bludgeon" against gay and lesbian people has given us the freedom to allow the voices of the people to give insights about the scriptures that keep them connected to God, Christ, and Christian community in spite of the oppression within the church.

Too often, gay and lesbian people are put on the defensive by the demands that we justify our lifestyle by giving our responses to the story of Sodom and Gomorrah, the holiness codes in Leviticus, and the writings of St. Paul in Romans and Timothy which are usually translated to read homosexuality in modern versions. Putting those aside, rich imagery has been raised up by gay and lesbian interpreters of biblical material who find guidance for their lives recorded in the other stories found there. Like others involved in liberation theology movements, gay and lesbian people find in Jesus of Nazareth one who came to bring freedom to the captives—in our case captives to homophobia and the resultant isolation and invisibility needed to survive. We hear in the good shepherd stories that "there are sheep who are not in this pen, who Christ will bring in so there will be one flock with one Shepherd." Jesus' message to Lazarus to "come out" takes on new meaning for gay and lesbian people who hear the message that there is freedom from our closet/tombs in life, resurrection, and the message of our Savior.

Wingspan has convened groups on Bible study and faith development and has held healing services in which a diverse group of congregation members participated. These times of sharing our life experiences have created a deeper understanding and bonding among community members. Weekend conferences provide the context for faith explorations in many arenas. Further work with biblical study will add to our communal understanding of the role of lesbian and gay persons in the church. "Embrace Hope" healing services are held regularly to help people prepare themselves spiritually in response to the AIDS crisis.

Building safe places of community among gay and lesbian persons, their family members, and friends has been a strength of the Wingspan Ministry. Wingspan staff act as liaisons for several groups which meet at St. Paul-Reformation: Parents and Friends of Lesbians and Gays, Lutherans Concerned/Twin Cities (the gay/lesbian caucus of Lutheran denominations), Gay Fathers' Support Group, Non-gay Spouses Support Group. Lesbian and Gay Youth Together is one example of groups with which Wingspan maintains a close working relationship. Facilitation is done in a supportive manner, and Wingspan does not run the programs or claim ownership of them. Giving people permission and space to explore their own needs and responses around gay and lesbian experience has been an important part of this evolving ministry of empowerment.

In contrast to ethnic minority groups, gay and lesbian people and their family members are isolated and invisible. Since there is no way to be sure of another person's affectional orientation until s/he acknowledges it for us, lesbian women and gay men may have a difficult time identifying others with whom they can feel safe to share their experiences and expectations. Family members live in the closet, too, and many actually feel more isolated than the lesbian or gay family member who has found support and friends in the lesbian or gay community.

The intergenerational sharing which provides history, continuity, perspective, and insight into the oppression felt by members of a minority community has been a virtual impossibility for lesbian and gay people, because so many have had to hide for so long. In situations where a Black, Hispanic, or Native American person might turn to family members for guidance about how to cope with a world that seemingly doesn't want them, lesbian and gay people often have nowhere to turn. The logical choice of family for another group could mean a painful rejection or disinheritance for gay men and lesbian women. Coming out to family members is often more difficult than telling strangers.

The concept of lesbian and gay elders who might provide such a familial role of continuity and education for younger gay and lesbian people is nearly unknown. Our culture has so closely connected active sexual involvement to the stereotype of what it means to be lesbian or gay that we virtually have no images of the elderly and few of adolescents or children who identify themselves as gay or lesbian people. It is a matter of conflicting stereotypes: gay and lesbian people are falsely labelled as totally sexual beings and adolescents and elders as asexual beings.

CONCLUSION

Breaking the conspiracy of silence which shrouds lesbian and gay existence is central to liberation theology for lesbian and gay people. The key lies in hearing the stories of gay and lesbian life and faith experience and responding to the needs raised by them. Some church communities have begun to realize the powerful impact of listening to the pain of hurting people. Gay and lesbian people are invited to share their stores in a forty-five-minute adult forum on a Sunday morning.

But simply hearing the stories is not enough. Without a component of advocacy and standing in a position of solidarity with gay and lesbian people in our pain about the injustice we face in society, the listening becomes an empty form of "churchly voyeurism" in which gay and lesbian people are further victimized. It is crucial to combat the homophobia, prejudice, and discrimination against gay men and lesbian women in our church and society, to break the conspiracy of silence supporting the status quo, and to extend a clear word of welcome in God's house for all peoples. To advocate with and on behalf of gay and lesbian persons in this manner is to extend to them the best that can be offered in pastoral care from a congregation.

RECOMMENDED READING

Edwards, George R. *Gay/Lesbian Liberation: A Biblical Perspective.* New York: Pilgrim, 1984.

Fortunado, John E. *Embracing the Exile: Healing Journeys of Gay Christians.* San Francisco: Harper & Row, 1982.
Heyward, Carter. *Touching Our Strength.* San Francisco: Harper & Row, 1989.
McCaffrey, Joseph A., ed. *The Homosexual Dialectic.* Englewood Cliffs, NJ: Prentice-Hall, 1972.
McNeill, John J., S.J. *The Church and the Homosexual.* Boston: Beacon Press, 1988.
Nugent, Robert, ed. *A Challenge to Love.* New York: Crossroad, 1978.
Scanzoni, Letha, and Virginia R. Mollenkott. *Is the Homosexual My Neighbor?* San Francisco: Harper & Row, 1980.

CHAPTER 17

The Empowering Spirit
of Religion

MERCY AMBA ODUYOYE

CONTEXT AND COMMITMENT

I am first and foremost an Akan, a member of a matrilineal society speaking the language of *Akan* found in Ghana and the Ivory Coast, brought up to believe in the centrality of woman to the human community. Brought up in the church and working with churches or teaching theology, my worldview has been shaped by a utopia that is Christocentric. But this does not mean that I am blind to all else. In fact it is as an African that I am Christian and I have no conflicts with that, only periodic depression with regard to how little the church in Africa concerns itself with social issues.

I have had problems with how the church, academia, and the patriarchal society into which I married assign roles to women. My definition of personhood and identity as an Akan has led me several times into conflicts with role-expectations of people around me. My cross-cultural experience of twenty years has fueled my commitment to the promotion of the visibility of women in church, academy, and society.

I have also developed and nursed a deep passion for relevant education. In Africa we continue to educate for unemployment, rural exodus, and brain-drain. It hurts me to see so many young lives we are inadvertently plotting to throw into the streets to struggle for their survival. Miseducation happens not only at the level of the economy—it seems to be an all-around disaster area. My experience teaching in certificate-oriented institutions that do very little to nourish creativity has been painful. So my working life has been divided between formal and informal education. I continue to advocate variety in educational opportunities. Education relates directly to the meaning and value of being human. It is as critical to me as the meaning of being a woman.

In Africa poor quality and lack of vision in creating alternatives can be partly attributed to the lack of resources. This lack of resources, the result of the exploitation of the continent, has been a major influence on theology. The bondage of Africa's human, material, and spiritual resources propels me to seek a theological approach that is contextual. The injustice experienced by young people and women is part of the larger challenge of global inequities.

My involvement in practical social work is very limited. I have tried to contribute through writing and speaking that challenges peoples to be critical and committed to effecting humanizing changes in their environment. I began this "ministry" with a study of alternatives in youth education and employment. I produced cartoons on these situations to help young people to analyze their communities and to see how they are placed and may be placed.

At the university I revised a traditional dogmatic Christian theology course into one that looked at contemporary theology in relation to society and to Africa in particular. Liberation theology of Latin America and black theology of the United States and South Africa enabled me to move my classes toward women's perspectives on Christian theology. I took every opportunity to speak, preach, or conduct Bible study, in order to challenge people to take another look at their community and see if the Spirit of Christ does not convince them to challenge the structures of death around them.

I have arrived at a point where I no longer wish to be patient with sexism, racism, and injustices against the dignity that rightly belongs to beings made in the image of God. These labels are losing their force, but the realities they point to, the burden and the evil we are naming, continue. Those who live under them feel their iron weight. I may not be classified materially poor in my own community, but as long as I am a woman and black and refuse to accept any condition or attitude toward me that makes me feel less than accepted and included, I stand with all who are trampled upon and with all who want to struggle to see the end of inhumanity in the human community.

CONSTRUCTION

The Christianity of the rank and file is not necessarily that of the priestly class, though it is the face of the church that the world sees. People of the church who are ordinarily in daily converse with one another are the carriers of religion. How they live and what they live by is what constitutes Christianity for the observer. If Christians read their Bibles, pray with the African Instituted Churches (AIC; churches in the charismatic tradition in western Africa) as well as the Roman Catholic priest, they reinforce the notion of openness of the spirit that moves all Christians. It is the popular beliefs and practices passed on from mothers to their children that build up a person's spirituality.

The religious lives of women in Africa are yet to be studied in any detail. General observation of the high proportion of women compared to men who practice distinctive types of spirituality suggests this as an important arena for investigation. Given that women of Africa visit shrines, diviners, holy persons, and traditional doctors, some preliminary questions are: Why do women follow religio-cultural rites and rituals that are sometimes physically risky? Why this keen awareness of a necessity to stay close to the mysterious forces behind creation? What makes women so vulnerable to the spiritual dimensions of life? The all-women cults in West Africa will also yield material for further understanding of spirituality. It is not enough to keep saying women are religious. One should also ask why they are and what benefit they derive from it.

This chapter explores spirituality (understood here as the energy by which one lives and which links one's worldview to one's style of life) in the lives of African women. It observes women at prayer in two religious traditions, the primal religions of Africa and Christianity, examining prayers and praise uttered by a Ghanaian woman, Afua Kuma, and moving into an exploration of songs as carriers of spirituality. The ways in which integration of this traditional spirituality takes place in the lives of Christian women are illustrated with examples from Malawi. I have concluded with my reflections on the significance of these prayers and songs for a distinctively African women's spirituality.

THE POWER OF A WOMAN'S PRAYER

A woman sat in an extended family meeting astonished at the lack of caring in the handling of the matter at hand. It all sounded to her most "untraditional." Another woman was being scolded in the presence of younger members of the family. Present at the meeting was a maternal uncle's son who, according to custom, was not a member of his father's family and therefore should not be at the meeting to witness the debating of what was a serious threat to the unity of the family.

When the astonished woman could not hold on to herself any longer she left the meeting room, which had belonged to the previous head of family who had passed away a decade or so ago. She put both hands on her head and cried out *"Nana ee bohwe woegyir"* ("Grandfather come and see/supervise what is going on here, now that you are gone"). It was the turn of the men sitting as judges in the hall of meeting to be distraught. "What is she doing, is she calling our uncle to come and punish us?" A cry of distress directed to the ancestors is bound to have repercussions if injustice is being done to a member of the family.

My reading of this situation and others like it is that women's alacrity and initiative in matters of religion arise out of the fact that they are usually the first or the most directly affected by catastrophe. In direct appeal to spiritual powers and praise of God, women are first to be moved by the spirit. It is in formal liturgy that women are pushed to the margins, usually by all-male performers of religious ritual.

In African religions the formal incantations that accompany sacrifice and in Christianity the recitation of prayers in sacramental rites are usually denied to women. The leaders of organized religion like their brothers in politics hesitate to empower women to perform. In Africa it is in African Instituted Churches, founded and led by African women and men, that this men's monopoly is beginning to break down. In the AIC, women are on a par with men in the matter of singing and praying. In the original languages, prayers from these churches do not make a gender differentiation. It is only when they have been "reduced" into English by "collectors" that the women are blotted out by the generic use of *man*. Let us see what a feminist consciousness reveals from these AIC prayers.

AFRICAN INSTITUTED CHURCHES-DESIGNATED SPIRITUAL

Mary Edet, a retired schoolteacher studying to become a Presbyterian minister, has had many encounters with the AIC. She describes the practices of the Christ Army Church founded by Elijah Garrick Braide in 1915 as a movement away from the Anglican Church of Bakan in the rivers state of Nigeria. Like several new Christian movements of the late nineteenth and early twentieth centuries elsewhere in Africa, it was born out of opposition to the racism and ethnocentrism of Euro-Americans on the continent. Edet finds its distinctiveness in the seriousness with which Acts 2:17 is appropriated: "Your sons and daughters shall prophesy." This has freed women from the imposed understandings of themselves as clients of a male priesthood. Not only that, they have appropriated the role of diviners, by prophesying in the context of worship.

In this church the healing ministry is in the hands of a prophetess called "Mother," and it is her ministry that draws members to the church. Through her ministrations people are able to have the causes of their many afflictions identified and remedies proposed. The system of healing she practices lends itself to the suspicion that "powers not altogether Christian" are being used. But then, I ask, who can fathom the deep roots of human spirituality amidst a religiously pluralist people? The fact is that prayer-healing is a central aspect of the life of AIC, resorted to by both women and men. It has established itself as a gift of the Holy Spirit, given to women and men alike.

Elizabeth Amoah contends that to get at "the vital aspects of women's experience of God" in Africa, one would have to take into account all the living religions in Africa. She contends further that cutting across all religions is the fact that women are more demonstrative of their spirituality and more ready to confess their dependence on the movement of the spirit. Writing on women in the AIC-designated "Spiritual Churches," Amoah says: "Women in these churches are very much convinced that true spirituality can be attained and sustained through vigorous fasting, praying and reflecting on the word of God. This they claim is the true way by which God grants them the spirit and the power to do the tasks ahead of them."[1] They rely on God for the spirit that empowers them. That women's spiritual powers are often calumnized as of the devil is nothing new. But women survive, strengthened by the sayings of Jesus: "By their fruits you shall know them"; "How can Satan cast out Satan?" These women add, "And by what spirit do men perform comparable deeds?"

Spirit-directed women appropriate the healing power of Jesus for the benefit of those who come to them. Women who face marital problems, tensions associated with barrenness, or trading problems, consult these spirit-directed women, who make new songs and pray effectively for every occasion. Like Edet, Amoah observes that "many people are attracted to them because they want to know what the future has for them."[2] The effectiveness of the spirit-directed life of the AIC and the efficacy of their prayers is acknowledged by many in Africa.

An Anglican laywoman and a Yoruba, Bisi Sowunmi, challenged a group of Nigerian theologians with the question, "Where is theology in Nigeria?" In her piece she refers to the "indigenous appellations of God" as "profound and inspiring" and points to their use in the AIC, "where prayers are more meaningful, deep and efficacious." The importance attached to names in Africa is such that the AIC are digging into extra-biblical materials and spirituality for more names of God, using Akan sources that give people confidence.

ONE WOMAN'S SPIRITUALITY

With this we are ready for Afua Kuma, a charismatic leader in the AIC, whose prayers are resplendent with potent names of God. Sowunmi asks Nigerian theologians whether they have considered using imagery from the Ifa corpus of divination poems. Afua does not have to resort to a collected version of an African corpus. She lives in the midst of it and can tap directly into it. She "uses the language of African customs and proverbs, and African traditions of worship and chieftaincy to praise the name of Jesus."[3] Her prayers are distinguished by the fact that even petitions are made implicit in praise. Her appellations for Jesus range from human titles of royalty and warriors to that of friend and mother, the highest praise a woman gives a man. She calls on Jesus as a strong presence in nature, mountains, rocks, pythons, or in dependable human creations like unsinkable boats. Even modern professionals like doctors, lawyers, teachers, police, and soldiers become image-bearers of the Christ figure. Jesus is "The Big Tree which enables the vine to see the heavens while shedding drops of water from its leaves to nurture the under-growth."[4] It is Jesus, the savior of the poor, who supports the poor and makes them into respected persons. Creepers and climbers all enjoy the mothering care of Jesus.

Between the trickster tradition of Akan folktales and the "wonder-workers" of the Bible, Afua Kuma has built up for herself and those with whom she prays a powerful image of "Jesus the wonder-worker" while holding on to the wise and intimate friend image. In times of difficulty a woman affirms "Jesus is the rock in times of trouble. He helps the poor very often (always)." With such a one for a friend, life's battles are won hands down. Afua Kuma's prayers are in the spirit of this "Efik woman's Thanksgiving":

> Jesus is my true friend
> He saved my soul from death
> He gave me everlasting life
> He is worthy to be praised
> O glorify Jesus Christ

Mmrane in Twi and *oriki* in Yoruba mean praise-names of one's forebears often associated with one's own name. These are less formal than the family and official histories of great deeds of generations. Recitation of *mmrane* provides one with courage and confidence to face the task at hand, heightens the will to live and to do so honorably and creatively. What Afua Kuma offers us is the *Mmrane of Jesus Christ.* Believers who hear this walk confidently in the power of those praise-names. Their spirits are lifted, their faith established, and their hope is strengthened. With all this, their strength is renewed for the tasks of life before them.

A spirituality which derives directly from one's personal experience of Jesus is sometimes questioned by the official clan priests, who see themselves as mediators of grace through prayer and sacrament. It is therefore no surprise that by the time one gets to the fourteenth page of Afua Kuma's *Mmrane* of Jesus, one meets the question:

> You and I have got Jesus
> What a precious find
> What about these priests?

Read in the original Twi language, the question *"Na Asofo yie?"* sounds like "and these priests, where do they come in?" It seems to be a characteristic of Jewish and Christian traditions for the priests to try to appropriate women's independent expression of spirituality and sanctify it by priestly presence (see 1 Samuel 1:1–19). Afua's *Mmrane* of Jesus turns toward the end to a gospel call. To share the source of one's strength is the sign of a life rooted in faith.

> Come, all you people, to Jesus
> And you too will shine.

This is followed by the interruption, "It is Jesus who has made the priests into shiney ones," which is evidence of priestly cooptation of women's spirituality. The priests have inserted themselves into the chant.

The attempts of the priestly investigators to coopt Afua's vivid christology is evidence of the genuine power derived from her spirituality which is expressed in the following:

> We have come to earth to tire ourselves out
> In Jesus we find rest.

and

> Jesus is the pod which explodes to scatter the beans
> That make the sterile beget twins.

THE POTENT PRAYER OF WOMEN

The way women pray, says Annie Nachisale of Malawi, has not changed very much. All Christian women have done is to pray through Jesus rather than through their grandmothers and great-grandmothers who have gone before them.[5] In her country, she says, women have more concern for serving God. "If God is sparing the world, it is because of the prayers of women." Whether traditional women or Christian, when women gather to pray, they pray first for the whole world, then for their leaders and their families, and only finally for themselves. The hearts of women in Africa meet in prayer. All women believe that because *they* are, that's why *we* are. Standing together is strength for women, and there are several women's praying groups in Malawi.

African women pray in times of sickness and health, for rain and for well-being of the community, and in thanksgiving. Prayers for children and appearances at every available shrine in order to secure them and keep them healthy are the prime essence of women's spirituality. Like men, they believe that life is meaningless unless one bears children. When the children are sick, women do not sleep, they pray the whole night as they nurse the sick child:

> Lord, you gave me this child as a gift.
> Let the child grow, so that it might also
> serve you and I might rejoice together
> with you. Please Lord, spare the child.

When a child is dead, women do not stop praying. They continue:

> Lord, we do thank you that you gave us a child that
> it may make us happy in our friend's family. It is
> a sorrow to see that it has pleased you to take what
> is yours. We pray, 'Help the mourners, remove their
> sorrow and tears from their eyes in the name of Jesus.'

When there is sickness in the village, a communal prayer is offered under the leadership of the village prophetess, who prays:

aa Nkazikunkholo, children are finishing in the
village. Let the children cry and make noise in our
houses. When the moon is shining, let the children
sing and dance outside our houses. Please
grandmother, hear our prayer. God have mercy on us.
Let the children grow.

Priestess and the people then pray:

Yes, yes, yes, *Mthini, yes, yes, yes, Maseko.*

Mthini and Maseko are names of respect for the clan's ancestor spirit. It is
an honor to appease the spirit by praising it.

When her husband dies, in her grief a woman laments "my husband,
you have abandoned me."[6] The dirges sung by women are full of praise
for the dead and regrets for the parting. They weep because "what death
holds on to, a human being cannot snatch," while they sing "human
beings would indeed be worth nothing if there was no death." Death is
both welcomed and abhorred. It is, however, accepted as inevitable after
every known cure has failed.

In a culture in which men don't cry, it is not easy to ascertain the nature
of men's grief and in what way it is verbalized. Men wear all the symbolic
trappings of mourning. But women's protest against the separation and
the disruption that death causes to the community is always loud and
clear.

Women are a rearguard of prayer and ritual performances at all of life's
many war fronts. In Africa rain is one such front. In Malawi when there is
no rain in the country, a woman functions as a prophetess with priestesses. They come together under a big tree, bringing with them a plate
of flour, some beer, and perhaps an animal they have sacrificed. The
prophetess, with her assistant priestesses, kneels down under the tree,
calling on the ancestor spirit:

Prophetess: *A Sofiva, a Nkazikunkholo, a Phalaro!!!*
Priestesses: *Sorry, Sorry, Sorry . . . ry!*
Prophetess: The country is dry, we have
drought, we need rain.
Please convey our plea to
God. We your children will
die of hunger.
Priestesses: Sorry, Sorry, Sorry . . . ry!
Prophetess: *A Nkazikunkholo,* do you want
all of us dead with hunger?
Who is going to continue the
clan's name? Give us rain.

Within a short time clouds start forming and later the rains fall—
sometimes even before they have finished praying. Women derive

strength from the knowledge that God hears and answers the prayers of sincere believers who are dedicated to the welfare of the whole community.

Women who operate entirely in the African religion are energized by the prayer, songs, and rituals of their traditions. They are both "clients" and "professionals," appropriating the strength emanating from the spirit-dimension to support them in the arduous duties of mothering the people. They develop a self-image of servants whose service is their source of honor and dignity. They are who they are because they make the community what it is. It is a spirituality of self-giving and a sense of justice and fair play. It is a spirituality founded on sharing all that is life-giving. As a Kenyan song says:

> Great love I found there
> Among women and children
> A bean fell to the ground—
> We split it among ourselves.

This is a spirit of *harambee* (cooperation and sharing that characterize self-help groups of urban or rural women in Africa) that women strain themselves to promote. This concern for wholeness in women's spirituality flows among Christian and Moslem women too, for it is embodied in traditional African womanness.

I do not wish to minimize the intensity of the spiritual contribution of women in the mainline churches of Africa that are more westernized. I call attention to the AIC because that is where the spirituality of women has found a wider range of expression. What we find in the AIC, however, could be said to apply to all Christian women, especially when they pray outside a formal church gathering.

The thanksgiving prayers of African Christians reflect the petitionary prayers of both the African religion and the AIC. However, since giving thanks under all circumstances is a demand of Christianity, there is added a petition "Let us not give thanks in sorrow." Women, like men, are nurtured in this spirituality and in that strength they confront the vicissitudes of life in Africa with unshakable faith.

In the AIC Jesus is the main recipient of prayer, although there are invocations of the Holy Spirit and thanksgivings to God. In these prayers Jesus seems much closer and is often addressed as an intermediary. An awareness of the complexity of Christian God-talk and the frailty of human vocabulary as compared with feeling and "certainty" is evident in these pages. We yearn to make affirmations of God for which we have no vocabulary. The poetry and rhythm in song becomes an effective carrier of deep spiritual affirmations.

THE POWER FROM SINGING

To explore the spirituality of a community, one must take into account all facets of its worship life, e.g., prayer and singing, as well as its ethical life. As in the prayers so in the songs of African spirituality one is unable to completely isolate the women's word. I am therefore depending on the popularity of these songs and the numerical preponderance of women in these assemblies to highlight them as words that give women the nourishment they need for struggle in the battle of life. Men and women alike are immersed in this spiritual exercise, but, judging from the enthusiasm and dedication of women singers in churches, one can say singing is mainly a women's avenue for ministry in African Christianity.

The songs are mainly prayer and praise and express the theology that corresponds to the African people's spirituality. They are based on a belief in the lively presence of God/Jesus. Some call on God to come, see, or hear. They expect God to enter our human experience, know how it feels in order to make the appropriate response. The experiences brought before God are many and varied, but they are all very real, daily needs of human life in the community of the living, expressed to the "God of Grace who saves us from the death of children, and from sudden deaths, protects us when we journey and brings us home safely." Prayer is a "telling it to God," as expressed in this lyric by a woman cantor:

> Jesus, when we touch anything it breaks.
> When we pull it snaps.
> You who still the sea, control the elements.
> Aid our efforts, direct our ways.[7]

A few of these African songs have been included in the African versions of the Western hymn books brought by missionaries. One finds in these additional hymns a strong belief in God who heals both physical and spiritual diseases.

Lyrics are often woven around the stories of Naaman, The Ten Lepers of the Gospel, and Bartimaeus. Jesus is the wonderful "compassionate healer in whose words people find comfort." The story of Hannah and Peninnah gets woven into lyrics that warn against gloating over other people's misfortune. Hannah, more so than the other mother-figures of the Bible, has captured the imagination of African women because of her polygynous marriage, a marriage that seemed to become intolerable to her. The themes of struggle, empowerment, and defeat of the oppressor are sounded in the prayers and songs in the name of Jesus, who is the reward for all who struggle for liberation.

THE FAITH OF AFRICA

The spirituality of African Christianity as it comes to us in prayer and song is a faith founded mainly on three affirmations. First, Satan is real and strong, but God is ultimate reality, and Satan cannot stand before God.[8] Secondly, all that brings pain can be conquered by God if we can tell it out. Thirdly, all that breaks community can be healed by God. African spirituality seeks fullness of life here and now, even as it hopes we shall have it in the other dimension of life. It has modified the eschatological interpretation of salvation with the cosmological one favored by traditional African religions. *Shalom* before God here on earth is as much God's will as the everlasting *shalom* before God in the hereafter.

Hymns from the Christ Apostolic Church in Nigeria express many of these concerns, using imagery also found in the Fanti *Compositions on Deliverance.* Jesus is the healer, the leader of the army, who goes ahead of us, but who is also behind. Such affirmations have become the theme of all choruses to hymns sung in the AIC. The power of Jesus is "super power"; all other powers are empty. The empty powers may be religio-political (Ogboni) or mystical (Osho witchcraft). Deliverance by Jesus is sure, and those who experience it call to all "those who know the goodness of Jesus, to join me and praise him."

Formalized "abuses," a test of language skills (mainly analogies) intended to defeat the opponent without resorting to physical combat, have found their way into Christian choruses as a source of power against evil. This battle of words is traditionally a device used by women. Men resort to wrestling.

> Satan you cannot be a match to God.
> Look at your feet, your hands, your face.
> Look at you, coming to compare yourself to God.

The phrase "look at you" alone is expected to reduce the enemy to nothing. That God is "super power" becomes the source of strength to those who sing the chorus, for while singing, they actually in their own mind's eye see the downfall of Satan. Confidence is re-established as they sing, "Only Jesus can save, the Diviner cannot save." The centrality of scripture is modified by the same affirmation that "only Jesus can save." Direct access to Jesus enhances the self-esteem of people who most of the time in the world have little to feed their self-worth. Thus empowered, they send out the mission call: "*Adasamina, monso nhwe na munnhu se Yehowa ye*" ("Mortal ones [human beings] taste and see that YHWH is good.")

Battles in the physical world are first won on the spiritual level, for the confidence that God is able to lead one out of misery enables the believers to rest secure. Assured of a God who never fails, they sing "Magnify the Lord, the Lord is able." Sometimes this confidence is established by observations from the natural order put in place by God, much in the style of the biblical psalms. The God who has done all this will never be thwarted by any other power. Therefore believers can depend on God to be faithful, just as the laws on which the universe is founded are dependable:

> None can stop the rain from falling in the rainy
> season, or quench the sun. None can take the light
> of the sun away nor prevent it from shining
> through the dry season: Nobody!

In this way Christians pray for rain but do not claim to be rainmakers. God is in control and in the hands of such a One, one cannot but rejoice and live a life of praise and thanksgiving.

Praise, hardly heard in African religions except in praise-names of God and in daily individual outbursts, has become a major expression of the spirituality of the AIC. People bring every individual success before the community to celebrate in song and dance. "Come join me to lift up my sorrow."

> God has done a lot for me,
> my legs dance, my heart should rejoice,
> my mouth should sing the glory of God.

In praise they worship Christ as the "King who does not allow the waves of life to overwhelm" them.

Those who join in celebration of victories won for others by God then turn to God in prayer. The God of AIC more so than in the Western churches of Africa is a "miracle-working God." Even the charismatic movement in some Roman Catholic churches in Africa exhibits this characteristic. At a healing Mass, people strive to get drops of holy water from the bishop's palm branches. They open bottles of olive oil, cologne, and water to receive the power that flows from the prayers and blessings of the bishop and take them home to use, convinced of their potency and efficacy. Faith in the efficacy of the words and actions of a cultic functionary pervades this Christianity, as it does African religions.

The power of God is very real and immediate. One can conclude that, apart from family tradition and inertia, the young people who sing these songs today do so because they derive strength from knowing that "it is not too much for God to do." Such is the affirmation that empowers people to make their own efforts. "While there is sun, and the rain has not stopped falling, we shall never lack, we shall get our share," also means getting on with the farming. For it is in getting on with your assignment as a human being that you stand on the side of God, and from that place then you can sing, "weeds shall not grow in our mouths," i.e., we shall not starve; and "our clothes shall not turn to rags." The spirituality of African religions in indigenous prayers and songs is a spirituality that empowers one to combat the powers that threaten to reduce human beings to nothing. This trust in the generosity and unearned grace of God is acknowledged in calling God "Okyeso Nyame"—God who leaves no one out of the distribution of good things.[9] To depend on such a God is sure security.

CONCLUSION

We have been focusing on the spirituality of African Christian women who have tapped deeply into the primal religious sources of their own communities. This is possible because Africans never saw the God of the Christian religion as different from the God they had known in their pre-Christian religions. Praying and singing in their own language, they have been able to retain this source of spiritual nourishment. In matters of religion African women have not been as completely subverted as in other aspects of life. Women's cults and women-founded Christian congregations are common developments. It is from this active involvement that we can observe the spirituality of African women.

African women have drawn on traditional sources and on the teachings of Western Christianity as passed on to them through Western missionaries and their collaborators. The examples from Malawi illustrate how African Christian women have integrated the various sources of spirituality and how they have derived strength from their religious life. African women believe in prayer as a form of "potent-speech" which once uttered releases power into the human community and reverberates throughout the cosmos.[10]

Together with fasting, ritual meals and objects, symbols and signs, African women live a life that is in every sense sacramental. Nothing is common; all occurrences may be seen as portents. This deep sense of the spirit-dimension of life is a source of strength for women. But much of what empowers African women may be described as a spirituality of sacrifice. Commitment to community well-being, beginning with the immediate family and expanding to the wider community, gives women a sense of participation in life-giving and life-protecting processes. Women's absence from overt displays of power and authority does not seem to affect women's sense of self-worth. After all, the spiritual powers most potent and instrumental in life are not seen to be physically present. African women's strength lies in the belief that the spirit-world is on the side of those who protect life and combat all that carries death in its wake.

In the spiritual dimension of life there is justice, for all are accounted and treated as the children of God. No human being has a God-given power to exploit or oppress others, for none of these things are hidden from God. God is the protector of the handicapped. God drives flies off the tailless animal. With the assurance of God as the final arbiter, African women do not hesitate to say what they see as inimical to the good of the community. African women are not bashful in resorting to the spirit-world for protection, comfort, strength in times of stress, and healing in times of sickness. They do not hesitate to call down the wrath of the spirit-world on all who would trample on their humanity and on the sense of community.

Society recognizes the potency of women's spirituality and has all sorts of devices to ensure that these powers are always used for the good of the community. The widespread accusation of witchcraft against women is evidence of the acknowledgement of this power, and women confess to being witches when they feel they have used these powers against others or solely for their individual advancement. African women believe in and operate in the context of human links to the spiritual world, and it is this that empowers them to cope with, combat, and control the harshly oppressive physical, economic, psychological, and political conditions of their continent.

RECOMMENDED READING

Abimbola, Wande. *Sixteen Great Poems of Ifa*. Paris: UNESCO, 1975.
Adegbola, E. A., ed. *Traditional Religion in West Africa*. Ibadan, Nigeria: Daystar, 1983.
Boesak, Allan A., and C. Villa-Vicencio. *When Prayers Make News*. Philadelphia: Westminster, 1987.
Idowu, Bolaji. *African Traditional Religion*. Maryknoll, NY: Orbis, 1973.
Mbiti, J. S. *The Prayers of African Religion*. London: SPCK, 1970.
Milingo, E. *The World in Between*. Maryknoll, NY: Orbis, 1984.
Oduyoye, Mercy Amba. *Hearing and Knowing*. Maryknoll, NY: Orbis, 1986.
Shaarawi, Huda. *Harem Years: The Memoirs of an Egyptian Feminist*. New York: Feminist Press, 1987.

PART 5C

The Scriptures

Introduction to Part 5C

Most churchgoers in North America do not think of Bible study as a revolutionary activity. Yet that is exactly how Bible study functions in base communities in Latin America and in other liberation communities around the world. Communities of resistance and solidarity gather to reflect on the scriptures in relation to all dimensions of their lives: social, political, economic, physicial, and spiritual—and on the conditions and possibilities of their lives in relation to the scriptural witness. Through this dynamic process they find their own voices, come to claim their identity, and are refreshed and renewed in their struggle.[1]

Not surprisingly, study of the Bible has also been at the center of the development of the theologies of liberation that have grown out of these communities. Whether sounding the biblical themes of exodus and promise, jubilee and new creation, or retelling biblical stories in narratives and pictures,[2] liberation theologians are claiming that God is on the side of the poor and the oppressed now, and has been since biblical times.

The new ways the scriptures are being interpreted in liberation communities and theologies is especially significant. Liberation theologians do not aim for an objective description of the meaning of the text either in its historical setting or in its contemporary context. Instead, with their commitment to the poor and the oppressed, they take what Elisabeth Schüssler Fiorenza has called an "advocacy stance." Liberation theologians hold that no value-neutral posture is possible, so "the interpreter must make her/his stance explicit and take an advocacy position in favor of the oppressed."[3]

According to Juan Luis Segundo, interpretation of a biblical text must move through a hermeneutical circle, a pattern of asking questions of the text and its previous interpretation. For Segundo, the hermeneutical circle begins with the social question. The interpreter has an experience that leads her or him to question the adequacy of prevailing interpretations of the text. Suspecting that they are not adequate, the interpreter takes this growing suspicion and applies it to the prevailing theology. The interpreter then moves to a new experience of reality with the realization that "the prevailing interpretation of the Bible has not taken important pieces of data into account."[4]

Feminist interpreters such as Elisabeth Schüssler Fiorenza or Sharon Ringe have observed that Segundo never turns his suspicions onto the text itself. "Segundo's model does not allow for a critical theological evaluation of biblical ideologies as 'false consciousness.'"[5] Ringe contends that biblical study needs to recognize "the androcentric nature of the communities that gave rise to the biblical texts."[6]

As the methods of liberation theology have traveled throughout the world, they have changed and broadened with the insights of the indigenous peoples who have been the recipients of Christian missionary efforts. Many of the Latin American theologians, like North American white feminists, have been trained through European methods. Chinese philosophical traditions are very different from those of the West, as Kwok Pui-lan observes. These perspectives were not as concerned with metaphysical or epistemological questions as the West is. Rather, the neo-Confucian tradition "emphasized the integral relationship between knowing and doing."[7] This shift gives rise to Kwok's method of "biblical interpretation as dialogical imagination," which is similar to Ro's dialogical method grounded in symbol, myth, and ritual (see chapter 3). In this method, indigenous stories are creatively interwoven with biblical stories and vice versa. No assumption of the universal truth of the Western biblical insights is entertained.[8]

Kwok's method is a useful one given the concerns that Ada María Isasi-Díaz raises about the role of the Bible in the lives of Hispanic women. The Bible has not played a central role in the religiosity of Hispanic women. But as they become more acculturated to the dominant American culture in which bibliocentric viewpoints prevail, Isasi-Díaz is concerned that Hispanic women will appropriate its anti-woman, anti-liberation bias. She offers a method of biblical study that will allow critical consciousness to emerge among Hispanic women.

As Segundo points out, experience of a new reality is the first step in freeing oneself from restrictive and oppressive biblical interpretation. Each of these chapters on the scriptures emphasizes this point while raising further questions about who identifies whose experience it is that plays such a central role. Thus we begin in this part with Isasi-Díaz's emphasis on the critical role of biblical study, move through Kwok's suspicions of the Western interpretation of scripture as part of the imperialist spread of Christianity, and end with Ringe's articulation of the parameters of a white North American feminist liberation hermeneutics.

CHAPTER 18

The Bible and *Mujerista* Theology

ADA MARÍA ISASI-DÍAZ

[Isasi-Díaz's Context and Commitment statement is found at the beginning of chapter 2.]

CONSTRUCTION

I write with the firm conviction that if one does not risk articulating some of the understandings that are part of the lived-experience of the community of faith, of the theologizing community to which one belongs, that faith and theology will never become explicit, will never become a part of the normative theological understandings of the Christian community at large and will remain marginal even for the community out of which they come. The work I present here has been gestating for the last three years. Like all my theological work, I consider it an attempt, a moment in the process of living, an articulation and clarification of the faith of my community of struggle.

This chapter examines the role the Bible has in the faith and theology of Hispanic women. I then suggest a feminist, Hispanic, liberative canon to which the use of the Bible must be submitted. I also suggest a model for an ethical method and, as part of that model, I attempt to sketch a methodology for dealing with the Bible as a resource for the struggle of Hispanic women. All of this will be done using as the general framework an articulation of *Mujerista* theology which some of us have been developing.

There are certain basic aspects of *Mujerista* theology that must be shared with the reader from the very beginning:

1. *Mujerista* theology is Hispanic women's theology.
2. *Mujerista* theology is a *mestizaje* (hybrid) born of the intersection of feminism, Hispanic culture, and the struggle for liberation.

3. *Mujerista* theology is a communal theology; the theologizing has been and is being done by groups of Hispanic women throughout the United States. Two of us who have academic theological training have served as theological technicians, articulating and synthesizing the theological understandings of the community. As full members of the theologizing community, we have afterwards met with some of the other women in the theologizing community and asked them for a critique of what we have written.

4. In the category of Hispanic women we include women whose cultural and historical roots are in Cuba, Mexico, and Puerto Rico, but who at present live in the United States. They now see their lives linked to this country and have a sense of being part of the resident Hispanic community in the United States.

5. When we refer specifically to Hispanic women, we are not claiming that we are unique, but that we are distinct. Therefore, some of what we say about Hispanic women may very well be true of Hispanic men and some of it may be true about women in general.

THE LIMITED ROLE OF THE BIBLE IN THE RELIGIOUS LIVES OF HISPANIC WOMEN

The Bible per se is extremely peripheral to the lives of Hispanic women. Though they are beginning to take it somewhat into consideration, another generation will probably pass before the Bible becomes significant. Why and how the Bible becomes significant for Hispanic women should be considered seriously. But before pursuing that subject, let us examine the reasons for the peripheral status of the Bible in Hispanic women's religious lives. The Bible plays such a small part not because Hispanic women are illiterate, negate the value of the Bible, or reject it, but because of cultural and historical reasons.

The Spanish Conquest

The first reason the Bible plays such a small part in the lives of Hispanic women has to do with the way that Christianity became a part of the Hispanic culture. Christianity came to Latin America at the time of the *conquista* (Spanish conquest) not in the form of an organized religion, but as an intrinsic part of the conquering culture. The *conquistadores,* among whom were priests, imposed their culture on the indigenous people without any consideration of their cultural heritage. This imposition of Spanish culture with Christianity as an intrinsic part of it gave the indigenous people no opportunity to accept it in an active way. The practices of the Christian religion were simply demanded of the indigenous population without requiring of them any previous understanding. Acquiescence instead of conversion was sought.

The Christianity of the *conquistadores* themselves was hardly based on the Bible. Their Christianity had to do with the doctrines, commandments, and practices of the church. Of course they claimed these were based on the Bible, but the fact is that the Bible was neither directly used nor often referred to in their Christianity. And those in charge of church programs did not teach the Bible to anyone. In short, the variety of Christianity that was planted and flourished in Latin America was a non-biblical Christianity. This is the Christianity into which Hispanic women were born and which they have practiced for most of their lives.

The Christianity of Hispanic women is a *mestizaje* of the nonbiblical Catholic religion of the *conquistadores* and the understandings and practices of African and Amerindian religions. The result is what is often referred to as "popular religiosity." Popular religiosity is often acknowledged but neither really valued nor fully accepted by the official church. On the other hand, *Mujerista* theology takes popular religiosity very seriously, because it is a real indicator of the religious understandings in the lives of Hispanic women. In popular religiosity the Bible does not play a role. Most Hispanic women do not read the Bible and only know popularized versions of biblical stories—versions told to make a point, and therefore often distorted.

The Centrality of the Saints

The second and main reason that Hispanic women do not use the Bible is that Jesus is not one of the main figures of popular religiosity. The practices and celebrations have to do much more with the saints than with Jesus. Many more Hispanics pray to saints than to Jesus, and they do not have a sense that as Christians they should try to emulate Jesus. Even in countries where the figure of Jesus plays a central role in popular religiosity, the Jesus that people pray to and revere is not related to the historical Jesus or to the Jesus of christology. In Peru, for example, the main devotion of the urban population is to *El Señor de Los Milagros* (The Lord of Miracles). The image of *El Señor de Los Milagros* consists of Jesus on the cross with Mary and John at his feet. But if one listens carefully to the prayers, songs, and stories of the miracles that *El Señor* has done for the people, this is not the same person as the biblical Jesus. They know *El Señor*, but they do not know the Jesus of the Bible. They have no concept that *El Señor* is God made flesh, or that there are other "persons" of this same God who have not become incarnate. What is important to the people is what *El Señor* has done for them and not who he is in himself.[1]

Why are the saints and not Jesus the focal point of popular religiosity? Because the legends of the saints cannot be controlled by the church officials. The saints of popular religiosity are shrouded in nebulous, nonhistorical facts, and some of them—St. Christopher, for example—most probably never existed. This lack of historical base for the saints allows the people to embellish the life stories of these saints with the qualities and functions of African and Amerindian deities—human qualities and functions which "official Christianity" does not emphasize, or even recognize in the lives of Jesus, Mary, and the saints.[2]

Although generally unsuccessful, church officials keep trying to control the legends of the saints. The identity of St. Lazarus in Cuba is a case in point. When the great majority of Cubans think of St. Lazarus, they are thinking of Babaluaye, one of the gods of the Lucumi religion—the religion of the Yoruba people who were brought to Cuba as slaves from Nigeria. Babaluaye is the god who controls epidemics and illnesses. For the common people, St. Lazarus is Babaluaye, who is the poor man covered with sores lying at the gate of the rich man in the parable of Jesus (Luke 16:19–31). Since they could not do away with this great popular devotion, church officials have attempted to control it by identifying Lazarus as the man Jesus brought back to life (John 11), not the man in the parable. It is the resurrected Lazarus, for example, whose statue is found in the shrine to Our Lady of Charity in Miami, the most important religious center for the Cuban refugees in the United States. This in no way has curtailed, either in Miami or in Cuba, devotion to Lazarus, the poor man covered with sores and identified with Babaluaye.[3]

The saints are a focal point of the popular religiosity of women for another important reason: because of the maleness of Jesus. In their day-to-day experience, Hispanic women hardly ever relate to men on an equal basis. Almost always, Hispanic women, at least in public, have to appear—whether they believe it or not—to be subservient to men. How, then, could Hispanic women be expected to relate to a male God? Once in El Paso, Texas, an old woman was asked whom she prayed to in time of trouble. She said she prayed to Our Lady of Guadalupe, the name people of Mexican extraction give to Mary. Asked why she did not pray to God, she looked up, smiled, and said, "God is a man and he does not understand women's problems!"

Finally, Hispanic women's popular religiosity emphasizes the saints because Jesus, and the Bible for that matter, belong to the world of priests. The priests are the ones who "know" how Jesus wants one to live. They are the ones who interpret for Hispanic women, and for everyone else, what Jesus' words and actions "mean." Yet the majority of these priests are not even part of the Hispanic community. Even many of those who were born and raised in the community seem to become aliens among their own people once they become priests.[4] The same thing happens to "their" Jesus: he is not immediately accessible to the Hispanic women whose struggle for survival is too real for them to trust in someone who must be approached through an intermediary. It is not that Hispanic women deny Jesus or his divinity; he simply is of no consequence for them. They have a sense that Jesus died for them, and they are grateful for his willingness to "die for me." But that happened long ago. If anything, they sympathize with his suffering, which in many ways parallels theirs. But they have no sense that what he did is normative for them, that they are supposed to follow in his footsteps.

Need for Self-Determination

The third reason for the peripheral role of the Bible in the lives of Hispanic women is because Hispanic women, not entirely unconsciously, do not want to give importance to something they do not understand and cannot control. Not paying attention to the Bible is a way of protecting their limited world of self-determination rather than a matter of rejecting dogmas or other church teachings.[5] Hispanic women know well the fallen human nature of those who speak in the name of the church. Therefore, they can consciously choose not to follow what the priests say without feeling totally sinful or unworthy of God's love, because they know that the priests and the church "make mistakes." On the other hand, if Hispanic women give importance to the Bible, if they accept the Bible as the word of God, then when they are told to do something "because the Bible says so," they can only feel guilty for not doing what God wants them to do. With what authority can they dispute the way the priests interpret the Bible? Do the priests not spend years studying the Bible? Is not the Bible the word of God and have not the priests consecrated their lives to God? And besides, the Bible is so complicated, so difficult to understand.

It is naive and counterproductive to presume that the Bible should become important and central in the lives of Hispanic women without fully understanding the reasons given above for its very peripheral role in their lives. Are these reasons valid? Can the Bible play a role without demeaning the importance of popular religiosity in the lives of Hispanic women? What kind of role should it play? Do Hispanic women have the training needed to interpret the Bible adequately, or will they have to depend on others who will then control them and their access to the Bible? Will that not diminish their moral agency? Can they keep the little bit of self-determination they have carved for themselves in their lives and at the same time accept the Bible as important? Will accepting the importance of the Bible enhance the moral agency of Hispanic women? Can they stay clear from a fundamentalist or pietistic approach to the Bible which promotes an exclusively deontological type of ethics?

THE URGENT NEED TO DEAL WITH THE ROLE OF THE BIBLE

There are four reasons why it is urgent to deal with the role of the Bible in the everyday religious lives of Hispanic women. First, the biblical tradition does play an indirect role in their lives. Hispanic women see themselves as, understand themselves as, and claim to be Christians. They do know that the Bible is important to Christianity, and that, therefore, they as Christians have something to do with the Bible, though most of them would find it difficult to explain this relationship. Further-more, though there are some differences, the basic understandings of popular religiosity are not antithetical to the core of the gospel message: i.e., justice and love. That is why the popular practices and beliefs use biblical stories and events which are modified and embellished to fit different situations—just as happened during the centuries of oral tradition which preceded the written biblical texts.

The second reason why there is an urgency regarding this whole issue has to do with the liturgical changes which took place in the Roman Catholic church in the 1960s. Before these changes occurred, the common people were neither encouraged nor given the opportunity to read the Bible. Because the Bible readings in the Sunday liturgy were in Latin, all the people really understood was what the priest would say about those readings in his sermon.[6] But since the 1960s, the Bible readings are in the vernacular, providing the people with at least an opportunity to hear what the Bible says.

Also, because of the Second Vatican Council which brought about these liturgical changes, there is a new or increased interest in the Bible on the part of the Roman Catholic church. This has led to the creation of several organizations designed by the clergy for the lay people in which the Bible plays a central role. Hispanic women participate quite exten-sively in these movements. It is alarming to note that in these organiza-tions the Bible is used mostly in a fundamentalist and pietistic way. Few if any attempts are made to provide the people with the tools needed to read the Bible correctly. The truth is that most of the clergy in charge of these organizations received their theological education before Vatican II or shortly thereafter and do not have adequate biblical training.

The third reason has to do with the cultural reality of Hispanic women in this country. Hispanic culture in the United States is a *mestizaje* of different Latin cultures as well as of elements of the dominant Anglo culture and the cultures of other groups such as Native Americans, Blacks, and Asian-Americans. Because the majority of the people living in the United States belong to Protestant denominations in which the Bible plays a prominent role, the ethos in which Hispanics live is one in which the Bible is referred to often, even outside church circles. Further-more, in this era in which television preachers play such a significant role in society, in which the so-called Moral Majority uses the Bible to claim authority regarding all sorts of societal issues, the Bible cannot help but have some impact on the lives of Hispanic women.

The fourth reason is related to the fact, that, for the majority of Hispanic women, life is a struggle. For them the main preoccupation is survival—whether both economic and cultural survival, or only cultural survival. Consciously or unconsciously, because of the centrality of the struggle for survival in their lives, Hispanic women deal with each situation according to what will help them in their struggle. They know that in this society the Bible carries authority, so they use it in their arguments more as a tactic than because of personal conviction. Oppressed people have no choice but constantly to defend themselves. The Bible for Hispanic women, often distorted according to the need at hand, is a weapon they can use in their struggle against those who seek to impose on them understandings and practices which are oppressive.

Given all of this, how *should* the Bible be used and promoted among Hispanic women? At present it should be used to promote the critical consciousness of Hispanic women without which they cannot carry on their struggle for liberation. The Bible should be integrated into their daily decision making, into their daily struggle for survival. But this process should take place with full consideration of the reasons why the Bible has up till now played an unimportant role for Hispanic women.

MUJERISTA THEOLOGY AND THE BIBLE

Mujerista theology is a praxis—critical, reflective action based on and dealing with questions of ultimate meaning which are the core of Hispanic women's faith, religion, and struggle for liberation. Because *Mujerista* theology is praxis, it does not use in its articulation the artificial separations insisted upon by academic theology, such as the division between scripture, theology, and ethics. All of these yield theological insights which come together in a variety of ways in *Mujerista* theology. Because it is a praxis, *Mujerista* theology demands three very clear and concrete commitments: to *do* theology; to do theology *as a communal process;* to do theology as a communal process from a *specific* perspective, that of Hispanic women.

To do theology is to recognize that the source of theology is human existence, its questions and preoccupations as well as beliefs. To do theology is to validate and uphold the lived experience of the oppressed—experience which the dominant cultures deny. To do theology as a communal process is to accept the fact that community is a central component of the experience of Hispanic women. One of the most pervasive themes in Hispanic culture in the community; *la comunidad* is the most immediate reality within which Hispanics function and find their personal identities. Theology as a communal process also has to do with the fact that liberation is a personal process that takes place within and through a community. This understanding of theology as a communal praxis makes *social* ethics an integral part of *Mujerista* theology.

To do theology as a communal process from the perspective of Hispanic women is to have at the core of this theology questions of survival, since this is their daily struggle. Survival has to do with more than barely making it. Survival has to do with the struggle *to be* fully. To survive one has to have "the power to decide about one's history and one's vocation or historical mission."[7] For Hispanic women this translates into two sets of questions: questions about physical survival and questions about cultural-historical survival.

Religion is central in this struggle for survival and liberation.

> No *true* liberation is possible unless persons are "religiously motivated" toward it. To be religiously motivated is to be drawn from the depths of one's being. This motivation, we concede, could be occasioned by alien ideologies, as history has often attested. But the peoples of the Third World will not spontaneously embark on a costly adventure unless their lives are touched and their depths stirred by its prospects *along the "cultural" patterns of their own "religious" histories.*[8]

It is precisely Hispanic women's deep sense of an existential interconnection between themselves and the divine that provides the "moods and motivations"[9] for their struggle for survival. Their religious understandings and beliefs can perhaps "be defined as a revolutionary urge, a psycho-social impulse, to generate a new humility."[10] Many Hispanic women "see their struggle for liberation as a way of 'holding fast to God,' to echo a phrase from Deuteronomy. . . . The fight for liberation is an option for life and a rejection of untimely and unjust death. What is more, the poor and exploited see this fight as an exigency of their faith in God the liberator."[11]

CONCLUSION

Hispanic women should and must accept the Bible as authoritative and use it as an intrinsic element in their religious understandings, insofar as it can enable them to *do* theology—to struggle for survival. The Bible cannot be ignored; it must be used.[12] *Mujerista* theology deals with the specific situation of survival, and in every given situation the Bible should and must be submitted to a Hispanic, feminist, liberative canon. Such a claim has two direct implications.[13] First, Hispanic women's experience and their struggle for survival, not the Bible, are the sources of *Mujerista* theology, a liberative praxis. Second, only those parts of the Bible which allow and enable a true liberative understanding of Hispanic women are accepted as revealed truth, as a "document of divine revelation relating to salvation."[14] In other words, Hispanic women need to analyze and test their lives against those sections of the Bible which are life-giving for them and not against *all* sections of the Bible.

RECOMMENDED READING

Gutiérrez, Gustavo. "Reflections from a Latin American Perspective: Finding Our Way to Talk About God." In *Irruption of the Third World,* edited by Virginia Fabella and Sergio Torres. Maryknoll, NY: Orbis, 1983.

Pieris, Aloysius. "The Place of Non-Christian Religions and Cultures in the Evolution of Third World Theology." In *Irruption of the Third World*, edited by Virginia Fabella and Sergio Torres. Maryknoll, NY: Orbis, 1983.

Wimbush, Vincent L. "Biblical Historical Study as Liberation: Toward an Afro-Christian Hermeneutic." *Journal of Religious Thought* (Howard University Divinity School) 42, no. 2 (Fall–Winter 1985–86).

CHAPTER 19

Discovering the Bible in the Non-Biblical World

KWOK PUI-LAN

CONTEXT AND COMMITMENT

As a citizen of Hong Kong, I always feel the depth of the marginality of existence. Situated at the boundary of China, Hong Kong was ceded to the British in 1842, and this "pearl of the Orient" has often been referred to as a "borrowed time and borrowed space." As part of the Chinese people, we live under British rule; as Asian Christians, we are treated as outsiders to the geopolitics of Christianity; as women, we are the silent majority of the church, and as an academic, I am one of the few Chinese women theologians trying to develop theology from a feminist perspective.

Claiming a boundary existence, I have come to understand that marginality should not been seen as a curse, but should be cherished and celebrated as an invitation to many possibilities. The struggles of marginalized people for justice, and the aspirations of the underdogs in history for human dignity are profound testimonies to the unceasing quest for freedom in human beings. Today, many Third-World women are aware of the need to join the struggle of oppressed people everywhere for more political participation, economic justice, and equal opportunity for women and men. We are also involved in the mountain moving task of articulating our own religious vision and social aspirations.

As an Asian woman, I am committed to pushing the boundaries which define our existence and circumscribe our power. I entered graduate school after marriage, challenging the "proper place" for a wife defined by Asian cultures. When my daughter was only two and a half years old, I brought my family across the ocean to begin the uphill struggle of doctoral studies. I have gladly accepted the many challenges in the multiple roles of student, lecturer, writer, wife, and mother, and hope to bequeath to future generations of women a legacy of greater freedom to live out their dreams.

In the Asian context, my commitment includes helping women to articulate our own theology and drawing the attention of the churches to sexism in the church and society. Through the ecumenical movement in Asia, with which I have been associated for many years, and through other women's gatherings, I have tried to develop theological reflections which speak to the Asian reality and which include the experiences of both women and men. In Hong Kong, I am committed to facilitate dialogues among women of different faiths to address our future.

As religious pilgrims on the earth, our struggles are interconnected and our dreams are intertwined. While studying in the United States, I helped to organize the Asian Women Theologians Network for mutual support among Asian and Asian-American women in theology and ministry. I am also concerned to build bridges to promote better understanding between Eastern and Western feminists, so that we may compare notes, share our visions, and identify our blind spots.

"The children expect the world from us!" For me, this means a life-long commitment.

CONSTRUCTION

"To the African, God speaks as if He [sic] were an African; to the Chinese, God speaks as if He [sic] were a Chinese. To all men and women, the Word goes out over against their particular existing environment and their several cultural settings." Thus spoke T. C. Chao, a Protestant theologian from China.[1] The central *problematik* of biblical hermeneutics for Christians living in the "non-Christian" world is how to hear God speaking in a different voice—one other than Hebrew, Greek, German, or English.

Christianity has been brought into interaction with Chinese culture for many centuries, but the Christian population in China has never exceeded one percent. Since the nineteenth century, the Christian missionary enterprise has often been criticized as being intricately linked to Western domination and cultural imperialism. Chinese Christians have been struggling with the question of how to interpret the biblical message to our fellow Chinese, the majority of whom do not share our belief.

In fact, this should not only be a serious concern to the Chinese, but a challenge to all Christians with a global awareness, and to biblical scholars in particular. For two-thirds of our world is made up of non-Christians, and most of these peoples are under the yoke of exploitation by the privileged one-third world. The interpretation of the Bible is not just a religious matter within the Christian community, but a matter with significant political implications for other peoples as well. The Bible can be used as an instrument of domination, but it can also be interpreted to support our liberation.

This chapter attempts to discuss some of the crucial issues raised by the interaction of the Bible with the non-Biblical world. I shall first discuss biblical interpretation in the context of the political economy of truth. The second part focuses on biblical interpretation as dialogical imagination based on contemporary reappropriation of the Bible by Asian Christians. Finally, I shall offer my own understanding of the Bible from a Chinese woman's perspective.

BIBLICAL INTERPRETATION AND THE POLITICS OF TRUTH

Biblical interpretation is never simply a religious matter, for the processes of formation, canonization, and transmission of the Bible have been imbued with the issues of authority and power. The French philosopher, Michel Foucault, helps us to see the complex relationship of truth to power by studying the power mechanisms which govern the production and repression of truth. He calls this the "political economy" of truth.[2]

Foucault's analysis leads me to examine the power dynamics underlying such questions as: What is truth? Who owns it? Who has the authority to interpret it? This is particularly illuminating when we try to investigate how the Bible is used in a cross-cultural setting.

Who Owns the Truth

In the heyday of the missionary movement of the late nineteenth century, John R. Mott, the chief engineer of what was called the campaign of the "evangelization of the world in this generation," and others saw the Bible as the revealed Word of God which had to be made known to all the "heathens" who were living in idolatry and superstition. The Bible was taken to be the "signifier" of a basic deficiency in the "heathen" culture. This is a Western construction superimposed on other cultures, to show that Western culture is the norm and it is superior. It might be compared to the function of the "phallus" as a signifier of the fundamental lack of females superimposed on women by men in the male psychological discourse.[3] It is not mere coincidence that missionary literatures describe the Christian mission as "aggressive work,"[4] and Western expansion as "intrusion"[5] and "penetration."[6]

The introduction of the Bible into Asia has been marked by difficulty and resistance, mainly because Asian countries have their own religious and cultural systems. The issue of communicating the "Christian message in a non-Christian World" was the primary concern of the World Missionary Conference in 1938. Hendrik Kraemer, the key figure in the conference, acknowledged that non-Christian religions are more than a set of speculative ideas, but are "all-inclusive systems and theories of life, rooted in a religious basis, and therefore at the same time embrace a system of culture and civilization and a definite structure of society and state."[7] But his biblical realism, influenced much by Karl Barth's theology, maintains that the Christian gospel is the special revelation of God, which implies a discontinuity with all cultures and which judges all religions.[8]

This narrow interpretation of truth has disturbed many Christians coming from other cultural contexts. T. C. Chao, for example, has stated: "There has been no time, in other words, when God has not been breaking into our human world; nor is there a place where men [sic] have been that He [sic] has not entered and ruled."[9]

In this battle for truth, many Chinese Christians reject the assumption that the Bible contains all the truth and that the biblical canon is rigidly closed. Po Ch'en Kuang argued in 1927 that many Chinese classics, such as the Analects, Mencius, and the book of Songs and Rites are comparable to the prophets, the Psalms, and the book of Deuteronomy of the Old Testament.[10] Since the Bible contains the important classics of the Jewish people which preceded Jesus, he could see no reason why the Chinese should not include their own classics. Others such as Hsieh Fu Ya[11] and Hu Tsan Yün[12] argue that the Chinese Bible should consist of parts of the Old Testament, the New Testament, Confucian classics, and even Taoist and Buddhist texts! For a long time, Chinese Christians have been saying that western people do not own the truth simply because they bring the Bible to us, for truth is found in other cultures and religions as well.

Who Interprets the Truth?

Another important question in the political economy of truth is, who has the power to interpret it? In the great century of missionary expansion, many missionaries acted as though they alone knew what the Bible meant, believing that they were closer to truth. The Gospel message was invariably interpreted as being the personal salvation of the soul from the sinfulness of humans. This interpretation reflects an understanding of human nature and destiny steeped in western dualistic thinking.

More importantly, this simplistic version of the gospel functions to alienate the Christians in the Third World from the struggle against material poverty and other oppressions in their society. But in the name of a "universal gospel," this thin-sliced biblical understanding was exported all over the world. The basic problem of the so-called "universal gospel" is that it not only claims to provide the answer, but defines the question too! If other people can only define truth according to the western perspective, then Christianization really means westernization!

Chinese Christians began a conscious effort to redefine what the Gospel meant for them in the 1920s, as a response to the Anti-Christian movement which criticized Christianity as "the running dog of imperialism." Chinese Christians became collectively aware that they had to be accountable to their fellow Chinese in their biblical interpretations, not just to the tiny Christian minority. They tried to show that biblical concepts such as *agape* were comparable to "benevolence" in Chinese classics and that the moral teachings of Jesus were comparable to the teachings of the Confucian tradition. As foreign invasion became imminent, the central concern of all Chinese was national salvation so the gospel message, too, became politicized.[13] Y. T. Wu, for example, reinterpreted Jesus as "a revolutionary, the upholder of justice and the challenger of the rights of the oppressed" in the mid 1930s, anticipating the kind of liberation theology that developed decades later.[14] These attempts of indigenization clearly show that biblical truth cannot be pre-packaged, but that it must be found in the actual interaction between text and context in the concrete historical situation.

What Constitutes Truth?

The last point I want to consider briefly concerns the norm by which we judge something as truth. Here again, Chinese philosophical tradition is very different from the west in that it is not primarily interested in metaphysical and epistemological questions. On the contrary, it is more concerned with the moral and ethical visions of a good society. The Neo-Confucian tradition in particular has emphasized the integral relationship between knowing and doing. Truth is not merely something to be grasped cognitively, but to be practiced and acted out in the self-cultivation of moral beings.

For most Chinese, the truth claim of the Bible cannot be based on its being the supposed revealed Word of God, for 99 percent of the people do not believe in this faith statement. They can only judge the meaningfulness of the biblical tradition by looking at how it is acted out in the Christian community. Some of the burning questions of Chinese students at the time of foreign encroachment were: "Can Christianity save China?" "Why does not God restrain the stronger nations from oppressing the weaker ones?" "Why are the Christian nations of the West so aggressive and cruel?"[15] These probing questions can be compared to what Katie G. Canon, an Afro-American ethicist, has also asked: "Where was the Church and the Christian believers when Black women and Black men, Black boys and Black girls, were being raped, sexually abused, lynched, assassinated, castrated and physically oppressed? What kind of Christianity allowed white Christians to deny basic human rights and simple dignity to Blacks, these same rights which had been given to others without question?"[16]

The politics of truth is not fought on the epistemological level. People in the Third World are not interested in whether or not the Bible contains some metaphysical or revelational truth. The authority of the Bible can no longer hide behind the unchallenged belief that it is the Word of God, nor can it appeal to a church tradition defined by white, male clerics. The poor, women, and other marginalized people are asking whether the Bible can be of help in the global struggle for liberation.

BIBLICAL INTERPRETATION AS DIALOGICAL IMAGINATION

To interpret the Bible for a world historically not shaped by the biblical vision, a new image is needed for the process of biblical interpretation. I have coined the term "dialogical imagination," based on my observation of what Asian theologians are doing.

Dialogue in Chinese means talking with each other. It implies mutuality, active listening, and openness to what the other has to say. Asian Christians are heir to both the Biblical story and to our own story as Asian people, and we are concerned to bring the two in dialogue with one another. Kosuke Koyama, a Japanese theologian, has tried to explain this metaphorically in the title of his latest book, *Mount Fuji and Mount Sinai*. He affirms the need to do theology in the context of a dialogue between Mount Fuji and Mount Sinai, between Asian spirituality and biblical spirituality.[17] Biblical interpretation in Asia, too, must create a two-way traffic between our own tradition and that of the Bible.

There is, however, another level of dialogue we are engaged in because of our multi-religious cultural setting. Our fellow Asians who have other faiths must not be considered missiological objects, but as dialogical partners in our ongoing search for truth. This can only be done when each one of us takes seriously the Asian reality, the suffering and aspirations of the Asian people, so that we can each share our religious insights to build a better society.

Biblical interpretation in Asia must involve a powerful act of imagination. Sharon Parks shows that the process of imagination involves the following stages: a consciousness of conflict (something not fitting), a pause, the finding of a new image, the repatterning of reality, and interpretation.[18] Asian Christians have recognized the dissonance between the kind of biblical interpretation we inherited and the Asian reality we are facing. We have to find new images for our reality and to make new connections between the Bible and our lives.

The act of imagination involves a dialectical process. On the one hand, we have to imagine how the biblical tradition which was formulated in another time and another culture can address our burning questions today. On the other hand, based on our present circumstances, we have to re-imagine what the biblical world was like, thus opening up new horizons hitherto hidden from us. Especially since the Bible was written from an androcentric perspective, we women have to imagine ourselves as if we were the audience of the Biblical message at that time. As Susan Brooks Thistlethwaite suggested, we have to judge critically both the text and the experience underlying it.[19]

I have coined the term "dialogical imagination" to describe the process of creative hermeneutics in Asia. It attempts to capture the complexities, the multi-dimensional linkages, the different levels of meaning in our present task of relating the Bible to Asia. It is dialogical, for it involves a constant conversation between different religious and cultural traditions. It is highly imaginative, for it looks at both the Bible and our Asian reality anew, challenging the established "order of things." The German word for imagination is *Einbildungskraft,* which means the power of shaping into one.[20] Dialogical imagination attempts to bridge the gap of time and space, to create new horizons, and to connect the disparate elements of our lives into a meaningful whole.

I shall illustrate the meaning of dialogical imagination by discussing how Asian theologians have combined the insights of biblical themes with Asian resources. We can discern two trends in this process today. The first is the use of the social biography of the people as a hermeneutical key to understand both our reality and the message of the Bible.

For some years now, C. S. Song, a theologian from Taiwan, has urged his Asian colleagues to stretch their theological minds and to use Asian resources to understand the depths of Asian humanity and God's action in the world. He says: "Resources in Asia for doing theology are unlimited. What is limited is our theological imagination. Powerful is the voice crying out of the abyss of the Asian heart, but powerless is the power of our theological imaging."[21] To be able to touch the Hindu heart, the Buddhist heart, and the Confucian heart, we have to strengthen the power of theological imaging.

C. S. Song demonstrates what this means in his book, *The Tears of Lady Meng.*[22] Song uses a well-known legend from China, the story of Lady Meng, weaving it together with the biblical themes of Jesus' death and resurrection. In one of his more recent books, *Tell Us Our Names,* Song shows how fairy tales, folk stories, and legends, shared from generation to generation among the common people, have the power to illuminate many biblical stories and other theological motifs. Song reminds us that Jesus was a master storyteller who transformed common stories into parables concerning God's kingdom and human life.[23]

The use of Asian resources has stimulated many exciting and creative ways of rereading the scripture. A biblical scholar from Thailand, Maen Pongudom, uses the creation folktales of the northern Thai to contrast with the creation story in Genesis, arguing that people of other faiths and traditions share certain essential ideas of creation found in the biblical story.[24] Archie Lee, an Old Testament scholar from Hong Kong, uses the role of the remonstrator in Chinese tradition to interpret the parable of Nathan in the context of political theology in Hong Kong. His creative rereading of the stories from two traditions shows that "story has the unlimited power to capture our imagination and invite the readers to exert their own feeling and intention."[25]

Asian women theologians are discovering the liberating elements of Asian traditions as powerful resources to re-image the biblical story. Padma Gallup reinterprets the image of God in Genesis 1:27–28 in terms of the popular image of Arthanareesvara in the Hindu tradition, an image which is an expression of male/female deity. She argues that "if the Godhead created humans in its image, then the Godhead must be a male/female, side by side, non-dualistic whole."[26] I myself have used Asian poems, a lullaby, and a letter of a woman prisoner to interpret the meaning of suffering and hope;[27] I have also used the story of the boat people in Southeast Asia to reappropriate the theme of the diaspora.[28]

The dialogical imagination operates not only in using the cultural and religious traditions of Asia, but also in the radical appropriation of our own history. We begin to view the history of our people with utmost seriousness in order to discern the signs of the time and of God's redeeming action in that history. We have tried to define historical reality in our own terms and we find it filled with theological insights.

In Korean *minjung* theology, Korean history is reinterpreted from the *minjung* perspective. *Minjung* is a Korean word which means the mass of people, or the mass who were subjugated or being ruled. *Minjung* is a very dynamic concept: it can refer to women who are politically dominated by men, or to an ethnic group ruled by another group, or to a race when it is ruled by another powerful race.[29] The history of the *minjung* was often neglected in traditional historical writing. They were treated as either docile or as mere spectators to the rise and fall of kingdoms and dynasties. *Minjung* theology, however, reclaims *minjung* as protagonists in the historical drama, for they are the subject of history.

Korean theologians stress the need to understand the collective spirit—the consciousness and the aspirations of the *minjung*—through their social biography. The social biography of the *minjung* has helped Korean Christians to discover the meaning of the Bible in a new way. Cyris H. S. Moon reinterprets the Old Testament story through the social biography of the *minjung* in Korea.[30] He demonstrates how the story of the Korean people, for example, the constant threat of big surrounding nations, and the loss of national identity under Japanese colonization, can help to amplify our understanding of the Old Testament. On the other hand, he also shows how the social biography of the Hebrew people has illuminated the meaning of the Korean *minjung* story. Through powerful theological imagination, Moon has brought the two social biographies in dialogue with one another.

The heremeneutical framework of the *minjung's* social biography also helps us to see in a new way the relationship between Jesus and the *minjung*. According to Ahn Byung Mu, the *minjung* are the *ochlos* [(the marginalized or abandoned)] rather than the *laos* [(the people of God)]. In Jesus' time, they were the ones who gathered around Jesus—the so-called sinners and outcasts of society. They might not have been the direct followers of Jesus and were differentiated from the disciples. They were the people who were opposed to the rulers in Jerusalem.[31] Concerning the relationship of Jesus to these *minjung*, theologian Suh Nam-dong says, in a radical voice. "[T]he subject matter of *minjung* theology is not

Jesus but *minjung*. Jesus is the means for understanding the *minjung* correctly, rather than the concept of *minjung* being the instrument for understanding Jesus."[32] For him, "Jesus was truly *a part of* the *minjung*, not just *for* the *minjung*. Therefore, Jesus was the personification of the *minjung* and their symbol."[33]

Social biography can also be used to characterize the hopes and aspirations of women, as Lee Sung Hee has demonstrated.[34] The question of whether Jesus can be taken as a symbol for the women among the *minjung* has yet to be fully clarified. Social biography is a promising hermeneutical tool because it reads history from the underside, and therefore invites us to read the Bible from the underside as well. Korean *minjung* theology represents one imaginative attempt to bring the social biography of *minjung* in Korea into dialogue with the *minjung* of Israel and the *minjung* in the world of Jesus. It shows how dialogical imagination operates in the attempt to reclaim the *minjung* as the center of both our Asian reality and the biblical drama.

LIBERATING THE BIBLE: MANY VOICES AND MANY TRUTHS

After this brief survey of the history of the politics of truth in the Chinese Christian community and a discussion of dialogical imagination as a new image for biblical reflection, I would like to briefly discuss my own understanding of the Bible. I shall focus on three issues: 1) the sacrality of the text, 2) the issue of canon, and 3) the norm of interpretation.

Sacrality of the Text

The authority of the Bible derives from the claim that it is the Scripture, a written text of the Word of God. However, it must be recognized that the notion of scripture is culturally conditioned and cannot be found in some other religious and cultural traditions, such as Hinduism and Confucianism. This may partly account for the relative fluidity of these traditions, which can often assimilate other visions and traditions. These traditions also do not have a crusading spirit to convert the whole world.

Why has the Bible, seen as sacred text, shaped western consciousness for so long? Jacques Derrida's deconstruction theory, particularly his criticism of the "transcendent presence" in the text and the logocentrism of the whole western metaphysical tradition offers important insights.

The notion of the "presence" of God speaking through the text drives us to discover what that "one voice" is, and logocentrism leads us to posit some ultimate truth or absolute meaning which is the foundation of all other meanings. But once we recognize the Bible as one system of language to designate the "sacred," we should be able to see that the whole biblical text represents one form of human construction to talk about God. Other systems of language, for example, the hieroglyphic Chinese, which is so different from the Indo-European languages, might have a radically different way to present the "sacred." Moreover, once we liberate ourselves from viewing the biblical text as sacred, we are free to test it and reappropriate it in other contexts. We will see more clearly how the meaning of the text is very closely related to the context, and we will expect a multiplicity of interpretations of the Bible, as Jonathan Culler says, "meaning is context-bound but context is boundless."[35]

The Issue of Canon

Canonization is the historical process which designates some texts as sacred and thus authoritative or binding for the religious community. This whole process must be analyzed in the context of religio-political struggles for power. For example, scholars have pointed out that formation of the canon of the Hebrew scripture was imbued with the power-play between the prophets and priests. The New Testament canon was formed in the struggle for orthodoxy against such heresies as Marcionism and Gnosticism. Recently, feminist scholarship has also shown how the biblical canon has excluded Goddess worship in the Ancient Near East and that the New Testament canon was slowly taking shape in the process of the growing patriarchization of the early church.

The formation of the canon is clearly a matter of power. As Robert Detweiler so aptly puts it: "A Text becomes sacred when a segment of the community is able to establish it as such in order to gain control and set order over the whole community."[36] This was true both inside the religious group as well as outside of it. Inside the religious community, women, the marginalized and the poor (in other words, the *minjung*), did not have the power to decide what would be the truth for them. Later, when Christianity was brought to other cultures, the biblical canon was considered to be closed, excluding all other cultural manifestations.

As a woman from a nonbiblical culture, I have found the notion of canon doubly problematic. As my fellow Chinese theologians have long argued, Chinese Christians cannot simply accept a canon which relegates their great cultural teachings and traditions to a secondary position. As a woman, I share much of what Carol P. Christ has said, "women's experiences have not shaped the spoken language of cultural myths and sacred stories."[37] Women need to tell our own stories, which give meaning to our experience. As Christ continues, "We must seek, discover, and create the symbols, metaphors, and plots of our own experience."[38]

I have begun to question whether the concept of "canon" is still useful, for what claims to safeguard truth on the one hand can also lead to the repression of truth on the other. A closed canon excludes the many voices of the *minjung* and freezes our imagination. It is not surprising that feminist scholars of religion are involved in the rediscovery of alternate truths or the formulation of new ones. Rosemary R. Ruether's recent book, *Womanguides,* is a selection of readings from both historical sources and modern reformulations that are liberating for women.[39] Elisabeth

Schüssler Fiorenza's reconstruction of the early Christian origins borrows insights from noncanonical sources.[40] Carol P. Christ describes women's spiritual experiences from women's stories and novels.[41] Black women scholars such as Katie G. Canon and Delores Williams have also emphasized black women's literature as resources for doing theology and ethics.[42] These stories of the liberation of women as well as other stories from different cultural contexts must be regarded as just as sacred as the biblical stories. There is always the element of holiness in the people's struggle for justice, but their stories are authenticated by their own lives and not the divine voice of God.

The Norm for Interpretation

Since I reject both the sacrality of the text and the canon as a guarantee of truth, I also do not think that the Bible provides the norm of interpretation in and by itself. For a long time, such "mystified" doctrine has taken away power from women, the poor, and the powerless, for it helps to sustain the notion that the "divine presence" is located somewhere else and not in ourselves. Today, we must claim back the power to look at the Bible with our own eyes and to stress that the divine is within us, not in something sealed off and handed down from almost two thousand years ago.

Because I do not believe that the Bible is to be taken as the norm by itself, I also reject that we can find one critical principle in the Bible to provide an Archimedian point for interpretation. Rosemary Ruether has argued that the "biblical critical principle is that of the prophetic-messianic tradition," which seems to her to "constitute the distinctive expression of biblical faith."[43] I think the richness of the Bible cannot be boiled down to one critical principle. The *minjung* need many voices, not one critical principle. I also do not think that the prophetic principle of the Bible can be correlated with women's experiences as Ruether suggests because this assumes that the prophetic principle can be lifted from the original context and transplanted elsewhere. Ruether fails to see that the method of correlation as proposed by Tillich and Tracy presupposes the Christian answer to all human situations, an assumption which needs to be critically challenged in the light of the Third World situation today.

Conversely, I support Elisabeth Schüssler Fiorenza's suggestion that a feminist interpretation of the Bible must "sort through particular biblical texts and test out in a process of critical analysis and evaluation how much their content and function perpetuates and legitimates patriarchal structures, not only in their original historical contexts, but also in our contemporary situation.[44]" The critical principle lies not in the Bible itself, but in the community of women and men who read the Bible and who through their dialogical imagination appropriate it for their own liberation.

The communities of *minjung* differ from each other. There is no single norm for interpretation that can be applied across all cultures. Different communities pose critical questions to the Bible and find diverse segments of it to address their situations. Our dialogical imagination has infinite potential to generate more truths, opening up hidden corners we have failed to see. While each community of *minjung* must work out their own critical norm for interpretation, it is important that we hold ourselves accountable to each other. Our truth claims must be tested in public discourse, in constant dialogue with other communities. Good news for the Christians might be bad news for the Buddhists or the Confucianists.

CONCLUSION

The Bible offers us insights for our survival. Historically, it has been more than simply a tool for oppression, because the *minjung* themselves have also appropriated it for their liberation. It represents one story of the slaves' struggle for justice in Egypt, the fight for survival of refugees in Babylon, the continual struggles of anxious prophets, sinners, prostitutes, and tax-collectors. Today, many women's communities and Christian-based communities in the Third World are claiming the power of this heritage for their liberation. These groups, which used to be peripheral in the Christian church, are revitalizing the church at the center. It is the commitment of these people which justifies the Biblical story to be heard and shared in our dialogue to search for a collective new religious imagination.

In the end, we must liberate ourselves from a hierarchal model of truth which assumes there is one truth above many. This biased belief leads to the coercion of others into sameness, oneness, and homogeneity which excludes multiplicity and plurality. Instead, I suggest a dialogical model for truth: each has a part to share and to contribute to the whole. In the so-called "non-Christian world," we tell our sisters and brothers the Biblical story that gives us inspiration for hope and liberation. But it must be told as an open invitation: what treasures have you to share?

RECOMMENDED READING

Russell, Letty M., Kwok Pui-lan, Ada María Isasi-Díaz, and Katie Geneva Canon, eds. *Inheriting Our Mothers' Gardens: Feminist Theology in Third World Perspective.* Philadelphia: Westminster, 1988.

Elwood, Douglas, J. *Asian Christian Theology: Emerging Themes.* Philadelphia: Westminster, 1980.

Fabella, Virginia, Jack Clancey, and John Ma, eds. *Theological Reflections on Asia's Struggle for Full Humanity.* Hong Kong: Plough, 1982.

Fabella, Virginia, and Mercy Amba Oduyoye. *With Passion and Compassion: Third World Women Doing Theology.* Maryknoll, NY: Orbis, 1988.

Katoppo, Marianne. *Compassionate and Free: An Asian Women's Theology.* Geneva: World Council of Churches, 1974.

Commission on Theological Concerns of the Christian Conference of Asia. *Minjung Theology.* Rev. ed. Maryknoll, NY: Orbis, 1983.

In God's Image, a quarterly journal by Asian Christian women. (Kowloon Hong Kong: Asian Women's Resource Centre for Culture and Theology, 566 Nathan Road, Kiu Kin Mansion 6/F).

Pobee, John, and Bärbel von Wartenberg-Potter, eds. *New Eyes for Reading: Biblical and Theological Reflections by Women from the Third World.* Bloomington: IN: Meyer-Stone, 1987.

Reading the Bible as Asian Women. Singapore: Women's Concerns Unit, Christian Conference of Asia, 1986.

Song, C. S. *Theology From the Womb of Asia.* Maryknoll, NY: Orbis, 1986.

Reading from Context to Context: Contributions of a Feminist Hermeneutic to Theologies of Liberation

SHARON H. RINGE

CONTEXT AND COMMITMENT

The sociological term for a North American, Caucasian, middle class clergywoman is "status inconsistency." Most of the characteristics of that social location point to privilege and dominance in the world community, except for the fact of being female. With that one detail, the insider is also outside, the dominant is subordinate, and the privileged has to struggle to find her history, has to be vigilant over economic and civil rights at best grudgingly granted, and has constantly to search for her space, for "a room of her own."

The anomalies of that social location are compounded by the fact that I teach in a Protestant seminary. At that boundary point of church and academy, where the primary vocation of the school is preparing women and men for the lay and ordained ministries of the church, concerns of academic responsibility and missional accountability are distinguished but never separated. In courses on the New Testament (the field in which I teach), canon, biblical authority, and hermeneutics are always being examined and tested in light of critical scholarship and of the human struggles that mark personal and corporate lives.

Within that context, the commitment that governs my work is a commitment to liberation and to the convergence of various global struggles for justice and peace. That commitment comes to expression in the present moment in work for human rights, for peace in Central America, against apartheid, and against the arms race of the superpowers. Locally, it has involved me in efforts to address personal and systemic expressions of racism, classism, sexism, and homophobia. In my professional life, this commitment has been focused on developing foundations in language and hermeneutics for structures and attitudes that affirm the full humanity of all women and men.

Discerning the path of that commitment has meant learning both the power of articulation and the art of silence. The first has come as I have worked with others to find our women's voice as citizens, as ministers, and as theologians. We have reclaimed language as our own, learned the stories of our foremothers, and dared to tell the stories of our own lives and journeys. *As women* we have had to learn to speak. But those of us who are also among the powerful people of the world because of our wealth, our race, or our nation have had also to learn the art of silence. In that silence we have begun to hear the voices of those people who are poor and powerless, who call us to account for the consequences of our lives, and who teach us about a world we fear to see.

For all of those reasons, my commitment includes seeking to understand the many points in common as well as the many differences between the liberation struggle of women like me and the struggles of poor people, of women and men of color, and of people from the dependent nations, for whom we represent the oppressor. The reflection which follows is a step into the stream of that commitment, to attempt to discern the particular contributions of feminist theology to the larger field of liberation hermeneutics.

CONSTRUCTION

To speak of "liberation theology" in the singular is a misnomer. Rather, we must speak of "liberation theologies" or of "theologies of liberation" in the plural. The methodological shift represented in these theological constructions, namely the affirmation of the significance of experience and social location in one's theological formulation, guarantees that no one expression of liberation theology can claim to speak for all. To listen to them is to hear not a chorus all speaking in unison, but rather a multi-voiced conversation. However, insofar as such theologies are the expression of "voices from below" on virtually any social hierarchy (class, race, sex, age, power, etc.), they do hold some agenda and perspectives in common. An examination of the role of scripture in the various liberation theologies discloses some of the basic contours of their common ground, as well as some of the ways feminist theology differs from theologies from the two-thirds world or the black community in North America.

To begin with some of the common ground occupied by black theology and the liberation theologians of the two-thirds world, one must certainly note their selection of biblical texts for consideration. Not surprisingly, these theologians can be seen to focus their work through the lens of texts in which persons who are poor or outcast from their societies figure as primary characters. Those texts which advocate justice and liberation constitute a canon-within-the-canon by which other portions of scripture are judged and on which subsequent theological reflection is based. The *content itself* of these key passages is the focal point: the prophets' cries for justice for the poor, for example, or the Exodus of the Israelites from slavery in Egypt to the promised land, or Jubilee and Sabbath Year legislation, or hymnic celebrations of God as advocate for the oppressed, or gospel proclamations of "good news to the poor."

In this focus on the liberating witness or teaching, historical critical questions (about such matters as the social and economic structure of the communities where the texts originated, or the function of the texts in the wider theological system, or religious experience and practice of those communities) may or may not be asked, depending on the perspective and background of the particular liberation theologian. Such critical questions are more apt to be raised relative to those portions of scripture where the poor and outcast fare less well, and the historical bias of the authors or contexts may be invoked to explain their apparent misrepresentation of the nature and will of God.

Liberation theologians are far from unique in identifying what might be called a prophetic voice as central to the biblical witness. What is new in their work is both their use of such passages as the lens through which the rest of scripture must be interpreted and their stress on the centrality of the agenda of those texts for the entire theological enterprise. This shift in accent is so significant that it constitutes virtually a change in content of the theological construction, as theology is identified with liberating praxis and as social consequences move to a center formerly occupied by questions of metaphysics. No longer can such consequences be relegated to a subsection on mission in a chapter on the nature of the church. Instead they establish criteria for decisions concerning authority and revelation and set parameters for discussions of the meaning of (among other topics) God, Christ, human nature, sin, grace, salvation, time, and eternity.

Women are of course included among the "voices from below" as determined by race, class, national origin, and other such criteria. Because that is true, the theological method and hermeneutical accent sketched above are ones in which women also can participate. Given what has been called the "feminization of poverty" and the disproportionate burden placed on women and children in times of a perceived or actual scarcity of resources, the affirmation of God's "preferential option for the poor" (in the language of the Puebla documents) is a particular word of liberation for women.

As women, however, our situation is not that simple. It is of course true that some feminist interpreters of scripture do give primary attention to a canon-within-the-canon consisting of texts dealing generally with liberation of oppressed people (perhaps supplementing or accenting that list with those texts which represent a positive attitude toward women).[1] On the other hand, many conclude that merely pointing to the portions of scripture whose content supports justice and liberation is not adequate, for these interpreters recognize that at the very heart of scripture itself women are on alien and even hostile ground. Much of feminist interpretation, therefore, has had a special interest in understanding the *contexts* of the biblical texts and not just their content, and in interpreting them from context to context.

Regardless of how we understand the nature of the authority of the Bible, that authority does not remove the fact that the library gathered in the Bible is a library of historically and culturally relative documents. The individual authors as well as the communities by and for whom the biblical documents were formulated, collected, and interpreted sought to express their own understanding of the nature of God, of the divine-human relationship, and of the faithful life. Their expressions of necessity fit their particular historical, social, and cultural contexts, for otherwise those formulations would have been both without meaning for those who heard them and without power to order or transform life. Whatever is of eternal validity in the biblical documents must be discerned by taking into account the particularity of their contexts and the influence of those contexts on the texts that emerged.

Proponents of historical-critical study of scripture have long recognized the truth of the preceding observations. They have advocated the use of tools developed by those critical disciplines as a way to get at what the various texts meant for the communities that created them, as well as to explore what were the historical circumstances reflected in them. The goal of such historical-critical study was (and is) as objective a reading as possible of the texts on their own terms, in order to avoid reading later doctrinal positions or modern questions and assumptions into the ancient literature.

Whether the desired objective reading is in fact possible is itself a moot point. No one can step out of time and space and observe these texts or data from a totally unbiased point of view. One's social location affects not only what one can see, but even what questions one thinks to ask about them. As natural scientists are well aware, even the most careful process of observation affects the subject being investigated. So much the more must one be wary of claiming to have arrived at objective truth when one is also professionally committed to the material being investigated.

Feminist interpreters, though they use many of the tools of historical criticism to investigate the Bible, generally differ from most other proponents of the historical-critical method in at least two ways. First, they do not claim objectivity, but instead they recognize that they, like their male colleagues, bring a bias to their work as a result of their contexts and experiences. Instead of denying or denigrating that bias, they affirm the value of the particular insights ensuing from their perspective and experience as women. Second, they recognize that, given the role of the Bible in the ongoing life of Judaism and Christianity, to stop at the descriptive task is inadequate. Because the Bible is literature recognized as having revelatory and normative force for those communities, study of the biblical texts requires study not only of their language and origins, but also of their function and consequences in people's lives, and particularly in the lives of women. The process of biblical interpretation itself cannot be seen as a value-neutral, descriptive task. Instead it both has theological consequences and embodies theological values.

Such observations about the process of reading and interpreting biblical texts touch the particular situation of women in at least two ways. First, historical-critical study compels the conclusion that in the biblical documents women are absent as subjects of their own religious experience.[2] Where women are referred to at all, it is as the objects of reflection and interpretation of men. The stories about women in the Bible are actually stories of their experience as it is perceived and evaluated by male authors in the context of a religious system where the experience of men is the norm. Laws affecting women reflect a codification of behavior embodying those same norms and values. Even metaphors for God similarly derive from the religious experience and reflection of men. A consequence of that silence as subjects is that women reading the Bible need always to be reading between the lines. To put it another way, for women the canonical function of scripture as a mirror of the identity of the community of faith breaks down, for the mirror does not reflect our own faces or the faces of our foremothers. Instead we see characters on the stage of a drama written for them by male authors: women of the biblical communities do not get to play themselves.

The second way women are touched by the preceding general observations about biblical interpretation is through a recognition of the androcentric nature of the communities that gave rise to the biblical texts. It is that male-centered context which underlies the absence of women as subjects of their own experience. That context also comes to expression in the prevailing negative assessment of women in the preponderance of the biblical texts, where the historically and culturally relative values of the community are virtually indistinguishable from the theology to which they give rise. With few exceptions, narrative portrayals of women and of the laws, logic, or injunctions relating to them or to their behavior agree in assessing women as evil, unclean, weak, emotional, silly, controlled by sexuality and sexual roles, valuable or troublesome pieces of property, and best kept out of sight, out of hearing, and out of mind—especially where important or religious matters were at stake.

To make matters worse, the documents embodying such perspectives came to be considered as scripture and hence in some way as normative for the theology and practice of Judaism and Christianity. Even though those documents probably do not give us insight into the experience or self-perception of women in the eras from which they have come, the values carried by those documents have formed part of the environment in which later generations of children, women, and men have had to live. Given the authority granted to these documents to define reality, to ascribe or withhold value, and to prescribe behavior, they have power both in and over human lives.

Because of that power which the Bible has, two other factors come to bear on the task of interpretation. First, not only the words of the text but their consequences in human lives need to be taken into account. An example will clarify this task. Careful exegetical study of Ephesians 5:21–33 reveals patterns of mutuality in the marriage relationship and revolutionary claims that men be self-giving in keeping with the model of Christ. These patterns set this text apart from the household codes of the surrounding culture, which it seems at first glance to echo. However, even a short time spent listening to the stories and reflections of battered women makes clear the fact that, whatever its intent, this passage has been used to grant a benediction to violence. To be responsible, an interpretation of the text must take that effect into account.

The second factor of which one cannot lose sight is that the Bible never really "speaks for itself," as one frequently hears urged. It is always interpreted. On one level that observation is a truism. No one comes to a document, event, experience, or another person without presuppositions or without the historical and cultural relativity of one's own social location. When the object encountered is one already vested with authority, the contribution of the interpreter is even greater. Thus the hermeneutical criteria one employs become key.

Several routes have been followed by feminist theologians in discerning hermeneutical criteria which can deal with the androcentric origins and the related value system enshrined in the biblical texts. For some feminist interpreters the preponderance of passages which simply mirror their contexts, and the continued acceptance of those passages within Christianity and Judaism as part of a canon revelatory of God, has led to a rejection of the entire Bible as of no value or negative value for women's religious experience and reflection. Those who do not reject the Bible outright identify theologically warranted criteria that allow them to evaluate and selectively to appropriate the biblical material in their reflection.

Of this latter group, some focus their attention on texts which stand in tension with their androcentric contexts—for example, texts in which women are portrayed as exercising leadership in the community or in which they or their activities are affirmed in other ways—as a counter-weight to the more negative portrayals.[3] Since there are in fact few such texts which can be read as affirming women, these texts are often claimed for theological reasons to be more central to or reflective of the true intent of scripture. These texts then become a sort of canon-within-the-canon, determined less by its specific content than by its contravention of the prevailing value system. Other feminist interpreters work primarily with passages where the prevailing patriarchy is reflected rather than challenged. They use tools of historical and literary criticism to look at the texts that chronicle women's experience as victims of male-centered values (the so-called texts of terror),[4] and at those that give hints of women's triumphs despite overwhelming odds (for example in the evidence of the *"ekklesia* of women" in early Christianity).[5] On the basis of such historical reconstruction, parallels can begin to be identified between ancient and modern contexts and experiences of women. The circumstances of modern women can thus be illumined by the suffering and struggles of their predecessors.

Despite their variety, these hermeneutical procedures share two per- spectives in common. First, they all honor insights into the nature of God and of the will of God deriving from the interpreters' own contexts and experiences. That theological authority allows the interpreters to approach the biblical traditions in dialogue rather than with the alter- natives of outright rejection or mute obedience. Second, these her- meneutical approaches all require that one approach the reading of scripture from praxis or engagement on the side of justice and advocacy for the poor and oppressed, and particularly for women.

The consequences of trust for one's own experience as a locus of revelation, and of attention to the authority of the praxis of justice, are epitomized in the "critical principle of feminist theology" articulated by Rosemary Radford Ruether: "The critical principle of feminist theology is the promotion of the full humanity of women. Whatever denies, diminishes, or distorts the full humanity of women is, therefore, appraised as not redemptive. Theologically speaking whatever diminishes or denies the full humanity of women must be presumed not to reflect the authentic nature of things, or to be the message or work of an authentic redeemer or a community of redemption."[6] In other words, theological criteria concerning the nature of God are invoked as the foundational authority, on which the authority of scripture itself depends. In addition, advocacy in light of those criteria is affirmed as part of a theologically responsible reading of the biblical documents.

Ruether's critical principle speaks specifically of women, whose full humanity is not denied in texts or other events that are truly revelatory. As she is quick to point out, however, that is not to say that the full humanity of men is unimportant, but simply that *as men* that humanity is not usually open to question. In fact, however, it cannot be assumed that the full humanity of all men is granted by all others, for other criteria such as race, class, physical condition, affectional preference, or national origin often serve as grounds for withholding such dignity and worth.

Many feminist interpreters are therefore widening the definition of the system they oppose from that of "androcentrism" (male-centeredness), where the accent is on an oppressive relationship of men to women, to "patriarchy." The term "patriarchy" is defined as encompassing the web of intersecting patterns of oppression which find systemic expression in racism, classism, imperialism, and other relationships of domination, as well as in the sexism to which the term seems more apparently to refer. These relationships of domination find philosophical expression in a dualistic ideology, according to which reality is perceived in patterns of opposition of male to female, rich to poor, powerful to powerless, pure to impure, white to black, "good" to "bad," and so forth.[7] Such dualistic categories identify not merely differences but also relative values, with qualities shared by persons possessing greater power understood as not just *other,* but also *better.*

CONCLUSION

The primary task of feminist theology in general and of feminist hermeneutics in particular can be summarized as the critique of patriarchy as it is known under this expanded definition. That critique involves discerning the presence and effect of dualistic systems and ideologies, and advocating alternative visions and structures which reflect more adequately the God who transcends all human categories and at the same time is found at the heart of our humanity. That task of discernment and advocacy is an appropriate hermeneutic key both to the biblical literature and its contexts of origin and preservation, and to the contexts and experiences of modern interpreters.

Far from being mere artifacts of a less sophisticated time, such dualistic systems and ideologies constitute the legacy of modern social and intellectual life, even to the very methodologies of our scientific and historical investigation. In fact, the system of dualism we are calling patriarchy is so much a part of what is seen as normal life that it often goes unrecognized, with the result that patriarchy is all the more powerful in its alienating effects. A sustained critique of the ideology of patriarchy and a commitment to engage in the struggle to change the social systems in which it is expressed are thus crucial to a feminist reading of the Bible, which is a reading from context to context.

RECOMMENDED READING

Brown, Robert McAfee. *Unexpected News: Reading the Bible with Third World Eyes.* Philadelphia: Westminster, 1984.

Collins, Adela Yarbro, ed. *Feminist Perspectives on Biblical Scholarship.* Chico, CA: Scholars Press, 1985.

Fiorenza, Elisabeth Schüssler. *In Memory of Her: A Feminist Theological Reconstruction of Christian Origins.* New York: Crossroad, 1983.

Gottwald, Norman K., ed. *The Bible and Liberation: Political and Social Hermeneutics.* Rev. ed. Maryknoll, NY: Orbis, 1983.

Mahan, Brian, and L. Dale Richesin, eds. *The Challenge of Liberation Theology.* Maryknoll, NY: Orbis, 1981.

Miranda, José Porfirio. *Marx and the Bible: A Critique of the Philosophy of Oppression.* Translated by John Eagleson. Maryknoll, NY: Orbis, 1974.

Russell, Letty M., ed. *Feminist Interpretation of the Bible.* Philadelphia: Westminster, 1985.

_____, ed. *The Liberating Word: A Guide to Nonsexist Interpretation of the Bible.* Philadelphia: Westminster, 1976.

Tolbert, Mary Ann, ed. *The Bible and Feminist Hermeneutics. Semeia* 28. Chico, CA: Scholars Press, 1983.

Trible, Phyllis. *God and the Rhetoric of Sexuality.* Philadelphia: Fortress, 1978.

_____. *Texts of Terror.* Philadelphia: Fortress, 1984.

CONCLUSION: DIRECTIONS
FOR THE FUTURE

Throughout this volume we have tried to call attention both to the points of convergence and to the points of divergence in theologies of liberation around the world. Rather than summarize here the points already made in the introductory essays to each of the major sections and the constructive chapters themselves, we conclude by suggesting possible directions for the future. Christian liberation movements and theologies around the world will continue to develop in response to the needs and issues arising in their specific contexts. This gathering of voices and songs raises two important questions related to that maturation. The first is a question of authentic diversity and the second a question of productive solidarity and alliances. How can necessarily different liberation movements and theologies support one another in their individual distinctive processes of social, economic, political, and spiritual transformation? And, how can they strengthen the bonds that draw them into community with one another?

It would be imperious (and impossible) for us to map out answers to these questions. For that work can and will only be done as members and representatives of these movements engage in the difficult task of ongoing critical dialogue with one another about their commitments, methods, decisive issues, and aims. What we can do is offer several observations about that dialogue.

1. In order for this dialogue to be effective, theologians of liberation must commit themselves to it and must continue to create new occasions for conversation with one another. Recognition of the necessity for such an ongoing dialogue is fundamental. Liberation theologians in North America have been slower than liberation theologians in other parts of the world to recognize that the future of their own movements and theologies depends on critical dialogue with others not like themselves. Creating more opportunities for this dialogue is also key. Recently the number of international con-

ferences bringing together theologians of liberation from a wide variety of contexts has increased, providing openings for mutual education, challenge, and support. This textbook provides another kind of opportunity for deepening one's understanding and commitment to one's particular justice struggle and for broadening one's connections with others struggling for justice.

2. For authentic community to occur among theologians and movements of liberation, the particularity of each must be appreciated and the diversity of all accepted as a positive and lasting feature of their unity. One of the questions that surfaces repeatedly in these essays, both by liberation theologians to other theologians and by liberation theologians to one another, addresses this issue directly: "Whose experience is it that you appeal to in the construction of your theology?" The future of liberation theologies will depend on the willingness and ability of its members and representatives to grapple together with that question.

3. Discussion of the question "Whose experience?" will require an ongoing openness to perceiving the limits as well as the possibilities of one's own limited experiential perspective. One of the main pillars of movements and theologies of liberation has been criticism of the assumption of First-World white male theologians that their experience is universal. What these liberation theologians are beginning to learn is that they too have often operated with an assumption of the universality and universalizability of *their own* experience of oppression and liberation, and that this assumption must be criticized with equal forcefulness. In other words, theologians of liberation must continue to expand their hermeneutics of suspicion to include their own assumptions, values, methods, commitments. Otherwise, they risk the danger of slipping into their own version of false universalism. A critical question for all theologies of liberation is how to continue to speak out of one's own particularities in ways that are powerfully disclosive and meaningful for one's own community and other communities *without* falling into a new false universalizing of one's limited perspective. The future of liberation theologies will depend on whether or not they take up this challenge to be open to criticism (both internal and external) of their own assumptions about experience.

4. In addition to expanding their hermeneutics of suspicion to include themselves, movements and theologians of liberation in all contexts will have to discuss how they can create and sustain communities that are open to continual self-criticism and self-transformation. If we are not to degenerate into another imperialism, we will have to discover ways to structure communities so that they will have clear sustaining identities and at the same time be open to nondefensive

dialogue with other communities about their structures, ideas, and visions.

5. As all movements and theologies deepen their awareness of their acute particularity, they will have to increase connections with one another. One of the essential tasks for the realization of this goal is giving greater attention to careful analysis of the ways in which different structures of oppression actually do reinforce one another. We seem to be at the stage now of asserting that economic, gender, and racial systems of exploitation are mutually interlocking and reinforcing. We need to press on from here and provide detailed analyses of how economic oppression affects racial, sexual, and age oppression and how racial oppression interlocks with sexual oppression. These examples are just the beginning. We need much more work in this direction if we are to move beyond monocausal theories of oppression that hinder more than aid the process of broadening the connections among different struggles for justice around the world.

6. For a critical dialogue that will lead simultaneously to deepening our particularities and increasing our connections, it is essential that all participants in the dialogue develop and refine one important skill: listening. We have tried in this volume to call attention to the necessity to "lift every voice," to provide occasions for those who have been silenced to speak. But for those who have been silenced to find their voices, or learn to sing God's song in new lands, is not enough. It is equally important that all of us *learn how to listen to voices and melodies that are unfamiliar to us.* We must acknowledge the sacred power and duty of speaking *and* of listening. One of the reasons we need to listen is so that we do not confuse our social location with an absolute perspective and our pride in our communities with *the* way to be the community called the church in the world. In addition, then, to our commitment to finding our voices and learning new songs, all Christians, whether members of liberation communities or not, will have to commit ourselves to develop the art and sacred obligation of listening to those who are different from us, particularly those who are despised and rejected.

7. To remain responsible participants in the critical dialogue within their communities and among liberation communities, theologians of liberation will have to take special care to stay rooted in the experiences of the vulnerable and oppressed in the struggle for justice and liberation. If we begin to neglect these wellsprings of our thought, it is inevitable that we will drift into our own forms of scholasticism. If we do not continue to be responsive and accountable to these primary communities, our theologies will lose the richness of their communal character. And if our exclusive or main

conversation partners become formally trained academic theologians, our theologies will lose their concrete character.

These seven observations about the future direction of theologies of liberation are necessarily provisional. Theologies of liberation are very much in the making, both individually and collectively. What we experience today and hear in the many chapters of this book is, in Carter Heyward's words, "an unfinished symphony of liberation."[1] The symphony will remain not only unfinished but cacophonous as long as we do not explore new ways to speak with one another and to hear one another, as long as we do not simultaneously develop our individual voices and work on making the connections among our voices. This volume is but a beginning in that direction. Less a definitive statement about liberation theologies individually and collectively, this book is more an invitation to pursue a conversation about what liberation theologies are individually and collectively, and what they might be. It is an invitation to gather together to seek new ways to sing the Lord's song in the many new lands in our own voices and in harmony with others. It is a call to live into the full and rich hope of the Christian tradition that invites us to "Lift every voice and sing, 'til earth and heaven ring / Ring with the harmonies of liberty."

Contributors

Steven Charleston is a citizen of the Choctaw Nation of Oklahoma. He is an Episcopal priest, currently on the faculty in Systematic Theology at Luther Northwestern Seminary in St. Paul, Minnesota. His most recent project has been the completion of a major children's curriculum based on the Old Testament of Native America.

James H. Cone is Briggs Distinguished Professor of Systematic Theology, Union Theological Seminary, New York City. One of the architects of modern American Black theology, Dr. Cone is a well-known author and lecturer. He is currently writing a book on Malcolm X and Martin Luther King, Jr.

Mary Potter Engel is Professor of Historical Theology at United Theological Seminary of the Twin Cities and a member of the Presbyterian Church U.S.A. She has published a five-part video series on theological perspectives on sexual and domestic abuse for use in seminaries, clergy-training workshops, and adult education in churches, as well as several articles in this area.

Robert M. Fukada was born in Riverside, California, in 1933. He grew up in Japan and received his education in the United States at Baker University (A.B.), Boston University (S.T.B. and S.T.M.), and the School of Theology at Claremont (D.Min.). He served as the director of Nishijin Community Center before he joined the faculty of the School of Theology at Doshisha University in 1966 as a Professor of Practical Theology. He is a member of the United Methodist Church (U.S.) as well as the United Church of Christ in Japan.

Bonganjalo Goba is Regional Secretary for Africa at the United Church Board for World Ministries in New York. He grew up in Westonaria, Western Transvaal, South Africa. He was a lecturer at the University of South Africa, Pretoria, in Social Ethics. He has also been an Associate Professor of Ethics at Chicago Theological Seminary.

Jacquelyn Grant is Associate Professor of Systematic Theology at the Interdenominational Theological Center and director of Black Women in

Church and Society. She has written several articles on womanist theology, black theology, and feminist theology, and a forthcoming volume entitled *White Women's Christ/Black Women's Jesus: White Feminist Christology and Black Womanist Response* (Scholars Press).

Carter Heyward was one of the first women to be ordained an Episcopal priest in 1974. She is Professor of Theology at the Episcopal Divinity School in Cambridge, Massachusetts, where she is one of the founders and resource faculty for a growing program in feminist liberation theology and ministry.

Anita C. Hill is Ministry Associate of St. Paul-Reformation, a Lutheran church with a reputation for diversity of membership and commitment to justice for all people. She has twelve years' experience in lesbian and gay advocacy and has been on the staff of Wingspan, a ministry with and on behalf of gay and lesbian people and their family members since 1983. She received an M.A. in religious studies from United Theological Seminary of the Twin Cities in 1987. Hill is treasurer for the Justice Network in the Lutheran Church and serves on the Board for Church in Society of the Saint Paul Area Synod of the Evangelical Lutheran Church in America.

Ada María Isasi-Díaz was born and raised in La Habana, Cuba, and came to the United States in 1960. She has studied in Peru, France, and the United States, and is at present a Ph.D. candidate at Union Theological Seminary in New York. Isasi-Díaz is an activist theologian working at developing a *Mujerista* theology—a Hispanic women's liberation theology. Her major concern is to find ways to provide a platform for the voices of Hispanic women, so they will be able to make a contribution to this society.

Kwok Pui-lan is a writer, lecturer, mother, and theologian. She teaches Religion and Society at the Chinese University of Hong Kong and is active in the ecumenical movement in Asia. She has edited *1997 and Hong Kong Theology* and coedited *Fullness of the Gospel* (both in Chinese). She has contributed several articles to *East Asian Journal of Theology* and *Journal of Feminist Studies in Religion*. She is completing a Th.D. dissertation for Harvard Divinity School on "Chinese Women and Christianity, 1860–1927."

Mercy Amba Oduyoye, Ghanaian, was educated at the University of Ghana and Cambridge University. She edited *With Passion and Compassion: Third World Women Doing Theology* with Virginia Fabella (Maryknoll, NY: Orbis, 1988) and is the author of *Hearing and Knowing: Reflections on Christianity in Africa* (Maryknoll: Orbis, 1986). She is Deputy General Secretary of the World Council of Churches in Geneva, Switzerland.

Mary D. Pellauer received her Ph.D. from the University of Chicago. She has worked as a seminary teacher and a freelance writer. She spent three years as a paraprofessional sexual assault counselor in Minnesota. She's presently a bureaucrat, earning a salary as Coordinator for

Research and Study at the Commission for Women of the Evangelical Lutheran Church in America.

Sharon H. Ringe is Professor of New Testament at Methodist Theological Seminary in Ohio. She was Vice-Chairperson of the Inclusive Language Lectionary Committee of the National Council of the Churches of Christ. She has written numerous articles on feminist hermeneutics and New Testament issues, as well as a book, *Jesus, Liberation, and the Biblical Jubilee: Images for Ethics and Christology* (Fortress). She is an ordained minister in the United Church of Christ.

Young-chan Ro is Associate Professor of Religious Studies in the Department of Philosophy and Religious Studies at George Mason University. He is the author of *Korean Neo-Confucianism of Yi Yulgok*, published by the State University of New York Press in 1989.

Rosemary Radford Ruether is Georgia Harkness Professor, Garrett Evangelical Seminary, and a member of the Graduate Faculty, Northwestern University, Evanston, Illinois. She is the author of over two dozen books, as well as numerous chapters and articles on feminist theology, history, and culture. Her most recent work, *The Wrath of Jonah,* is an analysis of the current Palestinian-Israeli crisis and its historical roots.

C. S. Song is Professor of Theology and Asian Cultures at Pacific School of Religion in Berkeley, California. He has served as associate director of the Faith and Order Commission of the World Council of Churches and as director of study for the World Alliance of Reformed Churches. His many publications include *Theology from the Womb of Asia* (Maryknoll, NY: Orbis, 1986) and *Tell Us Our Names: Story Theology from an Asian Perspective* (Maryknoll: Orbis, 1989).

Susan Brooks Thistlethwaite is Professor of Theology at the Chicago Theological Seminary, Chicago, Illinois. She is a former translator on the Inclusive Language Lectionary Committee of the National Council of Churches of Christ. An activist on issues of peace and violence, she is a counselor of abused women as well as a member of the Advisory Board of the Life and Peace Institute, Uppsala, Sweden. She has written several books and numerous articles on peace theology, feminism, inclusive language, and the church. Her most recent book (1989) is *Sex, Race, and God: Christian Feminism in Black and White* (Crossroads, 1989). She is an ordained minister in the United Church of Christ.

George E. Tinker holds a B.A. from New Mexico Highlands University, an M.Div. from Pacific Lutheran Theological Seminary, and a Ph.D. from the Graduate Theological Union. He was recipient of a Lutheran Brotherhood award for doctoral work and two Bacon Fellowships at the Graduate Theological Union. He joined the faculty of Iliff School of Theology in 1985. In addition to teaching he has served as Assistant Pastor at Grand Lake Lutheran Church for eight years and was director of Bay Area Native American Ministry for three years.

Leo Treadway was a founder of the Wingspan Ministry, and has been on the staff of St. Paul-Reformation Lutheran Church, as a Ministry Associate, since 1982. That congregation was the first member of the "Reconciled in Christ" Program of Lutherans Concerned/North America. This program represents actions taken by congregational councils to openly welcome and affirm lesbians, gay men, and their families in the full life and worship of the parish. Leo's active ministry with gay and lesbian people spans some fifteen years. Currently, he serves on the Minnesota Governor's Task Force on Prejudice and Violence, and is a member of the Health Commissioner's State AIDS Task Force.

Vítor Westhelle was born in the south of Brazil in 1952. He studied sociology and theology in Brazil. He received a Th.D. in Systematic Theology at the Lutheran School of Theology in Chicago, and was a visiting professor of Systematic Theology and Ethics at Luther Northwestern Theological Seminary in Saint Paul, Minnesota. He worked with peasants in a parish of the Evangelical Church of the Lutheran Confession in Brazil (ECLCB) and was coordinator of the Ecumenical Pastoral Commission on Land Problems (CPT-PR). He is currently Professor of Systematic Theology at the School of Theology of the ECLCB in São Leopoldo, Brazil.

Notes

Introduction: Making the Connections Among Liberation Theologies Around the World

1. See Paulo Friere's description of this in his *Pedagogy of the Oppressed*, trans. Myra Bergman Ramos (New York: Continuum, 1986), 30–32.
2. Alice Walker, "Only Justice Can Stop a Curse," in her *In Search of Our Mothers' Gardens* (Orlando, FL: Harcourt Brace Jovanovich, 1984), 342.
3. Juan Luis Segundo, *Theology and the Church: A Response to Cardinal Ratzinger and a Warning to the Church* (Minneapolis: Seabury, 1985), 150. The notion of "organic intellectual" is Antonio Gramsci's.
4. The Cornwall Collective, *Your Daughters Shall Prophesy: Feminist Alternatives in Theological Education* (New York: Pilgrim, 1980); The Mud Flower Collective, *God's Fierce Whimsy: Christian Feminism and Theological Education* (New York: Pilgrim, 1985); and the Amanecida Collective, *Revolutionary Forgiveness* (Maryknoll, NY: Orbis, 1987).
5. For a concise statement of this point, see J. J. Mueller, *What Are They Saying About Theological Method?* (Mahwah, NJ: Paulist, 1984), 63–65.
6. Shiva Naipaul, "The 'Third World' Does Not Exist," *Global Perspectives: A Newsletter of the Center for Global Education*, March/April 1987, 1.
7. *Ibid.*
8. *Ibid.*, 2.
9. See, for example, Jacquelyn Grant, "Black Theology and the Black Woman," in *Black Theology: A Documentary History 1960–1979*, ed. Gayraud S. Wilmore and James H. Cone (Maryknoll, NY: Orbis, 1979), 418–33.
10. See, for example, Elsa Tamez, *Against Machismo: Interviews by Elsa Tamez* (Bloomington, IN: Meyer-Stone, 1987).
11. Two recent collections of feminist writings that have challenged the assumed dominance of white North American feminist theology are *New Eyes for Reading: Biblical and Theological Reflections from the Third World*, ed. John S. Pobee and Bärbel von Wartenberg-Potter (Bloomington, IN: Meyer-Stone, 1987); and *Inheriting Our Mothers' Gardens: Feminist Theology in Third World Perspective*, ed. Letty M. Russell, Kwok Pui-lan, Ada María Isasi-Díaz, and Katie Geneva Cannon (Philadelphia: Westminster, 1988).
12. Gail Peterson, "Alliances Between Women: Overcoming Internalized Oppression and Internalized Domination," *Signs: A Journal of Women in Culture and Society* 12 (1986): 148.
13. Friedrich Schleiermacher, the "father" of liberalism, had quite a different view. In both his *Christian Faith* and *On Religion: Speeches to Its Cultured Despisers* he emphasized the communal context of religious practice and ideas.
14. Gustavo Gutiérrez, *A Theology of Liberation* (Maryknoll, NY: Orbis, 1973), 21–42.
15. The insight that knowledge is socially constructed is well introduced in Peter Berger and Thomas Luckman, *The Social Construction of Reality: A Treatise on the Sociology of Knowledge* (Garden City, NY: Doubleday-Anchor, 1967). This work, however, does not

address power and dominant group privilege and their importance in an analysis of the political-social construction of reality. See following note.

16. Michel Foucault, *Power/Knowledge: Selected Interviews and Other Writings, 1972–1977* (New York: Pantheon, 1980), 131. Foucault takes the concept of power very seriously in his epistemological discussions.

17. Mary Daly, *Gyn/Ecology, The Metaethics of Radical Feminism* (Boston: Beacon, 1978), 1.

18. Adrienne Rich, *Of Woman Born, Motherhood as Experience and Institution* (New York: Norton, 1976), 56.

19. Leonardo Boff and Clodovis Boff, *Liberation Theology: From Confrontation to Dialogue,* trans. Robert R. Barr (New York: Harper & Row, 1986), 18.

20. *Ibid.*

21. Frederick Herzog, *GodWalk: Liberation Shaping Dogmatics* (Maryknoll, NY: Orbis, 1988).

22. Ismael García, *Justice in Latin American Theology of Liberation* (Philadelphia: Westminster, 1987), 31.

23. For an argument for this in Latin American liberation theology, see Rebecca Chopp, *The Praxis of Suffering: An Interpretation of Liberation and Political Theologies* (Maryknoll, NY: Orbis, 1986).

24. Rosemary Radford Ruether, *Sexism and God-Talk: Toward a Feminist Theology* (Boston: Beacon, 1983); James H. Cone, *A Black Theology of Liberation* (Philadelphia: Lippincott, 1970); Juan Luis Segundo, in collaboration with the staff of the Peter Faber Center, *Theology for Artisans of a New Humanity,* trans. John Drury, 5 vols. (Maryknoll, NY: Orbis, 1973–74). Vol. 1, *The Community Called Church;* vol. 2, *Grace and the Human Condition;* vol. 3, *Our Idea of God;* vol. 4, *The Sacraments Today;* and vol. 5, *Evolution and Guilt.*

25. Dean Ferm's *Third World Liberation Theologies: A Reader* (Maryknoll, NY: Orbis, 1985), e.g., organizes essays by continent.

26. Friedrich Schleiermacher, *The Christian Faith,* trans. H. R. Mackintosh (Edinburgh: Clark, 1968; orig. pub. 1831), P. 28.2, pp. 120–121.

27. In common contemporary theological parlance this set of issues comes under the rubric of "Foundational" or "Fundamental" Theology. We have chosen, however, not to use the terms *Fundamental, Systematic,* and *Practical* (David Tracy) to distinguish the volume's contents since the entirety of liberation theology—foundational questions of methods, sources, and norms and all the systematic *loci*—is grounded in and directed toward the practical.

28. See, for example, the development of the meaning of the sacraments in Segundo et al., *The Sacraments Today* (Maryknoll, NY: Orbis, 1974).

29. Segundo, *Our Idea of God* (Maryknoll, NY: Orbis, 1974), passim. See also Leonardo Boff, *Trinity and Society* (Maryknoll, NY: Orbis, 1988). Feminist liberation theologians have been much more critical of the doctrine of the trinity than other liberationists, but there is not yet any published work reporting on this conversation.

30. Leonardo Boff, *Liberating Grace,* trans. John Drury (Maryknoll, NY: Orbis, 1979; first pub. 1976), 23.

31. *Ibid.*

32. Paul Tillich, *Courage to Be* (New Haven, CT: Yale University Press, 1952), 48, 52, 54, 75–77, 87, 90, 125–27, 132, 138, 169.

33. *Ibid.,* 24.

34. Audre Lorde, "The Master's Tools Will Never Dismantle the Master's House," in *This Bridge Called My Back: Writings by Radical Women of Color,* ed. Cherie Moraga and Gloria Anzaldúa (Watertown, MA: Persephone, 1981), 100.

35. From the famous black hymn written by James W. and J. Rosamund Johnson, available in many contemporary hymnals.

Introduction to Part 1

1. Gustavo Gutiérrez, *A Theology of Liberation* (Maryknoll, NY: Orbis, 1973), 11.

2. This recognition and claim is also common to feminist liberation theologies. See, for example, Letty M. Russell et al., *Inheriting Our Mothers' Gardens*; *The Mudflower*

Collective, *God's Fierce Whimsy;* and Ada María Isasi-Díaz and Yolanda Tarango, *Hispanic Women: Prophetic Voice in the Church* (San Francisco: Harper & Row, 1988).

3. David Tracy, "Theological Method," in *Christian Theology: An Introduction to Its Traditions and Tasks,* eds. Peter C. Hodgson and Robert H. King, 2d ed. (Philadelphia: Fortress, 1988), 35–60.

4. *Ibid.,* 8. The first chapter in his *The Liberation of Theology* (Maryknoll, NY: Orbis, 1973), 7–38, is an excellent statement of this method of mutually critical correlation.

5. Rosemary Radford Ruether, "Feminist Interpretation: A Method of Correlation," in *Feminist Interpretation of the Bible,* ed. Letty M. Russell (Philadelphia: Westminster, 1985), 111.

6. Juan Luis Segundo, *The Liberation of Theology* (Maryknoll, NY: Orbis, 1976), 33 (emphasis in original).

7. See Juan Luis Segundo, *Grace and the Human Condition* (Maryknoll, NY: Orbis, 1973), 58–99, 152ff.

8. Tracy, "Theological Method," 58.

Chapter 1

1. Allan Boesak, *Black and Reformed: Apartheid, Liberation and the Calvinist Tradition* (Johannesburg: Skotaville Publishers, 1984), 61–62.

2. Karl Barth, *Evangelical Theology: An Introduction* (New York: Holt, Rinehart and Winston, 1963), 100.

3. Standard Revised Version Bible, Luke 4:18–19.

4. Kairos theologians, *The Kairos Document,* 2d ed. (Grand Rapids, MI: Eerdmans, 1985), 7.

5. *Ibid.*

6. See the first volume of essays to be published on Black theology: *The Challenge of Black Theology in South Africa,* ed. Basil Moore (Atlanta, GA: John Knox, 1974).

7. Bonganjalo Goba, "The Black Consciousness Movement: Its Impact on Black Theology," in *The Unquestionable Right to Be Free,* ed. Itumeleng J. Mosala and Buti Tlhagale (Maryknoll, NY: Orbis, 1986), 58, quoting J. Deotis Roberts.

8. Simon Maimela, *Proclaim Freedom to My People* (Johannesburg: Skotaville, 1987), 104–5.

9. See Bonganjalo Goba, *An Agenda for Black Theology: Hermeneutics for Social Change* (Johannesburg: Skotaville, 1988).

10. See Bonganjalo Goba, "Corporate Personality: Ancient Israel and Africa," in *The Challenge of Black Theology in South Africa,* ed. Basil Moore, 65–73.

11. See especially G. D. Cloete and D. J. Smit, eds., *A Moment of Truth: The Confession of the Dutch Reformed Mission Church* (Grand Rapids, MI: Eerdmans, 1984).

12. Lebamang Sebidi, "The Dynamics of the Black Struggle and Its Implications for Black Theology," in *The Unquestionable Right to Be Free,* 15.

13. *Ibid.*

14. *Ibid.,* 17

15. *Ibid.,* 18.

16. Cornel West, *Prophesy Deliverance! An Afro-American Revolutionary Christianity* (Philadelphia: Westminster, 1982), 121–22.

17. *Kairos Document,* 29.

18. *Ibid.,* 30.

Chapter 2

I dedicate this chapter to Blanche Marie Moore, a sister in the Order of St. Ursula who died in the Bronx, New York, on December 10, 1987, as I was typing it. Blanche Marie was my high school teacher in Cuba. A person of great strength of character, her dedication and strong will caught my imagination and strongly influenced me. I will always be most grateful to her for imbuing in me a love of reading and studying. *In paradisum perducant te angeli,* Blanche.

1. See Isabel Carter Heyward, *The Redemption of God* (Washington, DC, 1982), 1–18.

2. In this chapter the terms *the poor* and *the oppressed* are at times used interchangeably and at times together. I would have preferred to use the term *nonperson*—those human beings who are considered less than human by society, because that society is based on privileges arrogated by a minority (Gustavo Gutiérrez, *The Power of the Poor in History* [Maryknoll, NY: Orbis, 1984], 92). But I am concerned that the ontological meaning of the word, "nonentity," would be read into my use of *nonperson*, regardless of the explanation provided. I thought of using only *the oppressed* but felt that some specificity needed to be added to that term for fear of creating the illusion that the oppressed are a classification, an abstraction, instead of concrete persons.

I then needed to decide what term to add to *the oppressed*. I thought of the term I use to identify my own oppression, *Hispanic women*, but felt that it was too specific and that what I say here could be understood to apply only to us. I decided to use *the poor* because, though the restricted meaning of the term relates to those who are economically oppressed, it often goes beyond that meaning and closely parallels the meaning of *the oppressed* even in everyday language. In the Bible, at least in the Book of Zephaniah 2:3, 3:12–13, "the poor" are identified with the *anawim*. The *anawim*, the poor, are "the portion of the community . . . upon which the possible future existence of the community depends (E. Jenni, "Remnant," *The Interpreter's Dictionary of the Bible*, ed. George Arthur Buttrick [Nashville, TN: Abingdon, 1965], 32–33). My usage of *the poor* in this chapter definitely includes this meaning.

3. *The Random House Dictionary of the English Language*, 2d unabridged ed. (New York: Random, 1987).

4. There are two reasons for not using the regular word employed by English Bibles, *kingdom*. First, it is obviously a sexist word that presumes that God is male. Second, the concept of kingdom in our world today is both hierarchical and elitist—which is why I do not use the word *reign*. The word *kin-dom* makes it clear that when the fullness of God becomes a day-to-day reality in the world at large, we will all be sisters and brothers—kin to each other.

5. Gustavo Gutiérrez, *A Theology of Liberation* (Maryknoll, NY: Orbis, 1973), 159.

6. *Ibid.*, 177.

7. Rebecca S. Chopp, *Praxis of Suffering* (Maryknoll, NY: Orbis, 1986), 25.

8. Gutiérrez, *Theology of Liberation*, 175.

9. William Werpehowski, "Justice," *The Westminster Dictionary of Christian Ethics*, ed. James F. Childress and John Macquarrie (Philadelphia: Westminster, 1986), 338.

10. Gutiérrez, *Theology of Liberation*, 177.

11. Synod of Bishops Second General Assembly, November 30, 1971, "Justice in the World," *The Gospel of Peace and Justice*, ed. Joseph Gremillion (Maryknoll, NY: Orbis, 1976), 514.

12. Sharon D. Welch, *Communities of Resistance and Solidarity* (Maryknoll, NY: Orbis, 1985), 53.

13. José Míguez Bonino, "Nueves Tendencias en Teología," in *Pasos* (1985), 22.

14. Gustavo Gutiérrez, *The Power of the Poor in History* (Maryknoll, NY: Orbis, 1984), 140.

15. *Ibid.*

16. *Ibid.*, 96.

17. Gutiérrez, *Theology of Liberation*, 289.

18. I use these three "isms" as inclusive categories and paradigms of oppression. Under sexism, for example, I include exclusive heterosexism. Under racism I include ethnic prejudice. Under classism I include militarism, etc.

19. I use strategy instead of practice here because of my insistence on the intrinsic unity between reflection and practice in praxis—which is what I claim solidarity is. I also use strategy because it carries with it the implication of political effectiveness which is intrinsic to solidarity as a praxis of liberation.

20. Janice Raymond, *A Passion for Friends* (Boston: Beacon, 1986), 22.

21. *Ibid.*, 214-15.

22. Gutiérrez, *Theology of Liberation*, 92.

23. Paulo Freire, *Pedagogy of the Oppressed* (New York: Seabury, 1973), 3.

24. Gutiérrez, *Theology of Liberation*, 92.
25. I have based this section about the relationship between the oppressor and the "friend" on Juan Carlos Scannone, *Teología de la Liberación y Praxis Popular* (Salamanca: Ediciones Sigueme, 1976), 133–86.
26. Scannone uses the word *brother.* I have used *friend* in translating into English in order to avoid a sexist term.
27. *Ibid.*
28. Scannone, 164. In translating I have used inclusive language even though the original uses sexist language.
29. Bell Hooks, *Feminist Theory: From Margin to Center* (Boston, South End, 1984), 159.
30. *Ibid.*
31. Margaret Farley, *Personal Commitments* (San Francisco: Harper & Row, 1986), 14.
32. *Ibid.*, 15.
33. *Ibid.*, 18–19.
34. *Ibid.*, 19.
35. This is what I understood Joan Martin to say recently about why the Black community does not use the word *mutuality* in their struggles.
36. See Farley, 36.
37. I find Gutiérrez wavering when he comes to this issue. In *Theology of Liberation*, 167, he says, "it is only in the temporal, earthly, historical event that we can open up to the future complete fulfillment." It is in this sense that I originally had written here that such betrayals *impede* the unfolding of the kin-dom of God. But Gutiérrez later insists on the contrary: "nor does it mean that this just society constitutes a 'necessary condition' for the arrival of the Kingdom, nor that they are closely linked, nor that they converge" (231). This is why I soften the claim I make here.

Chapter 3

1. Faith may not be reduced to a mere form of intellectual statement. In this sense, any form of an intellectual statement of faith may have an inherent limitation in expressing the nature of faith.
2. James H. Cone, for example, sees many resemblances between Black theology and *minjung* theology. See his Preface to *Minjung Theology: People as the Subjects of History*, ed. the Commission on Theological Concerns of the Christian Conference of Asia (Maryknoll, NY: Orbis, 1981), ix–xvii. See also J. Deotis Roberts, *Black Theology in Dialogue* (Philadelphia: Westminster, 1987), 104–33.
3. This is Hyun Young-hak's interpretation of Han's definition in *Minjung Theology*, xvii.
4. *Ibid.*, 184–85.
5. *Ibid.*, 184.
6. *Minjung Theology*, 55–72.
7. Suh Nam-dong, "Towards a Theology of Han," in *Minjung Theology*, 68.

Chapter 5

1. D. T. Suzuki, *Essays in Zen Buddhism* (second series), ed. C. Humphreys (London: Rider, 1949), 222–23.
2. G. van der Leeuw, *Religion in Essence and Manifestation*, trans. J. E. Turner (New York: Harper & Row), vol. 1, 43–44.
3. See *Suffering and Hope*, eds. Ron O'Grady and Lee Soo Jin (Christian Conference of Asia, 1978), 28.
4. *Ibid.*
5. *Genesis: A Commentary*, trans. John Marks (Philadelphia: Westminster, 1961), 275.
6. *Asia's Struggle for Full Humanity*, ed. Virginia Fabella (Maryknoll, NY: Orbis, 1980), 157.
7. "Towards a Christian Theology of Man in Nature," in *The Human and the Holy* (Maryknoll, NY: Orbis, 1980), 116.
8. *Compassionate and Free: An Asian Woman's Theology* (Geneva: World Council of Churches, 1979; Maryknoll, NY: Orbis, 1980), 9.
9. *Ibid.*, 65.

Introduction to Part 2

1. Juan Luis Segundo, *Our Idea of God* (Maryknoll, NY: Orbis, 1974), 5.
2. *Ibid.*, 3–11.
3. Kenneth Cauthen, *The Impact of American Religious Liberalism* (Washington, DC: University Press of America, 1983). Originally published by Harper & Row, 1962.
4. Leonardo Boff, *Trinity and Society* (Maryknoll, NY: Orbis, 1988), 20–33.
5. Gustavo Gutiérrez, *Theology of Liberation* (Maryknoll, NY: Orbis, 1973), 194.

Chapter 6

1. Albert Camus, *The Rebel*, trans. Anthony Bower (New York: Random House, 1956), 16–17.
2. Quoted in H. Richard Niebuhr, *The Social Sources of Denominationalism* (Cleveland, OH: Meridian, 1929), 249.
3. Trans. P. S. Watson (Philadelphia: Westminster, 1953).
4. Gordon Kaufman, *Systematic Theology: A Historicist Perspective* (New York: Scribner, 1968), 154.
5. Anders Nygren, *Agape and Eros*, 80.
6. C. H. Dodd, *The Johannine Epistles* (New York: Harper, 1946), 110.
7. Dietrich Bonhoeffer, *The Cost of Discipleship* (New York: Macmillan, 1961), 35.
8. Kaufman, *Systematic Theology*, 140.
9. Richard Rubenstein, *After Auschwitz* (New York: Bobbs-Merrill, 1966).
10. Paul Tillich, *Systematic Theology*, vol. 1 (Chicago: University of Chicago Press, 1951), 264, 267.
11. John Macquarrie, *God and Secularity* (Philadelphia: Westminster, 1967), 123.

Chapter 7

1. Peter Goodchild, *J. Robert Oppenheimer: Shatterer of Worlds* (London: BBC, 1980), 7.
2. For example, General Farrell, a military assistant to General Groves, military head of Los Alamos, likened the power of the first atomic explosion to the power of God; he described the "awesome roar which warned of doomsday and made us feel that we puny things were blasphemous to dare tamper with the forces heretofore reserved for the Almighty." William L. Laurence, *Dawn Over Zero: The Story of the Atomic Bomb* (New York: Knopf, 1946), 194. See also William L. Laurence, *Men and Atoms: The Discovery, the Uses and the Future of Atomic Energy* (New York: Simon and Schuster, 1959), 120; Victor F. Weisskopf, *The World According to Weisskopf* (Boston: WGBH Television Transcripts, 1984); Stanley A. Blumberg and Gwenn Owens, *Energy and Conflict: The Life and Times of Edward Teller* (New York: Putnam, 1976), 116–17; Nuel Pharr Davis, *Lawrence and Oppenheimer* (New York: Simon and Schuster, 1968), 116–17.
3. Robert Jay Lifton, *Indefensible Weapons* (New York: Basic Books, 1982), 87.
4. Ira Chernus, "War and Myth: 'The Show Must Go On,'" *Journal of the American Academy of Religion* 53, no. 3 (September 1985), 456–57.
5. *John Donne: Selected Poems*, ed. John Hayward (New York: Penguin, 1950), 171–72.
6. Chernus, "War and Myth." It should be noted that the years from 1963 to 1978 were by contrast devoid of nuclear imagery, possibly due to the country's preoccupation with the Vietnam War.
7. Quoted in Lifton, *Indefensible Weapons*, 11.
8. The anger is nowhere clearer than in the work of Hal Lindsey, *The Late Great Planet Earth* (New York: Dell, 1970).
9. Lifton, 104.
10. *Ibid.*
11. See, for example, Peter Berger, *The Sacred Canopy: Elements of a Sociological Theory* (Garden City, NY: Doubleday, 1967) or Karl Mannheim, *Essays on the Sociology of Knowledge*, ed. Paul Kecskemeti (London: Routledge and Kegan Paul, 1952). Both of these works show that theology as speech about God must read back from cosmos to the social location of human thought about God. Mannheim suggests that the sociology of

knowledge has for its principal thesis the assertion that there are modes of thought which cannot be adequately understood as long as their social origins are obscured.

12. C. Wright Mills, *The Power Elite* (New York: Oxford University Press, 1956), 171.

13. Quoted in Hannah Arendt, *On Violence* (New York: Harcourt Brace Jovanovich, 1969), 41.

14. *Ibid.*, 42.

15. *Ibid.*

16. Jo Vellacott, "Women, Peace and Power," in *Reweaving the Web of Life: Feminism and Non-violence* (Philadelphia: New Society, 1982), 32.

17. *Ibid.*, 38.

18. See Karl Rahner and Herbert Vorgrimler, *Dictionary of Theology* (New York: Crossroad, 1985), 27, 452.

19. See Yves Congar, "Classical Political Monotheism and the Trinity," in *God as Father? Concilium* (New York: Seabury, 1981), 31–36.

20. Jurgen Moltmann, *The Trinity and the Kingdom* (San Francisco: Harper & Row, 1981), 129–31.

21. Frederick Schleiermacher, *Christian Faith* (Edinburgh: T.&T. Clark, 1976), 738.

22. William Lloyd Newell, *The Secular Magi: Marx, Freud, and Nietzsche on Religion* (New York: Pilgrim, 1986).

23. *Ibid.*, 147–55.

24. Freud himself responded to the nuclear age by relating it to the death-wish drive that he postulated drove humanity to self-destruction. See Paul E. Stepansky, *A History of Aggression in Freud* (New York: International Universities Press, 1977), esp. chap. 1, "Thanatos and Aggression: The Strained Linkage." Erich Fromm in *The Anatomy of Human Destructiveness* (New York: Holt, Rinehart and Winston, 1973) follows Freud in postulating that the source of human violence is innate drives. The significant work of Alice Miller is an important correction. Miller's several works, *Thou Shalt Not Be Aware: Society's Betrayal of the Child* (New York: Farrar, Straus and Giroux, 1984) and *For Your Own Good: Hidden Cruelty in Child-Rearing and the Roots of Violence* (New York: Farrar, Straus and Giroux, 1983), identify the origins of human destructiveness in child abuse. According to Miller, destruction is *learned*, not innate.

25. *The Challenge of Peace: God's Promise and Our Response* (Washington, DC: United States Catholic Conference, 1982), see esp. 52–62.

26. Michael Novak, *Moral Clarity in the Nuclear Age* (Nashville, TN: Thomas Nelson, 1983), 37 (italics added).

27. *Ibid.*, 41 (italics added).

28. Other church-based discussions of peace theology follow suit. American Lutherans, in their document "Peace and Politics," stress "The root of war is sin" (3). "The church views war as a catastrophic consequence of sin against which God summons us all to strive" (4).

29. Lifton, *Indefensible Weapons*, ix.

30. *Ibid.*, esp. 10, 25, 27–28, 58.

31. Joanna Rogers Macy, *Despair and Personal Power in the Nuclear Age* (Philadelphia: New Society, 1983).

32. Gordon Kaufman, *Theology for a Nuclear Age* (Philadelphia: Westminster, 1985); Jonathan Schell, *The Fate of the Earth* (New York: Knopf, 1982); Sallie McFague, *Models of God: Theology for an Ecological, Nuclear Age* (Philadelphia: Westminster, 1987).

33. Kaufman, *Theology for a Nuclear Age*, 5–8.

34. McFague, *Models of God*, chapters 3 and 4.

35. Paul Tillich, *The Courage to Be* (New Haven: Yale University Press, 1952), 48, 52, 54, 75–77, 87, 90, 125–27, 132, 138, 169.

36. McFague, *Models of God*, xiv, 174ff.

37. The term thealogy is used to describe feminist reflections on the Goddess. *Thea* is the feminine form in Greek for the word for the divine. See Carol Christ, *The Laughter of Aphrodite: Reflections on a Journey to the Goddess* (San Francisco: Harper & Row, 1987), ix–xvii. Christ credits Naomi Goldenberg with coining this term. See ix, note 1.

38. Mary O'Brien, *The Politics of Reproduction* (London: Routledge and Kegan Paul, 1981), 29, quoted in Janet Kalven and Mary I. Buckley, *Women's Spirit Bonding* (New York: Pilgrim, 1984), 175.
39. *Ibid.*, 176.
40. See Rosemary Radford Reuther, "Eschatology and Feminism," chapter 8 in this volume.
41. *Ibid.*
42. *Ibid.*, 189.
43. Mary Daly, *Pure Lust: Elemental Feminist Philosophy* (Boston: Beacon, 1984), 48.
44. Christ, "Yahweh as Holy Warrior," in *Laughter of Aphrodite*, 73–81.
45. *Ibid.*, 70 (italics added).
46. James H. Cone, *A Black Theology of Liberation*, 2d ed. (Maryknoll, NY: Orbis, 1986), 63. See James H. Cone, "God Is Black," chapter 6 in this volume.
47. See Introduction to part 4 in this volume, "Creating and Governing Grace," for a further elaboration of this point.
48. Chrystos, "No Rock Scorns Me as Whore," in *This Bridge Called My Back: Writings by Radical Women of Color*, ed. Cherrie Moraga and Gloria Anzaldúa (Watertown, MA: Persephone, 1981), 245.

Introduction to Part 3

1. George Albert Coe, *A Social Theory of Religious Education* (New York: Scribner, 1917), 54ff.
2. Albert Schweitzer, *The Quest of the Historical Jesus* (London: Block, 1911).
3. Karl Barth, *The Epistle to the Romans* (London: Oxford University Press, 1933), 314. See also Jürgen Moltmann, *Theology of Hope: On the Ground and the Implications of a Christian Eschatology* (New York: Harper & Row, 1967), esp. chap. 1.
4. Juan Segundo critiqued Jürgen Moltmann's theology of hope, pointing out that "political theology" has a relativizing tendency with respect to all absolute experiences and ideologies and offers only a nonbinding, general future. See Juan Segundo, "The Choice Between Capitalism and Socialism as the Theological Crux," *Concilium* (Oct. 1974), as quoted in Jürgen Moltmann, "On Latin American Liberation Theology: An Open Letter to José Míguez Bonino," *Christianity and Crisis* 36, no. 5 (March 29, 1976): 58.

Chapter 8

1. Charlotte Perkins Gilman, *His Religion and Hers* (New York: Century, 1923).
2. *Ibid.*, vii.
3. *Ibid.*, viii.
4. *Epic of Gilgamesh*, Tablet X, 3, in *Religions of the Ancient Near East: Sumero-Akkadian Religious Texts and Ugaritic Epics*, ed. Isaac Mendelsohn (New York: Liberal Arts, 1955), 92.
5. "The Descent of Inanna," in *Inanna, Queen of Heaven and Earth: Her Stories and Hymns from Sumer*, eds. Diane Wolkskin and Samuel Noah Kramer (New York: Harper & Row, 1983), 52–71.
6. "The Poimandres of Hermes Trismegistus," in *The Gnostic Religion: The Message of the Alien God and the Beginning of Christianity*, ed. Hans Jonas (Boston: Beacon, 1963), 152–53.
7. Franz Cumont, *Astrology and Religion Among the Greeks and Romans* (New York: Dover, 1912), chap. 6.
8. Plato, *Phaedrus*, 246–49, from the *Dialogues of Plato*, vol. 1, ed. B. Jowett (New York: Random House, 1937), 250–54.
9. Plato, *Timaeus*, in *Dialogues of Plato*, ed. Jowett, vol. 2, 23.
10. For example, see 1 Enoch, v. 9, in *The Pseudepigrapha of the Old Testament*, ed. R. H. Charles (Oxford: Clarendon, 1913), 190.
11. *The Great Bundahis*, vol. 5, chap. 30 in *The Sacred Books of the East: Pahlavi Texts*, ed. F. Max Miller (Oxford: Clarendon, 1897).
12. Revelation, chap. 22.

13. 1 Corinthians 15:44.
14. Acts 2:17–18, from Joel 2:28–32.
15. See Elisabeth Schüssler Fiorenza, "Word, Spirit and Power: Women in Early Christian Communities," in *Women of Spirit: Female Leadership in the Jewish and Christian Traditions,* ed. R. Ruether and E. McLaughlin (New York: Simon and Schuster, 1979), 40–41.
16. *The Acts of Paul and Thecla,* in *Ante-Nicene Fathers,* vol. 8, eds. Alexander Roberts and James Donaldson (New York: Scribner, 1885–1897), 487ff.
17. Denis R. MacDonald, *The Legend and the Apostle: The Battle for Paul in Story and Legend* (Philadelphia: Westminster, 1983).
18. Plato, *Timaeus,* in *Dialogues of Plato,* ed. Jowett, vol. 2, 23.
19. "The Pseudo-Clementine Letters," in *The Ante-Nicene Fathers,* vol. 8, ed. Roberts and Donaldson, 75–360.
20. Augustine, *City of God* 22, 17; and Jerome, Epistle 108, 23.
21. Methodius, *Symposium,* Logos 3, 8, in *Ancient Christian Writers* (Westminster, MD: Newman, 1958), no. 27, 65–66.
22. Otto Semmelroth, *Mary: The Archetype of the Church,* trans. Maria von Eroes and John Devlin (New York: Sheed and Ward, 1963), 166–68.
23. Rosemary Radford Ruether, "Envisioning Our Hopes: Some Models for the Future," in *Women's Spirit Bonding,* eds. Kalven and Buckley, 325–35.
24. See Rosemary Radford Ruether, *Women-Church: Theology and Practice of Feminist Liturgical Communities* (San Francisco: Harper & Row, 1985), 112–13.
25. *Ibid.,* 213.

Introduction to Part 4

1. See, for example, Rosemary Radford Ruether, "Toward an Ecological-Feminist Theology of Nature," in her *Sexism and God-Talk: Toward a Feminist Theology* (Boston: Beacon, 1983), 85–92; and Dorothee Soelle with Shirley A. Cloyes, *To Work and to Love: A Theology of Creation* (Philadelphia: Fortress, 1984).
2. Vine Deloria, Jr., has been especially critical of Christianity's focus on the alienation of humankind from nature rather than on its fundamental relationship with nature. See his *God Is Red* (New York: Dell, 1973), 95.
3. Ruether, *Sexism and God-Talk,* 91.
4. Deloria, *God Is Red,* 91.
5. Ruether, *Sexism and God-Talk,* 91.
6. Compare this with the tendency of many North American feminist theologians (who are not all necessarily liberation theologians) to turn to psychology and the tendency of many process theologians to turn to biology.
7. He shares this concern with Jacquelyn Grant. See her chapter on christology in this volume.
8. For a similar approach to humankind's relation to one another and to nature through work, see Dorothee Soelle, "Work as Reconciliation with Nature," in *To Work and to Love,* Soelle and Cloyes, 103–13.
9. Compare Juan Luis Segundo's acknowledgment of the existence of entropy in the universe and its connection with sin and evil in *Evolution and Guilt* (Maryknoll, NY: Orbis, 1983) with Matthew Fox's more romanticized picture of nature as wholly good in *Original Blessing* (New Mexico: Bear, 1983).

Chapter 9

1. June Jordan, "Poem for South African Women," in her *Passion: New Poems, 1977–1980* (Boston: Beacon, 1980), 42–43 (italics in original).
2. Milton Schwantes, "Elementos para a compreensão de Gênesis 1 a 3: Uma introdução a concepção da passoa humana," in *Teologia no Brasil: Teoria e Prática,* ed. Odair Pedroso Mateus (Associação de Seminários Teológicos Evangélicos, 1985), 111–34. See also J. Severino Croatto, "Fé en la creación y responsabilidad por el mundo," in *Fé, compromiso y teología: Homenaje a José Míguez Bonino* (Buenos Aires: Isedet, 1985), 135–45.
3. Gustavo Gutiérrez, *La fuerza histórica de los pobres* (Lima: CEP, 1980), 337–94.

4. Carlos Drummond de Andrade, *Antologiá Poética,* 8th ed. (Rio de Janeiro: José Olympio, 1975), 12 (trans. by Westhelle).

5. "An die Nachgeborenen" (1938), in *Bertold Brechts Gedichte und Lieder* (Berlin: Suhrkamp, n.d.), 158.

6. César Vallejo, *Obras Completas VIII: Poemas Humanos* (Barcelona: Laia, 1977), 87.

7. Gustavo Gutiérrez, *Theology of Liberation* (Maryknoll, NY: Orbis, 1973), 173.

8. Alejo Carpentier, *Tientos y Diferencias* (Buenos Aires: Calicanto, 1976).

9. German Arciniegas, *Latin America: A Cultural History,* trans. Joan MacLean (New York: Knopf, 1970), 384–403, 424–27. See also Harold E. Davis, *Latin American Thought* (London: Free Press, 1974), 97–134.

10. Ernst Bloch, *Atheismus im Christentum* (Frankfurt am Main: Suhrkamp, 1968), 61.

11. Ernst Bloch, *Freiheit und Ordnung* (Hamburg: Rowohlt, 1969), 75–79.

12. According to John B. Cobb, Jr., this would be Whitehead's *theological* solution for the problem of transcendence and immanence without appealing to a God that is ideally above us. See Cobb's *A Christian Natural Theology* (Philadelphia: Westminster, 1965), 203–14.

13. John Reumann, *Creation and New Creation* (Minneapolis, MN: Augsburg, 1973), 95.

14. See Edith L. B. Turner, "Encounter with Neurobiology: The Response of Ritual Studies," *Zygon* 21, no. 2 (1986): 219–32.

15. Karl Marx, *Das Kapital,* 3 vols. (Berlin: Dietz, 1947), 1:192; see also 1:57; 3:723, 728, passim.

16. For further elaboration see my article "Labor: A Suggestion for Rethinking the Way of the Christian," *Word & World* 6, no. 2: 194–206.

17. *Hexaemeron,* 1.7. We may have problems with this analogy because of P's use of the verb *bara'*, which has God as its exclusive subject. But Claus Westerman, *Creation* (Philadelphia: Fortress, 1974), 114, comments that although it is "of utmost significance that this word *bara'* occurs in the Old Testament only with God as its subject . . . [it] is an exaggeration . . . [to] say that the biblical theology of Creation is contained in the notion behind *bara'* . . . and the exaggeration becomes obvious when we see that the priestly writing also uses the simple word *make* in the same sense."

18. See my article quoted in note 16, 204.

19. Marx, *Kapital,* 1:741. For an interpretation along these lines of the Cain and Abel story, see Gunter A. Wolff, "Una Historia de Luta entre o Pastor Abel e o Agricultor Cain," *Tempo e Presenca* 182 (1983): 22–24.

20. This is not the place to discuss the progressive disappearance of the worker as the one who intervenes directly in nature. The technological revolution is changing the characteristics of labor. But this change does not make human beings independent of nature—it only amplifies the distance between a need and the product for satisfying that need. This distance dramatizes and complicates the metabolic process, but in no sense eliminates it. An ethics of labor is therefore even more necessary than ever. Technological advances have blurred the metabolic criteria we need to work out questions that address both human justice and ecology.

21. John Leslie, "Anthropic Principle, World Ensemble, Design," *American Philosophical Quarterly* 19, no. 2 (1982): 141–51.

22. A. R. Peacocke, *Creation and the World of Science* (Oxford: Clarendon, 1979), 67–68.

23. For an introduction and summary of the debate see Philip Hefner, "The Creation" as the fourth locus of *Christian Dogmatics,* 2vols., ed. Carl E. Braaten and Robert W. Jenson (Philadelphia: Fortress, 1984), 1:323–39.

24. Erich Auerbach, *Mimesis* (São Paulo: Perspectiva, 1976), 15.

25. *Isto É,* 12 October 1977.

26. I am relying here on Hegel's dialectic of the master and the slave. See G. W. F. Hegel, *Phänomenologie des Geistes* (Frankfurt am Main: Suhrkamp, 1970), 145–55.

27. Reumann, *Creation,* 89–99.

28. Segundo, *The Community Called Church* (Maryknoll, NY: Orbis, 1973), 7.

Chapter 10

1. The process of aboriginal land claims can be followed in the Native American press, such as *Akwesasne Notes*. For an example of a specific case, see *A Song from Sacred Mountain*, ed. Anita Parlow (Lakota Nation: Oglala Lakota Legal Rights Fund, 1983).
2. This is not from Seathl's famous speech but from a letter written the following year to President Franklin Pierce. See *Native American Testimony*, ed. Peter Nabokov (New York: Harper and Row, 1978), 107–8.
3. Frank Waters and Oswald White Bear Fredericks, *The Book of the Hopi* (New York: Viking Press, 1963), 5, 12.
4. The *adam* (human being) is created out of the *adamah* (earth) in Genesis 2, but this rather striking word play is only treated in passing by most commentators as merely obvious.
5. See, for example, the collection of theological statements about the land published by the American Lutheran Church: *The Land: Statements and Actions of the American Lutheran Church* (1978–1982) which deals with the land and those who tend it (available through Augsburg Publishing House, Minneapolis).
6. *A Song from Sacred Mountain*, 3.
7. This distinction between temporal and spatial in Native American and immigrant cultures has been insightfully addressed by Vine Deloria, Jr., in *God is Red* (New York: Dell Publishing, 1973).
8. Sydney Mead, *The Lively Experiment: The Shaping of Christianity in America* (New York: Harper and Row, 1963) 5–7.
9. This is from the famous speech delivered at the signing of the Treaty of Medicine Creek, 1854. For the text, see *I Have Spoken: American History through the Voices of the Indians*, ed. Virginia I. Armstrong (Chicago: Swallow, 1971) 89ff.
10. S. Mead, *The Lively Experiment*, 5.
11. Ernest Thompson Seton, *The Gospel of the Red Man: An Indian Bible* (Los Angeles: Willig, 1948) 66.
12. Quoted from *I Have Spoken*, ed. V. Armstrong, 110.
13. Quoted from *Native American Testimony*, ed. P. Nabokov, 108.

Chapter 11

1. June Jordan, "Poem About My Rights," in her collection *Passion: New Poems, 1977–80* (Boston: Beacon, 1980), 89.
2. Barbara Chester, "The Statistics About Sexual Violence," in *Sexual Assault and Abuse: A Handbook for Clergy and Religious Professionals*, ed. Mary D. Pellauer, Barbara Chester, and Jane Boyajian (San Francisco: Harper & Row, 1987), 10–16.
3. E. N. Sargent, *The African Boy* (New York: Collier, 1963), 44.
4. Joy Bussert, *Battered Women: From a Theology of Suffering to an Ethics of Empowerment* (New York: Division for Mission in North America, Lutheran Church in America, 1986); Rita-Lou Clarke, *Pastoral Care and Battered Women* (Philadelphia: Westminster, 1986), 21ff.
5. Marie Marshall Fortune, *Sexual Violence, the Unmentionable Sin: An Ethical and Pastoral Perspective* (New York: Pilgrim, 1983), 213–15; Clarke, *Battered Women*, 77–82.
6. Fortune, *Sexual Violence*, 195–200.
7. I borrowed this term from Mary Midgeley, *Wickedness: A Philosophical Essay* (London: Routledge and Kegan Paul, 1984).
8. Paul Ricoeur, "Evil: A Challenge to Philosophy and Theology," *Journal of the American Academy of Religion* 53 (Fall, 1985): 635–48.
9. Michael Lerner, *Surplus Powerlessness: The Psychodynamics of Everyday Life and the Psychology of Individual and Social Transformation* (Oakland, CA: Institute for Labor and Mental Health, 1987), 152.
10. *Ibid.*, 153. See also Beverly Wildung Harrison, "The Power of Anger in the Work of Love," in her *Making the Connections: Feminist Essays on Social Ethics* (Boston: Beacon, 1985), 3–21.

11. Mary D. Pellauer, "Moral Callousness and Moral Sensitivity: Violence Against Women," in *Sexual Assault and Abuse*, 36.

12. Alice Miller, *Thou Shalt Not Be Aware: Society's Betrayal of the Child*. trans. Hildegarde and Hunter Hannum (New York: Farrar, Straus and Giroux, 1984), 95.

13. Toni Morrison, *The Bluest Eye* (New York: Washington Square, 1970), 158.

14. Martha Janssen, *Silent Scream: I Am a Victim of Incest* (Philadelphia: Fortress, 1983), 18.

15. Lark d'Helen, "Briefly," in *Voices in the Night: Women Speaking About Incest*, ed. Toni A. H. McNaron and Yarrow Morgan (Pittsburgh, PA: Cleis, 1982), 146.

16. Miller, *Thou Shalt Not Be Aware*, 319–20.

17. Margaret Farley, *Personal Commitments: Beginning, Keeping, Changing* (San Francisco: Harper & Row, 1986).

18. Lerner, *Surplus Powerlessness*, 41.

19. Tracy Nagurski, "To Daddy," *Voices in the Night*, 157–58.

20. Nagurski, *Voices in the Night*, 146.

21. *I Never Told Anyone: Writings by Women Survivors of Child Sexual Abuse*, ed. Ellen Bass and Louise Thornton (New York: Harper & Row, 1983), 249.

22. Victim of Brother Abuse, "Tamar and Amnon Revisited," *Daughters of Sarah* 13 (September/October 1987): 11.

23. See, for example, *I Never Told Anyone*, 136.

24. See Valerie Saiving Goldstein, "The Human Situation: A Feminine View," *Journal of Religion* 90 (1960): 100–112; Judith Plaskow, *Sex, Sin, and Grace: Women's Experience and the Theologies of Reinhold Niebuhr and Paul Tillich* (Washington, DC: University Press of America, 1980); Susan Nelson Dunfee, "The Sin of Hiding: A Feminist Critique of Reinhold Niebuhr's Account of the Sin of Pride," *Soundings* 65 (1982): 316–27; and H. R. Niebuhr, *The Responsible Self* (New York: Harper & Row, 1963), 137–38.

25. Paul Tournier, *The Violence Within* (San Francisco: Harper & Row, 1982), 154; see also 154–59.

26. For this theme, see Lerner, *Surplus Powerlessness*, 2–17, and Elizabeth Janeway, *Powers of the Weak* (New York: Morrow Quill, 1981).

27. This is not to be understood as autonomy, for it involves a continuing awareness of our ability and need to care for others in healthful ways. See Jean Grimshaw, *Philosophy and Feminist Thinking* (Minneapolis, MN: University of Minnesota Press, 1986), 174ff.; and Jean Baker Miller, *Toward a New Psychology of Women* (Boston: Beacon, 1976), 60–73.

28. See, for example, Fortune, *Sexual Violence*, 79–80, where she speaks of sin as "alienation, brokenness, and estrangement" and "rupture of relationship." Later she shifts her language to "violation of right relationship" (83–87).

29. Albert Memmi, for example, in his *Dependence* (trans. Philip A. Facey [Boston: Beacon, 1984] 5–6), observes that there is a large difference between the alienation a dependent person experiences in relation to her/his provider and the alienation a subjected person experiences in relation to her/his dominator.

30. Maya Angelou, *I Know Why the Caged Bird Sings* (New York: Bantam, 1969), 73.

31. Ella Radke, *Child Cry*, unpublished manuscript.

32. Judith Lewis Herman, with Lisa Hirschman, *Father-Daughter Incest* (Cambridge: Harvard University Press, 1981) 22–35.

33. Memmi, *Dependence*, 150.

34. Miller, *Drama of the Gifted Child: How Narcissistic Parents Form and Deform the Emotional Lives of Their Gifted Children*, trans. Ruth Ward (New York: Basic Books, 1981), ix.

35. Morrison, *Bluest Eye*, 159–60.

36. Herman, *Father-Daughter Incest*, 218.

37. Memmi, *Dependence*. See also the argument in Martha C. Nussbaum, *The Fragility of Goodness: Luck and Ethics in Greek Tragedy and Philosophy* (Cambridge: Cambridge University Press, 1986).

38. Memmi, *Dependence*, 155.

39. Morrison, *Bluest Eye*, 127.

40. *Ibid.*, 159.

41. Miller, *Drama of the Gifted Child*, 69.

42. Radke, *Child Cry.*
43. This way of framing the issue comes from Memmi, who says, "The history of the species has been that men solve the problem of dependence by dominating women and women solve it by subjecting themselves to men" (*Dependence,* 155). This is not always the case, however. Jean Grimshaw has argued in *Philosophy and Feminist Thinking* that some feminists, especially early feminists such as de Beauvoir and Daly, reacted to male expectations of women as dependent by rejecting all dependence or need and imitating male forms of independence, hoping for a life "uncorrupted by dependencies" (142ff.).
44. *I Never Told Anyone,* ed. Bass and Thornton, 182.
45. Memmi, *Dependence,* 155. Jean Baker Miller suggests that society as a whole might learn this consent from women's often positive acknowledgement of vulnerability, weakness, and helplessness that does not lead to subjection but to the release of greater creativity of life (*Toward a New Psychology of Women,* 29–38).

Introduction to Part 5

1. Leonardo Boff, *Liberating Grace* (Maryknoll, NY: Orbis, 1979), 3.
2. *Ibid.,* 4–5.

Introduction to Part 5.A

1. *Womanist* is a term coined by Alice Walker. "Womanist 1. From *womanish.* (Opp. of 'girlish,' i.e., frivolous, irresponsible, not serious.) A black feminist or feminist of color. From the black folk expression of mothers to female children, 'You acting womanish,' i.e., like a woman. Usually referring to outrageous, audacious, courageous or *willful* behavior. Wanting to know more and in greater depth than is considered 'good' for one." In *Search of Our Mothers' Gardens* (San Diego, CA: Harcourt Brace Jovanovich, 1983), xi–xii.
2. Reginald H. Fuller, *The Foundations of New Testament Christology* (New York: Scribner, 1965), 143.
3. Schleiermacher, *Christian Faith,* ed. H. R. Mackintosh and J. S. Stewart (Edinburgh: T. & T. Clark, 1968), 88, 94.
4. See Barth's *Epistle to the Romans,* trans. Edwyn C. Haskins (New York: Oxford University Press, 1977).
5. See Karl Barth, *Christ and Adam: Man and Humanity in Romans 5* (New York: Macmillan, 1956); and *The Humanity of God* (Richmond, VA: John Knox, 1960).
6. Karl Barth, *The Theology of Schleiermacher,* trans. Geoffrey W. Bromeley (Grand Rapids, MI: Eerdman's, 1982), 191.
7. John B. Cobb, *Christ in a Pluralistic Age* (Philadelphia: Westminster, 1975), 171.

Chapter 13

1. I am especially grateful to Kelly Brown, Beverly Harrison, Pat Shechter, Ann Wetherilt, Delores Williams, and students in my christology classes.
2. All theology is to some extent a reaction against an author's perceptions of earlier theological distortions, excesses, or errors. For example, the "crisis" theologian Karl Barth (1886–1968) reacted against the relativism of such liberals as Albrecht Ritschl (1822–1989) Liberation theologian Dorothee Soelle (1928–) reacted in one of her first books, *Political Theology,* trans. John Shelly (Philadelphia: Fortress, 1971), against the individualism of existential theologian Rudolf Bultmann (1884–1976).
3. For helpful discussions of dualism as a theological and ethical problem, see Ruether, *Sexism and God-Talk,* esp. 72–92; Joan L. Griscom, "On Healing the Nature/History Split in Feminist Thought," 85–98; and Toinette M. Eugene, "While Love Is Unfashionable," in *Women's Consciousness, Women's Conscience* (Minneapolis, MN: Winston, 1985), 121–41.
4. I am aware that for *many* "Christian women of different colors, cultures, and classes," Jesus/Christ is redemptive in that he "saves" them from a sense of personal despair. From the perspective of *liberation* theology, however, redemption (or salvation) involves

the ongoing creation of justice. It is within the context of this process that personal salvation (from despair, loneliness, meaninglessness, etc.) is available.

5. This point is made with compassion and clarity by Tom F. Driver, *Christ in a Changing World: Toward an Ethical Christology* (New York: Crossroad, 1981).

6. H. S. Reimarus (1694–1768), *On the Intention of Jesus*, reissued by American Theological Library, 1962; and David Friedrich Strauss (1808–1874), *The Life of Jesus Critically Examined* (Philadelphia: Fortress, 1972; first pub. 1831–38).

7. In this broad inclusive sense, "the historical Jesus" or "Jesus of history" is assumed by all Christian liberation theologians to be fundamental to christology.

8. Isabel Carter Heyward, *The Redemption of God: A Theology of Mutual Relation* (New York: University Press of America, 1982), 31.

9. Schleiermacher, *Christian Faith*, ed. H. R. Mackintosh and J. S. Stewart (Edinburgh: T. & T. Clark, 1968).

10. Rudolf Bultmann, *Jesus Christ and Mythology* (New York: Scribner, 1958).

11. Frederick Denison Maurice, *Theological Essays* (London: James Clarke, 1957; first pub. 1853); *Kingdom of Christ, or Hints to a Quaker Respecting the Principles, Constitution and Ordinances of the Catholic Church*, 2 vols. (London: SCM, 1958; first pub. 1838–42).

12. For example, Richard Hurrell Froude (1803–1836), John Keble (1792–1866), John Henry Newman (1801–1890), and Edward Bouverie Pusey (1801–1882).

13. Consider the following passage from Desmond Tutu's *Hope and Suffering*:

> The Gospel of Jesus Christ is a many-splendoured thing, a jewel with several facets. In [certain] situation[s] . . . the aspect of the Gospel that will be relevant is the Gospel as reconciliation. [But] if you are oppressed and the victim of exploitation, then the Gospel for you will be liberation. . . .
>
> Black and White Christians look at Jesus Christ and they see a different reality. It is almost like beauty, which is said to be in the eye of the beholder. . . .
>
> . . . Christianity knows nothing about pie in the sky when you die, or concern for man's soul only. That would be a travesty of the religion of Jesus of Nazareth, who healed the sick, fed the hungry, etc. . . . *Jesus showed that for the spiritual God, His Kingdom must have absolute centrality; but precisely because that was so, because He turned Godwards, He of necessity had to be turned manwards. He was the Man for others precisely because He was first and foremost the Man of God* ([Grand Rapids, MI: Eerdmans, 1985], 84–85, italics mine).

14. Maurice, *Theological Essays*, 81.

15. *Ibid.*

16. *Ibid.*

17. Albert Schweitzer, *The Quest of the Historical Jesus: A Critical Study of Its Progress from Reimarus to Wrede*, trans. W. Montgomery (New York: Macmillan, 1979), 62–67.

18. *Alienation* is a term in Marxist theory which denotes "negation of productivity." Erich Fromm writes,

> Alienation (or "estrangement") means, for Marx, that man does not experience himself as the acting agent in his grasp of the world, but that the world (nature, others, and he himself) remain alien to him. They stand above and against him as objects, even though they may be objects of his own creation. Alienation is essentially experiencing the world and oneself passively, receptively, as the subject separated from the object (Erich Fromm, *Marx's Concept of Man* [New York: Ungar, 1961], 44).

19. Reference is specifically to the bronze sculpture "Christa" by English artist Edwina Sandys.

20. The development of this idea was initiated in the third century by Cyprian, bishop of Carthage, a student of Tertullian. Trying to secure the *unity* of the church in an era of its persecution by the Roman state, Cyprian identified the presence of the church with the person of the bishop. *Letters*, 66.8, in *The Fathers of the Church (A New Translation)*, vol. 51 (Washington, DC: Catholic University of America, 1964), 228–29.

21. This is the primary theme of Tom F. Driver's christological work (1981). Tom Driver was my teacher and mentor at Union Seminary in New York. I continue to appreciate and learn from his christological wisdom.

Chapter 14

1. Zora Neale Hurston, *Their Eyes Were Watching God* (Philadelphia: Lippincott, 1939).
2. Gloria T. Hull, Patricia Bell Scott, and Barbara Smith, eds., *All the Women Are White, All the Blacks Are Men, but Some of Us Are Brave: Black Women's Studies* (Old Westbury, NY: Feminist Press, 1982).
3. From the poem, "I Am a Black Woman," in *I Am a Black Woman: Poems by Mari Evans* (New York: Morrow, 1970), 12.
4. Carter G. Woodson, *The Mis-Education of the Negro* (Philadelphia: Hakim, 1922).
5. James H. Cone, *God of the Oppressed* (New York: Seabury, 1975), 108–9.
6. *Ibid.*
7. James H. Cone, *A Black Theology of Liberation* (Philadelphia: Lippincott, 1970), 198.
8. J. A. Johnson, "The Need for a Black Christian Theology," *Journal of the I.T.C.* 11 (Fall 1974): 25.
9. Albert Cleage, *The Black Messiah* (New York: Sheed and Ward, 1968), 3.
10. *Ibid.*
11. Cone, *Black Theology*, 214–15.
12. Gayraud Wilmore, "The Black Messiah: Revising the Color Symbolism of Western Christianity," *Journal of the Interdenominational Theological Center* 2 (Fall 1974): 13–14.
13. William Eichelberger, "Reflections on the Person and Personality of the Black Messiah," in C. Eric Lincoln's *The Black Church Since Frazier* (New York: Schocken, 1979), 6, 61.
14. Barbara Hilkert Andolsen, *Daughters of Jefferson, Daughters of Bootblacks: Racism and American Feminism* (Macon, GA: Mercer University Press, 1986), see chap. 3.
15. Quoted in Andolsen, *Daughters of Jefferson*, 17.
16. *Ibid.*
17. Nancy Cott, *The Bonds of Womanhood: Women's Sphere in New England, 1780–1835* (New Haven, CT: Yale University Press, 1972), 126ff.
18. "The General Association of Massachusetts (Orthodox) to the Churches Under Their Care, 1837," in *Feminist Papers: from Adams to de Beauvoir*, ed. Alice Rossi (New York: Columbia University Press, 1973), 305.
19. Sarah Grimké, "Letter on the Equality of the Sexes and Condition of Women," in *Feminist Papers*, ed. Rossi, 107. Both Grimké sisters were active women's rights advocates (as well as abolitionists). They spoke out for the rights of women, including the right to speak on any issue—be it Negro or women's suffrage. See also Angelina E. Grimké, *An Appeal to the Christian Women of the South* (New York: American Antislavery Society, 1836).
20. Leonard Swidler, *Biblical Affirmation of Women* (Philadelphia: Westminster, 1979).
21. Leonard Swidler, "Jesus Was a Feminist," *South Asia Journal of Theology* 13 (1971): 106.
22. See Kathleen Storrie, "New Yeast in the Dough: Jesus Transforms Authority," *Daughters of Sarah* 10 (January/February 1984). In this article Storrie draws on the work of Elizabeth Schüssler Fiorenza, *In Memory of Her* (New York: Crossroad, 1983), and Dorothee Soelle, *Beyond Mere Obedience* (Minneapolis, MN: Augsburg, 1970).
23. Swidler, "Jesus Was a Feminist," 103.
24. Rosemary Radford Ruether, "Feminism and Christology: Can a Male Savior Help Women?" in *Occasional Papers* (Nashville, TN: United Methodist Board of Higher Education and Ministry, 1976), 1–9.
25. Rosemary Radford Ruether, in *To Change the World: Christology and Cultural Criticism* (New York: Crossroad, 1981), 47.
26. Rosemary Radford Ruether, *Sexism and God-Talk: Toward a Feminist Theology* (Boston: Beacon, 1983), 135.
27. Ruether, *To Change the World*, 47.
28. Ruether, "Feminism and Christology," *Occasional Papers*.
29. *Ibid.*

30. Ruether, *Sexism*, 135.
31. *Ibid.*
32. *Ibid.*, 138.
33. *Ibid.*
34. *Ibid.*
35. This word was used by El Savadoran activist Marta Beñarides in describing the need for a theology of accompaniment vs. empowerment. For black women, I would argue, as I see evidences in black women's religious experiences, for both a theology of accompaniment and empowerment.
36. William Eichelberger, *The Black Church*, 54.
37. Harold A. Carter, *The Prayer Tradition of Black People* (Valley Forge, PA: Judson, 1976). Carter, in referring to traditional black prayer in general, states that Jesus is revealed as one who is "all one needs!"
38. *Ibid.*, 49.
39. *Ibid.*
40. *Ibid.*
41. Olive Gilbert, ed., *Sojourner Truth: Narrative and Book of Life* (1850, 1875; reprint, Chicago: Johnson's, 1970), 118.
42. *Ibid.*, 119.
43. *Ibid.*
44. *Ibid.*, 122.
45. Cone, *God of the Oppressed*, 135.
46. *Ibid.*, 136.
47. Jarena Lee, *Religious Experiences and Journal of Mrs. Jarena Lee* (Philadelphia, 1849), 15–16.
48. *Ibid.*, 16.
49. Sojourner Truth, "Ain't I a Woman," in *Feminism*, ed. Miriam Schneir (New York: Vintage, 1972), 94.

Introduction to Part 5.B

1. Juan Luis Segundo, *The Hidden Motives of Pastoral Action: Latin American Reflections*, trans. John Drury (Maryknoll, NY: Orbis, 1978), 70ff. See also Leonardo Boff, *Ecclesiogenesis* (Maryknoll, NY: Orbis, 1988); and Juan Luis Segundo, *The Community Called Church*, trans. John Drury (Maryknoll, NY: Orbis, 1973).
2. See Rosemary Radford Ruether, *Women-Church: Theology and Practice of Feminist Liturgical Communities* (Boston: Beacon, 1987); and Elisabeth Schüssler Fiorenza, *In Memory of Her: A Feminist Theological Reconstruction of Christian Origins* (New York: Crossroad, 1983), for elaboration of feminist liberation ecclesiologies.
3. Letty M. Russell, *Growth in Partnership* (Philadelphia: Westminster, 1981), and *Household of Freedom* (Philadelphia: Westminster, 1987).
4. For a brief summary of this development, see Lynn N. Rhodes, *Co-Creating: A Feminist Vision of Ministry* (Philadelphia: Westminster, 1988), 122–26.

Chapter 15

1. Nakane's ideas are summarized in Yoji Inoue, "Problems of Acceptance of Christianity in Japan," *Jurist Magazine* (A Special Issue on Religion and the Contemporary Person [in Japanese]), no. 21 (Winter 1981): 73–78. Article first published 1967.
2. *Ibid.*
3. Ruth Benedict, *The Chrysanthemum and the Sword* (Boston: Houghton Mifflin, 1946), 222.
4. *Ibid.*, 223.
5. Suzuki Norihisa, "Tsumi to Haji" ["Sin and Shame"], in *Kiku to Katana to Jujika to* [*Chrysanthemum, Sword and the Cross*] (Tokyo: Nippon Kirisuto Kyodan Publishing House, 1976), 44–47.
6. Doi Takeo, *The Anatomy of Dependence* (Kobunso, 1971; in English, New York: Kodansha International, 1986).

7. Toshio Yamazaki, *Oyano nai Tensaitachi* [*Geniuses Without Parents*] (Kyoto: Rugaaru-sha, 1987).
8. Ichiro Hori, ed., *Japanese Religion* (New York: Kodansha International, 1974), 209.
9. *Ibid.*, 210.
10. *Ibid.*
11. Kenneth J. Dale, *Circle of Harmony: A Case Study in Popular Japanese Buddhism* (Tokyo: Seibunsha, 1975), 91.
12. Nikkyo Niwano, "Kotoku o tsumukotoga shiawase no michi" ["To accumulate virtues is the way to happiness"], *Shukyo Jyoho* 17 (March 1988): 22.

Chapter 16

1. Irving Bieber, *Homosexuality: A Psychoanalytical Study of Male Homosexuals* (New York: Random House, 1965), 12.
2. *Ibid.*, 319.
3. Albert Ellis, "The Effectiveness of Psychotherapy with Individuals Who Have Severe Homosexual Problems," in *The Problem of Homosexuality in Modern Society*, ed. Hendrik Ruitenbeek (New York: Dutton, 1963).
4. Bieber, *Homosexuality*, 4.
5. George Weinberg, *Society and the Healthy Homosexual* (New York: Anchor Press/ Doubleday, 1973), chap. 3.
6. George R. Edwards, *Gay/Lesbian Liberation: A Biblical Perspective* (New York: Pilgrim, 1984), 16.
7. Richard Lovelace, *Homosexuality and the Church* (Old Tappan, NJ: Revell, 1978), 19.
8. Michael Guinan, "Homosexuals: A Christian Pastoral Response Now," in *A Challenge to Love*, ed. Robert Nugent (New York: Crossroad, 1978), 69.
9. Weinberg, *Healthy Homosexual*.
10. *Open Hands, Journal of the Reconciling Congregation Program*, Affirmation: United Methodists for Lesbian/Gay Concerns (Fall 1987), 9.
11. Weinberg, *Healthy Homosexual*, 70; authors added female referents.
12. C. A. Tripp, *The Homosexual Matrix* (New York: New American Library, 1975), 253.
13. Ann and Barry Ulanov, *Religion and the Unconscious* (Philadelphia: Westminster, 1975), 165.
14. *Ibid.*
15. Thomas Szasz, "The Product Conversion—From Heresy to Illness," in *The Homosexual Dialectic*, ed. Joseph A. McCaffrey (Englewood Cliffs, NJ: Prentice-Hall, 1972), 110.
16. Ulanov, *Religion and the Unconscious*, 143.
17. James B. Nelson, *Embodiment* (Minneapolis, MN: Augsburg, 1978), 197.
18. Guinan, "Homosexuals," in *Challenge to Love*, 73.
19. Letha Scanzoni and Virginia R. Mollenkott, *Is the Homosexual My Neighbor?* (San Francisco: Harper & Row, 1980), 135.
20. As quoted by Nelson, *Embodiment*, 198.
21. Edwards, *Gay/Lesbian Liberation*, 129.
22. Carter Heyward, *The Redemption of God* (Lanham, MD: University Press of America, 1982), 1–2.

Chapter 17

1. Elizabeth Amoah, "The Vital Aspects of Women's Experience of God," paper presented to Continental Consultation on Theology from the Third World: Women's Perspective, 19–23 August 1986, CIWA, Port Harcourt, Nigeria.
2. See note 1 above.
3. Adebisi Sowunmi, "Where Is Theology in Nigeria?" in *The State of Christian Theology in Nigeria*, ed. Mercy Amba Oduyoye (Ibadan, Nigeria: Daystar, 1986), 1–13.
4. Afua Kuma, *Jesus of the Deep Forest*, trans. and ed. Peter Kwasi Ameyaw, Fr. Jon Kirby, et al. (Accra, Ghana: Asempa, n.d.).
5. Interview at Union Theological Seminary, New York, 1986.
6. J. S. Mbiti, *The Prayers of African Religion* (London: Heineman, SPCK, 1970), 148.

7. Mercy Amba Oduyoye, *Hearing and Knowing* (Maryknoll, NY: Orbis, 1985). This lyric is from the repertoire of the Dwenesie Singers of Accra, directed by Dinah Reindorf, a Ghanaian Methodist.

8. J. S. Pobee and B. von Wartenberg-Potter, eds., *New Eyes for Reading: Biblical and Theological Reflections by Women from the Third World* (Oak Park, IL: Meyer-Stone, 1986).

9. Huda Shaarawi, *Harem Years: The Memoirs of an Egyptian Feminist* (New York: Feminist Press, 1987).

10. E. A. Adegbola, ed., *Traditional Religion* (Maryknoll, NY: Orbis, 1973), 203–34.

Introduction to Part 5.C

1. One of the most striking examples of this process to be published in North America is Ernesto Cardenal, ed., *The Gospel in Solentiname*, vol. 1 (Maryknoll, NY: Orbis, 1976).

2. See, for example, Gustavo Gutiérrez, *Theology of Liberation*, esp. part 4,143–250. Gutiérrez's most recent book, *On Job: God-talk and the Suffering of the Innocent* (Maryknoll, NY: Orbis, 1987), is biblical commentary. Ernesto Cardenal, *The Gospel in Solentiname*, 4 vols. (Maryknoll, NY: Orbis, 1982), and Philip Scharper and Sally Scharper, eds., *The Gospel in Art by the Peasants of Solentiname* (Maryknoll, NY: Orbis, 1984) are retellings of the biblical narratives with a political consciousness of their meaning. Most other Latin Americans have made biblical themes of liberation central: Elsa Tamez, *Bible of the Oppressed* (Maryknoll, NY: Orbis, 1982), and José Miranda, *Marx and the Bible* (Maryknoll, NY: Orbis, 1974), etc. These are summarized in J. A. Kirk, "The Bible in Latin American Liberation Theology," in *The Bible and Liberation*, ed. Norman K. Gottwald and Antoinette C. Wire (Berkeley, CA: Radical Religion, 1976).

3. Elisabeth Schüssler Fiorenza, "A Feminist Biblical Hermeneutics," in *The Challenge of Liberation Theology*, ed. Brian Mahan and L. Dale Richesin (Maryknoll, NY: Orbis, 1981), 100.

4. Segundo, *Liberation of Theology*, trans. John Drury (Maryknoll, NY: Orbis, 1976), 9.

5. Schüssler Fiorenza, "Hermeneutics." 101.

6. Sharon H. Ringe, chapter 20 in this volume.

7. Kwok Pui-lan, chapter 19 in this volume.

8. Nonwhite, non-Western biblical interpretation has greatly increased since the Gottwald and Wire summary in the 1970s. See Mercy Amba Oduyoye, *Hearing and Knowing: Theological Reflections on Christianity in Africa* (Maryknoll, NY: Orbis, 1986); Desmond Tutu, *Hope and Suffering: Sermons and Speeches* (Grand Rapids, MI: Eerdmans, 1984); C. S. Song, *Tell Us Our Names: Story Theology from an Asian Perspective* (Maryknoll, NY: Orbis, 1984); C. S. Song, *Theology from the Womb of Asia* (Maryknoll, NY: Orbis, 1986).

Chapter 18

I would like to thank the Hispanic women who have shared their religious understandings with me. I am also indebted to Beverly Harrison and Norman Gottwald, who helped me to develop this work.

1. When I lived in Peru in the 1960s, I had the immense privilege of working with two adult groups in a parish. These two groups—one for women, one for men—were charged with the responsibility of promoting devotion to *El Señor de Los Milagros*. Once a year, the two groups organized a procession which lasted for two days and traveled through the whole parish. Since I was the "spiritual adviser" of both *hermandades,* as the groups are called, I walked in the procession immediately in front of the image which was being carried. But I could not turn my back to *El Señor,* so I walked backwards for two days. The first time I participated in the procession, my attitude was condescending and patronizing. I thought I would do what pleased them so I would be accepted by them. Then I would teach them about the gospel and the church. Somewhere about midway through the second day I was converted. I was deeply touched and moved by the faith of the people. Once and for all I came to realize that their expression of faith was not any less important to the unfolding of the reign of God than mine, indeed, that their faith was much stronger than mine. From then on I have respected and have

valued popular religiosity. It was not the gospel story but the faith of those poor people which taught me to say, "God, help my unbelief."

2. For example, Our Lady of Regla, an invocation of the Virgin Mary sanctioned by "official" Christianity in Cuba, is identified in popular religiosity with Yemaya, the goddess of the sea in the Lucumi religion—one of the African religions. "Yemaya is the strong, powerful and serious mother of the rest of the deities, goddess of fertility but not of love. In spite of her wisdom and prudence, sometimes Yemaya is passionate and sensual" (Juan J. Sosa, "Religiosidad Popular y Sincretismo Religioso: Santería y Espiritismo," *Documentaciones Sureste*, no. 4 [Marzo, 1983]: 18). Passion and sensuality are not attributes which "official" Christianity ascribes to Mary. Maybe if it did, Christianity would have a much more realistic understanding of the morality of sexuality.

3. In conversations in Cuba in January of 1987, both Frei Betto and Professor Castellanos of the Seminario Ecuménico in Matanzas clearly indicated the ongoing importance ot African religious beliefs and practices in Cuba today. The main written source for understanding these practices and beliefs is the work of Lydia Cabrera. See especially *El Monte* (Miami: Ultra Graphics, 1983).

4. Roman Catholic doctrine teaches that the sacrament of ordination leaves an indelible mark on the soul of a priest. This has led many to postulate that an ontological change takes place in the person at the moment of ordination. I remember a few years ago teaching in a Roman Catholic seminary and being surprised—I was naive!—when I learned that some of the young seminarians still believed that ordination sets them apart, that it radically changes them.

5. Vincent L. Wimbush, "Biblical Historical Study as Liberation: Toward an Afro-Christian Hermeneutic," *The Journal of Religious Thought* (Howard University Divinity School) 42, no. 2 (1985–1986): 9.

6. Even in this day and age Sunday sermons do not necessarily refer to the scripture readings. When the priests do use the scripture readings, hardly ever do their sermons show any real exegetical work.

7. Juan Carlos Scannone, "Teología Cultural Popular y Discernimiento," in *Cultura Popular y Filosofía de la Liberación* (Argentina: Fernando García Cambeiro, 1975), 253–54.

8. Aloysius Pieris, "The Place of Non-Christian Religions and Cultures in the Evolution of Third World Theology," in *Irruption of the Third World*, ed. Virgina Fabella and Sergio Torres (Maryknoll, NY: Orbis, 1983), 127 (italics added).

9. Clifford Geertz, *The Interpretation of Culture* (New York: Basic Books, 1973), 90.

10. Pieris, "Place of Non-Christian Religions," *Irruption*, 134.

11. Gustavo Gutiérrez, "Reflections from a Latin American Perspective: Finding Our Way to Talk About God," in *Irruption*, 233.

12. Elisabeth Schüssler Fiorenza, *Bread Not Stone* (Boston: Beacon, 1984), 84.

13. These implications are adapted from the implications Schüssler Fiorenza surmises from a feminist liberationist canon. See *Bread*, 87–92. See also Elisabeth Schüssler Fiorenza, *In Memory of Her: A Feminist Theological Reconstruction of Christian Origins* (New York: Crossroad, 1983), 30.

14. Bruce Vawter, C.M., "The Bible in the Roman Catholic Church," in *Scripture in the Jewish and Christian Traditions*, ed. Frederick E. Greenspahn (Nashville, TN: Abingdon, 1982), 128.

Chapter 19

I am grateful to Kesaya Noda for editing the manuscript and to the Asian Women Theologians, U.S. Group, for mutual support and challenge.

1. T. C. Chao, "The Articulate Word and the Problem of Communication," *International Review of Mission* 36 (1947): 482.

2. Michel Foucault, *Power/Knowledge*, ed. Colin Gordon (New York: Pantheon, 1980),131.

3. "Jacques Lacan and the école freudienne," *Feminine Sexuality,* ed. Juliet Mitchel and Jacqueline Rose, trans. Jacqueline Rose (New York: Norton, 1982), 74–85.

4. R. H. Graves, "How Shall the Native Church Be Stimulated to More Aggressive Christian Work?" in *Records of the General Conference of the Protestant Missionaries of China Held at Shanghai, May* 10–24, 1877 (Shanghai, China: Presbyterian Mission Press, 1877), 339.

5. P. W. Pitcher, *A History of the Amoy Mission, China* (New York: Board of Publication of the Reformed Church in America, 1893), 47.

6. Hendrik Kraemer, *The Christian Message in a Non-Christian World,* 3d ed. (Grand Rapids, MI: Kregel, 1956), Table of Contents, 4.

7. *Ibid.,* 102.

8. Hendrik Kraemer, "Continuity or Discontinuity," in *The Authority of the Faith* (New York: International Missionary Council, 1939), 1–21.

9. T. C. Chao, "Revelation," in *The Authority of the Faith,* 42.

10. Po Ch'en Kuang, "Chung-kuo ti chiu-yüeh" ["Chinese Old Testament"], *Chen-li yu sheng-ming [Truth and Life],* 2, no. 9 (1927): 240–44.

11. Hsieh Fu Ya, "Kuan-hu chung-hua chi-tu-chiao sheng-ching ti pien-ting wen-t'i" ["On the issues of editing the Chinese Christian Bible"], in *Chung-hua chi-tu-chiao shen-hsüeh lun-chi [Chinese Christian Theology Anthology]* (Hong Kong: Chinese Christians Book Giving Society, 1974), 39–40.

12. Hu Tsan Yün, "Liang-pu chiu-yüeh" ["Two Old Testaments"], in *Chung-hua chi-tu-chiao shen-hsüeh lun-chi,* 67–71.

13. Ng Lee Ming, "The Promise and Limitation of Chinese Protestant Theologians, 1920–50," *Ching Feng* 21–22 (1978–79): 178–79.

14. Y. T. Wu, "The Orient Reconsiders Christianity," *The Christian Century* 54, no. 26 (1937): 837.

15. *Ibid.,* 836.

16. Katie G. Cannon, "A Theological Analysis of Imperialistic Christianity," in *An Ocean with Many Shores: Asian Women Making Connections in Theology and Ministry,* ed. Nantawan Boonprasat Lewis (New York: Asian Women Theologians, Northeast U.S. Group, 1987), 25.

17. Kosuke Koyama, *Mount Fuji and Mount Sinai: A Critique of Idols* (Maryknoll, NY: Orbis, 1984), 7–8.

18. Sharon Parks, *The Critical Years: The Young Adult Search for a Faith to Live By* (San Francisco: Harper & Row, 1986), 117.

19. Susan Brooks Thistlethwaite, "Every Two Minutes: Battered Women and Feminist Interpretation," in *Feminist Interpretation of the Bible,* ed. Letty Russell (Philadelphia: Westminster, 1985), 98.

20. Parks, *The Critical Years,* 113.

21. C. S. Song, *Theology from the Womb of Asia* (Maryknoll, NY: Orbis, 1986), 16.

22. C. S. Song, *The Tears of Lady Meng* (Geneva: World Council of Churches, 1981).

23. C. S. Song, *Tell Us Our Names: Story Theology from an Asian Perspective* (Maryknoll, NY: Orbis, 1984), Preface, x.

24. Maen Pongudom, "Creation of Man: Theological Reflections Based on Northern Thai Folktales," *East Asia Journal of Theology* 3, no. 2 (1985): 227.

25. Archie C. C. Lee, "Doing Theology in the Chinese Context: The David-Bathsheba Story and the Parable of Nathan," *East Asia Journal of Theology* 3, no. 2 (1985): 254.

26. Padma Gallup, "Doing Theology—An Asian Feminist Perspective," *Commission on Theological Concerns Bulletin, Christian Conference of Asia* 4 (1983): 22.

27. Kwok Pui-lan, "God Weeps with Our Pain," *East Asia Journal of Theology* 2, no. 2 (1984): 228–32.

28. Kwok Pui-lan, "A Chinese Perspective," in *Theology by the People: Reflections on Doing Theology in Community,* ed. Samuel Amirtham and John S. Pobee (Geneva: World Council of Churches, 1986), 78–83.

29. Kim Yong Bock, ed., *Minjung Theology: People as the Subjects of History* (Singapore: Commission on Theological Concerns, Christian Conference of Asia, 1981), 186.

30. Cyris H. S. Moon, *A Korean Minjung Theology: An Old Testament Perspective* (Maryknoll, NY: Orbis, 1985).

31. Ahn Byung Mu, "Jesus and the Minjung in the Gospel of Mark," in *Minjung Theology*, ed. Kim, 138–39.

32. Suk Nam Dong, "Historical References for a Theology of Minjung," in *Minjung Theology*, ed. Kim, 160.

33. *Ibid.*, 159.

34. Lee Sung Hee, "Women's Liberation Theology as the Foundation for Asian Theology," *East Asia Journal of Theology* 4, no. 2 (1986): 2–13.

35. Jonathan Culler, *On Deconstruction: Theory and Criticism After Structuralism* (Ithaca, NY: Cornell University Press, 1982), 128.

36. Robert Detweiler, "What Is a Sacred Text?" *Semeia* 31 (1985): 217.

37. Carol P. Christ, "Spiritual Quest and Women's Experience," in *Womanspirit Rising*, 229 30.

38. *Ibid.*, 231.

39. Rosemary Radford Ruether, *Womanguides: Reading Toward a Feminist Theology* (Boston: Beacon, 1985).

40. Schüssler Fiorenza, *In Memory of Her: A Feminist Theological Reconstruction of Christian Origins* (New York: Crossroad, 1983).

41. Carol P. Christ, *Diving Deep and Surfacing: Women Writers on Spiritual Quest* (Boston: Beacon, 1980).

42. Katie Geneva Cannon, "Resources for a Constructive Ethic in the Life and Work of Zora Neale Hurston," *Journal of Feminist Studies in Religion* 1, no. 1 (1985): 37–51; Delores Williams, "Black Women's Literature and the Task of Feminist Theology," in *Immaculate and Powerful: The Female in Sacred Image and Social Reality*, ed. Clarissa W. Atkinson, Constance H. Buchanan, and Margaret R. Miles (Boston: Beacon, 1985), 88–110.

43. Rosemary Radford Ruether, "Feminist Interpretation: A Method of Correlation," in *Feminist Interpretation of the Bible*, 117.

44. Elisabeth Schüssler Fiorenza, "The Will to Choose or to Reject: Continuing Our Critical Work," in *Feminist Interpretation of the Bible*, 131.

Chapter 20

1. Katherine Doob Sakenfeld, "Feminist Uses of Biblical Materials," in *Feminist Interpretation of the Bible*, ed. Letty Russell (Philadelphia: Westminster, 1985), 55–64; see esp. 59–61.

2. Bernadette J. Brooten, "Early Christian Women and Their Cultural Context: Issues in Method of Historical Reconstruction," in *Feminist Perspectives on Biblical Scholarship*, ed. Adela Yarbro Collins (Chico, CA: Scholars Press, 1985), 65–81.

3. Sakenfeld, "Feminist Uses," 57–59.

4. See the rhetorical critical study of several such passages in Phyllis Trible, *Tests of Terror* (Philadelphia: Fortress, 1984).

5. See both the methodological contributions and the historical study in Elisabeth Schüssler Fiorenza, *In Memory of Her: A Feminist Theological Reconstruction of Christian Origins* (New York: Crossroad, 1983).

6. Rosemary Radford Ruether, *Sexism and God-Talk: Toward a Feminist Theology* (Boston: Beacon, 1983), 18–19.

7. Sheila Collins, *A Different Heaven and Earth* (Valley Forge, PA: Judson, 1974), 166–67.

Conclusion

1. Carter Heyward, "An Unfinished Symphony of Liberation: The Radicalization of Christian Feminism Among White U.S. Women," *Journal of Feminist Studies in Religion* 1 (1985): 99–118.

Index